Econo-Legal Studies

Takashi Yanagawa · Hiroshi Takahashi ·
Shinya Ouchi
Editors

Econo-Legal Studies

Thinking Through the Lenses of Economics and Law

Springer

Editors
Takashi Yanagawa
Faculty of Economics
Setsunan University
Neyagawa, Osaka, Japan

Hiroshi Takahashi
Graduate School of Law
Kobe University
Kobe, Hyogo, Japan

Shinya Ouchi
Graduate School of Law
Kobe University
Kobe, Hyogo, Japan

ISBN 978-981-16-5144-1 ISBN 978-981-16-5145-8 (eBook)
https://doi.org/10.1007/978-981-16-5145-8

This Springer imprint is published by the registered company Springer Nature Singapore Pte Ltd.
The registered company address is: 152 Beach Road, #21-01/04 Gateway East, Singapore 189721, Singapore

Preface to the English Edition

The authors of the English language edition of the Econo-Legal Studies textbook are delighted with its publication by Springer. The textbook was originally published in Japanese by Yuhikaku Publishing in 2014. A Chinese language edition was published by China Machine Press in 2017. The Chinese language edition was translated by nine lawyers and economists, most of whom hold a Ph.D. in law or economics from Kobe University. This English language edition was translated by the authors, and study questions were added at the end of each chapter to assist in learning.

This textbook was written for the Econo-Legal Studies Program that is jointly offered by the Faculties of Law and Economics at Kobe University. This undergraduate program was launched in 2010 and has been completed by many students. Drawing on this decade of experience, the university established the Econo-Legal Studies Graduate Program in 2019 under Kobe University's Center for Interdisciplinary Programs. The program has been a pillar of interdisciplinary study at the university. Although this textbook was originally written with undergraduate readers in mind, the content will be beneficial to graduate students as well. For graduate students who already possess knowledge of both economics and law, this textbook can offer deeper insight into the significance of the connection between the two fields, and for those who have studied only one of the two disciplines, this textbook offers the chance to explore the possibilities and benefits of thinking through the dual lenses of economics and law.

Over the past decade, new international movements have focused on the connection between economics and law. Guido Calabresi, an eminent authority on law and economics, noted in one of his books that this field of study offers more novel possibilities compared to the economic analysis of law. A slightly lengthy excerpt from this book is presented below:

> What I call Economic Analysis of Law uses economic theory to analyze the legal world. It examines that world from the standpoint of economic theory and, as a result of that examination, confirms, casts doubt upon, and often seeks reform of legal reality.
>
> What I call Law and Economics instead begins with an agnostic acceptance of the world as it is, as the lawyer describes it to be. It then looks to whether economic theory can explain that world, that reality. And if it cannot, rather than automatically dismissing that world as irrational, it asks two questions.

> The first is, are the legal scholars who are describing the legal reality looking at the world as it really is? Or is there something in their way of seeing the world that has led them to mischaracterize that reality?
>
> If, however, even a more comprehensive view of legal reality discloses rules and practices that economic theory cannot explain, Law and Economics asks the second question. Can economic theory be amplified, can it be made broader or more subtle (without thereby losing characteristics that give it coherence and make it as powerful as it is) so that it can explain why the real world of law is as it is? If such a more nuanced theory can do this, Law and Economics then proposes that this expanded economic theory be used more broadly. It suggests that the changes imposed on economic theory to make it capable of explaining a specific legal reality be made part of economic theory generally.[1]

Calabresi sees law and economics as holding different possibilities from those of the economic analysis of law, as described by Richard A. Posner, and he attempts to explore the desired future direction for law and economics. In contrast, we view the current state of law and economics as synonymous with that of the economic analysis of law. We therefore seek to establish econo-legal studies as a distinct academic field. In this regard, Calabresi's approach differs from ours; however, the two approaches are similar in that they both question the current status of law and economics and seek new possibilities. Through repeated discussions by legal and economic scholars, the econo-legal studies discipline accounts for the differences between the silent assumptions of both economics and law in terms of value judgments and thought patterns. It seeks to utilize the two fields' respective strengths and perspectives to resolve complex issues facing modern society. As Calabresi notes, this work may lead to new developments in economics. However, it may lead to other outcomes as well. This field of study can not only enrich and develop economics by incorporating the achievements of law but may also bring about advances in law by incorporating the achievements of economics. Furthermore, assuming that economics and legal studies have differences in values, mutual comparisons of the conclusions drawn by each discipline may lead to better understanding. Nevertheless, legal and economic scholars collaborating on complex social issues, taking interdisciplinary perspectives, and deepening their understandings of each other's fields to contribute to solutions is a very hopeful prospect. We will be delighted if this textbook is part of the first step in such an attempt.

Finally, we are deeply grateful to Prof. Michela Riminucci of Kobe University for her sincere contribution in coordinating the English language edition. We would also like to thank Ms. Juno Kawakami of Springer, Editage (www.editage.com), and all of the administrative staff at the Center for Interdisciplinary Programs for their tremendous assistance in the preparation of this English language edition.

Kobe, Japan
March 2021

Takashi Yanagawa
Hiroshi Takahashi
Shinya Ouchi

---

[1] Calabresi G (2016) The future of law and economics. Yale University Press, New Haven, pp. 2–4.

Preface to the Japanese Edition

Many societal problems are frequently discussed separately by individual academic fields, such as economics, law, and political science. However, each of these academic fields has a different perspective, and, thus, their areas of concern, analysis methods, and values related to these problems all differ, as do their proposed solutions. Economics and legal studies have especially large differences, and the opinions of these two fields are frequently at odds. With the development of law and economics as an academic field, especially in the United States, the legal studies field in Japan has also proactively incorporated elements of economics. However, the law and economics field has mainly focused on economic analyses of the law, and many Japanese legal scholars reject this kind of analysis. Although calls have been made to recognize the importance of interdisciplinary education and some universities recommend studying both economics and law, students are typically responsible for filling gaps in their knowledge, which is no easy task.

Recognizing this problem, the Kobe University Faculties of Law and Economics jointly established the Econo-Legal Studies Program so that selected students from both departments can study economics and law together in the same classroom. The class included 30 students from the economics and law departments, and legal scholars and economists shared their various viewpoints with the students for discussion in each session. Through the classes, the students were exposed to legal and economic perspectives related to problems in a variety of different fields. The program not only explained the commonalities and differences of the two fields but also explored the origins of these differences.

From these experiences, the students came to understand the importance of interdisciplinary thinking that considers both economic and legal perspectives. This field of study, which develops expressions with a mutual understanding of achievements and which strives to enable students to apply knowledge from both law and economics with consideration for differences in terminology, unspoken value judgments, and thought patterns, was named "econo-legal studies" to differentiate it from the simple combination of law and economics. Econo-legal studies include legal studies that incorporate economic findings and economics research that incorporates legal findings. This combined field of study shifts between the two disciplines and viewpoints, taking an interdisciplinary perspective while remaining cognizant of the commonalities and differences of legal and economic thought. With this unique outlook on the complexities of modern society, this field strives to contribute to the resolutions of various problems.

This book is a product of this program. It covers the major problems that modern society currently faces using content that both students and working adults will find interesting. This book will help the reader to develop an understanding of the characteristics of both legal and economic thinking and experience the atmosphere of lectures at Kobe University. We hope that readers can develop the ability to view society more comprehensively with this interdisciplinary perspective.

The book is organized so that the reader can proceed directly to any section of interest after reading Chap. 1. The appendix titled "Elements of Economics" is included to explain the fundamentals of economics. Columns related to the content are included in each section to provide fundamental legal knowledge. The explanations of the legal system in this book are current as of 2021.

Yuhikaku Publishing's Daisuke Ozaki served as this book's editor, and he made significant contributions to the book. His numerous revisions improved its readability. We are grateful for his assistance. We would also like to express our gratitude to Prof. Hironobu Asano (Kobe University) for his detailed comments on the column covering The Constitution of Japan. The Econo-Legal Studies Program received special assistance from Japan's Ministry of Education, Culture, Sports, Science, and Technology in 2010–2011 and 2013–2014. We hope that the publication of this book is the first step in a new leap forward.

Kobe, Japan
February 2014 (updated March 2021)

Takashi Yanagawa
Hiroshi Takahashi
Shinya Ouchi

Contents

1 Introduction to Econo-Legal Studies: The Dual Views of Economics and Law ... 1
Hiroshi Takahashi and Takashi Yanagawa
1.1 Introduction ... 2
1.1.1 Aims of This Book and This Chapter ... 2
1.1.2 Historical Background ... 3
1.2 Economics and Law in Opposition: An Example ... 3
1.2.1 When and How Does the Market for Real Estate Leasing Function? ... 3
1.2.2 The Purpose of the Law: Benefit Society as a Whole or Provide Justice in Specific Transactions? ... 6
1.3 The Pursuit of Value in Economics and Law ... 10
1.3.1 The Value Pursued by Economics ... 10
1.3.2 The Value Pursued by the Law and Legal Studies ... 12
1.3.3 Economics and Law: Similarities and Differences ... 13
1.3.3.1 Values Pursued ... 13
1.3.3.2 Political Views ... 14
1.3.3.3 Methodologies ... 15
1.4 Contents of This Book ... 18
References ... 22

2 The Right to Own Things: Intellectual Property Law ... 23
Ryo Shimanami and Kenta Nakamura
2.1 Outline and Significance of Ownership Systems ... 24
2.1.1 What is Ownership? ... 24
2.1.2 History of and Reasons for the Existence of Ownership Systems ... 25
2.2 Outline of Intellectual Property Law Systems ... 26
2.2.1 What is Intellectual Property? ... 26
2.2.2 What Are Intellectual Property Laws? ... 27

2.2.3 Why Do the Patent Act and the Copyright Act Exist? ... 28
2.2.4 Characteristics of Intellectual Property Laws ... 29
2.3 Economic Analysis of the Patent System ... 31
2.3.1 Knowledge as a Public Good ... 31
2.3.2 Benefits of Patents ... 31
2.3.3 Social Costs of Patents ... 32
2.3.4 Patents as an Appropriability Mechanism ... 34
2.3.5 Pro-Patent Policy: The Case of Software Patents ... 37
2.4 Economic Analysis of Copyright Protections ... 37
2.4.1 Extensions of Copyright Protections ... 38
2.4.2 Unlawful Downloads of Digital Content ... 39
References ... 42

3 The Rules Governing the Relationships Among a Company's Stakeholders: Company Law ... 45
Motohiro Sakaki and Hidefusa Iida
3.1 Introduction ... 46
3.1.1 What is a Company? ... 46
3.1.2 The Underlying Outlook of the Companies Act ... 46
3.1.2.1 The Purpose of the Companies Act ... 46
3.1.2.2 The Nature of the Companies Act ... 47
3.1.3 Typical Conflicts ... 48
3.1.4 Economic Positioning ... 49
3.1.4.1 Agency Theory ... 49
3.1.4.2 Conflicts of Interest Between Directors and Shareholders ... 49
3.1.4.3 Conflicts of Interest Between Controlling and Minority Shareholders ... 50
3.2 Conflicts of Interest Between Directors and Companies ... 51
3.2.1 General Remarks ... 51
3.2.2 Conflicting Interest Transactions ... 51
3.2.2.1 Situations with Conflicting Interests ... 51
3.2.2.2 Liability for Damages ... 52
3.2.2.3 Should Conflicting Interest Transactions Be Prohibited? ... 52
3.2.2.4 Rules of the Companies Act ... 53
3.2.2.5 Application of the Companies Act Rules ... 54
3.2.2.6 Summary ... 55
3.2.3 Derivative Lawsuits and the Business Judgment Rule ... 55
3.2.3.1 Functions and Purpose of a Derivative Lawsuit ... 55

3.2.3.2 The Problem with Derivative Lawsuits: Profits from Taking Risks and Directors' Personal Responsibility ... 56
3.2.3.3 Business Judgment Rule ... 57
3.2.3.4 Summary ... 57
3.2.4 Remuneration Regulations ... 58
3.2.4.1 Traditional Thinking ... 58
3.2.4.2 Questions About Traditional Thinking ... 59
3.2.4.3 Recent Developments ... 59
3.2.4.4 Economic Analysis ... 60
3.2.4.5 Summary ... 61
3.3 Protection of Minority Shareholders ... 62
3.3.1 Exploitation of Minority Shareholders by Controlling Shareholders ... 62
3.3.2 Legal Systems for the Abuse of Majority Votes ... 64
3.3.3 Economic Implications of Protecting Minority Shareholders ... 64
3.4 Conclusion ... 66
References ... 70

4 The Rules for Fair Competition: Antimonopoly Law ... 71
Fumio Sensui and Takashi Yanagawa
4.1 Summary and Purposes of Antimonopoly Law ... 72
4.1.1 The Antimonopoly Act ... 72
4.1.2 Defining Purposes of Antimonopoly Law ... 73
4.1.3 Economic Analysis of the Antimonopoly Act ... 75
4.2 Resale Price Maintenance ... 76
4.2.1 Resale Price Maintenance Explained ... 76
4.2.2 Legal Background ... 76
4.2.3 Economics of RPM ... 77
4.2.3.1 Anticompetitive Effects of Resale Price Maintenance ... 77
4.2.3.2 Procompetitive Effects of RPM ... 78
4.2.3.3 Summary of the economic effects of RPM ... 79
4.2.4 Supreme Court Decision on RPM: The Wakodo Case ... 80
4.2.5 Justifiable Cause for RPM: The Economic Case ... 82
4.2.6 Exemptions to RPM Laws ... 84
4.2.7 RPM of Books Overseas ... 85
4.3 Tie-In Sales ... 86
4.3.1 What is Tying? ... 86
4.3.2 An Economic Assessment of Tying ... 87
4.3.2.1 Reasons for Tying ... 87
4.3.2.2 Tying for the Purpose of Price Discrimination ... 87

4.3.2.3 Tying for the Purpose of Gaining Power in a Competitive Secondary Product Market ... 89
4.3.2.4 Tying for the Purpose of Gaining Power in a Noncompetitive Secondary Product Market ... 90
4.3.2.5 Tying for the Purpose of Maintaining Market Power in Markets for Primary Products ... 91
4.3.3 Explanations and Precedents of the Antimonopoly Act: Acts that Constitute Tying ... 92
4.3.4 Explanations and Precedents of the Antimonopoly Act: (Unjustly) Impeding Fair Competition ... 94
4.4 Conclusion ... 96
References ... 99

5 Determining the Desirable Rules for the Labor Market: Labor Law ... 101
Shinya Ouchi and Kazufumi Yugami
5.1 Introduction ... 102
5.1.1 What is Labor Law? ... 102
5.1.2 Labor Law Systems ... 104
5.1.3 The Need for Rules Governing the Labor Market ... 105
5.2 Minimum Wage Systems as Measures to Address Poverty ... 108
5.2.1 The Minimum Wage Act ... 108
5.2.2 Law and Economics of the Minimum Wage System ... 109
5.2.3 Why Does the Minimum Wage Exist? ... 111
5.3 Employment Protection Legislation and the Labor Market ... 112
5.3.1 Definition of Dismissal ... 112
5.3.2 Impact of Dismissal Regulations ... 114
5.3.3 Why Do Dismissal Regulations Exist? ... 116
5.4 Conclusion ... 118
References ... 118

6 Equity and Efficiency in the Safety Net: Social Security Law ... 121
Yuki Sekine and Takashi Oshio
6.1 An Outline of the Social Security System and Its Significance ... 122
6.1.1 Why is Social Security Necessary? ... 122
6.1.2 Risk Diversification and Risk Mitigation ... 123
6.1.3 Minimum Living Standard ... 124
6.1.4 The Social Security System ... 125
6.1.5 The Administrative Bodies that Implement Social Security: The Distribution of Competences Between National and Local Governments ... 126
6.1.6 Social Security Benefits and Financial Resources ... 127

6.1.7 The Insurance and Welfare Principles ... 128
6.1.8 Social Security and Income Redistribution ... 129
6.1.9 Legal Nature of Social Security Benefits and the Settlement of Disputes ... 130
6.2 Principles and Roles of Social Insurance ... 131
6.2.1 Risk-Averse Individuals and Expected Utility ... 131
6.2.2 The Significance of Social Insurance ... 132
6.2.3 Principles of Social Insurance ... 133
6.2.4 Justifications for Compulsory Enrollment ... 134
6.2.5 The Issues of Forced Enrollment and Moral Hazard ... 135
6.3 Structure of and Issues with the Current System ... 136
6.3.1 Structure of Public Pensions ... 136
6.3.2 Public Pension Sustainability and Intergenerational Inequality ... 137
6.3.3 Generational Accounting ... 138
6.3.4 Structures of Medical and Long-Term (Old-Age Dependency) Care Insurance ... 139
6.3.5 Problems with Health and Long-Term Care Insurance ... 141
6.3.6 The Structure of Public Assistance (or Livelihood Protection) ... 142
6.3.7 Problems with Public Assistance and Optimal Low-Income Support Measures from an Economics Perspective ... 143
6.4 Conclusion ... 145
References ... 148

7 When is Breaking a Promise Allowed? Contract Law ... 149
Akira Saito, Hiroshi Tanaka, and Yoshinobu Zasu
7.1 Introduction ... 150
7.2 Legal Theories of Remedies for Breaches of Contract: A Comparative Study of Japanese and English Law ... 152
7.2.1 A Breach and Its Remedies ... 152
7.2.2 Right to Demand Performance ... 153
7.2.2.1 Right to Demand Performance Under Japanese Law ... 153
7.2.2.2 Right to Demand Performance Under English Law ... 154
7.2.3 Right to Claim Damages ... 155
7.2.3.1 Right to Claim Damages: Requirements ... 155
7.2.3.2 Scope of Damages ... 156
7.2.3.3 Possibility of Compensation Reduction ... 156
7.2.4 Right to Avoid Contracts ... 157
7.2.4.1 Right to Avoid Contracts Under Japanese Law ... 157

7.2.4.2 Avoidance of Contracts Under English Law ... 159
7.2.5 Underlying Concepts of Contract Law: The Grounds and Scope of Binding Power ... 159
7.3 Suitability of Remedy Methods: Analysis of Two Cases ... 160
7.3.1 Two Typical Cases of Buying and Selling ... 162
7.3.2 Obligation of a Buyer Who Can Use the Market to Purchase a Substitute Product ... 163
7.3.3 Logic for Legitimizing the Substitute Transaction Obligation ... 163
7.3.4 Obligation to Mitigate Damages as the Market Use Norm ... 169
7.3.5 Explanation from Historical Examples ... 170
7.4 Contract Law: An Economic Approach ... 171
7.4.1 Role of Contract Law ... 171
7.4.2 Example 1: Vehicle Contract ... 171
7.4.2.1 Complete Contract ... 172
7.4.2.2 Incomplete Contract (With Specific Performance as the Remedy) ... 173
7.4.2.3 Incomplete Contract (With Compensation for Expectation Interest as the Remedy) ... 174
7.4.2.4 Compensation for Damages When the Court Cannot Make an Accurate Judgement ... 175
7.4.2.5 Inaccurate Expectation Damages and Obligations to Mitigate Damages ... 176
7.4.3 Example 2: The Painting Contract ... 177
7.4.3.1 Complete Contract ... 177
7.4.3.2 Incomplete Contract (With Specific Performance as a Remedy) ... 179
7.4.3.3 Incomplete Contract (with Compensation for the Expectation Interest as the Remedy) ... 179
7.4.3.4 Inaccurate Expectation Interests as the Remedy ... 180
7.5 Conclusion ... 181
References ... 183

8 The Meaning of Compensating Damages: Tort Law ... 185
Takayuki Furutani and Shinjiro Miyazawa
8.1 Introduction ... 186
8.1.1 What is Tort Law? ... 186
8.1.2 This Chapter's Objective ... 186
8.2 Summary of the Tort System ... 187

8.3 Legal and Economic Perspectives on Tort Law 189
8.3.1 Legal Perspectives 189
8.3.1.1 Purpose of the Tort Law System 189
8.3.1.2 Characteristics of Legal Approaches 191
8.3.2 Perspective of Economics 192
8.3.2.1 Characteristics of an Economics Approach 192
8.3.2.2 Evaluating Ex Post Functions: Remedies, Sanctions, and Income Redistribution 192
8.3.2.3 Evaluating Ex Ante Functions: Deterrence and Risk Allocation 194
8.3.3 Legal and Economic Perspectives 197
8.4 Principle of Negligence Liability 198
8.4.1 What is Negligence? 199
8.4.2 Why is Liability for Negligence a Principle? 200
8.4.2.1 Principle of Negligence Liability and Its Exceptions: A Legal Perspective 200
8.4.2.2 Comparison of the Strict and Negligence Liability Rules: An Economics Perspective 201
8.5 Conclusion 204
Appendix: Optimal Deterrence in the Case of Bilateral Precaution 205
References 208

9 Appropriate Rules for Protecting the Environment: Environmental Law 209
Narufumi Kadomatsu, Takeshi Shimamura, and Kenji Takeuchi
9.1 Issues Discussed in This Chapter 210
9.2 Waste Management and Recycling 210
9.2.1 Economic Approach to Waste Management 211
9.2.1.1 External Diseconomies and Pigouvian Taxes 211
9.2.1.2 Pigouvian Tax: Charging Garbage Disposal Fees 212
9.2.1.3 Two Ways to Impose Garbage Disposal Fees 214
9.2.2 Economic and Legal Approaches to Recycling: The Recycling of Home Appliances 215
9.2.2.1 Home Appliance Recycling 215
9.2.2.2 Economic Approach to Recycling 216
9.2.3 Designing Recycling Law Systems 218
9.2.3.1 Containers and Packaging Recycling Law 218
9.2.3.2 Home Appliance Recycling Law 219
9.2.3.3 Automobile Recycling Law 219

9.2.4 Evaluating the Home Appliance Recycling Law 219
9.2.4.1 Evaluation from the Perspective of EPR 219
9.2.4.2 Efficiency: Evaluation from an Economic Perspective 220
9.2.4.3 Rationality of Existing Recycling Laws 221
9.3 Landscapes 223
9.3.1 An Economics Approach to Landscape Problems 223
9.3.2 Landscape Issues and the Legal System 225
9.3.2.1 Sample Case 225
9.3.2.2 Land Ownership and Landscape: The Constitution and the Guarantee of the Right to Property 226
9.3.2.3 Private Law Restrictions on Land Ownership 227
9.3.2.4 Administrative Legal Limitations on Land Ownership: City Planning 229
9.3.3 The Law and Economics of Landscape Problems 232
9.3.3.1 Landscapes as Commons 232
9.3.3.2 Social Dilemmas 233
9.3.3.3 Coase Theorem 234
9.3.3.4 Discussion and Coordination-Oriented City Planning 234
9.4 Conclusion 235
References 237

10 Appendix: Elements of Economics 239
Noritsugu Nakanishi
10.1 Incentives and Rational Choice 239
10.2 Preferences, Expected Utility, and Attitudes Toward Risk 241
10.3 Demand and Supply and Market Efficiency 243
10.4 Strategic-Form Games and Nash Equilibria 248
10.5 Extensive-Form Games and Subgame Perfect Equilibria 250
10.6 Externalities 252
10.7 Public Goods and the Tragedy of the Commons 254
10.8 Monopolies and Oligopolies 257
10.9 Asymmetric Information: Adverse Selection, Moral Hazard, and the Hold-Up Problem 260
10.10 Discounted Present Value 262

Index 267

Editors and Contributors

About the Editors

Takashi Yanagawa is a professor at the Faculty of Economics at Setsunan University and a professor emeritus at Kobe University. He received his Ph.D. from the University of North Carolina at Chapel Hill and focuses on industrial organization. He was a professor at the Graduate School of Economics at Kobe University until 2021 and was the director of the Interfaculty Initiative in the Social Sciences at Kobe University from 2014 to 2016. As well, he was the vice-dean of the Organization for Advanced and Integrated Research at Kobe University from 2016 to 2020 and the president of the Japan Economic Policy Association from 2016 to 2019. He is a co-editor of the *International Journal of Economic Policy Studies* (Springer).

Hiroshi Takahashi is a professor at the Graduate School of Law at Kobe University. He received his LL.M. from The University of Tokyo. His major academic focus is the sociology of law. He was the secretary general of the Japanese Association of Sociology of Law from 2017 to 2020, a member of the editorial board of the *Journal of Japanese Arbitration and ADR* from 2016 to 2019, and the vice-dean of the Graduate School of Law at Kobe University from 2019 to 2021.

Shinya Ouchi is a professor at the Graduate School of Law at Kobe University. He received his Ph.D. from The University of Tokyo and specializes in labor law and employment policy. He became the director of the Center for Interdisciplinary Programs, Kobe University, in 2020, and is a board member of the Japanese Industrial Relations Research Association (JIRRA). He received the 22nd Annual Award for Research Monographs on Labour from the Japan Institute for Labour Policy and Training (JILPT) in 2000. The focus of his recent research includes the impacts of digitalization, robotics, and artificial intelligence on the labor market. Dr. Ouchi's co-edited works include *Labour Law in Motion: Diversification of the Labour Force and Terms and Conditions of Employment* (Roger Blanpain and Takashi Araki, co-editors;

Kluwer 2004); *Decentralizing Industrial Relations and the Role of Labor Unions and Employee Representatives* (Roger Blanpain and Takashi Araki, co-editors; Kluwer 2007); *Reconsidering unfair dismissal in Japan: Design of the monetary compensation system* (Daiji Kawaguchi, co-editor; Yuhikaku, Tokyo, 2018); and *Severance Payment and Labor Mobility: A Comparative Study of Taiwan and Japan* (Tatsuo Hatta, co-editor; Springer Nature, Singapore, 2018).

Contributors

Takayuki Furutani Faculty of Law, Kyoto Sangyo University, Kyoto, Japan

Hidefusa Iida Graduate Schools for Law and Politics, University of Tokyo, Tokyo, Japan

Narufumi Kadomatsu Graduate School of Law, Kobe University, Kobe, Hyogo, Japan

Shinjiro Miyazawa Faculty of Business Administration, Hosei University, Tokyo, Japan

Kenta Nakamura Graduate School of Economics, Kobe University, Kobe, Hyogo, Japan

Noritsugu Nakanishi Graduate School of Economics, Kobe University, Kobe, Hyogo, Japan

Takashi Oshio Institute of Economic Research, Hitotsubashi University, Tokyo, Japan

Shinya Ouchi Graduate School of Law, Kobe University, Kobe, Hyogo, Japan

Akira Saito Graduate School of Law, Kobe University, Kobe, Hyogo, Japan

Motohiro Sakaki Graduate School of Law, Kobe University, Kobe, Hyogo, Japan

Yuki Sekine Graduate School of Law, Kobe University, Kobe, Hyogo, Japan

Fumio Sensui Graduate School of Law, Kobe University, Kobe, Hyogo, Japan

Takeshi Shimamura Graduate School of Law, Kobe University, Kobe, Hyogo, Japan

Ryo Shimanami Graduate School of Law, Kobe University, Kobe, Hyogo, Japan

Hiroshi Takahashi Graduate School of Law, Kobe University, Kobe, Hyogo, Japan

Kenji Takeuchi Graduate School of Economics, Kobe University, Kobe, Hyogo, Japan

Hiroshi Tanaka Graduate School of Law, Kobe University, Kobe, Hyogo, Japan

Takashi Yanagawa Faculty of Economics, Setsunan University, Neyagawa, Osaka, Japan

Kazufumi Yugami Graduate School of Economics, Kobe University, Kobe, Hyogo, Japan

Yoshinobu Zasu Faculty of Economics, Kansai University, Suita, Osaka, Japan

Chapter 1
Introduction to Econo-Legal Studies: The Dual Views of Economics and Law

Hiroshi Takahashi and Takashi Yanagawa

Contents

1.1 Introduction 2
1.1.1 Aims of This Book and This Chapter 2
1.1.2 Historical Background 3
1.2 Economics and Law in Opposition: An Example 3
1.2.1 When and How Does the Market for Real Estate Leasing Function? 3
1.2.2 The Purpose of the Law: Benefit Society as a Whole or Provide Justice in Specific Transactions? 6
1.3 The Pursuit of Value in Economics and Law 10
1.3.1 The Value Pursued by Economics 10
1.3.2 The Value Pursued by the Law and Legal Studies 12
1.3.3 Economics and Law: Similarities and Differences 13
1.4 Contents of This Book 18
References 22

This book has two key objectives. One is to focus on the basics of legal and economic thinking and convey their commonalities and differences. The other is to allow the reader to understand the fundamentals of both legal and economic studies. Applying these thought processes in practice necessarily requires knowledge of economics and law in the context of specific issues and subjects. However, at a minimum, this book intends to convey the essence of legal and economic thinking. Moreover, by comparing these two approaches in the context of different domains, such as intellectual property, corporate, antitrust, labor, social security, environmental, and civil law, we intend to highlight the characteristics of each approach.

H. Takahashi (✉)
Graduate School of Law, Kobe University, 2-1 Rokkodai-cho, Nada-ku, Kobe 657-8501, Hyogo, Japan
e-mail: hiroth@kobe-u.ac.jp

T. Yanagawa
Faculty of Economics, Setsunan University, 17-8 Ikeda-Nakamachi, Neyagawa 572-8508, Osaka, Japan
e-mail: takashi.yanagawa@setsunan.ac.jp

T. Yanagawa et al. (eds.), *Econo-Legal Studies*,
https://doi.org/10.1007/978-981-16-5145-8_1

This chapter serves as an introduction to the book and begins by describing specific court decisions pertaining to legal and economic thinking. We first introduce two cases in which economics and law may be seen as being in opposition. These cases illustrate the diametric opposition of economics and law in terms of their recognition and appraisal of the free market's purposes. Then, we consider why these differences arise and discuss the points on which the two fields differ and the points that they have in common. We compare the pursuit of value, political views and methodologies of economics and law. Finally, we briefly describe the contents of this book.

1.1 Introduction

1.1.1 Aims of This Book and This Chapter

What sorts of people may read this book? We expect our readers to include law students, economics students, working people, and perhaps reading aficionados. Some may have selected this book for practical motives, whereas others may have chosen it out of intellectual interest. Regardless of their specific motivations, however, we expect our readers to want to understand not just law or economics but rather both in tandem.

How can this small book convey the key points of these two fields in the social sciences? Of course, it is impossible to provide painstakingly detailed information. An alternative option is to take a surface-level approach and convey only the most salient, important aspects of each domain. However, that sort of light fare leaves little lasting impression on the reader. Thus, we need to find another alternative.

This book opts to focus on the basics of legal and economic thinking while conveying their commonalities and differences. Some aspects of legal studies and economics mutually constitute part of the broader field of social sciences, but the two disciplines also differ substantially. The goal of this book is to guide the reader to better utilize these two domains and thought processes while still remaining aware of their differences, that is, to acquire an interdisciplinary understanding of legal studies and economics. In this book, we refer to the use of insights from both legal studies and economics to explore possible solutions to societal problems as "econo-legal studies." This terminology is intended to imply a distinction from the methodologies informed by the study of law and economics, that is, methodologies that focus solely on the use of economic methods to analyze legal phenomena and systems. Such methodologies are essentially a one-way adaptation from economics to the law.

This chapter serves as an introduction to the book and begins by describing specific court decisions pertaining to legal and economic thinking. We first introduce two cases in which economics and law may be seen as being in opposition. These cases illustrate the diametric opposition of economics and law in terms of their recognition and appraisal of the free market's purpose.

1.1.2 Historical Background

"Modern Western Law," the basis of the Japanese legal system since the Meiji era, developed from special characteristics of European society and history. With an affinity for capitalist market economies, it may appear from a historical starting point that economics and legal studies in the first half of the nineteenth century were not particularly contradictory. "Civil Law/*Bürgerliches Recht*" meant "laws for citizens," and the civil society in which those citizens lived was a capitalist society.

However, the honeymoon period for economics and law ended with the development of the capitalist economy. A free market is built on a framework of principles that include "inviolability of ownership" and "freedom of contract." It is regarded as a place where free and equal individuals compete to exchange products in a personally beneficial manner. In the latter half of the nineteenth century, however, it became clear that as the numbers of parties and goods in a capitalist economy expand, some aspects of the free and competitive market cease to function. Economists and lawyers have begun to discuss dysfunction in the free market, but they have not come to an agreement regarding the definition of "dysfunction" in the free market and the appropriate measures to take if the market is dysfunctional. To better understand this disagreement, we now introduce an example in which economics and law are in opposition.

1.2 Economics and Law in Opposition: An Example

1.2.1 When and How Does the Market for Real Estate Leasing Function?

Owing to real estate's considerable value, it is not only sold but is also often leased. In the case of a lease, the lessee generally pays rent to the lessor according to the lease period (usually monthly in the case of residential real estate). Moreover, depending on the region, the lessor may request a deposit of so-called "caution money" or "key money" in addition to rent. Consider the following case and, specifically, the payment of these fees.

Assume that a person (i.e., a lay citizen who, for our purposes, we call Mr. Rokkō) concludes a contract to rent an apartment for two years through a real estate broker (i.e., a specialist company that we call "Sumiyoshi Homes" in this example). Mr. Rokkō rents the apartment at a monthly rate of 56,000 Japanese yen (JPY), which is approximately 510 United States dollars (USD). Mr. Rokkō pays a deposit of 300,000 JPY (2,760 USD) in rent to Sumiyoshi Homes. At the end of this contract, Sumiyoshi Homes subtracts 250,000 JPY (2,300 USD) from this deposit and must return the remainder to Mr. Rokkō (who substantively receives 50,000 JPY or 460 USD). Mr. Rokkō agrees to this provision when he enters into the rental contract.[1]

However, suppose that Mr. Rokkō decides to cancel the contract within six months, a much shorter time frame than the initially scheduled contract period, and Sumiyoshi Homes therefore returns the 50,000 JPY to Mr. Rokkō. Many would find this response utterly natural, as Sumiyoshi Homes is simply performing its obligations as per the original contract. Moreover, an economics-informed approach also finds this conduct viable (Yanagawa 2006). From an economics perspective, because the market for rented real estate is free and competitive, Mr. Rokkō is deemed to have chosen the property that best met his desires and budget from the various options available. Requiring a deposit equivalent to nearly five months' rent is Sumiyoshi Homes' monetary expression that it is seeking long-term renters. Mr. Rokkō presumably concluded the contract with the lessor with this understanding, and if Sumiyoshi Homes were to hypothetically seek a vast and unreasonable amount of caution money from Mr. Rokkō, Mr. Rokkō would not consent to such a one-sided agreement. Put differently, the monthly rent over a given period of time is effectively reduced to the extent that the lessee pays caution money. The market economy exists to prevent parties from reaching an unreasonable outcome that benefits only one party. If the genuine intentions of two parties who come to an agreement through market forces are not respected and realized, then the market economy is distorted.

Nevertheless, in a trial in Japan (Kobe District Court Judgment, July 14, 2005, 1901 *Hanrei Jihō* 87) in which a renter like Mr. Rokkō sued a broker like Sumiyoshi Homes for a refund of the entirety of the 250,000 JPY deposit, the court fully upheld the claim. The reader should take a moment to consider the logic under which Mr. Rokkō's claim stands.

The party in this case made wide-ranging claims, and the court's rationale was also fairly complex. However, in terms of the aforementioned economic theory, the logic provided in the court decision can be summarized as follows:

> If the caution money in this case were intended to reduce the monthly rent, it might be deemed legally valid. However, making this claim would require the lessor to clearly explain to the lessee the extent to which the rent would be reduced relative to the rent to which the parties would ordinarily agree in a normally operating market. In this case, however, no such explanation was found to have been made. Furthermore, in the Kansai region, lessors of real estate compel lessees to pay such caution money, meaning that the terms of the agreement could hardly be said to have been entered freely (summarized by the authors).

Thus, the court's logic can be interpreted as follows. Under certain circumstances, the real estate rental market does not function as a perfect market as defined by economists; thus, when unfeasible transactions are made under terms that are detrimental to one party who is compelled to accept them, that party must be legally protected from harm insofar as the law is concerned. We must note that the actual

[1] Some readers may find this notion difficult to believe. However, this provision is referred to as a "deposit" or "caution money" (*shikibiki*), and this practice is common in the Kansai region, including Osaka and Kobe; the Kyushu region, including Fukuoka and Nagasaki; and other cities in Japan.

rationale given by the court according to the terms of Article 10 of the Consumer Contract Act (*Shōhisha keiyaku hō*) was more elaborate. We describe this case merely to highlight the court's perspective on the market and its functions.

This discussion leads to several conclusions:

(1) To reiterate the original premises, both economics and legal studies agree on emphasizing and respecting the free market.

(2) Given this agreement, the law sees its role as *actually* establishing a free market, providing an institutional framework for the free market, and regulating actions that may interfere with the establishment and function of a free market. Conversely, the economics discipline considers the conditions for the establishment of free markets *from a theoretical perspective* and seeks to identify phenomena that inhibit the functioning of free markets. Thus, in the case described above, economists view the return of only 50,000 JPY as valid conduct by the real estate broker.

(3) However, legal and economic interpretations of whether the free market is functioning as intended can sometimes diverge. From an economics perspective, the free market functioned as intended in the case described above. The real estate rental market includes many suppliers (lessors) and consumers (lessees), and supply and demand dictate the price (i.e., rent and deposit money). If the price is set too high, supply is too high and demand is too low, and lessors fail to find lessees, placing downward pressure on prices. If a transaction is highly profitable for a lessor, new suppliers will emerge in search of that profit, which will eventually place downward pressure on the price. Conversely, if prices are too low, supply will decrease and demand will increase. Thus, individual transactions are conducted at a price that balances supply and demand. Even if this balance temporarily deviates, the deviation is unlikely to last, and the market will self-correct. The fact that many real estate lease agreements in Japan's Kansai region include a mechanism for caution money indicates a balanced market; if the market were not balanced, caution money would not prevail as a general mechanism. In fact, when the vacancy rate increases owing to a decline in lessees during a recession, rent does fall, as does the amount of caution money.

(4) Conversely, from a legal perspective, these conditions do not constitute a free market, as the above example shows. Thus, it is necessary to understand the legal studies perspective on specific economic actions (and the decisions made by the parties thereto) in the absence of a free market. A key role of the law in this context is rendering a judgment on the legal validity of economic actions taken by individual actors. Trials are an archetypal form of this role. Thus, economic actions taken in situations in which free markets do not function tend to prioritize the interests of those with relatively fewer resources, including information. For this reason, the lessee's claim was upheld in the case described above. Here, a certain dynamism is working to restore fairness between parties in an unfair equilibrium. The market is meant to be a site for fair covenants between parties. Both legal studies and economics view agreements made in

such a market as promises that must be kept. However, legal studies aim only to protect covenants made within a free market, and this field's definition of a free market is more stringent.

1.2.2 *The Purpose of the Law: Benefit Society as a Whole or Provide Justice in Specific Transactions?*

The conflict between economics and law does not only arise in the understanding of the free market. These disciplines also commonly disagree on the purpose of the law. In this section, we again provide an explanation based on an actual court decision (Supreme Court (Third Petty Bench) Judgement, April 3, 2007, 61 *Minshū* 967).

Some of this book's readers may have studied a foreign language at a foreign language school. A foreign language learner can hardly expect to see results after just one or two lessons. Such courses typically take a long time, and one can reasonably expect the cost of a course to reflect the large amount of time required. The following case addresses a dispute between a foreign language school and a former student.

The foreign language school industry is very competitive, and, thus, schools try to attract potential students via a variety of measures. A device pioneered by a leading foreign language school in Japan is the adoption of a "points" system for tuition payment. Under this system, points cost less if a student purchases more points in advance. However, it is unclear how to handle pre-purchased points if a student decides to leave the course before he or she uses all of the paid points. We consider a specific example.

In this example, the fee structure is established as follows:

(1) A student pays for points in advance as a tuition fee. One point can be used for one lesson.
(2) If 200 points are purchased, then the cost per point is 2,000 JPY (totaling 400,000 JPY or around 3,660 USD).
(3) However, if more points are purchased in advance, then the cost per point decreases. A student can purchase 400 points for 1,500 JPY each (totaling 600,000 JPY or approximately 5,500 USD) and 600 points for 1,200 JPY each (totaling 720,000 JPY or approximately 6,600 USD).

In this case, we ask what happens if Ms. Maya, a hypothetical student, pays 720,000 JPY for 600 points but decides to quit the course after taking only 300 lessons. How should the tuition fee be adjusted?

In this specific case, a clause concerning the adjustment of tuition fees was included in the contract between the foreign language school, which we call "SOVA" in this case, and the student. According to this clause, SOVA subtracts the equivalent amount of points used before the student left the program (i.e., canceled her contract) from the total tuition amount paid and return the remainder. This requirement makes perfect sense. However, the amount to be returned varies greatly depending upon how the cost of a point is calculated. The problem lies in the system for determining the value of a point.

Ms. Maya may envision the system as follows:

> I used exactly half of the points that I paid for. The amount of points used therefore equals 1,200 JPY × 300, for a total of 360,000 JPY (approximately 3,300 USD). Thus, I should receive half of what I paid, or 360,000 JPY.

However, SOVA handled it this way:

> When Ms. Maya signed up, we explained the settlement provisions. These provisions state that the point price shall be determined using the closest rank below the actual number of points used. Because Ms. Maya used 300 points, she qualifies for reimbursement as if she had purchased 200 points (the nearest level below 300). Thus, the calculation is 2,000 JPY × 300, for a total of 600,000 JPY, and the amount to be refunded is 720,000 minus 600,000, a total of 120,000 JPY (approximately 1,100 USD).

The gap between the appropriate amounts according to each party creates a serious conflict. Whose argument do you find persuasive? Please take a moment to think about it before proceeding.

Economically speaking, this case can be evaluated as follows (Yanagawa 2008). SOVA's fee structure offers discounts for bulk purchases, which is similar to purchasing a suit at a discount suit store. If two suits are purchased together, the second suit is half price. If the price of the first suit is 40,000 JPY, then the second suit costs 20,000 JPY. The effective cost of each suit can be thought of as 30,000 JPY. Under normal conditions, selling or purchasing suits in this way does not cause problems. Selling two suits for the price of 1.5 suits is beneficial for both the seller and the purchaser, which is why this sales method is common. Offering a reward to customers who purchase in bulk makes everyone happy.

At a more granular level, however, it is important to understand what "purchasing in bulk makes everyone happy" means. Economically speaking, a lower price per suit is clearly beneficial for purchasers who desire two or more suits. From the seller's perspective, selling two suits to one customer reduces overhead (e.g., the cost of bringing in a new customer) relative to selling one suit each to two customers. Furthermore, some customers may think, "If the price per suit is lower when I buy two suits together, then I guess I will purchase two suits." If these types of customers are prevalent, then the shop's income will increase as well. As long as the price is set appropriately (i.e., if the total sale price is not lower than the actual cost of the suits), then sales will increase if the store offers this deal. In other words, if reducing the per-unit cost for bulk purchases leads to the seller making more money and the buyer saving money, then the needs of both the seller and the buyer are satisfied, and the situation works out better for everyone. This concept is the essence of desirability, and the key phrase in this case is "overall profit."

Consider what would happen if a buyer said, "I purchased two suits, but I want to return this one. The per-suit cost was 30,000 JPY, so I would like to be refunded 30,000 JPY instead of 20,000 JPY." If a store catered to this kind of request, then a single suit would essentially cost 30,000 JPY instead of 40,000 JPY, and it would be impossible for the store to stay in business. In this case, a store could no longer offer a second item for half price, and, thus, it is appropriate for a seller to refuse a request for a 30,000 JPY refund.

Economically speaking, the same reasoning should apply to the case of SOVA vs. Ms. Maya. The fee structure is beneficial for both SOVA and Ms. Maya (or any other student). If it is appropriate for SOVA to honor Ms. Maya's refund request, then it is optimal for every student to purchase 600 points for 720,000 JPY (assuming the student can procure the funds). As a result, the cost of one point, which is equivalent to one class, is effectively 1,200 JPY (approximately 11 USD). In this case, SOVA may not be able to remain in business. The fee structure was originally developed based on the assumption that some students would initially purchase 200 or 400 points. In this way, from an economics perspective, it is natural and correct for SOVA to respond as described above rather than being bound by Ms. Maya's request.

At first glance, this logic is very convincing. However, the legal approach is entirely different. Currently, according to a judgement by the Japanese Supreme Court, Ms. Maya's argument, rather than SOVA's argument, is correct. To understand why, we start by looking at the basic idea of the decision:

> Japanese law distinguishes between foreign language schools and suit sellers. Under existing laws, the method by which SOVA calculated the settlement amount reduces the consumer's benefit and is therefore invalid.

Here, we can see that the legal way of thinking is based on legal sources (i.e., individual laws and precedents) and that the law does not attempt to view economic acts as a whole and render uniform justice. Instead, it handles each case differently depending upon the nature of the specific economic activity and the personalities involved. We consider this distinction in more detail.

The law that plays an important role in this case is the Act on Specified Commercial Transactions (ASCT, or *Tokutei shōtorihiki ni kansuru hōritsu*). Like its predecessor, the Act on Door-to-Door Sales (*Hōmon hanbai tō ni kansuru hōritsu*), this law was established to protect consumers from malicious sales. This law covers all types of transactions, but the transaction type referred to as "specific continuous services" applies to this case.

Specific continuous services are businesses, such as foreign language schools, cram schools, aesthetic salons, and marriage agencies, whose continued services are expected to lead to a future result. These services have existed for a long time, but a particular social problem arose in the 1990s in Japan. Customers of such businesses who did not realize an improvement (e.g., improved language skills, improved beauty, etc.) or achieve a satisfactory result owing to poor service tried to cancel their contracts, but they repeatedly found that cancellation incurred a penalty, and they were unable to cancel their services in a satisfactory manner. To decrease the risk to consumers of malicious sales, the ASCT was revised in 1999 to add a provision addressing premature contract cancellations. The provision falls under Article 49 of this law,[2] and it directly affects the case that we are currently discussing.

---

[2] Article 49 of the Act makes the following stipulation (http://www.japaneselawtranslation.go.jp/law/detail/?id=3340&vm=04&re=01&new=1): "(1) If a service provider has entered into a specified continuous service contract, the recipient of the specified continuous services may effect a

Nevertheless, an objection from an economic standpoint surely comes to mind. According to economic thought, discounts for bulk purchases are generally considered desirable. In response to this objection, the question from a legal perspective is why economists are trying to judge the legality of a discount for bulk purchases in a general sense. It is possible to distinguish between inappropriate and appropriate categories for bulk purchases based on the details of the system in question.

We again compare specific continuous services with the suit example. A buyer can directly determine the outcome of purchasing a suit immediately after its purchase. Furthermore, the buyer and seller of a suit have a mutual understanding regarding its important points (e.g., size, material, and design). As such, the purchaser of a suit may not return after the suit's purchase. Conversely, with certain services, such as foreign language schools, beauty salons, and marriage agencies, buyers generally do not know when the effect will come out and what the outcome will be. Additionally, characteristics of the service that affect its outcome (e.g., the skill of the teacher or practitioner; the intervals between classes, treatments, or matching; and the degree of effort required of the user) are largely unknown to the buyer at the time of purchase. Furthermore, owing to the difficulty of achieving a satisfactory outcome, it is normal for a purchaser to be concerned about spending a large amount of money and achieving the desired result. Consumers who use specific continuous services

---

prospective cancellation of the contract in question once eight days have passed after the date on which the recipient of the specified continuous services has received the document referred to in Article 42, paragraph (2) (if the recipient of the specified continuous services did not cancel the specified continuous service contract under the provisions of paragraph (1) of the preceding Article by the relevant time limit because the recipient of the specified continuous services was under the misapprehension that information about canceling the specified continuous service contract under the provisions of the paragraph that the service provider had misrepresented to the recipient of the specified continuous services, in violation of the provisions of Article 44, paragraph (1), was true, or because the recipient of the specified continuous services was overwhelmed due to the service provider's use of intimidation, in violation of the provisions of Article 44, paragraph (3), then once eight days have passed after the date on which the recipient of the specified continuous services received a document delivered thereto by the service provider, pursuant to the provisions of order of the competent ministry, that contains a notice to the effect that the recipient of the specified continuous services may cancel the specified continuous service contract under the provisions of paragraph (1) of the preceding Article).

(2) If a specified continuous service contract is canceled pursuant to the provisions of the preceding paragraph, the service provider may not demand that the recipient of the specified continuous services pay an amount of money that exceeds the aggregate of the amount specified in each of the following items for the event listed therein and the amount of the relevant damages for delay based on the statutory interest rate, even if there is an agreement for liquidated damages or a provision for a penalty:

(i) if the specified continuous service contract is canceled after the specified continuous services began to be provided: the total of the following amounts:

(a) the amount equal to the consideration for the specified continuous services that were provided; and

(b) the amount specified by Cabinet Order referred to in Article 41, paragraph (2) in accordance with each of the services specified therein as the amount of damages that are normally caused by the cancellation of the relevant specified continuous service contract.".

typically have these concerns, and the providers of these services certainly understand these concerns. However, some service providers take advantage of consumers' feelings and think only of personal profit. The ASCT was created based on this background. Operators of specific continuous service businesses must provide these services responsibly, and consumers who decide that the quality of a service is not meeting their expectations must have the right to cancel their contracts. This is the aim of Article 49 of the ASCT.

In this way, the bar for providing a continuous service under the provisions of the ASCT is higher than that for providing services that are not covered by these provisions. Because Article 49 of the ASCT was designed to protect consumers of specific continuous services, the spirit of the law must be respected. Here, we can see the importance of emphasizing individual legislation and the legislative purpose of each article.

Additionally, because this law requests that business owners not engage in acts that can be considered unfair based on economic rationality, we can identify another special quality of legal thought. The law often expects a certain degree of ethics from actors and considers the righteousness of social relationships between specific parties. The law is not content merely with *overall* profit growth in the market; rather it focuses as much as possible on the fairness and justice of *specific and concrete* transactions. Article 49 of the ASCT is the legal manifestation of the idea that the consumer of a specific continuous service generally has fewer resources than the provider or operator of the service, and, thus, the consumer's well-being must be vigorously protected.

In summary, if the key phrase that summarizes economics is "overall profit," then the key phrase that summarizes legal thought is "adherence to the purpose of each law," with an orientation toward judging the righteousness of specific transactions.

1.3 The Pursuit of Value in Economics and Law

1.3.1 The Value Pursued by Economics

Thus far, we have examined the differences between economic and legal thought. Now, we consider why these differences arise. To determine the reasons for these differences, we begin with a point that both legal scholars and economists can agree on: they both probably hope to achieve a certain value in their academic work. Starting from this idea that both economics and law aim to pursue value, clarifying the paths that each field takes to achieve this goal can help us to mutually understand economics and law and help them to cooperate with each other using an appropriate division of labor. In other words, knowing the similarities of and differences in the pursuit of value in economics and law and understanding the possibilities and limitations of each field will enable economics and legal studies to share roles and cooperate. Thus, we must ask why economics and law prioritize different values. First, we consider this question from an economic perspective.

The value pursued by economics is the economic welfare of society as a whole. In other words, it seeks to improve the economic well-being of all people in society. For that reason, economics emphasizes the importance of realizing economic efficiency and fairness. Although human desire is infinite, the available resources (i.e., labor, capital, and natural resources) are limited, and, thus, "maximizing efficiency" means using these available resources effectively. In other words, the resources should be allocated to produce the goods desired by consumers, output should be increased to create as many consumer goods as possible, and the goods that are produced should be consumed by those who need them the most. However, it is thought that income redistribution is necessary for consumable goods to be distributed equally. The meaning of 10,000 JPY is very different for a rich person and a poor person. From a social perspective, 10,000 JPY has more value for a poor person; thus, redistributing wealth to the poor by taxing the rich is desirable to improve economic welfare.

When efficiency is defined based on the strong assumptions that it is possible to assign a monetary value to utility, a measure of a person's degree of satisfaction, and to compare utility levels across people, proposals for and evaluations of laws and policies that affect economic welfare become simple. Efficiency can also be defined such that it does not measure utility or require assumptions about individuals' different levels of satisfaction. The latter definition has merit in that the assumptions are weak enough to describe a more general situation, but proposing concrete laws and policies under this definition involves many difficulties. An important theorem is that a perfectly competitive market gives rise to efficiency regardless of the assumptions (see Sect. 3 of the Appendix "Elements of Economics").

There are three main definitions of fairness in economics according to different opinions as to the meaning of the word "fair" (Mankiw 2020, Chap. 20). The first definition relates to utilitarianism, which is the idea of maximizing happiness for the maximum possible number of people, as defined by Jeremy Bentham, an English philosopher, economist, and jurist of the eighteenth and nineteenth centuries. As stated earlier, if we assume that the value of money decreases for an individual as that individual's income increases, then redistributing income from high earners to low earners increases an entire society's economic welfare. The second definition relates to liberalism, represented by John Rawls, an American political and moral philosopher of the twentieth century, who states that judgements should be made from an "original position" under a "veil of ignorance" (Rawls 1999). Rawls suggests considering a point in time before an individual is born. At this stage, it is impossible to know whether that individual will be rich or poor in the future. The concern that this individual may be disadvantaged should lead a society to seek to improve the economic welfare of the lower class. This theory underpins income redistribution as social insurance. The third definition relates to libertarianism. Rather than seeking equality as an economic outcome, this definition prioritizes equal opportunities for economic behavior. In other words, by this definition, it is important to preserve the rights and freedoms that allow individuals to demonstrate their own talents rather than redistributing the income that individuals earn. An important caveat at this juncture is that when fairness is debated in economics, the issue of income distribution often arises. Debates on fairness generally treat the economic activity of individuals and corporations as though they are entities with independent intentions.

Economics considers laws and systems with both efficiency and fairness to be desirable, but typically prioritizes efficiency in practice in most cases. A major reason for this prioritization is that most people have the same definition of efficiency. Thus, it is easy to come to an agreement on efficiency and to analyze it economically. Conversely, people have differing views on the meaning of the word "fair," meaning that reaching an agreement can be difficult. For that reason, when debating efficiency, it is important to remain conscious of the other underlying value of fairness. Additionally, efficiency and fairness often have trade-offs, and it is important to remember that increasing fairness may lead to a loss of efficiency and vice versa.

1.3.2 The Value Pursued by the Law and Legal Studies

Next, we consider value according to the law and legal studies. These fields pursue many values, but two important concepts that are especially relevant are the equality and freedom of the autonomous individual. In the Constitution of Japan, Articles 13 and 14[3] deal with respect for individuals and their equality and rights under the law, and Articles 19–23 define a variety of guaranteed freedoms.[4] Furthermore, in Article 3(1) of the Civil Code, "the enjoyment of private rights commences at birth" defines individual equality in law. The article includes "principles of private autonomy," which encompass the principle of contract freedom, as a basic principle of modern private law.

---

[3] The Constitution of Japan makes the following stipulations:

Art. 13. All of the people shall be respected as individuals. Their right to life, liberty, and the pursuit of happiness shall, to the extent that it does not interfere with the public welfare, be the supreme consideration in legislation and in other governmental affairs.

Art. 14. All of the people are equal under the law and there shall be no discrimination in political, economic or social relations because of race, creed, sex, social status or family origin [the rest omitted].

[4] Art. 19. Freedom of thought and conscience shall not be violated.

Art. 20. Freedom of religion is guaranteed to all. No religious organization shall receive any privileges from the State, nor exercise any political authority [the rest omitted].

Art. 21. Freedom of assembly and association as well as speech, press and all other forms of expression are guaranteed [the rest omitted].

Art. 22. Every person shall have freedom to choose and change his residence and to choose his occupation to the extent that it does not interfere with the public welfare.

Freedom of all persons to move to a foreign country and to divest themselves of their nationality shall be inviolate.

Art 23. Academic freedom is guaranteed (http://www.japaneselawtranslation.go.jp/law/detail/?id=174&vm=04&re=01&new=1).

1.3.3 Economics and Law: Similarities and Differences

1.3.3.1 Values Pursued

With an understanding of the values pursued by economics and legal studies, as outlined above, we discuss the points on which the two differ and the points that they have in common.

Freedom is a prerequisite for the efficiency prioritized by economics, and equality is a prerequisite for fairness. In this sense, the concept of "efficiency and fairness" in economics is not inconsistent with that of "freedom and equality" emphasized by law. However, efficiency and fairness in economics mainly relate to the pursuit of economic happiness. Conversely, the values of freedom and equality emphasized by legal scholars primarily relate to rather non-economic spaces. For example, constitutional law scholars often emphasize the significance of personal freedoms, including freedom of thought, conscience, religion, and expression (see Column 15). Both constitutional and civil law place importance upon respecting equality. Unlike civil law, however, economics does not pay special attention to equality. Rather, these issues are considered a premise for economics. Additionally, if legal scholars emphasize freedom, we may observe a tendency to prioritize the freedom of the socially weaker party in any given dispute, as outlined in the previous section.

A value that has been traditionally consecrated in the area of civil law that includes the Civil Code, the Commercial Code, and the Companies Act is that of "security of transaction," which can prevent confusion when a transaction is cancelled or invalidated. In some cases, this value improves efficiency in economic activity. Additionally, economic efficiency is valued in many areas of patent and antimonopoly law (see Chaps. 2 and 4). From this perspective, efficiency also plays in important role in legal studies, and legal studies and economics may appear to have some affinity. However, in certain cases, lawyers, including legal scholars, emphasize other values besides efficiency, resulting in judgements that can be seen as inefficient from an economics perspective. Such judgements may, in turn, lead to disputes between economists and legal scholars, as we discussed in the previous section.

Finally, we should touch on the model individual that each field envisions. Court decisions often include references to the "average person." The average person as defined by the law is *not* a person who always makes flawless cost-benefit judgements. In other words, the average person in the legal world is not "rational" in an economic sense. The rational individual in economics is understood as a type of superhuman from a legal perspective. For example, in discussions surrounding the SOVA case, the economic viewpoint is that given the views of the Supreme Court, the discounted bulk sale system will become untenable, and businesses will no longer adopt it. From a legal standpoint, however, it does not necessarily follow that all consumers will begin to request that refunds be calculated based on the purchase price after such a judgement, causing the general bulk purchase discount system to fail. In other words, average humans will not cancel contracts so frequently that the system is likely to collapse.

1.3.3.2 Political Views

By now, the reader should appreciate that an understanding of the market and the relation of the law to the economy is pivotal to understanding approaches informed by economics and legal studies. Nevertheless, with both the market and the law, events do not occur in a social vacuum; it goes without saying that they are strongly influenced by the national political process that dictates their establishment. Thus, when considering the natures of economics and law, it is necessary to understand their relationships with politics. We therefore compare the role of politics and the government in the context of legal studies and economics.

Economics is typified by its treatment of the government, the main political actor, as a chiefly benevolent ruler. From this perspective, the legislative and executive branches of the government unify to create and implement policy for the betterment of the populace's welfare. The following chapters evaluate existing legislation, systems, policies, and their amendments and propose policies that the government should adopt from an efficiency (and, in some cases, fairness) standpoint. These ideas are intended to suggest actions for the government to take as a benevolent ruler in service of the people and are intended as strong recommendations of ways to create the necessary governance mechanisms for those ends.

The role of the state has been interpreted by economists differently throughout history. As such concepts as Adam Smith's invisible hand show, in the nineteenth century, economists posited that the government should take a laissez-faire approach, provided that the market has an inbuilt mechanism for self-regulating economic activity. From this perspective, governments should be small and focus mainly on national defense, police, and the judiciary. In the twentieth century, economists began focusing on efficiency and fairness and began advocating for government intervention in market failures that the market could not resolve (see Sect. 3 of the Appendix "Elements of Economics"). Moreover, economists do not always assume that the government acts as a benevolent ruler. In the second half of the twentieth century, the idea emerged that the people's economic welfare is sacrificed when legislators and administrators pursue their own interests (this situation is called "government failure," an analogue to market failure). The existence of government failure leads to the question of what systems must be devised to enable the government to act as a benevolent ruler, leading back to the notion that perhaps the market, rather than the government, is a better approach. In this way, economists' view of the government has changed over time.

By contrast, the fundamental notions of modern Western law come from the idea of the primacy of private law and also incorporate elements of European (particularly French) governance systems. The Civil Code, a general form of private law, is a constitution not in the sense of a foundational document for a nation but in the broader sense of constituent principles of society. In this context, the central actors are citizens who can make their own decisions and form relationships with other citizens. This principle therefore assumes that the government should play a laissez-faire role so as not to inhibit people's autonomous activity. Here, the basic idea of legal studies concurs with the idea of a small government, strongly seeks ways to suppress governmental activity to keep the government small, and seeks to control the government by separating the legislative, executive, and judicial branches. The latter idea is known as the "rule of law." From this premise, the problem of market failure and the political response to this problem became a concern of legal studies, and the eventual expansion of administrative power led to the inevitable restructuring of modern political concepts. Since the twentieth century, maintaining a balance between citizens' freedoms and national regulations has been an ongoing challenge in the legal, social, and national spheres. Nevertheless, it is reasonable to conclude that legal studies are generally distanced from the idea espoused by economics that the government is a benevolent ruler. Lawyers and legal scholars focus on how the political system and the government control politics and remain aware of the benefits posed to and risks of violating citizens' rights.

1.3.3.3 Methodologies

Next, we compare the two fields from a methodological perspective.

Methodologies in economics are largely categorized as positive or normative analyses. A positive analysis is a method of logical positivism that involves forming a hypothesis based on actual facts and then verifying it with data. In most cases, this process involves using logical analysis to create a hypothesis and then verifying it by performing quantitative analysis on a set of data. For example, an analysis may start from the assumption that consumers will react rationally. If the price of a certain good is lowered, then the demand for that good should increase. This derived proposition supposes a causal relationship between two economic variables (i.e., price and demand). Actual data can then be used to verify whether this proposition is valid. It is wonderful when a mathematically derived theory can be verified statistically. When such verification is not possible, however, logically hypothesizing causal relationships between important economic variables and then attempting to verify those relationships with historical and experiential data is an important analytical method in economics as well. Normative analysis, in contrast, is also called "welfare economics" and is based on value judgements. Specifically, it examines desirable economic conditions or policies according to basic values. As an example, to preserve a certain level of tax income without sacrificing efficiency, economists may discuss the relationship between goals and methods to understand the relative desirability of a consumption or individual excise tax. In economics, it is normal for students to debate without making their own basic values clear, but in normative economics, it is important to illuminate the values underpinning a debate.

Conversely, methodologies in the study of law can largely be categorized as discussions aiming for legislation and discussions aiming for interpretation. Legislation is the study and practice of the letter of the law and aims to determine which laws and regulations should be implemented to achieve policy objectives appropriately. Interpretation is a practice based on the idea that existing laws (including statutes, case law, and legal theory) should be examined from the standpoint of logic and systematic consistency to ensure that problems are resolved concretely in accordance with their content. Studying law at a university requires devoting a large amount of time to the process of acquiring the ability to interpret the law (Columns 10 and 13 describe various methods of legal interpretation). It can also be said that interpretation is one of the main duties of expert legal scholars.

Based on these definitions, we take a closer look at the different roles and unique features of economics and law.

1.3.3.3.1 Economic Methods

First, we consider economics. Positive analysis, as defined in the field of economics, can clarify the relationship between economic variables. Using that information, one can predict the resulting changes to those economic variables when laws or systems change. In particular, if a law or system is changed, positive analysis can consider not only direct and short-term influences but also indirect and long-term influences. Additionally, normative analysis is useful for clarifying the influence of changes to economic variables concerning laws and systems on set policy goals. As such, if a realistically achievable economic end goal is defined, the appropriate law or system for achieving that goal can be determined. The goal does not necessarily need to involve efficiency. Regardless of the goal, normative analysis can be used to identify the methods for best achieving that goal. As such, economics can be effectively used for advanced analysis to provide guidance on legislation and administration.

Economics can consider both direct and long-term influences, and its ability to discuss these matters from a standpoint of economic rationality is one of its special features. The importance of direct and long-term effects in economics is partially due to the unique characteristics of its analytical methods. We explain these characteristics in a bit more detail. Economic analysis involves identifying a problem that needs to be solved, determining the economic variables that have major influences on that problem, and analyzing the mutual relationships among those variables. An example is the changes that will result from the implementation of a certain law. In particular, if the law directly changes a certain variable, economic analysis can also check if the law indirectly affects any other variables. Then, this analysis can also identify any long-term effects of these indirect changes. The law influences people because people act according to incentives. In other words, people who operate under existing legal frameworks can be expected to act in their own self-interest.

In this way, economic analysis can be seen as playing a role in legal interpretation as well. Legal interpretation involves looking at past conflicts and, establishing the specific validity of individual cases based on established laws and past case laws. However, the meaning of the term "specific validity" changes depending upon the economic and social situations at the time.

We therefore emphasize the importance of practicing and learning the analytical methods of economics. To examine an economic problem logically, one must identify the major economic variables associated with that problem and then analyze the mutual relationships among those variables. Thus, it is important to capture the major essential elements and consider their relationship to the problem, ignoring unessential details. Logical analysis often involves mathematical analysis, but it is important to note that the relationships between variables can be intuitively inferred as well. Even when using difficult mathematics, a researcher has not truly found the essence of a problem if he or she cannot intuitively explain the conclusions reached.

1.3.3.3.2 Legal Methods

Next, we discuss legal methods. One pillar of the study of law is discussions concerning legislation. These discussions involve looking to the future to make desirable legal amendments, and they have a high affinity with economic analysis in that respect. Thus, it should be possible for economics and law to cooperate to create legislation that is useful and desirable to society. For example, it clearly makes sense to question the stipulations of the ASCT from the perspective of economic efficiency. In fact, even if consumers should be protected in a general sense, in the case that formed the basis of the SOVA decision, the consumer who filed the lawsuit initially purchased 600 points and cancelled after using almost 400 points. Whether this consumer should have been protected by the law is questionable from an economic perspective and is probably controversial even among legal scholars.

However, these principles only apply to discussions concerning legislation. Discussions of legal interpretation are different. As previously stated, interpreting the law is one of the primary duties of lawyers and legal scholars. Furthermore, the legal system, and particularly the judicial system, is only invoked when a specific problem arises (or is assumed). In other words, the law mainly deals with problems after they have occurred, and legal interpretation is carried out in that context and is expected to exert its power. An additional, closely related point is that the law has developed a unique conflict resolution mechanism called "adjudication." Moreover, to address an essential need, the adversary system was created. Two adversaries must be guaranteed an opportunity to submit evidence and state their arguments before a judge. Then, having listened to the arguments and considered the evidence of the opposing parties, a judge issues a judgment as to which party's argument is more convincing along with the reasons for that decision (Fuller 1963).

Accordingly, the legal decisions in an adjudication are driven by the claims and arguments of the two parties. As such, each decision has characteristics related only to the specific matter at hand. During an adjudication, the direct impacts on the parties involved are weighted heavily (this weighting is natural because the judgement is being made with regard to those parties), but little attention is paid to the indirect impacts on other parties or the long-term implications of the decision. In the case of the foreign language school, it may be reasonable to predict that a certain judgement will make it impossible for the foreign language school to remain in business and, thus, will negatively impact many students. Nevertheless, that prediction does not have a primary influence on the decision-making process. It is commonly held that the parties who appear before a judge cannot appropriately represent the circumstances and interests of any other stakeholders except themselves. An observer can notice and review a wide range of possibilities from the perspective of an economist, but that viewpoint naturally differs from that of a party in a specific adjudication.

1.4 Contents of This Book

We have covered many topics already, and we encourage the reader to keep these ideas in mind when reading the following chapters, as these ideas will greatly aid in understanding. To close this chapter, we briefly describe the contents of this book.

From a legal perspective, the organization of this book is quite unorthodox starting from the next chapter. The two chapters pertaining to the Civil Code, which is the main body of legislation covering all aspects of citizens' lives, appear at the end of this book (Chaps. 7 and 8), whereas the chapters concerning legislation applied to specific domains or social relationships related to markets and transactions appear at the beginning of the book (Chaps. 2–6). However, the inevitability of this sequence can be understood based on the introduction provided thus far. Laws that apply to markets and transactions under specific domains or social relationships (often referred to as "special laws," discussed in Column 7) are enacted because legal scholars may have identified cases in which a fair market has not been achieved (leading to antimonopoly law, see Chap. 4), because there is marked reason to impel various actors to behave appropriately following market growth (leading to intellectual property laws and amendments to the Companies Act, see Chaps. 2 and 3, respectively), or because the conditions under which citizens should be subject to legal protections as actors in the market have been reconsidered (although this category can include refinements to consumer protection legislation in general, here we focus on consumer protections in the context of labor legislation and protections of the right to lead a healthy and cultured life in society; see Chaps. 5 and 6, respectively). In other words, these laws are enacted to calibrate the market to function as intended. That being the case, this orientation in legal studies can be reconciled with economics; we can therefore conclude that legal studies and economics have a relative affinity in these domains. Chaps. 2–6 are intended to lead the reader to explore these domains and identify the general similarities between economics and legal studies while also appreciating the inevitable conflicts that sometimes occur. In particular, Chaps. 2–4 focus on domains in which economics and legal studies show particular affinity and exhibit a sort of internalized integration, referred to herein as econo-legal studies. By contrast, Chaps. 5 and 6 describe domains in which there are both opportunities for and challenges to the integration of these two disciplines.

The situation is slightly different in the case of the Civil Code, a general set of laws that act as the underlying premise for special laws (see Column 7 for details on general laws). Nevertheless, as mentioned earlier, civil law is fundamentally necessary for the smooth functioning of the market in a capitalist society, meaning that it *should* provide a sufficient set of rules for the market's autonomous operation. If we assume that it does, then it follows that an economics perspective is *not* necessary for the functioning of civil law. Moreover, at least in Japan, economics and law have little dialogue on topics directly related to the Civil Code. However, this varying conflict and coordination between economics and law, with each bringing its own characteristics to the table, leads to the development of key social values, including an exploration of what these values may be. Chaps. 7 and 8 deal with the two basic pillars of civil law, contracts and torts, and serve as a jumping-off point for the exploration of econo-legal studies.

Lastly, in Chap. 9, we focus on the environment, a domain in which numerous laws work together, and we describe how econo-legal studies may handle contemporary issues that are fraught with complexity and conflict. Column 1 provides details on how each chapter is structured from the perspective of economics.

Today, many complex problems are rich in both the legal and economic dimensions, and, thus, attempting to resolve them solely from the standpoint of a single discipline falls short; the combined efforts of both disciplines are required. It goes without saying that in many cases, numerous other disciplines must be used in conjunction with economics and law. Economists and legal scholars frequently differ in their general opinions, and we cover those general differences as well as specific issues and problems on which their opinions are divided. We also note that the opinions of economists and legal scholars frequently differ on issues within their own disciplines. We hope that the reader can take this fact into account when observing both the similarities of and differences between economics and law. Readers who identify discrepancies in opinions on complex legal issues are urged to investigate the basis for those discrepancies. Lastly, we hope that this book allows the reader to cultivate the ability to view ideas and problems through the interdisciplinary lens of legal studies and economics.

Column 1. The structure of this book from an economics perspective

Now that we have explained the organization of each chapter's contents from a legal perspective, we will briefly outline the organization of each chapter from an economics perspective. Various laws influence people's economic activities as regulations based on legal rules. Thus, to determine these laws' roles, it is important to consider what would occur without them.

Chapter 2 discusses the granting of property rights. Goods can be classified as public goods, club goods, common resources, or private goods, and the nature of a good changes when property rights are granted. Information is considered a public good if property rights are not granted, but it becomes a club good when intellectual property rights are granted (see Sect. 7 of the Appendix).

Chapter 3 focuses on addressing the market failures caused by information asymmetry within the Companies Act (see Sect. 9 of the Appendix).

Chapter 4 explains how to regulate the exertion of monopoly power under the Antimonopoly Act (antitrust law) in response to the market failures caused by monopolies and oligopolies (see Sect. 8 of the Appendix).

Chapters 5 and 6 focus on labor and social security law, respectively. The concept of fairness is at the forefront for these types of law, although efficiency issues, such as information asymmetry (see Sect. 9 of the Appendix) in labor law and risk sharing (see Sect. 2 of the Appendix) in social security law, also arise.

Chapter 7 deals with incomplete contracts, that is, the response of contract law to the fact that contracts cannot be expected to predict every possible situation at the time of signing.

Chapter 8 explains how tort laws serve to internalize acts that produce external effects (see Sect. 6 of the Appendix).

Finally, Chap. 9 discusses environmental law and measures that create incentives to solve problems caused by externalities, particularly in relation to recycling and landscapes (see Sects. 1 and 6 of the Appendix).

Column 2. Interpretation in economic thought

As explained in the introduction, interpretation plays a key role in the law, but it is also necessary within the realm of economic thought. For example, we outlined the case of a foreign language school being treated in the same way as a discount business suit store; however, from an economics perspective, the two certainly differ in some ways. With business suits, the offer to buy one and get one for 50% off is set by the trader, with the result that when a consumer buys two suits for 60,000 JPY each, the price of one suit is halved to 30,000 JPY. Conversely, in the case of SOVA, the school set the condition that students purchasing 600 points were charged 1,200 JPY per point when they signed their contracts. However, if a student canceled the contract after 300 points were used, those points were instead valued at 2,000 JPY each. In other words, SOVA nearly doubled the price of a point at the time of cancelation compared to the time that the contract was first signed. However, the question arises of whether SOVA can set prices as in the suit example, that is, by offering students who buy 400 points for 600,000 JPY the opportunity to buy the next 200 points for 120,000 JPY.

This concept is an important device to avoid disadvantageous legal judgments from an economics perspective. When setting a price in this way, it is possible to set essentially the same overall price while still avoiding the doubled price that was judged problematic by the court owing to the different prices when points were sold and canceled. Similarly, in the case of a landlord refunding a deposit, if the landlord properly presents two (or more) options, such as relatively high monthly rent with a relatively low deposit and relatively low monthly rent with a relatively high deposit, and if the court finds that the tenant has chosen an option voluntarily after careful consideration, the contract may not be considered legally invalid even if the deposit when the tenant moves out is high (although this choice must be reasonable from the court's perspective). These examples show that taking rational steps to factor in legal judgments is important in business and is therefore a true benefit of learning more about economic studies, although the authors hope that society as a whole will also benefit from the wisdom gained from econo-legal studies.

Column 3. If you go to court: Civil and criminal law

Directly observing actual legal proceedings is a good way to better understand the law. Doing so is simple—just go to court. We take Japanese courts as an example. As Article 82 of the Japanese Constitution stipulates, court proceedings are open to the public, even during the COVID-19 pandemic. When a visitor arrives at a court in Japan, he or she will find a case list (*kaiteihyō*) posted near the entrance that indicates which different types of cases are currently in session. This list will include two types of courts: civil and criminal. For those attending a case for the first time, it is better to attend a criminal case, especially if the first trial date for that case is being held on that day (such cases are designated as "new cases" on the list). The first trial dates for criminal cases are generally interesting and relatively easy to understand (it is not uncommon for such proceedings to move very quickly, sometimes taking just tens of minutes). It is also important to understand what the terms "civil" and "criminal" mean. Clearly, the fact that these divisions are separated within the court means that these classifications are very fundamental.

Most of the topics covered in this book are classified as civil law. Rules governing the rights of and obligations between citizens are termed "private law" (not to be confused with the Civil Code, which is the name of a particular statute that, along with commercial law, is an important part of private law). The litigation procedure based on private law as the standard for determining these rights and obligations is known as a "civil lawsuit." In a civil lawsuit, both parties (i.e., the plaintiff and the defendant) act essentially as citizens. Note that the term "citizen" in this case does not necessarily refer to a human being, as organizations, such as companies, are also often described by this term as well.

Conversely, criminal proceedings evaluate whether a defendant is proven guilty of a crime, decide whether to impose a sentence, and determine the nature and severity of the sentence. These proceedings all use criminal law as the standard. One party within a criminal trial is a citizen (i.e., the accused), and the other is a public prosecutor with the authority to investigate and prosecute crimes on behalf of the state. Like civil lawsuits, criminal proceedings are generally presided over by a judge or body of judges, but in criminal proceedings that meet certain requirements, members of the general public may be required to make legal decisions as lay judges (i.e., jury members), as some readers may know if they have been required to fulfill this societal obligation.

Incidentally, the expression "civil law" can also refer to a law that is responsible for regulating various procedures for establishing and realizing rights and obligations under private law, such as the Code of Civil Procedure. We realize that these divisions are not exactly as clear as they could be, but we will explain them in a bit more depth in Column 9.

Study Questions

1. Briefly explain the point of the judgement in the appeal of the deposit refund case (Kobe District Court Judgment, July 14, 2005, 1901 *Hanrei Jihō* 87) and why the legal and economic perspectives may differ using the terms "free market" and "fairness."
2. Briefly explain the decision made in the SOVA case (Supreme Court Judgement, April 3, 2007, 61 *Minshū* 967) and why the legal and economic perspectives may differ using the terms "bulk purchases" and "purpose of the legislation."
3. Compare economics and legal studies according to the values that they prioritize and their ways of thinking.
4. Explain your own thoughts regarding the deposit refund case and the SOVA case.

References

Fuller LL (1963) The adversary system. In: Berman HJ (ed) Talks on American law. Vintage Books, New York
Mankiw NG (2020) Principles of economics 9 Cengage Boston
Rawls J (1999) A theory of justice Cambridge Belknap
Yanagawa T (2006) Shijōka shakai wo sasaeru hō to hōritsuka no yakuwari: keizaigaku no shiten kara (The role of law and lawyers in market societies: from an economic perspective). Kōbe Hōgaku Zasshi 56(1):119–137 [publication in Japanese]
Yanagawa T (2008) NOVA jiken hanketsu to suiheiteki chitsujo (The sentence of NOVA's case and horizontal order). Kōbe Hōgaku Zasshi 58(1):39–52 [publication in Japanese]

Chapter 2
The Right to Own Things: Intellectual Property Law

Ryo Shimanami and Kenta Nakamura

Contents

2.1 Outline and Significance of Ownership Systems 24
2.1.1 What is Ownership? 24
2.1.2 History of and Reasons for the Existence of Ownership Systems 25
2.2 Outline of Intellectual Property Law Systems 26
2.2.1 What is Intellectual Property? 26
2.2.2 What Are Intellectual Property Laws? 27
2.2.3 Why Do the Patent Act and the Copyright Act Exist? 28
2.2.4 Characteristics of Intellectual Property Laws 29
2.3 Economic Analysis of the Patent System 31
2.3.1 Knowledge as a Public Good 31
2.3.2 Benefits of Patents 31
2.3.3 Social Costs of Patents 32
2.3.4 Patents as an Appropriability Mechanism 34
2.3.5 Pro-Patent Policy: The Case of Software Patents 37
2.4 Economic Analysis of Copyright Protections 37
2.4.1 Extensions of Copyright Protections 38
2.4.2 Unlawful Downloads of Digital Content 39
References 42

The legal bases for the idea that an entity can own something are ownership systems, which concern material (i.e., tangible) items, such as wristwatches and land, and intellectual property systems, which concern immaterial (i.e., intangible) items, such as ideas and brands. Even ownership systems, whose rationale for existing is rarely

R. Shimanami
Graduate School of Law, Kobe University, 2-1 Rokkodai-cho, Nada-ku, Kobe 657-8501, Hyogo, Japan
e-mail: ryo@kobe-u.ac.jp

K. Nakamura (✉)
Graduate School of Economics, Kobe University, 2-1 Rokkodai-cho, Nada-ku, Kobe 657-8501, Hyogo, Japan
e-mail: knakamura@econ.kobe-u.ac.jp

T. Yanagawa et al. (eds.), *Econo-Legal Studies*,
https://doi.org/10.1007/978-981-16-5145-8_2

questioned in contemporary Japan because it is self-evident, have some grey areas, such as forbidding the organ trade. Furthermore, the contents of intellectual property systems, such as patent and copyright laws, are greatly swayed by other aspects, such as a country's industrial policies. Thus, an understanding of these systems that links back to their reason for existing is particularly necessary. Economic analysis plays an important role in this understanding. Taking the perspective of efficiency, which is considered the premise of economics, is vital for constructing a system that stimulates the production or creation of information goods that benefit society, such as inventions and works of art, by providing monopoly rights. At the same time, the system must not overly restrict their enjoyment by society. In this chapter, we examine this perspective by comparing ownership and intellectual property rights based on actual patent and copyright systems.

2.1 Outline and Significance of Ownership Systems

2.1.1 What is Ownership?

Ownership is the right to exclusively use, obtain profit from, and dispose of something (Civil Code, Article 206). A landowner may live on (use) land, lease it to another person (obtain profit from it), or transfer it to someone else (dispose of it).

Along with the contract and tort systems, the ownership system is one of the basic property protection systems provided by the Civil Code, and we can say that it sets the premise for the contract and tort systems because it determines the subject and object of property rights, which are the targets of trades and infringement. For example, the validity of a wristwatch sales contract can only be determined once the wristwatch's ownership is established. Likewise, an unauthorized entrance cannot be classified as a tort until the physical boundaries (including not only a surface but also the space above it and the ground below it) of an area that falls under land ownership rights are established.

The Civil Code relates to tangible things, that is, clusters of atoms that a person can touch with his or her hands (Civil Code, Art. 85), and these things can be divided into real estate (land and buildings) and movables (Civil Code, Art. 86(1) 1 and (2)). In contrast, legal protection for intangible items, that is, ideas and things that cannot be physically touched or held (i.e., intellectual property, such as inventions, works of art, and brands) is provided not by the ownership system in the Civil Code but by intellectual property law systems, such as patent, copyright, and trademark law.

It is important to clarify the actual meaning of ownership being the right to exclusively use, obtain profit from, and dispose of a tangible thing. The relevant article says, "An owner has the rights to freely use, obtain profit from and dispose of the Thing owned, subject to the restrictions prescribed by laws and regulations" (Civil Code, Art. 206). Thus, it may seem that the article gives an owner the right to use, obtain profit from, and dispose of a tangible thing without interference from other people, but this understanding is not quite accurate. For example, if someone throws you down in a nelson hold as you try to get in your car, thereby stopping you, it is not be an infringement of your car ownership rights (of course, this act is not legal and is treated separately as a tort). Infringement of a person's car ownership rights occurs when someone enters or breaks that person's car without permission. In other words, the effect of ownership rights is not that they allow owners to use, obtain profit from, or dispose of the things that they own without interference (i.e., a positive effect) but rather that they can stop unauthorized use, profit, or disposal by others (i.e., a negative effect).

We have thus explained the ownership system determined by the current Civil Code. However, if we consider the broader meaning of "owned" as describing "a thing that is mine," numerous present-day issues, including some very difficult problems, arise. For example, current laws and regulations do not allow the purchase or sale of organs and blood even though people feel very strongly that their bodies are their own. Other examples of present-day issues are the ownership of babies borne by surrogate mothers and the level of control people should have over their private information. Most of these issues pertaining to the right to self-determination relate to the idea of ownership in its broader sense. Furthermore, the question of who owns a company (e.g., its shareholders, its employees, or possibly society at large) recently became a subject of controversy as corporate mergers and acquisitions started becoming more frequent. Furthermore, many environmental problems involve questions regarding the ownership rights to the pleasant aspects of a region's environment. Thus, the position and contents of the right of determination related to companies and the environment are also a type of ownership issue in the broader sense.

2.1.2 History of and Reasons for the Existence of Ownership Systems

Next, we discuss how the concept of the ownership of tangible things was formed and why this concept became legally protected. Textbooks on the Civil Code generally do not touch on ownership's history and grounds for justification. Until now, the concept of ownership and ownership systems has been considered a given premise in positive law, and its history and reasons for existence have been researched entirely by adjacent academic fields, such as basic legal theory, sociology, anthropology, and economics.

Of course, researchers who view history from a progressive perspective, such as a Marxist perspective, have a different understanding of the rationale for ownership systems as a means and tool for achieving a goal. Their viewpoints have been met with approval from even researchers who specialize in, for example, economic analysis of the law. One of the foremost law and economics researchers of that time considered ownership systems to be a means for improving social welfare and divided the rationale for the existence of such systems into six points: (1) the incentive to work; (2)

the incentive to preserve and improve things; (3) the incentive to transfer things to others; (4) avoiding the need for disputes, protection of one's possessions, or seizures of others' possessions; (5) protection from risk; and (6) the realization of a desirable distribution of wealth (Shavell 2004).

However, other systems and bases that justify private ownership do not start from such an exclusively instrumental and utilitarian understanding.

2.2 Outline of Intellectual Property Law Systems

2.2.1 What is Intellectual Property?

Of the several legal systems pertaining to ownership in its broad sense, we now focus specifically on intellectual property law systems, which relate to intellectual property as an intangible entity. Intellectual property is information with a proprietary value. Information, unlike a wristwatch or land, is an intangible item that cannot be physically touched. For example, a new invention (i.e., a technical idea) is information with an extremely high economic value in contemporary society, but an invention cannot be physically touched even if the machines that embody it are tangible. In the same way, works of art, such as novels or music, and trademarks, such as brands, are also forms of information that cannot be physically touched. Inventions, works of art, and trademarks are all typical examples of intellectual property (Table 2.1).

Taking the more concrete example of smartphones and cellphones, the devices themselves are movables (i.e., tangible objects), and ownership rights protect them. Accordingly, a stolen device can be returned to the original owner, as stealing is an infringement of a person's property rights. In other words, a person has the right to demand restitution under real rights. In contrast, if the technical ideas embodied by a device, such as an internal setup that enables efficient communication, fulfill the requirements for patentability, which include novelty and inventiveness, then they will pass through an application, screening, and registration process at the Patent Office and become inventions that are protected by patent rights. The music, videos, and games that are downloaded onto a smartphone or cellphone are protected by copyrights as works of art. In addition, the Apple or NTT Docomo logo engraved on

Table 2.1 Examples of tangible and intangible objects

Property (Tangible objects)	Intellectual property (Intangible objects)
Machinery, equipment, chemicals	Inventions (Ideas for technologies)
Paperback Bbooks, CDs, sculptures	Expressive works (Novels, musical compositions, art, etc.)
Clothes, food, cars	Trademarks (Brands)

the back of a smartphone or cellphone is a trademark registered at the Patent Office and is the object of trademark rights.

2.2.2 *What Are Intellectual Property Laws?*

Intellectual property laws are laws that regulate the interests of the parties related to intellectual property. These parties include the people who created a piece of intellectual property, the company that employs those people, the entities who use the created intellectual property (e.g., production, sales, publication, or broadcasting companies), and the individuals who want to use or appreciate the intellectual property. The interests of these parties sometimes conflict, and, thus, the government has established rules to regulate such conflicts in the form of laws.

However, no one law is called the "Intellectual Property Act." Instead, intellectual property law is a general term that covers separate laws, such as the Patent Act, the Copyright Act, and the Trademark Act, and describes this field of jurisprudence. The various individual laws that are categorized as intellectual property laws can be roughly classified as either creation laws, which provide incentives for creative work, and trade indication laws, which maintain order in market transactions (Table 2.2).

Because inventing new technologies and creating works of art are desirable activities that benefit society, the government promotes them by establishing creation laws and granting artificial monopoly rights, such as patent rights and copyrights. Furthermore, as in the case of the manufacturing and sale of fake brands, using another person's trademark without permission and free riding on their accumulated business credit is an undesirable act that inhibits fair market competition. Thus, trade indication laws are created as a means to prevent such actions.

Table 2.2 Main types of intellectual property and the related acts

Category	Acts	Objects
Creation laws	Patent act	Inventions
	Utility model act	Utility model
	Design act	Designs
	Copyright act	Expressions
Trade indication laws	Trademark act	Trademarks
	Unfair competition prevention act (in part)	Indication of goods or business

2.2.3 *Why Do the Patent Act and the Copyright Act Exist?*

As mentioned above, the Patent Act and the Copyright Act are both categorized as creation laws, and they grant monopoly rights as an incentive to promote creative activities (i.e., the production of information, such as inventions and works of art). A natural question is why such artificial incentives are necessary.

Unlike tangible items, such as movables, which can be put in a safe and locked away, or real estate, which can be fenced in, intellectual property information has no natural exclusivity. Thus, it is difficult to exclude unauthorized use, and no additional costs are incurred even if it is not excluded.

We know that inventions and works of art of this nature will be undersupplied by the market economy without incentives (see Sect. 2.3). For example, suppose for the sake of argument that the car is a single invention (even though many thousands of patents are embodied in cars). In the era before cars existed, it was necessary to invest a great deal of effort in research and development (R&D) to invent the first car.

Then, to actually manufacture a car, one must cover the costs of purchasing production facilities and raw materials and labor costs for the workers. In other words, for inventors to sell their inventions in the market and recover their investments, they must bear both the necessary R&D costs to create their intangible inventions and the necessary production costs to manufacture the resulting tangible products. In contrast, a person who buys a car that an inventor produced and sold and copies its mechanism without permission bears no R&D costs. This person bears only the production costs needed to manufacture a car and, thus, can sell a car with the same structure and performance at a lower price. If such copying of inventions is not stopped, it becomes extremely difficult for the person who first arrives at an idea to beat someone who copies the idea in market competition.

The cases of novelists and movie directors are similar. Writing a novel or making a movie requires a certain amount of investment, but once those intangible items are created, it is far cheaper to manufacture a pirated version of, for example, a Blu-ray movie disc or a paperback book, which are both tangible objects (recall the unit price of paper or a blank disc). If the pirated versions of movies or books start circulating at a low price or for free, the legitimate products will no longer be purchased, and writers and movie directors will have a hard time earning a living. This principle not only applies to traditional works of art but is also especially relevant to industrial works handled by companies, such as computer programs or databases.

Intellectual property laws play a role in this context by prohibiting other people from copying someone's work. Patent and copyright laws place an artificial monopoly (i.e., the right to prohibit copying) on the use of created work to enable creators to recover the costs of their creations. These laws thereby promote the invention of new technologies and the creation of works of art, both of which are types of information that benefit society.

However, monopolies also lead to social costs. First, direct partners who are banned from copying (e.g., persons in the same business) are harmed by not being able to use the information, and society as a whole (e.g., consumers) suffers the disadvantage of having to purchase patented products and reproductions at higher, monopoly prices (consumers would prefer to freely buy cheap pirated versions of these works). Furthermore, when inventions and works of art are created by building on previous work, it is not necessarily fair to give a creator a full monopoly over the use of the creation.

From this perspective, the importance of balancing the monopoly (prohibition of copying) and use (free copying) of intellectual property information is clear. Thus, although patent and copyright laws provide incentives to create in the form of monopoly rights, measures restricting these incentives have been taken. Examples include limiting the term of validity (in principle, patent rights expire 20 years after an application and copyrights expire 70 years after the author's death) and restricting rights in various situations (e.g., producing another person's patented product for tests and research, that is, reverse engineering and reproducing work for private use are both allowed). For more details about the Patent Act and the Copyright Act in Japan, see Shimanami et al. (2021, 2014).

2.2.4 Characteristics of Intellectual Property Laws

Next, we discuss the characteristics of the field of intellectual property laws. The main ideas are easy to understand by comparing these laws with ownership laws, which only appear to be similar.

Whether they are creation or trade indication laws, intellectual property laws aim to protect intellectual property by borrowing from the system of ownership law. In other words, intellectual property laws consider information, which cannot be physically touched, as intangible. These laws define property rights to enable the transfer and collateralization of rights and grant a rights holder the power to prohibit (forbid) unauthorized use. Both of these aspects of these laws are modeled after the ownership laws for tangible items described above. Notably, intellectual property rights, like ownership rights, do not have a positive effect, which would allow a rights holder to freely use intellectual property, but rather have only a negative effect, which forbids unauthorized use by other people.

However, intellectual property rights are also specific because their objects are intangible items. For example, unlike a tangible item, which is an object of ownership, an intangible item does not have clear physical limits. Thus, the definition of unauthorized use that constitutes an infringement of intellectual property rights is not unequivocally determined. In the case of land, it is clear that taking even one step over a border, such as a fence or a wall, constitutes a possible infringement on land ownership rights. In contrast, inventions, which are merely conceptual, technical ideas, have no borders in a physical sense, and, thus, it is not easy to determine whether a patented technology has been used. Thus, for example, the application form for a patent includes an annex called "patent claim scope." By describing the invention in that annex when applying for a patent, an inventor can linguistically clarify the object of the patent right as much as possible.

Two additional differences between the characteristics of intellectual property laws and those of the ownership rights system are as follows.

First, intellectual property laws are a policy-related field of jurisprudence. As mentioned earlier in this section, the current mainstream understanding is that creative laws are established to provide an incentive for creative work (this point is reconsidered from an economics perspective in the following section), and marking laws are established to maintain the market's competitive order. This line of thought is an attempt to explain intellectual property law systems from an economics perspective as means and tools for enhancing social welfare by providing incentives to create and maintain competitive order.

As we mentioned when describing the basis for the justification of ownership, intellectual property rights are sometimes justified according to the natural rights school of thought in addition to instrumental and utilitarian justifications (this tendency is especially strong for copyright laws, which express provisions for an author's personal rights). However, at least in separate concrete systems, the actual state shows that system changes (i.e., law amendments) are carried out relatively flexibly to reflect policy. In this case, the restraints of the law's state-ownership dogma are weak, and policies in each sector based on economics and management actually have a stronger influence.

Furthermore, intellectual property laws are an international field of jurisprudence. Both the Industrial Property Act (under the Paris Convention for the Protection of Industrial Property), which includes the Patent Act and the Trademark Act, and the Copyright Act (under the Berne Convention for the Protection of Literary and Artistic Works) fall under international conventions. Intellectual property laws are among the fields of jurisprudence with the most detailed definitions and the earliest international rules. Additionally, the World Trade Organization's Agreement on Trade-related Aspects of Intellectual Property Rights was recently concluded.

This agreement was made because both products that embody intellectual property and intellectual property itself are being traded across borders (e.g., songs by American singers can be purchased for download through iTunes worldwide), and, thus, it is necessary to set uniform rules for protecting intellectual property globally. It is also advantageous for developed countries to apply their intellectual property laws to developing countries as well. An apparent ban on piracy and fakes from developed countries will be reflected in developing countries as though an ownership system for intellectual property, which is information that is essentially free to use, is being imposed. The North–South problems related to intellectual property rights, which are typically exemplified by the issue of pricing the cure for AIDS, a patented product, in developing countries, are difficult from an international justice perspective and cannot be solved using economics.

Thus far, we have outlined ownership law and intellectual property law. In the next section, we focus on two intellectual property laws that are central to creative laws—the Patent Act and the Copyright Act—and attempt some economic analysis. The Patent Act and the Copyright Act are particularly suitable for economic analysis, even relative to other intellectual property laws, because they are strongly bound to policy. We aim to economically understand the world of creative laws, which change peoples' behavior by giving them monopoly rights to incentivize creative activities.

2.3 Economic Analysis of the Patent System

2.3.1 Knowledge as a Public Good

The economic rationale for the patent system stems from the theory of market failure based on the assumption that new technological knowledge is analogous to a public good (Arrow 1962). Traditionally, public goods are thought to have two defining characteristics. First, they are non-rival in consumption, implying that the use of a public good by one person does not reduce the supply available for others. Second, they are non-excludable, meaning that consumers cannot be excluded from using them either physically or with pricing once they are available. Common examples of pure public goods include national defense, police, and the justice system.

Knowledge is a public good because, first, its use by one person does not reduce the amount available to be used by others and, second, in the absence of patent protection, inventors have no feasible way of preventing third parties from using knowledge without their consent once it has been discovered and published. Thus, knowledge, including patentable inventions and similar types of information, appears to have both characteristics of a public good.

In a well-functioning market, the price for any good or service should equal the marginal social cost of consumption, meaning that the socially optimal price of knowledge use is zero in a static equilibrium. Hence, knowledge utilization is below the socially optimal level if its price is positive rather than zero. It is clear, however, that if knowledge were freely available in society, potential inventors would be reluctant to invest any of their own money in R&D because they would have no effective ways to recover their costs from free riders benefiting from their work. Thus, investment in generating new knowledge would be too low owing to knowledge's public good nature even though new knowledge is the primary driver of innovation and future welfare. These problems related to knowledge utilization and creation are a well-known example of market failure, which occurs when the market fails to align incentives to produce an optimal outcome; thus, government intervention is needed to overcome this market failure.

2.3.2 Benefits of Patents

Patent systems are designed to spur innovation and technological progress. The underlying objectives can be summarized in patent protections and disclosures of research findings. Patents provide temporary exclusion rights, which enhance private incentives to invest in R&D by offering a promising opportunity to appropriate the returns from R&D. Owing to this function, the patent system may be a way to mitigate or eliminate the market failure that arises from other parties' incentives to free ride on R&D efforts.

In return for the temporary monopoly provided by a patent, an inventor must disclose the nature of an invention. These disclosures contribute to the diffusion of ideas and encourage technological progress. In Japan, the Japan Patent Office (JPO) publishes the content of a patent application in the *Official Gazette* 18 months after the date of filing; similar systems have been introduced by many patent offices worldwide. When considering the significance of these disclosures, it is crucial to note that without patent protection, inventors can protect their intellectual property by keeping their discoveries secret. When disclosure incentives are exchanged for patent protection, however, other inventors can avoid duplicative research efforts by using existing findings, thereby developing more innovations based on prior work (although disclosures may induce so-called "inventing around" patents as well, as explained in the next section).

Moreover, the term of a patent is generally set at 20 years from the application date to balance patent protection and disclosure. The exclusive rights that the patent system confers are not infinite but instead last only for a finite period, after which a patented invention becomes part of the public domain and promotes cumulative innovations.

2.3.3 Social Costs of Patents

Although the patent system provides social benefits, such as inducing more innovation and knowledge spillovers, the exclusive rights of patent holders also create some social costs. First, when a given invention is subject to patent rights, firms can be restricted from using that technology, which, in turn, decreases the supply of products using that technology. As mentioned above, knowledge intrinsically has non-rivalry. For this reason, it is naturally more advantageous to provide knowledge to society at no cost. However, the patent system creates incentives to invent by artificially restricting access to knowledge. In other words, there are trade-offs between the use of knowledge and knowledge creation.

Furthermore, in many cases, R&D is cumulative. When patent rights are granted for a particular technology, new R&D based on that technology may be hindered because potential users of a patented technology expect the rights holder to charge license fees. In particular, when a basic technology is patented, third parties may be severely constrained from pursuing further R&D. For example, Kyoto University has stated that it has applied for many patents related to induced pluripotent stem cells (also known as iPS cells, pioneered by Shinya Yamanaka's lab in Kyoto, Japan, in 2006) because if the university, rather than a company, holds these patents, it can license the technology to anyone at a low cost, which will ultimately bring iPS cells closer to practical use (Nihon Keizai Shimbun, electronic version, July 18, 2011).

Second, the patent system may encourage duplicative R&D investments for several reasons. The patent system incentivizes R&D by inducing competition among firms to obtain a technology first through a mechanism called "first-to-file" (i.e., if two parties apply for a patent for the same invention, the first party to file is granted the patent). However, such a patent race may also lead to the overprovision of R&D from a social perspective. We first consider a case with no patent races (i.e., only one firm conducts R&D). Suppose that the expected profit from the outcome of R&D is greater if the R&D is pursued earlier because the discounted present value of the profit is smaller the later the result is realized. Conversely, if R&D is pursued earlier, then its cost is greater because less information and equipment that are useful for R&D are available in earlier periods. Under these circumstances, a firm should conduct R&D when the difference between the profit and the cost is maximized. Next, we consider a situation in which multiple firms are developing the same technology (i.e., a patent race with multiple players) and determine when it is optimal to conduct R&D. If one firm increases its R&D expenditures, the possibility of technological anticipation increases. Thus, rival firms have an incentive to increase their investments to succeed in R&D as quickly as possible. As a result of this competition, the optimal R&D timing is when the difference between the profit and cost of the R&D is zero. Competition accelerates technological progress relative to the case of no patent race, but it also generates socially excessive R&D investment.

As mentioned in the previous section, the disclosures associated with patents reduce duplicative R&D investments in the same invention. However, once a technology is protected by a patent, third parties cannot implement it without the patent rights holder's permission. Thus, disclosures may inspire a company to invent around a patent, which is beneficial to that company but can be regarded as duplicative by society. Socially unnecessary duplications of investments are especially extensive when existing patent rights are narrow because, in that case, it is easy to invent around patents. Additionally, the long protection period of a patent encourages investments in reproduction owing to the high necessity of seeking acceptable alternatives to the legally encumbered technology.

The costs of defensive applications and the cost of maintaining the patent system itself are also included in the social cost of the patent system. A defensive application is an application for a patent that a company does not intend to use. These applications aim to reduce the risk that a competitor will enter the market with a technology that substitutes for the company's patented technology. In some cases, companies obtain patents in domains that are peripheral to other firms' patents to increase their bargaining power if a competitor brings a patent infringement suit. The costs of these strategic filings can be avoided if competitors can cooperate, but such cooperation is generally difficult to broker. Furthermore, the patent system is a mechanism for granting property rights to intangible inventions, which is far more complicated and costly than establishing property rights to physical and measurable tangible objects, such as land, vehicles, and equipment.

The discussions in this section thus far can be summarized by reconfirming the significance of the patent system. First, it seems entirely appropriate to achieve the socially optimal level of R&D investment without exercising market power and with sufficient diffusion of technology, but doing so is not easy given that knowledge has the characteristics of a public good. However, because knowledge is a public good, it may be possible for the government to conduct R&D using public funds and publish the results for free, as is the case with other public goods. In fact, the government directly funds research at universities and public research institutes with the intention of generating fundamental knowledge. This funding is because the divergence between private and social returns is greater for many basic research projects and technologies. The government may also commit funds to stimulate applied and development research. However, government support in these fields may not necessarily be efficient because the government has less information on the commercialization of the candidate technologies than the private sector does. Another issue is that the government has minimal incentives to reduce the expenses associated with R&D. In other words, R&D suffers from not only market failures but also government failures. Despite the variety of social costs involved, however, many countries adopt a patent system as the second-best solution on the basis that it is the least expensive way to incentivize innovation.

2.3.4 Patents as an Appropriability Mechanism

Section 2.3.2 states that one of the primary purposes of the patent system is to increase incentives for R&D by protecting inventions. It is true that after a patent is granted, no unit or individual may use the patented invention without permission from the patent holder. However, for the patent system to increase incentives to invent, it is not sufficient for patents to protect inventions. What really matters to a patent applicant is whether the patent can be used to appropriate the benefits from the invention.

It is important to note that the protection of an invention by a patent does not always coincide with the benefits of innovation provided by a patent. We explain this distinction using the example of a pencil that does not roll off tables (Marushima 2008, pp. 17–18). First, assume that only pencils with totally round cross-sections exist. Next, suppose that a company invents a pencil with a triangular form and files a patent application, thinking that it can earn greater profits by creating a pencil that does not accidentally roll away. If the patent is granted, the company will have exclusive rights to manufacture and sell triangular pencils. However, it is unlikely that this patent will perfectly capture the value of the non-rolling pencil innovation. It is easy to see that the cross-section of a non-rolling pencil does not need to be triangular. Such a pencil can be square, hexagonal, or even elliptical. Furthermore, it may be possible to create a pencil with a perfectly circular cross-section that does not roll by shifting the center of gravity. Thus, in many cases, technologies or products can be invented that come as close to the boundaries of a patent as possible without crossing them. This activity is referred to as "inventing around" a patent.

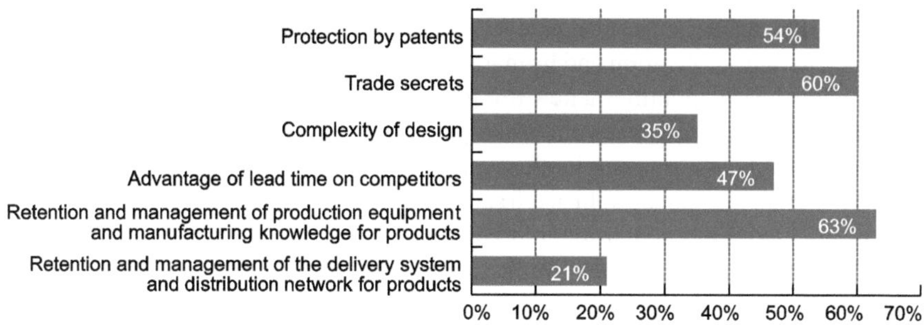

Fig. 2.1 Methods to ensure a profit from innovation activities for the most important product innovation: proportion of all product innovators, defined as large firms in all industries (%)
Note This figure shows the percentage of product innovator firms responding that the effect of each appropriation mechanism is "high" or "medium"
Source Japanese National Innovation Survey 2003, National Institute of Science and Technology Policy

Given the possibility of inventing around a patent, it is natural to ask to what extent patenting is effective for appropriating the profits from an innovation. The term "appropriability" refers to the ability of an innovator (i.e., a firm or individual) to capture the profits generated by an innovation. Levin et al. (1987) and subsequent researchers have identified several means by which firms can attempt to appropriate the gains from innovation.

Figure 2.1 shows the effectiveness of various appropriation mechanisms for firms' important product innovations based on the Japanese National Innovation Survey (Ijichi et al. 2004). Of the respondents, 54% stated that patents are effective at protecting innovation, implying that although patents are useful to a certain extent, they are not seen as a foolproof means of protection. The respondents rated two mechanisms as being more effective than patents. The first is control of complementary assets (63%), which refers to the assets or capabilities, such as manufacturing capacity, distribution channels, and after-sales service, that are necessary to successfully commercialize a technology (Teece 1986). The second is secrecy (60%). Respondents said that the next most useful tool after patents is having a lead-time advantage over competitors (47%). These results suggest that firms have a diverse set of appropriation mechanisms in addition to patents. As described in the previous section, the patent system has certain social costs. Thus, in designing a patent system, it is crucially important to consider the validity of other appropriation mechanisms.

As the Japanese National Innovation Survey and other data clearly show, the effects of patents differ widely by industry, technological field, and type of innovation. For example, patents are well known to have high appropriability in the pharmaceutical industry. In the survey, 85% of large firms in this industry responded that patents are useful, which is much higher than the total rate of 54% shown in Fig. 2.1 (Ijichi and Odagiri 2006). This difference is because the core technical feature of a pharmaceutical product is the active substance, which is protected by a strong patent called a substance patent. Under the substance patent system, if a basic patent protects a substance (i.e., a substance patent), then it protects the use of the chemical substance for any application and its manufacture by any process. Thus, for example, even if a third party identifies a new-use invention of a known substance, this invention cannot be implemented without the patentholder's consent. When a substance patent expires, however, generic alternatives to the previously patented drugs can enter the market and can be sold at a fraction of the price of branded drugs. Thus, the sales of branded drugs can drop rapidly in a phenomenon known as a "patent cliff." This phenomenon is a testament to the fact that patents protect innovation interests in the pharmaceutical industry exceedingly effectively.

It is also known that patents are more relevant for product than for process innovation. The difference in the strengths of these legal protections arises for several reasons. First, patents' effectiveness as appropriability tools depends in part on the object of rights as defined by the Patent Act. This dependence is because the scope of inventions protected by patents and the requirements for their registration can change owing to amendments to the Patent Act or revisions to the guidelines for the examination practice within the Intellectual Property Office. In fact, the aforementioned substance patents were first introduced in Japan in 1976; previously, pharmaceutical inventions were generally protected by patents on manufacturing methods (i.e., process patents). Thus, companies that developed branded drugs could not prevent new entrants from producing equivalent drugs using other manufacturing methods that did not infringe on incumbents' patents.

Second, the definability of an invention is a major factor in the effectiveness of patents as appropriability mechanisms. To obtain patent protection, an inventor must describe the content of an invention in writing because intellectual property offices, including the JPO, recognize only written descriptions and do not accepts submissions of products or oral explanations. However, some techniques may be challenging to describe in writing. For example, artisan skills often involve intuitive elements (i.e., tacit knowledge), which are difficult to codify or explain in text form. Conversely, some knowledge can be easily expressed through diagrams or text (i.e., explicit knowledge). Naturally, the latter knowledge is more likely to be patentable.

Third, the enforceability of patent rights is at least an equally important factor in a patent's effectiveness for appropriability. This outcome relates to the fact, confirmed by extensive empirical work, that product innovations are more likely to be patented than process innovations are. A product innovation is an innovation related to a product itself, and its features are easy to recognize visually; thus, patent infringement in product innovation is relatively easy to detect and prove. By contrast, it is difficult to identify an infringement of process innovation merely by looking at a downstream product. It is also hard to demonstrably prove infringement in court. Thus, in the case of process innovation, enforcing one's patent rights against infringement can be difficult, which tends to decrease the effectiveness of patents as appropriability mechanisms.

2.3.5 *Pro-Patent Policy: The Case of Software Patents*

As mentioned in the previous section, the appropriability of a patent also depends on the nature of the underlying patent system. Thus, it makes sense to ask whether increasing patent protections leads to greater incentives to pursue R&D. Beginning with the United States in the 1980s, many countries have trended toward increasing patent protections, and several empirical analyses have assessed the impacts of pro-patent policies. Here, we discuss Bessen and Hunt (2007) research on software patents in the United States.

In the past, United States patent law did not protect computer programs; instead, computer programs were mainly protected by copyrights. However, in the 1981 *Diamond v. Diehr* judgment, the United States Supreme Court suggested moving toward applying patent protections to software-related technologies, which gradually opened up the use of software patents. In 1996, after several landmark decisions by this court, such as the decision in *In Re Alappat* (Fed. Cir. July 29, 1994), the United States Patent and Trademark Office issued examination guidelines for computer-related inventions, and the availability of software patents has rapidly relaxed since then. Bessen and Hunt (2007) analyze whether introducing patent protections to the software domain indeed increased incentives to invest in R&D.

According to their analysis, relaxing barriers to software patents significantly increased the number of patent filings. However, growth in R&D inputs and productivity improvements explain very little of this increase; instead, the ease of obtaining a software patent contributed significantly to the increase in software patent applications. In other words, Bessen and Hunt (2007) conclude that strengthening patent protections did not increase incentives to invest in R&D. Although more than a few studies have produced similar results for pro-patent policies (Boldrin and Levine 2008, Chap. 8), one interpretation of this result is that strengthening patent rights has a small marginal effect because most empirical studies of pro-patent policies are conducted in countries with well-developed patent systems (Yamada 2009, p. 247).

2.4 Economic Analysis of Copyright Protections

In the preceding section, we explained that protecting inventions using patents leads to trade-offs; although patents provide incentives to conduct R&D, they also incur social costs. However, these trade-offs do not exclusively apply to patents but rather apply to intellectual property rights as a whole, including the copyright system discussed in this section. The positive aspect of the copyright system is that it encourages the creation of new works by reducing copying, whereas its negative aspects are the costs of limiting access to creative works and the administrative and enforcement costs of operating the system. In this section, we discuss extensions of copyright protections and a recent amendment of Japanese copyright law to prevent illegal downloads of pirated music or films to obtain insights on the ideal form of copyright protection.

2.4.1 *Extensions of Copyright Protections*

The discussion of extending the protection period for copyrighted works in Japan originated from the Copyright Term Extension Act (CTEA) of 1998, which extended copyright terms in the United States. First, it is crucial to understand the Berne Convention (formally known as the International Convention for the Protection of Literary and Artistic Works), which is an international agreement governing copyrights that was first accepted in Berne, Switzerland, in 1886. One of the basic principles of the Berne Convention is that of "automatic protection," which means that copyright protection exists automatically when a work is fixed in a tangible medium, such as paper, film, or a silicon chip, without any specific formalities, such as a registration process. Furthermore, the convention requires that the copyright protection period span the author's lifetime and 50 or more years after the author's death. Thus, the over 150 countries that are parties to the convention have stipulated that a copyright exists once a work is created and lasts for at least 50 years after the author's death.

In the United States, the Copyright Act of 1976 stipulated that a copyright lasted for the author's lifetime plus the next 50 years. For a work of corporate authorship, a copyright lasted for 75 years after an author's death. The CTEA of 1998 sought to extend post-mortem protections for non-corporate works by 20 years. It also sought to extend protections for works of corporate authorship to 120 years after creation or 95 years after publication, whichever ended earlier. The CTEA is called the Sonny Bono Copyright Term Extension Act, after its proposer, and is also derisively called the Mickey Mouse Protection Act because Disney lobbied to extend the provisions to cover the copyrights for Mickey Mouse, who first appeared in 1928. In 1999, the year after the CTEA was promulgated, internet publisher Eric Eldred, the lead petitioner, and other publishers and librarians brought the lawsuit *Eldred v. Ashcroft* to obtain an injunction on the enforcement of the act. However, the Supreme Court ruled in 2003 that the act was constitutional. Currently, the term of copyright protection is 70 years after an author's death in many European countries and in the United States. In Japan, the revised Copyright Act came into effect on December 30, 2018, when the Comprehensive and Progressive Agreement for Trans-Pacific Partnership came into effect. The term of protection in Japan was thereby extended to 70 years after an author's death.

In general, when the term of copyright protection is too short, the creator's potential profits are insufficiently protected, which may reduce the incentive to create. At the same time, because works are often created based on prior achievements, an overly long protection period can inhibit the creation of new work. It is reasonable to ask whether extensions of copyright protections, such as the CTEA of 1998, increase the incentive to create. Thus, George Akerlof, who is known for "The Market for

Lemons," his work on asymmetric information, and who won the 2001 Nobel Memorial Prize in Economic Sciences, estimated the impact of extensions along with his colleagues in an amicus brief in the *Eldred v. Ashcroft* case (Akerlof et al. 2002).

Suppose that an author lives for 30 years after creating a work. The annual revenue generated from the copyrighted work is constant, and the discount rate is 7%. In this scenario, the increase in revenue, that is, the increase in the present discounted value of the income flow from the work, when the copyright is extended from 50 to 75 years after the author's death is only 0.33%. Akerlof's estimation therefore implies that the discounted present value of earnings in the distant future is so small that the copyright extension cannot be expected to increase incentives to create. Additionally, Landes and Posner (2003) find that the term extensions of the United States Copyright Act of 1962 and 1998 did not increase the number of creative works. Tanji (2008) investigates the publication status of Japanese works after their authors' deaths and finds that the life spans of many works are shorter than the terms of copyright protection.

2.4.2 *Unlawful Downloads of Digital Content*

In Japan, the revised Copyright Act, which came into effect on January 1, 2010, made it illegal to download music or video files that were uploaded without the copyright holder's permission, knowing that such files are unlawful. Prior to 2010, the unauthorized uploading of copyrighted content to the Internet without the rights holder's consent was treated as an illegal infringement on reproduction and public transmission rights, which are part of a copyright. A typical case involved peer-to-peer file-sharing networks or unauthorized uploads to video sites, such as YouTube. The 2010 amendments made the downloading of illegal files, even for private use, illegal. In addition, illegal downloads were criminalized under the amended Copyright Act of October 1, 2012. Reflecting the activities of pirate websites, such as Mangamura, the applicable scope of the regulation on downloading copyrighted works that were uploaded illegally was expanded from music and video to manga, books, essays, and computer programs, among others, in January 2021. This case can be regarded as an intriguing natural experiment in which copyright protections, which had generally grown stronger for many years, were substantively weakened by the emergence of a new technology, that is, the Internet.

According to the Recording Industry Association of Japan's "Usage Survey on Illegal Distribution" (RIAJ 2011), the number of downloads of illegal music files is estimated to be 4.36 billion, about ten times the size of legitimate music distribution. Furthermore, based on the sales price of legal music distribution, the potential estimated revenue from these illegal downloads if they were instead purchased legally is 668.3 billion JPY, which is about eight times the annual sales of music that was legally distributed over the Internet, which were 86 billion JPY in 2010. The Computer Entertainment Supplier's Association also provides estimates regarding illegally copied game software (CESA 2010). Their survey reports that between 2004 and 2009, total domestic losses in Japan from illegal downloads of Nintendo DS and PlayStation Portable software were 954 billion JPY; worldwide damages were estimated to be 3,816 billion JPY. The damage to creators from these illegal downloads (i.e., the effect of illicit copies substituting for legitimate products) is the rationale for the recent legal amendments.

However, it is theoretically possible that sharing files of music and other goods and unauthorized uploads and downloads to a digital platform can increase the demand for legitimate goods. First, if creative content, such as music, videos, and books, is an experience good, that is, a good whose quality can be understood only after consuming it, then file sharing allows a user to gain information about a content or creator and, thus, may increase a user's willingness to pay for the legitimate version of a product or other work by the same creator (Shapiro and Varian 1999). This effect can be described as a consumer learning effect. Second, even if a standalone consumer's willingness to pay does not exceed the retail price of an information good, if the aggregate willingness to pay within a small-scale social sharing group does exceed the retail price, then sharing will markedly increase the seller's profits (Bakos et al. 1999).

Based on this description, the effects of illegal copying on sales of information goods are not apparent a priori but rather are an empirical issue. Empirical research in this field is still ongoing, and Oberholzer-Gee and Strumpf (2007), for example, find that the effect of illegal downloading on CD sales cannot be confirmed. Waldfogel (2010), however, estimates that illegal copies of a music file reduce its download sales by one sixth to one third. Waldfogel (2010) also suggests that because the music obtained via illegal downloading is generally not highly valued by consumers, if only an authentic version existed, these consumers would be unlikely to purchase it. This suggestion is meant to imply that file sharing does not reduce the music industry's profits but rather creates a surplus of consumers.

To reiterate, no consensus has been reached on the impacts of piracy and illegal copies on legitimate copies. Even if illegal copies decrease revenue from CDs and other media, it is not clear that the incentives to create, publish, or release works have concomitantly declined. It is also possible that the emergence of new technologies can motivate artists and the entertainment industry to transition from traditional sources of revenue to complementary sources to compensate for illegal copies. For example, YouTube provides a business model that monetizes secondary uses of content (i.e., illegal uploads). Specifically, when a legitimate copyright holder registers video information with YouTube in advance, the service automatically identifies copyright-infringing videos and allows the holder to choose to block the content (i.e., delete it), track the content (i.e., monitor where and how it is used), or monetize it (i.e., display advertisements on it to generate revenue). In the United States, many copyright holders reportedly elect to monetize infringing videos rather than deleting them. The South Korean rap artist PSY, who released the song "Gangnam Style" in July 2012, chose to monetize infringing content. This music video, which was the first in YouTube history to surpass 1 billion views, earned over 8 million USD in advertising revenue on YouTube. Because 50% of the advertising revenue on YouTube goes to the video publisher, PSY earned 4 million USD (Nihon Keizai Shimbun, electronic edition, February 22, 2013).

The optimal level of copyright protection is the level that maximizes social welfare. In other words, the most important metric is the extent to which new works are created, released, and distributed. It is therefore important to consider that strengthening copyright protection based on discussions that focus on sales in a limited market may reduce social welfare due to excessive protections.

Column 4. Who are the readers of the law? Mandatory and voluntary laws

The terms "mandatory laws" (*kyōkō hōki*) and "voluntary laws" (*nin'i hōki*) appear in Chap. 3 (see also Column 5), and some readers may find them confusing. Who is mandated (or forced) by certain laws? In what sense are some regulations voluntary, and for whom are they voluntary?

The provisions of private law generally serve quite effectively as judicial standards primarily because judges are one of principal readers of them, and judges in certain cases simply enforce these laws. Even if regulations are voluntary, they are enforced in the same way every time. However, if citizens decide to establish rights and obligations in their own contracts that differ from those stipulated in voluntary regulations (i.e., they decide to exclude the effects of the provisions of the law) and the contracts are also approved by the court, then the court will enforce these contract regulations. Citizens are legally permitted to voluntarily establish rights and obligations related to such provisions regardless of the law's provisions.

Thus, from the court's perspective, the mandatory provisions of the law are the provisions that must be enforced regardless of the content of an agreement between parties, whereas any voluntary provisions that differ from the content of an agreement are viewed with respect for the voluntary nature of the agreement. From the perspective of the parties to an agreement, mandatory provisions are those that are enforced by the court, and voluntary provisions are those that can be voluntarily excluded if they both agree. Thus, laws are not necessarily always dictates imposed on citizens from above. Additionally, whether a means of enforcement based on a court decision is equipped is not as relevant because if voluntary provisions are enforced through a court, they can be enforced through the power of the state. This discussion therefore becomes somewhat complicated. In short, although mandatory and voluntary provisions are widely accepted among lawyers, they may not be as simple as they seem, nor is the idea that laws are compulsory orders imposed by the state.

Finally, a few related points are worth considering. First, determining whether specific provisions under private law are mandatory or voluntary requires judgment through informed interpretation. It is difficult to distinguish between the two solely by reading the text of a law. Second, the provisions of public law are essentially all mandatory, with some exceptions, such as

Article 11, paragraph 1 of the Code of Civil Procedure. Third, even mandatory provisions are not legally enforced unless they are subject to a judgment in court proceedings. A judge rules on whether provisions offend public order and morals, and a contract between parties can also be valid even if the matter does not lead to a court proceeding. Fourth, both mandatory and voluntary provisions can exert de facto influence and action-regulation power over citizens, as occurs sometimes when citizens decide not to enter into a contract that offends public order and morals (in particular, some argue that law in the twentieth century shifted its focus toward regulating citizens' actions rather than providing a judicial basis, which is also related to the changes in political and governmental roles explained in the introduction). Fifth, close attention to the powerful influence that laws can exert over action-regulation will reveal many points of contact between the law and economic thought, which seeks to focus on people's economic activities (see Sect. 1 of the Appendix). Some readers may want to ask the important question, "Why does the law stipulate in detail the provisions that allow parties to voluntarily exclude that same law from becoming effective?" The most important clue io answering that question is the notion of providing incentives to those involved (see Chap. 2 and Sect. 1 of the Appendix).

Study Questions

1. Explain the difference between property rights and intellectual property rights.
2. Technological knowledge has the characteristics of a public good. Thus, the government should bear the cost of R&D. Discuss the pros and cons of this opinion.
3. A patent protecting an invention is not necessarily the same as a patent protecting the profits from an innovation. Explain why.
4. Greater levels of protection for intellectual property rights are not necessarily desirable. Explain the social costs of patents and copyrights.

References

Akerlof GA et al. (2002) Brief of George A. Akerlof et al. in support of petitioners, Eldred v. Ashcroft, 537 U.S. 186 (2003) (No. 01–618)

Arrow K (1962) Economic welfare and the allocation of resources for invention. In: Universities-National Bureau Committee for Economic Research and Committee on Economic Growth of the Social Science Research Council (ed) The rate and direction of inventive activity: economic and social factors. Princeton University Press, Princeton, pp 609–626

Bakos Y, Brynjolfsson E, Lichtman D (1999) Shared information goods. J Law Econ 42:117–155. https://doi.org/10.1086/467420

Bessen J, Hunt RM (2007) An empirical look at software patents. J Econ Manag Strat 16:157–189. https://doi.org/10.1111/j.1530-9134.2007.00136.x
Boldrin M, Levine DK (2008) Against intellectual monopoly. Cambridge University Press, New York
Computer Entertainment Supplier's Association (CESA) (2010) Ihō fukusei Game Soft no Download ni kansuru shiyō jittai chōsa (Survey on the actual status of the use of downloading of illegal copies of videogames). https://www.cesa.or.jp/information/release/201006041803.html. Accessed 25 Apr 2021 [publication in Japanese]
Ijichi T, Odagiri H (2006) Zenkoku Innovation chōsa ni yoru iyakuhin sangyō no hikaku bunseki (A comparative study of the Japanese pharmaceutical industry with the National Innovation Survey data). Discussion Paper No. 43, National Institute of Science and Technology Policy [publication in Japanese]
Ijichi T, Iwasa T, Odagiri H, Keira H, Koga T, Goto A, Tawara Y, Nagata A, Hirano Y (2004) Zenkoku Innovation chōsa tōkei hōkoku (Statistics on innovation in Japan: report on the Japanese National Innovation Survey 2003, J-NIS 2003). Research Material No. 110, National Institute of Science and Technology Policy [publication in Japanese]
Landes WM, Posner RA (2003) The economic structure of intellectual property law. Harvard University Press, Cambridge
Levin RC, Klevorick AK, Nelson RR, Winter SG (1987) Appropriating the returns from industrial research and development. Brook Pap Econ Act 3:783–831
Marushima G (2008) Chizai, kono hito ni kiku (Ask them about intellectual property), vol 1. Japan Institute of Invention and Innovation, Tokyo [publication in Japanese]
Oberholzer-Gee F, Strumpf K (2007) The effect of file sharing on record sales: an empirical analysis. J Political Econ 115:1–42. https://doi.org/10.1086/511995
Recording Industry Association of Japan (RIAJ) (2011) Ihō haishin ni kansuru riyō jittai chōsa, 2010 nen ban (Survey on the actual status of the use of illegal distribution). https://www.riaj.or.jp/f/pdf/report/web/20110309report.pdf. Accessed 25 Apr 2021 [publication in Japanese]
Shapiro C, Varian HR (1999) Information rules: a strategic guide to the network economy. Harvard Business School Press, Boston
Shavell S (2004) Foundations of economic analysis of law. Harvard University Press, Cambridge
Shimanami R, Ueno T, Yokoyama H (2014) Tokkyohō nyūmon (Patent law in Japan). Yuhikaku, Tokyo [publication in Japanese]
Shimanami R, Ueno T, Yokoyama H (2021) Chosakukenhō nyūmon (Copyright law in Japan), 3rd edn. Yuhikaku, Tokyo [publication in Japanese]
Tanji Y (2008) Hon no horobikata: hogokikanchū ni shoseki ga kiete yuku katei to shikumi (The perishing of books: the process and mechanism of book disappearance during the protection period). In: Tanaka T, Hayashi K (eds) Chosakuken hogo kikan: enchō wa bunka wo shinkō suru ka? (Copyright protection period: does the extension promote culture?). Keiso Shobo, Tokyo, pp 29–57 [publication in Japanese]
Teece DJ (1986) Profiting from technological innovation: implications for integration, collaboration, licensing and public policy. Res Policy 15:285–305. https://doi.org/10.1016/0048-7333(86)90027-2
Waldfogel J (2010) Music file sharing and sales displacement in the iTunes era. Inf Econ Pol 22:306–314. https://doi.org/10.1016/j.infoecopol.2010.02.002
Yamada S (2009) Tokkyo no jisshō keizai bunseki (Empirical economic analysis of patents). Toyo Keizai Inc, Tokyo [publication in Japanese]

Chapter 3
The Rules Governing the Relationships Among a Company's Stakeholders: Company Law

Motohiro Sakaki and Hidefusa Iida

Contents

3.1 Introduction 46
3.1.1 What is a Company? 46
3.1.2 The Underlying Outlook of the Companies Act 46
3.1.3 Typical Conflicts 48
3.1.4 Economic Positioning 49
3.2 Conflicts of Interest Between Directors and Companies 51
3.2.1 General Remarks 51
3.2.2 Conflicting Interest Transactions 51
3.2.3 Derivative Lawsuits and the Business Judgment Rule 55
3.2.4 Remuneration Regulations 58
3.3 Protection of Minority Shareholders 62
3.3.1 Exploitation of Minority Shareholders by Controlling Shareholders 62
3.3.2 Legal Systems for the Abuse of Majority Votes 64
3.3.3 Economic Implications of Protecting Minority Shareholders 64
3.4 Conclusion 66
References 70

M. Sakaki (✉)
Graduate School of Law, Kobe University, 2-1 Rokkodai-cho, Nada-ku, Kobe 657-8501, Hyogo, Japan
e-mail: sakaki@boar.kobe-u.ac.jp

H. Iida
Graduate Schools for Law and Politics, University of Tokyo, 7-3-1 Hongo Bunkyo-ku, Tokyo 113-0033, Japan
e-mail: hidefusa@j.u-tokyo.ac.jp

T. Yanagawa et al. (eds.), *Econo-Legal Studies*,
https://doi.org/10.1007/978-981-16-5145-8_3

3.1 Introduction

3.1.1 *What is a Company?*

One of a company's fundamental goals is to generate profit via business; in other words, to pursue efficiency. To function, a company requires people and money above all else. Joint-stock companies, which are one of the most important company types, have four relevant parties. They are the directors, who form the board of directors and manage the company; the shareholders, who invest in the company; the creditors, who have claims on the company; and the employees, who work for the company.

3.1.2 *The Underlying Outlook of the Companies Act*

3.1.2.1 The Purpose of the Companies Act

The Companies Act's objective is to provide rules to reasonably balance the interests of the relevant parties to maximize a company's profits (Ochiai 2016, pp. 44–49). The Companies Act deals with three issues: conflicts of interest between a company's shareholders and directors, conflicts of interest between a controlling shareholder and minority shareholders, and conflicts of interest between shareholders and other stakeholders, principally creditors. This chapter deals mainly with the first and second of these conflicts.

The separation of ownership from management is the starting point for the first issue. Shareholders own a company, but they do not manage it. Instead, the task of managing a company is entrusted to a board of directors. It would be inefficient to assemble all of a company's shareholders to make operating decisions, as a public company may have ten thousand or more shareholders. Furthermore, although shareholders, as investors, may have expertise and skill in investing, they are not necessarily experts in management. Thus, it is more efficient to entrust a company's management to several individuals who specifically specialize in management. Under the Companies Act, shareholders have the power to decide on only certain essential matters, such as the appointment and dismissal of board members and company reorganizations (e.g., mergers). The authority to make other decisions concerning a company's management falls to the board of directors. For example, day-to-day business matters, such as factory locations and quantities of products or services to sell, are left to the management's discretion. However, if the board of directors makes management decisions for its own private benefit, shareholders' interests may be harmed. Thus, it is crucial to design a system that appropriately balances management efficiency and not harming shareholders' interests.

In regard to the second issue, the principle of "one share, one vote" is a good illustration of how the Companies Act reconciles conflicts of interest among shareholders. Decisions about a company are made via majority rule at a general meeting of the company's shareholders. Rather than giving one vote to each person, as in a parliament, majority decisions at a general meeting of shareholders operate on the principle of one share, one vote. This principle grants voting rights in proportion to a shareholder's investment in the company. Previously, the theory underlying the Companies Act held that the principle of one share, one vote was a manifestation of shareholder equality, as each share is treated as equivalent to each other share. Recently, however, some scholars have argued that the one share, one vote principle functionally grants more votes to shareholders who have a greater incentive to exercise their rights to maximize the company's profit. In other words, a shareholder who has invested heavily in a company can earn greater profits when the company performs better and, conversely, will suffer greater losses if the company performs poorly. Accordingly, shareholders who invest heavily in a company have incentives to exercise their voting rights to increase rather than reduce that company's value.

3.1.2.2 The Nature of the Companies Act

The Companies Act has not only default rules but also mandatory rules. For example, the relationship between a company and its directors is governed by the provisions of the mandate, which the Civil Code defines. Under the Civil Code, "[a] mandatary shall assume a duty to administer the mandated business with the care of a good manager compliance with the main purport of the mandate."[1] If a director violates this duty of care, then that director may be required to compensate the company for damages. Thus, a director's duty of care is understood to be a mandatory rule of the Companies Act. For a typical mandate contract under civil law, the principle of freedom of contracts applies. Thus, a contract that eliminates any responsibility to compensate the mandator for damages, even if the mandatary breaches the duty of care, is valid. However, the Companies Act does not account for contracts that eliminate all of a director's responsibilities by wholly exempting that director from any duty of care, even if the company and the director both agree to the contract. Such a contract would be regarded as invalid. In other words, agreements not accounted for by the Companies Act are invalid; a contract cannot supersede the Companies Act's mandatory rules (see Column 5, Mandatory Laws).

We can explain the inclusion of mandatory rules in the Companies Act by noting that they apply common rules to all public companies, providing the advantage that these rules are standardized. Mandatory rules can reduce the costs for shareholders seeking to invest in a company and other parties who do business with the company in researching the mechanisms that are involved in its operations. Thus, this standardization through mandatory rules improves efficiency. Additionally, public companies premised on the separation of ownership and management are likely to have participation from various shareholders. At least one of these shareholders is likely to fail to understand why, for example, the company's articles of incorporation contain

[1] Civil Code, Art. 644. Also see Companies Act, Art. 330.

a clause exempting directors from a duty of care. Thus, limiting the principle of freedom of contracts and rendering such a clause void protects such shareholders.

Column 5. Mandatory laws

Mandatory laws refer to laws that render contract provisions or articles of incorporation invalid when they differ from the provisions of the Companies Act. This concept is the opposite of the concept, default rules; if an agreed contract differs from a default rule, the contract can still be valid. In other words, if a party concludes a contract that contradicts a default rule, the content of that contract is still binding for that party, whereas if the party concludes a contract that contradicts a mandatory law, the content of that contract is not binding for the parties involved; instead, the mandatory laws apply to the parties to the contract.

Column 6. The duty of due care of a prudent manager

Although the duty of due care of a prudent manager is an abstract idea, a director committing an action that violates a law (i.e., an illegal act), for example, is a violation of the duty of due care of a prudent manager. To cite a real-world example as precedent, when a food sales company sold food in violation of the Food Sanitation Law and a director of the company knowingly concealed this action, the court ruled that this director had violated the duty of due care of a prudent manager. This ruling determined that the duty of due care of a prudent manager requires making efforts to prevent the loss of company credit and restoring consumers' trust through such measures as discontinuing sales of foods that violated the Food Sanitation Law, reporting to the relevant authorities, alerting purchasers, and openly sharing information. The court found that these efforts were not made and, thus, that the duty of due care was neglected (Osaka High Court decision, January 18, 2007).

3.1.3 Typical Conflicts

The separation of ownership and management and the principle of one share, one vote are believed to fundamentally contribute to companies' efficiency. However, they can also have a deleterious effect on a company. This effect is known as the "conflicts of interest problem."

The conflicts of interest problem arises, for example, when a party to a contract is not only able to make decisions on its own behalf but can also affect the decisions made by the contract's counterparty. Thus, the former party can conduct business to its own advantage and to the counterparty's disadvantage. This chapter discusses two types of conflicts of interest.

First, we consider cases of conflicts of interest between directors and shareholders. When a company's ownership is separated from management and decisions on most matters are delegated to the board of directors, the directors can abuse this power and effectively pursue private benefits at the expense of shareholders. We discuss how company law handles these problems in Sect. 3.2.

Second, we discuss how the principle of one share, one vote can allow controlling shareholders to arbitrarily control the decisions made at a general meeting of shareholders if they own enough shares. Under the capital majority rule, controlling shareholders can effectively implement decisions that are disadvantageous to minority shareholders, who hold only a small number of shares, and are advantageous only to controlling shareholders. We review how company law addresses conflicts of interest between controlling and minority shareholders in Sect. 3.3.

3.1.4 Economic Positioning

3.1.4.1 Agency Theory

From an economics perspective, it is useful to analyze the relationship between directors and shareholders using agency theory. Agency theory analyzes how an agent's behavior can affect a principal's profits. The basic premise is that when a contract or other relationship exists between an agent and a principal, the agent can behave in ways that maximize the agent's rather than the principal's profits. In the director–shareholder relationship, the agent is the director, and the principal is the shareholder. The directors are delegated the task of managing the company to produce profits for the shareholders. However, directors may pursue their own profits instead.

3.1.4.2 Conflicts of Interest Between Directors and Shareholders

A premise in agency theory is that information is asymmetric; although greater efforts by an agent may produce better results, a third party cannot observe whether the agent is making such efforts. It remains debatable whether a contract that ties compensation to results is ideal in the case of information asymmetry.

Take as an example a company hiring directors under a contract that awards them 10% of the company's profits as compensation. In this case, if the cost of effort is sufficiently small for directors, directors can maximize their own compensation, that is, their own profits, by making efforts rather than shirking. Thus, the directors will put in an effort and the company and its shareholders can expect greater profits as a result.

However, this type of compensation agreement cannot completely resolve conflicts of interest. For example, consider a director selling her car to her company for 300 when its true value is only 100. In this case, the company loses 200. As a result, the director's compensation is reduced by 20 (= 200 × 10%). However, the director also earns 200 in profit by selling the car, and that profit exceeds the decrease in her compensation as director of the company.

Thus, although tying compensation to performance may prevent directors from inefficiently shirking their duties, it cannot completely eliminate behaviors created by the conflicts of interest between directors and shareholders. If directors are allowed to freely engage in behaviors that represent their conflicts of interest, they may have incentives to shirk their duties and engage in conflicting interest transactions rather than working hard and generating profits for the company. In that case, the company will fail to improve its results.

3.1.4.3 Conflicts of Interest Between Controlling and Minority Shareholders

In the relationship between controlling and minority shareholders in which controlling shareholders can affect minority shareholders' interests via their voting rights, minority shareholders may be regarded as principals, and controlling shareholders can be regarded as agents. Minority and controlling shareholders do not have a contractual relationship, but they do have a relationship as shareholders in the same company because real decision-making power is delegated to majority shareholders. The principle of one share, one vote carries the expectation that shareholders who have invested heavily in a company will make decisions that increase the company's profits. However, this principle is powerless to prevent acts stemming from conflicts of interest. If controlling shareholders transfer the company's profits into their personal control, the company's share value will decrease, harming both controlling and minority shareholders' economic interests, but the controlling shareholders may still profit overall.

For example, suppose that the controlling shareholder in Company S, who owns 90% of Company S's shares, seeks to merge with Company S. Company S's shares have an actual value of 100, but the controlling shareholder stipulates that it will only pay 70 per share under the terms of the merger. This stipulation is detrimental to Company S's minority shareholders but is profitable for the controlling shareholder The controlling shareholder is in a position to buy the 10% of Company S's shares held by minority shareholders, and it stands to gain a profit of 30 per share via this merger. Conversely, the minority shareholders stand to lose 30 per share. Nevertheless, this merger may be approved at a general meeting of Company S's shareholders because the controlling shareholder, by definition, has control over the vote.

Minority shareholders may expect such an outcome to occur and opt not to invest in the company in the first place, anticipating that their shares may be valued below their intrinsic value. Thus, a company that needs investments from minority shareholders may find it difficult to obtain them because of the risk of conflicts of interest. This problem leads to inefficiency.

3.2 Conflicts of Interest Between Directors and Companies

3.2.1 General Remarks

We can consider two example cases involving conflicts of interest between a director and shareholders. In the first example, a director sacrifices the company's interests in favor of personal or third-party interests through transactions, such as buying a luxury car from the company at a very low price or selling land to the company at an inflated price (see Sect. 3.2.2). In the second example, a director serves his or her own interests or the interests of a third party at the expense of the company's interests through remuneration, such as submitting a proposal to the shareholders' meeting for higher director compensation than is appropriate (see Sect. 3.2.4). In the following sections, we review the rules included in corporate law to address these two example situations.

If a director causes damage to the company by neglecting his or her professional duties, as in the case of transactions involving conflicts of interest, the director is liable to the company. However, if the company does not file a claim against the director for damages, the shareholders can do so on their own behalf (a derivative lawsuit). In Sect. 3.2.3, we consider the function of derivative lawsuits and, conversely, the business judgment rule that prevents directors from being held liable for errors in their management decisions.

3.2.2 Conflicting Interest Transactions

3.2.2.1 Situations with Conflicting Interests

Consider a case in which a company and a representative director (or another company represented by a representative director) make a transaction. The representative director has the authority to represent the company and to perform any activity related to the company's business (Companies Act, Art. 349(4)). Thus, as a representative of the company, this director also has the authority to do business with the other directors. If a company's representative director is also the representative director of another company, then the director can represent both companies and conduct transactions between the two. Thus, a representative director has substantial authority, and if this director uses this authority for personal interests, it may cause damage to the company.

3.2.2.2 Liability for Damages

Even if there were no rules directly regulating conflicts of interest, representative directors are liable to their companies for any damages due to neglect of their duties. A company can hold its representative director liable. Moreover, even if a company does not hold its representative director liable, the shareholders can exercise the right to claim damages on behalf of the company in a derivative lawsuit. In other words, a representative director has a mandated relationship with the company, bears duties of care (Companies Act, Art. 330, and Civil Code, Art. 644) and loyalty (Companies Act, Art. 355) to the company, and is liable for any damages caused to the company by breaching these duties (Companies Act, Art. 423(1)).

However, even if a claim for damages is in the interests of a company and its shareholders, the company may not pursue that claim if other directors will not oppose the representative director owing to feelings of protectiveness for their colleague, feelings of appreciation toward their colleague for having given them their positions, or concerns about possible retaliation. Thus, the Companies Act allows individual shareholders to exercise their right to enforce a director's liability for damages to the company and file a shareholder derivative lawsuit on behalf of the company (Companies Act, Art. 847).

However, if a shareholder files a derivative lawsuit, the entity that wins damages is the company. The plaintiff shareholders receive economic benefits only through their share ownership, as the value of their shares increases when the company receives damages. Suppose that a plaintiff shareholder holds, for example, only 1% of all issued shares. In that case, the plaintiff shareholder can only receive a financial return of 1% of the total compensation for damages despite paying at least some of the litigation costs. The financial merits of such a lawsuit are therefore low for plaintiff shareholders. The shareholders filing a suit have to put in time and effort. Although they can seek reimbursement of their costs by the company if they win the case, Article 852, paragraph 1 of the Companies Act states that shareholders can only claim "an amount that is found to be reasonable," and the plaintiff shareholder must bear any costs above that amount. Moreover, if the shareholders lose the lawsuit, they must bear all of the costs. Thus, it is conceivable that individual shareholders have little incentive to file derivative lawsuits against representative directors because it is not in their financial interest to do so. In Japan, derivative lawsuits are often filed for non-financial reasons by, for example, a shareholder ombudsman (Milhaupt 2004; Puchniak and Nakahigashi 2012).

Thus, liability for damages cannot entirely solve the problem of conflicts of interest between directors and companies.

3.2.2.3 Should Conflicting Interest Transactions Be Prohibited?

Conversely, consider a rule that prohibits any conflicting interest transactions because they may damage a company. Such a rule would mean that companies would no longer lose money owing to conflicting interest transactions, but it may also mean that companies can no longer conduct some transactions that are beneficial. This problem is even more acute when a representative director represents multiple companies within the same corporate group. In this case, a rule that completely prohibits conflicting interest transactions would prohibit transactions that could benefit two companies within the group. This prohibition creates a loss for both companies and weakens their existential value as group companies. Thus, it is not desirable to prohibit all conflicting interest transactions.

3.2.2.4 Rules of the Companies Act

Thus, when conflicts of interest between a company and its representative director may arise, liability is not a complete solution, but prohibiting all transactions with conflicts of interest may not be in the company's best interest either. Thus, the Companies Act requires control by the board of directors by obliging a director who enters into a conflicting interest transaction to obtain the board's approval and to report information on such transactions to the board (Companies Act, Arts. 365, 356). It also strengthens directors' responsibility in the event of damages caused by conflicting interest transactions (Companies Act, Art. 423(3)).

Specifically, a director who intends to engage in a conflicting interest transaction is required to report the material facts regarding the transaction to the board of directors in advance and to obtain the board's approval (Companies Act, Arts. 365(1), 356(1)). This director must also report to the board of directors after the transaction (Companies Act, Art. 365(2)). Here, the term "conflicting interest transaction" refers to situations in which a director engages in a competitive transaction (e.g., when a director of a company that operates restaurants also runs a restaurant (Companies Act, Art. 356(1)(i)), a direct transaction (e.g., when a representative director buys land from the company (Companies Act, Art. 356(1)(ii)), or an indirect transaction (e.g., when the company intends to guarantee the representative director's debts (Companies Act, Art. 356(1)(iii)).

We consider a simple direct transaction. Conflicting interest transactions are not necessarily disadvantageous for a company, but they carry the risk that a director will exercise discretion in his or her favor, resulting in transactions that are disadvantageous for the company. For example, if a company sells land to a representative director at an objectively reasonable price, it will not suffer a loss. However, if it sells land below a reasonable price, the representative director gains a benefit equal to the difference from a reasonable price, and the company suffers a loss. Because the representative director has the authority to determine the terms of the transaction and has conflicts of interest with the company in terms of how the price is set, this director is obliged by the rules to report the details of the transaction in advance and obtain approval from the other members of the board of directors even though he or she does have the authority to execute operations in principle.

3.2.2.5 Application of the Companies Act Rules

Next, we describe the application of these rules. First, directors, including the representative director, are obliged to comply with laws and regulations,[2] and obtaining approval from the board of directors when conducting a conflicting interest transaction is one of these legal compliance obligations. Thus, if a director causes damage to the company by neglecting his or her duties (which is a violation of the law in this case), the other directors are liable to the company for damages (Companies Act, Art. 423(1)). Furthermore, directors are obliged to supervise other directors' compliance with laws and regulations, including general rules, such as the duties of care and loyalty. According to precedent,

> as the board of directors of a stock company is in a position to monitor the execution of operations of the company, the directors that make up the board of directors have a duty to monitor not only matters included on the agenda, but also the general execution of operations by the representative director and, if necessary, themselves convene the board of directors or require them to gather and ensure that operations are being executed properly through the board of directors.[3]

If we apply this principle to a conflicting interest transaction, the representative director neglects his or her duty by carrying out a conflicting interest transaction without board approval. Even if a conflicting interest transaction is approved, if it causes damage to the company, it may still be neglect of the representative director's duty. Additionally, if the representative director requests approval for a conflicting interest transaction, the other directors should monitor the transaction to ensure that it is appropriate. If the representative director tries to carry out a conflicting interest transaction without board approval, the other directors must investigate and monitor whether a conflicting interest transaction is about to take place if they find indications of such a transaction. Failing to do so may result in a breach of the obligation to monitor, and the other directors may therefore become liable for damages.

As described above, representative directors who engage in conflicting interest transactions may be considered to have neglected their duties and may be liable for damages owing to their failure to obtain approval and the inappropriate terms of the transaction. Thus, representative directors must accept appropriate controls by reporting material details before and after transactions and must ensure that the details of transactions are appropriate. Failing to do so will result in a penalty of liability for damages. The other directors are also responsible for monitoring the details of a transaction at the time of approval to ensure that they are appropriate. If an unapproved transaction is carried out, they are obligated to take measures to prevent further losses to the company.

Furthermore, conflicting interest transactions are typically considered high risk. Thus, the Companies Act prescribes several rules to encourage careful judgment by both the representative directors who carry out conflicting interest transactions and the directors who approve these transactions. If a transaction causes damage to

[2] Companies Act, Art. 355.

[3] Supreme Court Judgment, May 22, 1973, 27 Minshū 655.

a company, it is presumed that both the representative director who carried out the transaction and the directors who approved it have neglected their duties (Companies Act, Art. 423(3)). This rule shifts the burden of proof onto the directors. In other general cases, the shareholder seeking to enforce a director's liability is responsible for proving that the director has failed to perform his or her duties. However, because the risk of conflicting interest transactions is typically high, it is presumed that the directors neglected their duties, and the directors who are being held liable must prove that they were not neglectful to avoid liability. In this respect, the presumption of neglect of duty means that the plaintiff does not need to prove neglect, thereby reducing the cost of establishing proof and facilitating the enforcement of liability. Furthermore, the director who carried out the direct transaction cannot escape liability for damages because the Companies Act imposes strict liability on such directors (Companies Act, Art. 428). Enforcing compensation for damage to the company indicates the severity of the Companies Act in situations of conflicting interests.

3.2.2.6 Summary

In the case of conflicting interest transactions between companies and directors, the Companies Act requires the person carrying out a transaction to report the details to the board of directors in advance, obtain their approval, and report the details again after the transaction. This requirement provides a mechanism for the board of directors to control these typically high-risk transactions. The other directors have a duty to monitor conflicting interest transactions to ensure that they do not damage the company. If these laws are violated, a greater burden of responsibility is imposed on these directors. Reducing the cost of establishing proof and facilitating shareholders' enforcement of liability through derivative lawsuits increases the likelihood that liability will be enforced through such a lawsuit. These systems provide an incentive for directors to adhere to the framework established in the Companies Act. Thus, reconciling interests to give the board more effective control is preferable to banning conflicting interest transactions.

3.2.3 Derivative Lawsuits and the Business Judgment Rule

3.2.3.1 Functions and Purpose of a Derivative Lawsuit

Next, we discuss derivative lawsuits, which are a means for shareholders to enforce the directors' liability. Derivative lawsuits have two functions. First, they compensate for damages to a company. A shareholder seeks to enforce a director's liability on behalf of a company through a derivative lawsuit when the company is not enforcing that liability.

Second, they serve to deter directors from breaching their fiduciary duties. Suppose that a director expects to be held liable by the company or its shareholders after carrying out a self-serving conflicting interest transaction. Then, when deciding whether to carry out a transaction that would damage the company, the director should choose not to do so.

Thus, derivative lawsuits not only are useful ex post (i.e., after a director carries out a conflicting interest transaction and exploits the company) but also perform an important function ex ante (i.e., before a director decides to engage in a conflicting interest transaction and exploit the company), as they act as a restraint to prevent damage to a company. Derivative lawsuits can both compensate for damages and act as a deterrent against the negligence of duties, but their deterrent function is overwhelmingly more important. That is, the possibility of enforcing liability ex post deters the negligence of duties ex ante. In the case of certain large companies, the ability of a lawsuit to compensate for damage is relatively low. A company and an individual director may differ greatly in terms of economic power. Although a company may suffer tens of billions of yen in damages owing to a director's negligence of duty, an individual director cannot compensate for such large damages. Thus, the deterrent function of a derivative lawsuit is more important than its compensation function in this context.

3.2.3.2 The Problem with Derivative Lawsuits: Profits from Taking Risks and Directors' Personal Responsibility

We now extend this line of thinking. A person running a business may succeed or fail. If a director exploits and causes damage to a company, then that director should be held liable. However, if directors are held liable for taking risks that are desirable for the company and carrying out projects that ultimately fail and damage the company, directors will avoid taking risks that would be desirable for the company for their own protection.

Consider an example in which a director must decide whether to carry out a project that has a 20% chance of generating a profit of 10,000 and an 80% chance of resulting in a loss of 1,000. If the project is not undertaken, the company receives no profit or loss. If the company undertakes this project, its expected profit is 1,200 (= 10,000 × 0.2 – (1,000) × 0.8). Thus, carrying out this project is beneficial for the company and its shareholders.

Suppose further that if this project is carried out and fails, the director is liable for the full amount. However, the director does not receive any additional compensation if it succeeds. In this case, the expected benefit to the individual director of carrying out the project is –800 (= –(1,000) × 0.8), whereas the benefit of not undertaking the project is zero. Thus, the director does not carry out the project owing to the risk of being held liable even though the project is desirable for the company's shareholders.

In terms of legal theory, carrying out such a project is desirable, implying that the director is not neglecting any duties and should not be held liable. However, the director's court defense may fail or be subject to an incorrect decision,[4] and having to defend a lawsuit imposes a large financial burden on the director. Even if the company decides not to pursue the director's liability owing to the potential of losing the case and the possible reputational costs, a derivative lawsuit is always a possibility because even shareholders who own only a single share have the right to file a derivative lawsuit. A shareholder whose personal, political, or social interests differ from those of other shareholders has the ability to file such a lawsuit and may therefore decide to sue.

3.2.3.3 Business Judgment Rule

In such situations, the legal principle that prevents directors from being held individually liable as a result of taking risks that are desirable for a company is called the "business judgment rule." This rule was developed in the United States, and Japanese law has imported the basic idea, although the business judgment rule differs somewhat between Japan and the United States. For brevity, we introduce only the business judgment rule applied in the United States and do not explain its differences from the business judgment rule applied in Japan.

In the United States, the business judgement rule is to respect the business judgment of the board of directors even if a project fails and the company is damaged. The court does not consider the director liable as long as there are no conflicts of interest between the company and the director, the director gathered sufficient information, and the director made decisions using the appropriate procedures. At worst, the business judgment rule may be viewed as a way for a company's managers to protect themselves, but, in many countries, the possibility of failure is considered inherent to business judgment and is a necessary part of taking appropriate risks.

The requirement of no conflicts of interest is a key to the business judgment rule applied in the United States. In situations with conflicts of interest, directors may seek to serve their own interests even in transactions that seem fair at first glance, and, thus, the business judgment rule is not applied.

3.2.3.4 Summary

The concept of eliminating conflicts of interest from the decisions made by a board of directors is not limited to the business judgment rule. For example, in Japan, directors who have a special interest in a board of directors resolution are not allowed to participate in that resolution (Companies Act, Art. 369(2)). In the event of conflicts of interest with a company, directors may exercise discretion in their own favor and will be strongly suspected of doing so ex post. It cannot be known for certain ex post

[4] Although readers may be surprised to hear that courts make mistakes, that possibility should always be considered in corporate law. A court's decisions are not always better than those of directors or shareholders.

whether damage to a company occurred owing to an intentional act or as a result of taking a necessary risk, and the difficulty of making such judgments with hindsight is why an ex ante rule is established.

3.2.4 Remuneration Regulations

3.2.4.1 Traditional Thinking

Another situation in which conflicts of interest between a company and its directors may be a problem relates to directors' remuneration. Directors receive compensation from a company in exchange for performing their duties, and decisions about their remuneration, similar to employee salaries, can be thought to fall under the directors' authority as part of the company's business operations. However, directors who set their own remuneration will be tempted to increase it at the company's expense. Greater remuneration is in a director's own interest, and the other directors also benefit from increasing their remuneration. Thus, directors may not be able to effectively control the appropriateness of each other's remuneration (i.e., there is a risk of *otemori*, or self-approved payment plans), leading to conflicts of interest between the company and the directors regarding the amounts they are paid. To address this conflict of interest, it is required that shareholders determine remunerations in the articles of incorporation or through a resolution of the general meeting of shareholders (Companies Act, Art. 361(1)).[5]

This description explains the traditional rules in Japan, and the courts have focused on the dangers of self-approved payment plans and have formed case law principles on the regulation of remuneration. For example, individual directors' remuneration does not have to be specified in the articles of incorporation or at the general meeting of

[5] The reform to the Commercial Code in 2002 introduced the system of a company with committees to enable companies to choose corporate governance following the style in the United States. A company with committees is any company that has nominating, audit, and compensation committees (Companies Act, Art. 2(xii)). Before 2002, a Japanese company with a board of directors was required to also have a board of auditors. The 2002 reform enabled companies with a board of directors to choose whether to have a board of auditors or be a company with committees. A company with committees has a different governance structure from that of a company with a board of auditors. Specifically, a company with committees has a compensation committee with a majority of outside directors that sets the remuneration of executive officers and directors (Companies Act, Art. 404(3)), thereby reducing the risk of conflicts of interest. Although outside directors are more independent than directors who were employees, they receive more information about other directors' execution of their duties than shareholders do through board of directors meetings. The members of the compensation committee, the majority of whom are outside directors, have more information than shareholders and can more easily observe the abilities and effort levels of the directors and executive officers. They are less likely to provide unnecessarily high compensation because of their independence from other directors and executive officers. As long as the company with committees system is functioning, the agency problem should be properly solved. Although the number of such companies is small, the company with committees structure may be superior to the company with a board of auditors structure in terms of solving the agency problem.

shareholders; instead, it is sufficient to set the maximum amount of total remuneration for all directors and entrust the board of directors to allocate that amount across the individual directors (Supreme Court Judgement, March 26, 1985, 144 Shūmin 247). This distinction is because a company's directors setting their own remuneration is a problem when the company pays compensation above a reasonable level (i.e., profits are transferred from the shareholders to the directors) owing to self-approved payment plans. Thus, it is assumed that if the maximum total amount paid to directors is determined, then no further transfer of profits will occur, and shareholders will not suffer any damage even if the specific allocation to individual directors is the responsibility of the board of directors. Traditionally, it is also widely believed that revealing the amount of each director's remuneration is a violation of the directors' privacy.

3.2.4.2 Questions About Traditional Thinking

The reader may view this traditional belief as rather unnatural. The amount of remuneration is a measure of an executive's performance, as a company may provide greater compensation to its best executives and reduce compensation if business performance is lackluster. If shareholders do not determine each director's compensation, then they have insufficient control over directors' remuneration. Even in the case of conflicts of interest, it is insufficient to consider director remuneration only in terms of avoiding these conflicts. The ability to determine only the total amount of remuneration for directors and not individual compensation cannot be sufficient to give shareholders confidence.

3.2.4.3 Recent Developments

In this regard, developments in recent years have departed from the traditional rules. The rules emphasizing the dangers of self-approved payment plans attach importance to controlling total remuneration. However, shareholders also care about the relationship between remuneration and performance. As the number of foreign investors increases, shareholder proposals that require the disclosure of individual remuneration (Companies Act, Arts. 303, 304, and 305) have become prominent. Most of these proposals have been rejected by a majority of shareholders, but in some companies, over 40% of shareholders have voted for them. Furthermore, based on an amendment of the Cabinet Office Order on the Disclosure of Corporate Affairs, Etc. in fiscal year 2010, listed companies are obliged to disclose individual remuneration if their directors' remuneration exceeds 100 million JPY. Thus, as of disclosures of individual remuneration reduce the persuasiveness of privacy infringement claims and that interpretation is becoming weaker, investors are moving to modify the traditional rules.

3.2.4.4 Economic Analysis

We consider these changing movements from the perspective of agency theory. The agency problem arises when the principal (shareholders) cannot observe the level of effort of the agent (director). If the goal is to prevent the transfer of profits from shareholders to directors through excessive remuneration, then the problem can be solved simply by regulating total remuneration. The traditional explanation holds up to this point. However, it is more desirable for shareholders to observe the directors' levels of effort and determine whether they are incentivized by their remuneration to work hard.

In a company with separate ownership and management, it is difficult for smaller shareholders to observe directors' levels of effort, and shareholders are forced to evaluate directors' performance based on results. Thus, it is natural for a shareholder, as the principal, to alleviate the agency problem by linking each director's performance to his or her remuneration. Moves to demand disclosures of individual remuneration are a means of exercising control or establishing a performance-linked remuneration system.

For example, consider a game-theoretic analysis (Tanaka 2001). In this example, a director can choose to either make an effort or make no effort. If the director works hard, the company has an 80% chance of making a profit of 1,000 and a 20% chance of making neither a profit nor a loss (for example, the effort fails owing to the market environment). By contrast, if the director makes no effort, the company has a 20% chance of making a profit of 1,000 and an 80% chance of making neither a profit nor a loss. The director incurs a cost of 100 by making the effort. This cost represents the monetary value of the director's time and effort invested.

Conversely, if the director does not make an effort, then he or she receives a so-called "slacking benefit" equivalent to 100. For example, it is easy to imagine how enjoyable it is to avoid work and have fun, and doing so brings a kind of happiness. Additionally, if we assume that the company is unable to observe whether the director has worked hard, then the shareholders can only conclude that the director made an effort based on whether a profit is made. If no profit is made, then the shareholders do not know whether the failure was due to a lack of effort or if the director made an effort that did not lead to success.

From the company's perspective, it is clearly desirable for the director to work hard. The company's expected profit when the director works hard is 800 ($= 1{,}000 \times 0.8$), whereas its expected profit without the director's effort is 200 ($= 1{,}000 \times 0.2 + 0 \times 0.8$). However, if we assume that the director receives a fixed remuneration of 150 from the company regardless of his or her level of effort, then the total benefit from working hard is only 50 because working hard incurs a cost of 100. Conversely, the director receives a remuneration of 150 with certainty even if he or she makes no effort, and, thus, it is better for the director to not make any effort (assuming that the possibility of reappointment and reputational concerns are not taken into account).

The natural question arises of how shareholders can incentivize directors to work hard. One solution is to contractually require hard work or to establish such a rule in the Companies Act. However, such a rule cannot clearly show whether a director has worked hard. For example, a business failure due to the market environment may lead shareholders to conclude that the director caused the problem. Thus, entering into a contract to work hard is not sufficient to guarantee hard work.

However, if remuneration can be set so that the benefits to an individual director from working hard are greater than the benefits from making no effort, then directors will work hard of their own accord. For example, consider performance-based compensation that pays 30% of a company's profits to directors in addition to their fixed remuneration. If a director works hard, then he or she receives 240, which is 30% of the expected profit of 800, in addition to the fixed remuneration of 150. After subtracting the cost of working hard, which is 100, the director receives a benefit of 290 (= 150 + 240 − 100). Conversely, if the director does not make an effort, he or she receives the fixed remuneration of 150 along with an additional 60, which is 30% of the expected profit of 200. Although the director does not bear the cost of 100 for working hard in this case, he or she still only earns an expected benefit of 210 (= 150 + 60). In this situation, the director chooses to work hard to receive the performance-based compensation (however, if the director is risk averse or if the costs are higher, the director may still not make any effort).

Based on this example, performance-based compensation may seem to be a very good idea, but it has problems as well. For example, the external environment may have a greater influence on the result than the director's effort does. To illustrate this situation, we assume that the chance of making a profit of 800 is 40% regardless of whether the director makes an effort and only increases to 60% if the director does work hard. In this configuration, the expected remuneration from working hard is the fixed remuneration of 150 plus 30% of the expected profit of 480, or 144. After subtracting the cost of effort, the overall expected benefit is 194 (= 150 + (480 × 0.3) − 100). Conversely, the expected remuneration for no effort is 150 plus 30% of the expected profit of 320, or 96. As there is no cost of effort, the expected benefit is 246 (= 150 + (320 × 0.3)). In this situation, a director cannot be encouraged to work hard. Furthermore, directors' remuneration may fluctuate significantly owing to other factors besides their effort, such as the company's external environment. The risk of changes in the market environment is therefore borne more by risk-averse directors than by the company in this case.

3.2.4.5 Summary

Regulating directors' remuneration has two purposes: preventing conflicts of interest and providing an incentive for directors to work hard. On one hand, traditional explanations of corporate law are persuasive and have led to the formation of precedents. On the other hand, from a contemporary viewpoint (or a perspective that is independent from the unique ideas of traditional corporate law, such as an economics perspective), the artificiality of that interpretation leads to many questions. The gradual retreat of a legal interpretation that emphasizes conflicts of interest is one example of the contemporary perspective gaining traction. Throughout the course of this book, we will come across several other interesting issues.

3.3 Protection of Minority Shareholders

3.3.1 Exploitation of Minority Shareholders by Controlling Shareholders

An underlying premise for shareholders is that their voting rights are not subject to any restrictions. Shareholders have incentives to exercise their voting rights in ways that increase the value of their shares, and, thus, they can generally be left to their own devices. For example, if a controlling shareholder with 80% of all voting rights votes in favor of a proposal that would be detrimental to the company at a general meeting of shareholders, then the economic value of the controlling shareholder's shares also decreases. We can therefore expect that a controlling shareholder will not vote in a way that disadvantages the company. Thus, minority shareholders' interests are protected in the sense that resolutions that are disadvantageous to the company are generally not made.

However, if the controlling shareholder is a trading partner in business with the company, this logic does not hold. Consider the following scenario.

Scenario 1

Suppose that the value of a share in Company T is 100 and that Company A is the controlling shareholder of Company T. Suppose also that companies A and T have undergone a merger. The terms of the merger, as established in the merger agreement, are that Company A pays 30 per share in cash to the shareholders of Company T. At a general meeting of the shareholders of Company T, Company A, the controlling shareholder, votes in favor of the merger and, thus, the merger is approved.

The terms of this merger lead to Company A purchasing shares in Company T, which are ordinarily valued at 100, from the other shareholders for just 30. Company A therefore accrues profits of 70 per share, whereas the minority shareholders in Company T lose 70 per share.

Under the Companies Act in Japan, these sorts of resolutions at general meetings of shareholders are considered grossly improper and should be revoked (Companies Act, Art. 831(1)(iii)). Different jurists may have different opinions regarding the specific conditions for a grossly improper resolution, but most scholars agree that Scenario 1 describes grossly unfair conditions.

Next, consider an alternate scenario.

Scenario 2

Suppose that the corporate value of Company X is 600 and that the value of Company Y is 400. However, when the two companies merge, the merged company's value is 1,500, which is greater than the simple sum of the two companies' standalone values owing to synergies. The corporate values of Companies X and Y sum to 1,000 (= 600 + 400) before the merger but 1,500 after the merger. The difference between the two totals, which is 500 in this example, is referred to as the synergies.

Incidentally, if Company X is the controlling shareholder of Company Y, then even if Company Y's shareholders are paid only the current corporate value of Y (i.e., 400), Company X, as the controlling shareholder, can vote in favor of the merger at a general meeting of

Company Y's shareholders, rendering a majority vote in favor of the merger. Doing so allows Company X to monopolize the synergies.

Corporate law scholars disagree on how to address scenarios like Scenario 2, in which a controlling shareholder monopolizes the synergies of a merger. However, the prevailing opinion is that this behavior is unfair. A 2005 amendment to the Companies Act introduced a system in which the synergies must be distributed fairly if a minority shareholder of Company Y exercises an appraisal right under conditions like those in Scenario 2 (Companies Act, Arts. 785, 797, and 806). An appraisal right is the right of shareholders who oppose certain proposed actions of a corporation (e.g., mergers) to have the fair value of their shares appraised by a court and demand that the company purchase their shares at this appraised value. In Japan, this right is available in organizational restructurings, such as mergers, share exchanges, share transfers, corporate splits, sales of the business, and cash-outs.

Appraisal rights have existed since 1950. The concept of fair value was reformed in 2005. Before the 2005 reform, the court had to determine the fair value as the value of the stock that would have prevailed had the merger not taken place. Thus, in Scenario 2, if minority shareholders holding 10% of the outstanding shares in Company Y exercised their appraisal right, their shares would have been appraised at 40, which is 10% of Company Y's pre-merger value (i.e., 400), before the reform. Under pre-2005 rules, Company Y's minority shareholders who were dissatisfied with Company X's monopolization of the synergies were not able to resolve their dissatisfaction even by exercising their appraisal right. In Scenario 2, they would receive the same amount from the merger regardless of whether they exercised their appraisal right.

As a countermeasure, the 2005 Companies Act amendment requires an appraisal to account for both the company's value in the absence of the merger (i.e., 400 for Company Y in Scenario 2) and the additional synergies obtained as a result of the merger (i.e., 500 in Scenario 2), and it must distribute the synergies fairly. An consensus interpretation of a fair allocation of synergies has not been established, but one approach is to distribute synergies according to the merger parties' corporate values. By this interpretation, because Company X's corporate value was 600 and Company Y's corporate value was 400, the synergies should be distributed on a three to two basis. Of the 500 in value created by synergies, a fair distribution is to allocate 300 to Company X and 200 to Company Y. Then, suppose that a minority shareholder holding 10% of Company Y's total issued shares is unsatisfied with Company X's monopolization of the synergies. In that case, a minority shareholder can exercise the right of appraisal at the expected value of Company Y (400) plus a fair distribution of the synergies (an additional 200), resulting in an appraisal price of 60 for that shareholder's shares (10% of 600). Thus, Company Y's minority shareholders who are dissatisfied with the controlling shareholder monopolizing the synergies are protected by a fair redistribution of those synergies.

3.3.2 Legal Systems for the Abuse of Majority Votes

In the Companies Act, a few rules correspond to actions in which a controlling shareholder exercises its voting rights to pursue interests that are detrimental to minority shareholders (i.e., abuses the majority vote). For our purposes, we focus on two of these rules.

First, when a grossly improper resolution is passed as a result of a shareholder with special interests[6] exercising its voting rights at a general meeting of shareholders, as in Scenario 1, the resolution is nullified if a court upholds a lawsuit for the revocation of the vote (Companies Act, Art. 831(1)(iii)). Thus, if a controlling shareholder abuses its capital majority, minority shareholders who suffer a disadvantage can file a revocation lawsuit to nullify the relevant resolution and prevent this disadvantage.

The second rule is appraisal rights, as discussed in relation to Scenario 2. In restructuring scenarios, such as mergers, shareholders who opposed a resolution at a general meeting of shareholders can exercise their appraisal rights to require the company to buy back their shares at a fair price (Companies Act, Arts. 785, 797, and 806). If a merger agreement under unfair conditions is approved by a resolution of the general meeting of shareholders, minority shareholders who disagree with the resolution can exercise their appraisal rights to sell their shares for cash at a fair price. This rule ensures that minority shareholders do not suffer losses.

3.3.3 Economic Implications of Protecting Minority Shareholders

Now, we reconsider the above discussion from an economics perspective.

First, Scenario 1 merely entails a transfer of profits between the controlling and minority shareholders and, thus, does not appear problematic from an efficiency standpoint; however, corporate law scholars appear to find these merger terms unfair. Efficiency refers to the total surplus in this context. Even if the seller suffers a loss of 70, the net change in efficiency is zero if the buyer accrues a profit of 70. Thus, this act does not affect efficiency in any way. In this case, the law has no reason to intervene from an efficiency standpoint.

In terms of the distribution of synergies in Scenario 2, legal intervention may actually impair efficiency by reducing the controlling shareholder's incentive to conduct a merger. The allocation of synergies is merely an issue of allocating the surplus among the parties to a merger. However, the ideal allocation remains insufficiently clear both theoretically and in practice. A court intervening to redistribute synergies more fairly a posteriori can aggravate the problem. Let us tentatively accept the hypothesis that Company X monopolizing the synergies from a merger is problematic. If the ideal allocation is unknown, however, then it is reasonable to conclude that making no

[6] In Scenarios 1 and 2, Companies A and X may be shareholders with "special interests" under the Companies Act, Art. 831(1)(iii).

legal intervention is preferable to intervening. Suppose that Company X works to achieve the merger between Companies X and Y precisely because it can monopolize the synergies. If the court intervenes ex post, then Company X, predicting this action, may make only the minimum effort to achieve a merger with Company Y, impeding a merger that can create synergies worth 500. Thus, a legal intervention on the grounds of unfair distribution may inhibit efficiency.

However, a counterargument is that enacting legislation to protect minority shareholders enables them to invest and enhances efficiency (La Porta et al. 1997). Ensuring that parties are willing to invest despite being minority shareholders allows a company to accrue much more capital. A scenario in which the controlling shareholder exercises its rights solely in its own interest is likely to be disadvantageous to minority shareholders and may minimize their incentive to invest. Preventing a company from raising the necessary funding is disadvantageous to the controlling shareholder. In other words, efficiency is impaired. Thus, to create incentives for minority shareholders to invest, the controlling shareholder must commit to not taking opportunistic actions. Legislation governing the protection of minority shareholders acts as this commitment, thereby increasing efficiency.

For example, suppose that an entrepreneur of a startup company wishes to specify in the articles of incorporation that governing shareholders will not exploit minority shareholders. However, it is difficult to establish a company's articles of incorporation based on projections of specific types of future conduct that must be avoided. Even if diverse scenarios can be predicted ahead of time, minority shareholders are not likely to believe these promises. Because the controlling shareholder controls the general meeting of shareholders, the possibility that this shareholder will change the articles of incorporation to exploit minority shareholders cannot be entirely discounted.

However, if the Companies Act stipulates certain rules for the protection of minority shareholders, then these shareholders see that they are protected under its scope and feel confident in their ability to invest in stocks. Such rules protecting minority shareholders are also useful for controlling shareholders who have no intention of exploiting minority shareholders in the future.

The degree to which a company depends on investment from minority shareholders varies. Nevertheless, the legal rules protecting minority shareholders apply uniformly to all companies. Thus, the question arises as to what extent legal provisions should prescribe rules to protect minority shareholders.

Uniform regulations carry no guarantee of achieving first-best outcomes. Different companies have different capital needs. Some controlling shareholders may prefer much more stringent rules against controlling shareholders' abuse of power than prevail in many jurisdictions because they want to receive more investment from minority shareholders. One may argue that the following mechanism would address this issue. Legal regulations set forth minimum minority shareholder protection provisions that are required of all companies. Companies that need more investment from public investors voluntarily include rules to protect minority shareholders in their articles of incorporation, and these rules cannot be changed without unanimous agreement by all shareholders. The requirement of a unanimous agreement for revisions renders it impossible for a controlling shareholder to change these rules in the future to the detriment of the minority shareholders. This system makes it possible for controlling shareholders to commit not to harm minority shareholders' interests in the most suitable manner for each company's conditions.

However, general interpretations of the Companies Act do not take this position, and, thus, rules are uniformly applied to protect shareholders.

3.4 Conclusion

This chapter examined two aspects of conflicts of interest in public companies: conflicts between directors and shareholders and conflicts between controlling and minority shareholders. Traditionally, corporate law studies follow the logic that obtaining profit through conflicts of interest is unjust and unfair in and of itself, but the discussion thus far has provided justification for legislation designed to handle conflicts of interest in terms of efficiency losses due to these conflicts.

This juxtaposition leads to the question of whether fairness and efficiency are oriented in the same direction, which is a key question from this book's perspective. Contemporary jurisprudence related to corporate law is increasingly unlikely to emphasize the protection of minority shareholders solely for reasons of unfairness. Some corporate law jurists find that efficiency should be the fundamental basis for decisions and argue that laws inhibiting efficient transactions because they are unfair are unjustifiable (Tanaka 2013). Even if we do not pursue this line of thinking this far, the notion of "fairness" is not inherently clearly defined, and, thus, increasingly many corporate law jurists believe that the fairness argument is not necessarily persuasive.

Nevertheless, it is ill-advised to conclude that such a challenging question has been answered before obtaining a full understanding of corporate law rules, and we will avoid making such recommendations here. We want to emphasize that the reader may find it advantageous to keep the following points in mind in future jurisprudence or economic studies of corporate law.

First, when studying corporate law, it is essential to define "fairness" as concretely as possible. The term "fairness" is sometimes used to simply mean right, but in terms of a merger distribution, "fairness" generally refers to the proportion of the corporate value allocated to the parties thereto. The term also has many other definitions. For example, Kanda (1985) suggests the following three definitions of fairness. First, it is fair to protect the reasonable expectations of shareholders; second, a state of fairness is one in which a specific shareholder does not begrudge other shareholders; and third, it is fair to enact rules to minimize the costs arising when a court of law engages in fact finding that diverges from truthful facts.

In any event, when considering the question of whether fairness and efficiency are the same or in opposition, verifying the exact concept of fairness used in corporate law is essential to reaching a consistent line of logic. To understand corporate law, it is critical to tease out the inquiry further rather than simply ending the thought process at the term "fairness" by continually asking how it relates to the concept of efficiency in concrete terms.

When studying corporate law from an economics perspective, it is also beneficial to consider the context of efficiency. For example, efficiency may be related to decisions around a merger or whether investors should invest in a particular stock. The timing of this efficiency matters. Analyses that are informed by an efficiency standpoint can be extremely effective. When considering whether efficiency aligns with or diverges from fairness in the legal sense, more than a few scenarios may arise in which ex-post fairness in a legal sense is also justified in the sense of ex-ante efficiency.

Analyzing corporate law rules from the standpoint of both fairness and efficiency can, in turn, provide a better understanding of the subject. Although this book aims to highlight differences in the perspectives of jurisprudence and economics in the aid of each discipline, overemphasizing these differences in terms of corporate law is unreasonable. Rather, we believe that understanding the essentials of each discipline and engaging in an internal inquiry of each discipline's strengths and weaknesses can inform new developments in both fields.

Furthermore, as Sect. 3.2 explains, approaches that were previously viewed as implicitly correct may become less persuasive when viewed from an economics perspective, which may provide fundamental changes to traditional legalistic interpretations (e.g., the shift toward treating the risks associated with arbitrary compensation decisions and other compensation issues as privacy-related problems in the regulation of compensation). Of the legal domains discussed in this book, corporate law is one in which economics and jurisprudence are very proximate and in which economic analyses of the law have made considerable strides (Miwa et al. 1998; Fujita 2002–2003). Although some textbooks incorporate an economic analysis of the law, many still opt for a traditional interpretation. In studying corporate law, it is interesting to consider whether these theories continue to enjoy support today because they are genuinely persuasive or whether they contain inherent vulnerabilities. Although arriving at a quick conclusion may be more efficient and aid rapid learning, considering a range of perspectives is, in fact, an efficient way of arriving at a deeper and more accurate understanding. The reader will obtain some of these techniques, albeit partially, by continuing to read this book.

Column 7. Einstein's laws: general and special laws

The problem of formulating physical laws for every co-ordinate system was solved by the so-called general relativity theory; the previous theory, applying only to inertial systems, is called the special relativity theory. The two theories cannot, of course, contradict each other, since we must always include the old laws of the special relativity theory in the general laws for an inertial system.[7]

Within modern science, a proper understanding of the contrast between the general/*allgemein* and the special/*speziel* seems to be an important requirement in both the natural and the social sciences. The domain of law is no exception in this respect, as it includes the concepts of "general" and "special" law. This contrast, however, differs from the contrast between civil and criminal law explained in Column 3. For example, commercial law is a special law of civil law, and civil law is a general law of commercial law. This relationship is because the Civil Code stipulates general regulations regarding transactions and the Commercial Code sets regulations regarding commercial transactions in particular. With regard to the Financial Instruments and Exchange Act (*Kin'yū shōhin torihiki hō*), however, the Commercial Code acts as a general law, and the Financial Instruments and Exchange Act is a special law of the Commercial Code, as the Financial Instruments and Exchange Act regulates only commercial transactions relating to financial products. In other words, whereas civil and criminal law are considered exclusive counter-concepts (i.e., if a law is civil, it is not criminal, and vice versa), general and special law are relational concepts that express the relationships between multiple concrete laws. Thus, this concept can only really be discussed when multiple laws overlap in terms of the scopes or problem areas that they cover. For example, the relationship between general and special law does not apply to civil and criminal law.

We can distinguish between general and special law because a special law is established when the provisions (groups) of certain laws or regulations are deemed inappropriate in situations belonging to a particular category. The Act on Specified Commercial Transactions mentioned in the introduction is considered a special law of the Civil Code, meaning that the cooling-off cancellation system, which is not stipulated in the Civil Code, is legally effective as long as the Act on Specified Commercial Transactions applies. General law provides principles, whereas special law provides exceptions that prevail over those general principles.

Study Questions

1. Fill in the Blanks Labeled (1) Through (3) in the Following Text.

   A risk-neutral director has signed a performance-based contract stating that he will receive 80% of the company's profit as compensation.
   If the situation is as shown in Table 3.1, will the director exert effort? Suppose that the cost of the director's effort (i.e., the disutility calculated in monetary terms) is 1 million JPY.
   When the director exerts effort, there is a 70% probability that the reward will be 10 million JPY and a 30% probability that the reward will be zero. The cost of effort is 1 million JPY with a 100% probability. Thus, the director's expected compensation is (1) ______________ JPY.
   When the director does not exert effort, there is a 30% probability that the reward will be 10 million JPY and a 70% probability that the reward will be zero. The

[7] Taken from Einstein A, Infeld L (1938) The evolution of physics. Cambridge University Press, Cambridge, pp 224–225.

Table 3.1 The director's effort and the probability of business success

	The business succeeds and earns 10 million JPY in profit	The business fails and earns 0 JPY in profit
Director exerts effort	Probability 70%	Probability 30%
Director does not exert effort	Probability 30%	Probability 70%

Table 3.2 The company's payoff and the director's effort (Question 1)

	The business succeeds (50% probability)	The business fails (50% probability)
Director makes an effort	1,000 in profit is created	600 in loss is created
Director makes no effort	600 in profit is created	400 in loss is created

cost of effort is zero with a 100% probability. Thus, the director's expected compensation is (2) _____________ JPY.
Thus, in choosing whether exerting or not exert an effort, the director decides to (3) _____________.

2. Question 1. If the situation is as shown in Table 3.2, is it desirable for the director to make an effort? Does the director make an effort? Assume that the director and the shareholders are both risk neutral and that exerting effort incurs a cost (disutility) of 100 in monetary terms.

   (1) What happens when the director's fixed compensation is 200 and performance-based compensation is zero?
   (2) What happens when the director's fixed compensation is 0 and performance-based compensation is 60% of profits?
   (3) What happens when the director's fixed compensation is 0 and performance-based compensation is 50% of profits?
   (4) What happens when the director's fixed compensation is 0 and performance-based compensation is 40% of profits?
   (5) What happens when the director's fixed compensation is 100 and performance-based compensation is 40% of profits?

   Question 2. What happens in scenarios (1) through (5) in Question 1 under the circumstances given by Table 3.3?
   Question 3. What conclusions can be drawn from Questions 1 and 2?
3. Question 1. Are shareholder derivative lawsuits beneficial for maximizing shareholders' profits? Discuss the positive and negative aspects of the system as well as your own views.
   Question 2. Why do investors invest in companies with controlling shareholders even when they know they will be minority shareholders?

Table 3.3 The company's payoff and the director's effort (Question 2)

	The business succeeds (50% probability)	The business fails (50% probability)
Director makes an effort	1,000 in profit is created	1,000 in loss is created
Director makes no effort	600 in profit is created	400 in loss is created

References

Fujita T (2002–2003) Law and economics kaishahō (Law and economics on corporate law) (1)-(12). Hōgaku Kyōshitsu Voll. 259–270 [publication in Japanese]

Kanda H (1985) Gappei to kabunushi kan no rigai chōsei no kijun: Amerikahō (Standards for adjustment of interests between mergers and shareholders: American law). In: Egashira K (ed) Hachijūnendai shojihō no shosō, Ōtori Tsuneo sensei kanreki kinen[Various aspects of commercial law in the eighties, commemoration of the 60th birthday of Professor Tsuneo Otori]. Yuhikaku, Tokyo, p 331 [publication in Japanese]

La Porta R, Lopez-De-Silanes F, Shleifer A, Vishny RW (1997) Legal determinants of external finance. J Finance 52:1131–1150

Milhaupt CJ (2004) Nonprofit organizations as investor protection: economic theory and evidence from East Asia. Yale J Int Law 29:169–207

Miwa Y, Kanda H, Yanagawa N (1998) Kaishahō no keizaigaku (Economics of corporate law). University of Tokyo Press, Tokyo [publication in Japanese]

Ochiai S (2016) Kaishahō yōsetsu (Company law outline), 2nd edn. Yuhikaku, Tokyo [publication in Japanese]

Puchniak DW, Nakahigashi M (2012) Japan's love for derivative actions: irrational behavior and non-economic motives as rational explanations for shareholder litigation. Vanderbilt J Transnatl Law 45:1–82

Tanaka W (2001) Kaishahō no keizai bunseki (Economic analysis of company law). Hōgaku Kyōshitsu 253:81–86 [publication in Japanese]

Tanaka W (2013) Sūji de "wakaru" to wa dō iu koto ka (What does it mean to "understand" by numbers?). In: Tanaka W (ed) Sūji de wakaru kaishahō(Numerical analysis of corporate law). Yuhikaku, Tokyo, pp 1–13 [publication in Japanese]

Chapter 4
The Rules for Fair Competition: Antimonopoly Law

Fumio Sensui and Takashi Yanagawa

Contents

4.1 Summary and Purposes of Antimonopoly Law 72
4.1.1 The Antimonopoly Act 72
4.1.2 Defining Purposes of Antimonopoly Law 73
4.1.3 Economic Analysis of the Antimonopoly Act 75
4.2 Resale Price Maintenance 76
4.2.1 Resale Price Maintenance Explained 76
4.2.2 Legal Background 76
4.2.3 Economics of RPM 77
4.2.4 Supreme Court Decision on RPM: The Wakodo Case 80
4.2.5 Justifiable Cause for RPM: The Economic Case 82
4.2.6 Exemptions to RPM Laws 84
4.2.7 RPM of Books Overseas 85
4.3 Tie-In Sales 86
4.3.1 What is Tying? 86
4.3.2 An Economic Assessment of Tying 87
4.3.3 Explanations and Precedents of the Antimonopoly Act: Acts that Constitute Tying 92
4.3.4 Explanations and Precedents of the Antimonopoly Act: (Unjustly) Impeding Fair Competition 94
4.4 Conclusion 96
References 99

F. Sensui
Graduate School of Law, Kobe University, 2-1 Rokkodai-cho, Nada-ku, Kobe 657-8501, Hyogo, Japan
e-mail: sensui@kobe-u.ac.jp

T. Yanagawa (✉)
Faculty of Economics, Setsunan University, 17-8 Ikeda-Nakamachi, Neyagawa 572-8508, Osaka, Japan
e-mail: takashi.yanagawa@setsunan.ac.jp

T. Yanagawa et al. (eds.), *Econo-Legal Studies*,
https://doi.org/10.1007/978-981-16-5145-8_4

The Antimonopoly Act, which defines the rules governing competition between companies, is among the most fertile fields of cooperation between legal and economic scholars in terms of its theoretical interpretation and practical applications. The authorities responsible for its application have backgrounds in jurisprudence and economics, and it is not unusual for legal scholars and economists to collaborate on joint research in this field. Although jurisprudence and economic interpretations of the many issues surrounding the Antimonopoly Act align in many cases, they sometimes do not. In this chapter, we address prototypical examples of this misalignment: resale price maintenance and tying. The principal driver of the diverging opinions on this issue is that economists use efficiency as a basis for their opposition to strict regulation, whereas legal scholars emphasize distributors' right to set prices against resale price maintenance and consumers' right to choose consumption goods against tying. Legal scholars believe that conduct that impedes these rights should be restricted. In this way, the two groups' foundations for evaluating these cases differ in essence.

4.1 Summary and Purposes of Antimonopoly Law

4.1.1 The Antimonopoly Act

In this chapter, we discuss the Antimonopoly Act (formally called the "Act on Prohibition of Private Monopolization and Maintenance of Fair Trade"), which was established in 1947. Antitrust law was first established in 1890 in the United States and is referred to by various names in different countries; the term "competition law" is universally understood.

The Japanese Antimonopoly Act bars or restricts four types of conduct: private monopolization, the unreasonable restraint of trade, corporate mergers that restrict competition, and unfair trade practices. The Antimonopoly Act is operated and executed by the Japan Fair Trade Commission (JFTC).

First, the law defines private monopolization as the exclusion or control of another business entity's business activities, thereby substantially restraining competition in a particular field of trade against the public interest (Antimonopoly Act, Art. 2(5)). For example, the Japanese Society for Rights of Authors, Composers, and Publishers collected broadcast fines in a way that effectively blocked other copyright management organizations.

Second, an unreasonable restraint of trade is an act that substantially restricts competition in a particular field of trade against the public interest by restraining or enforcing the business activities of enterprises jointly and mutually (Arts. 2(6), and 3). Typical examples of such acts are price fixing and bid rigging.

Third, the category of corporate mergers includes not only mergers but also concurrent appointments of officers and transfers of a business to another party in ways that substantively restrain competition in a particular field of trade (Arts. 10, 13,

14, 15, 15–2, 15–3, and 16). Past examples include the merger of Nippon Steel Corporation with Sumitomo Metal Industries to create Nippon Steel & Sumitomo Metal Corporation and Panasonic's acquisition of Sanyo. The latter case was reviewed in the United States, the European Union, China, and numerous other countries, with legal fees estimated to have reached nearly 10 billion JPY.

Finally, unfair trade practices are manifold and are restricted when they tend to impede fair competition (Art. 2(9)). For example, in 2011, the JFTC issued a cease and desist order to DeNA, the operator of the Mobage platform, for exerting pressure on software development companies to withhold their games from rival mobile gaming sites; this action was treated as an unfair trade practice against DeNA's competitors. In another example from 2011, the JFTC issued a cease and desist order against Sanyo Marunaka and ordered it to pay 200 million JPY in surcharges for allegedly leveraging its position to unfairly force delivery companies to return inventory of specialty goods and dispatch personnel during peak times, such as sale periods. However, the Tokyo High Court reversed the order in the Sanyo Marunaka case in 2021, citing procedural defects. Cease and desist orders and surcharges were also brought against Toys "R" Us in December 2011, Edion in 2012, and Ralse in 2013. A surcharges of 4 billion JPY was imposed on Edion.

4.1.2 Defining Purposes of Antimonopoly Law

The intended purpose of the Antimonopoly Act is defined in Article 1. It states:

> The purpose of this Act is to promote fair and free competition, stimulate the creative initiative of enterprise, encourage business activity, heighten the level of employment and actual national income, and thereby promote the democratic and wholesome development of the national economy as well as secure the interests of general consumers by prohibiting private monopolization, unreasonable restraint of trade and unfair trade practices, preventing excessive concentration of economic power and eliminating unreasonable restraints on production, sale, price, technology, etc. and all other unjust restrictions on business activity through combinations, agreements, etc.

The Act lists a range of interests to be protected by the law, including fair and free competition, business activity, the democratic and wholesome development of the national economy, and the interests of general consumers. It is useful to understand the relationships among these elements.

The accepted theory is that the Antimonopoly Act's immediate purpose is promoting fair and free competition (i.e., economic order of free competition) and that the listed values pursuant to this goal are mere effects or functions of promoting fair and free competition. In contrast, a Supreme Court decision (Second Petty Bench of the Supreme Court, decision on February 24, 1984) described the Antimonopoly Act's immediate purpose as the promotion of fair and free competition and its ultimate purpose as the promotion of the democratic and wholesome development of the national economy. The court stated that in exceptional cases in which the ultimate purpose supersedes the immediate purpose, acts that obstruct fair and free competition do not contravene the Antimonopoly Act.

This chapter does not explore whether such exceptions exist or the cases in which they would apply; generally, interpretations of Article 1 (i.e., the purposes) of the Antimonopoly Act do not diverge from the idea that, as a rule, the Act promotes fair and free competition and offers a range of protections connected with creation, employment, and consumers' benefit. We investigate how the act functions to achieve these goals.

As an example, one may ask why the Antimonopoly Act bars price fixing. To answer this question, we consider the case of ice cream manufacturers colluding to raise the price of ice cream and describe the likely results of this collusion.

First, the price of ice cream rises. In turn, consumers who purchase ice cream at this inflated price are subject to damages. Second, the quantity of ice cream provided decreases, and precious resources cease to be used. Third, innovation to produce new, more delicious types of ice cream may stop altogether.

Law scholars believe that pricing cartels should be barred because, as described in this example, they place consumers at a disadvantage and contravene standards of fairness and justice. However, they do not generally cite the reduced production as grounds for their argument against cartels. In contrast, scholars of economics argue that because the price increase resulting from a cartel's formation does not inhibit economic efficiency and is simply an income distribution issue, the problem can be resolved by redistributing income. Instead, they tend to focus on the reduction in quantity because it creates an inefficient resource distribution (i.e., it decreases social welfare) and reduces supply. Finally, some scholars of economics speculate that if a cartel does monopolize a market, it may use this monopoly position to actively innovate (the so-called "Schumpeterian hypothesis").

Even if we define the purposes of the Antimonopoly Act as ensuring an efficient allocation of resources and an increased supply, providing a fair distribution of income, and protecting consumers, if a pricing cartel, bid rigging, private monopolization, or corporate merger occurs in contravention of the Act, all three purposes are simultaneously nullified. Thus, regardless of which purpose is emphasized, the conclusion as to whether an act is illegal does not change.

For this reason, debating which purpose is the actual intended purpose of the Act offers little practical benefit. The fields of jurisprudence and economics appraise the vectors of efficiency, income distribution, justice, and fairness differently with respect to the Antimonopoly Act, and they may provide very different rationales for restricting certain conduct. Nevertheless, in terms of the law's ultimate application, they are likely to reach similar conclusions.

However, the conclusions arrived at by jurisprudence and economics with respect to the Antimonopoly Act do diverge in several cases. The signature examples of this divergence are resale price maintenance and tying. We explain these examples in more detail in the following sections. First, however, we provide an economic analysis of the Antimonopoly Act.

4.1.3 Economic Analysis of the Antimonopoly Act

When analyzing issues posed by the Antimonopoly Act, an economics perspective places more emphasis on efficiency than on fairness. Efficiency is evaluated based on such metrics as Pareto efficiency and surplus, and improved efficiency indicates increased economic benefits. As we explain in the preface, this thinking is analogous to that used in economic analyses of other policies. However, the reader should pay careful attention to the treatment of monopolies; in terms of economic benefits, monopolistic markets generate deadweight loss, a key form of market failure (see Sect. 8 of the Appendix). From an efficiency perspective, a fully competitive market is desirable, and even in the absence of a fully competitive market, some competition is generally considered more desirable than a monopoly. For this reason, monopolistic conduct must be restricted. Nevertheless, the Antimonopoly Act does not aim to forcibly transform monopolistic or oligopolistic markets into competitive ones. At a fixed point in time, monopolies are inefficient, but over the long term, they aim for innovation, which drives economic growth and ultimately benefits the economy. Aiming to monopolize a market and using a range of strategies is an engine for growth that improves economic efficiency. The Antimonopoly Act does not bar a company from providing affordable, high-quality products and services to increase its market share and then raising the price of its products; instead, it bars artificial manipulation to create, maintain, and strengthen market control.

Typical economic analyses focusing on surplus use the total surplus, that is, the sum of the consumer and producer surpluses. Economic analyses in the context of the Antimonopoly Act usually focus on the total surplus, but some scholars note that it is preferable to use the consumer surplus as a baseline vector. This opinion is based on the fact that United States antitrust law emphasizes benefits to consumers and European Union competition law is also based on consumer benefits, and it essentially applies that thinking to economic reasoning (note that Japan does not exclusively use a consumer surplus-based system). The determination of illegality in a particular case changes based on whether the total surplus or just the consumer surplus is considered. For example, mergers and acquisitions may increase the total surplus by increasing only the producer surplus, with the consumer surplus instead decreasing. Such mergers and acquisitions are seen as favorable when considering the total surplus but not when considering the consumer surplus. Ordinarily, when a corporation aims to obtain profits, the producer surplus should increase. If the consumer surplus increases, the total surplus increases; however, the total surplus may still increase even if the consumer surplus does not increase. In this way, using the consumer surplus in an analysis means that when a corporation engages in a certain activity that absolutely increases the total surplus, it can be treated as lawful conduct (although the consumer surplus may unexpectedly drop in some cases). Some argue that the total surplus should be analyzed because if the total surplus increases, some of that surplus can be redistributed to consumers, with economic benefits accruing to both producers and consumers. However, although such redistribution may be possible in macroeconomies, it is difficult to redistribute profits to individual actors in localized economies. Thus, regardless of whether redistribution occurs, using the consumer surplus as a basis is a better solution in terms of fairness when trying to avoid cases in which one party (i.e., producers) benefits and one party (i.e., consumers) loses.

4.2 Resale Price Maintenance

4.2.1 Resale Price Maintenance Explained

This section discusses resale price maintenance (RPM), an act that falls within the category of unfair trade practices. For example, suppose that a manufacturer manufactures a product, a wholesaler buys it from the manufacturer and (re)sells it, and a retailer buys it from the wholesaler and (re)sells it to consumers. RPM occurs when the manufacturer binds the price at which the wholesaler can resell the product to the retailer or the price at which the retailer can resell the product to the consumer (i.e., the retail price). In Japan, as we shall see, RPM is illegal in principle.

Please consider your answers to the following questions:

1. When is RPM treated as illegal?
2. Is RPM intended to avoid free rides and double margins, which are considered illegal?
3. How is RPM restricted in countries outside of Japan?
4. Is it illegal to sell printed matter and music CDs at their list prices?
5. Although printed matter and music CDs have list prices, university cooperative associations sell them at a discount. How is this possible?

4.2.2 Legal Background

RPM is treated as an unfair trade practice and is illegal in principle. It is barred by the terms of Article 19 of the Antimonopoly Act. Paragraph 9 of Article 2 defines unfair trade practices. It states, "The term 'unfair trade practices' as used in this Act means any act falling under any of following items." Item (4) in that list states:

> supplying goods to a party who purchases the relevant goods from oneself and imposing one of the restrictive terms listed below without justifiable grounds: (a) causing the party to maintain the selling price of the goods that one has determined or otherwise restricting the party's freedom to set the selling price of the goods or (b) requiring the party to force an enterprise to purchase the goods from the party to maintain the selling price of the goods that one has determined or otherwise causing the party to restrict the relevant enterprise's freedom to set the selling price of the goods.

The Antimonopoly Act employs the following sanctions related to RPM. First, a cease and desist order (Art. 20) is used to order the cessation of the activity, and prevent its recurrence as an administrative procedure. Second, the act includes a surcharge payment order (Art. 20-5); if RPM is repeated within 10 years, the government will collect 3% of the amount earned from RPM as a surcharge to the national treasury. This order is also treated as an administrative measure. Third, the Antimonopoly Act provides for a special system of compensation for damages (Art. 25), and victims can also pursue liability in tort under the Civil Code (Art. 709). This damage is claimed by a person who was forced to buy a product at a higher price owing to RPM (i.e., the victim). Fourth, the victim may request the court to enjoin the violation (Antimonopoly Act, Art. 24).

4.2.3 Economics of RPM

4.2.3.1 Anticompetitive Effects of Resale Price Maintenance

We consider the economic effects of RPM on market competition and economic welfare. We first discuss its anticompetitive effects and then discuss its procompetitive effects. The main anticompetitive effect that reduces economic welfare is the use of RPM to avoid competition, namely, the greater ease with which retailers' and manufacturers' cartels can be formed and maintained using RPM.

First, we consider the case of retailers forming a dealer cartel and using RPM to restrict "intra-brand" competition among retailors over products of a certain brand. The retailers can easily decide to form a cartel, launch it, and fix a good's retail price by asking RPM of manufactures. RPM makes it easier to prevent other retailers from deviating from the cartel, thereby increasing its effectiveness. However, from the manufacturers' perspective, dealer cartels do not lead to profits. For a given shipped price, manufacturers want retailers to sell more products. In terms of efficiency, dealer cartels do not promote competition, as we explain later, and they are thought to worsen economic welfare.

Second, we consider the case in which RPM enables manufacturers to more easily maintain manufacturers' cartels and allows them to restrict "inter-brand" competition among manufacturers over certain brands. We suppose that manufacturers wish to use the cartel to raise and maintain prices. In this case, the shipped price greatly exceeds the marginal cost, meaning that every manufacturer has an incentive to leave the cartel and sell more units. Manufacturers will therefore furtively break the cartel by lowering their prices. However, with RPM, a manufacturer lowering its shipping price will not reduce the retail price, as lowering the retail resale price would help other manufacturers to more easily notice the break from the cartel. Thus, manufacturers who fear oppositional pricing cannot extricate themselves from the cartel, enabling its continuation.

Furthermore, because RPM restricts intra-brand pricing competition, prices may increase even in the absence of a deliberate cartel.

4.2.3.2 Procompetitive Effects of RPM

At the same time, RPM can also promote competition and improve economic welfare for a variety of reasons. Below, we discuss the following effects in turn: the avoidance of double marginalization, the prevention of free riders, the promotion of non-price competition, the promotion of new entrants and new products, the promotion of franchise sales, management of uncertain demand, and the evasion of loss leading.

First, we consider a market in which both a manufacturer and a retailer hold monopolies. In this case, the consumer is subject to double margins by two market-dominant companies before purchasing a product from these companies. The avoidance of double marginalization protects against cases in which both the manufacturer and retailer add margins into the price such that the resulting price is too high for the manufacturer and fewer items are sold. If maximum RPM is possible, the manufacturer will lower the retailer's margin, that is, the retail price, to the level that maximizes the manufacturer's profits, thereby increasing the quantity sold. The resulting outcome is desirable for not only the manufacturer but also for consumers.

Next is the prevention of free riders. After receiving a service from a retailer that provides that service at cost, a consumer may purchase the same product from a retailer that does not expend these service costs and offers the product at a lower price. Put differently, a retailer that does not provide a service can free ride on a retailer that offers that service. Free riding often occurs in the case of explaining a product prior to a purchase; an explanation increases a consumer's understanding and desire to purchase. The formation of a brand also fits into this category; at franchises, department stores, and well-known retailers, consumers can inspect the quality of items before purchase, meaning that other retailers that sell those items can free ride on the brands of such stores. The displays and installations of trial products and services, such as electric appliances and books, also fall into this category. When another retailer can free ride on this service by simply offering the same product at a lower cost, the original provider is unable to continue providing those services, which, in turn, reduces consumer demand. With RPM, retail prices become uniform, and when a consumer purchases a product from a retailer that provides added services, that retailer can, in turn, offer more services, which increases demand and economic efficiency. In the past, it was difficult for consumers to seek out and find retailers offering the same goods at inexpensive prices, meaning that such free riding was uncommon. With the Internet, however, consumers can readily obtain price information from numerous stores. When shipping is inexpensive, the risk of frequent free riding or showrooming is even higher.

Third, RPM promotes non-price competition. If prices exceed marginal costs and remain fixed at that point, retailers will invest in non-price services to sell more units, promoting non-price competition. Japanese booksellers can open vast stores stocking ample selections of items and compete in the vicinities of premier districts because of RPM. In the absence of price competition, retailers can expand their stores and improve their selections of inventory, enticing consumers and increasing revenue. Although fixed airfares are not an example of RPM, when airfares were fixed, the number of flights serving a route and the onboard services offered were an active form of non-price competition among carriers. However, although non-price competition increases consumption and improves economic welfare, excess competition over services does not necessarily translate into gains for consumers; in some cases, price competition provides a greater benefit to consumers even if it means lowering the standard of service.

Fourth, RPM can promote new entrants and products. When manufacturers use RPM to secure ample retail margins, they guarantee that the major expenses borne by the retailer associated with the sale of the products will be covered. Thus, retailers can actively pursue selling, thereby promoting the entry of new manufacturers and products. For example, RPM is helpful for relatively unknown firms that require active sales activities or for famous manufacturers that need to launch a campaign in advance of a release of new products.

The fifth way that RPM promotes competition is through the promotion of franchise sales. When 7-Eleven, McDonald's, and other franchises and chain stores launch sales promotion campaigns, such as a 100 JPY sales run at all locations, RPM is effective. In its absence, a campaign can only succeed if all franchisees autonomously agree with the franchisor's suggestion.

Sixth, RPM enables the management of uncertain demand. The production of Nintendo videogame software cartridges originally took considerable time, and, thus, retailers had to stock up on units before they could assess actual demand. If the market price were determined by setting supply equal to demand, low demand would cause prices to plunge, and high demand would cause them to spike. If a minimum resale price can be set, the price does not plummet even if demand is low, and, thus, retailers can secure fixed and stable profits. A minimum resale price can therefore enable retailers to stockpile inventory before its release date and can also weaken price hikes when demand is high. Minimizing price fluctuations in this way translates into gains for consumers.

Finally, the seventh point, the evasion of loss leading, has notably been cited in Japan as a basis for defending RPM. When a retailer sells attractive products (i.e., loss leaders) at a discount, other shops' profit margins shrink. Furthermore, if the lower price of these loss leaders is generally accepted, they can no longer be sold at the original, higher price. As more shops cease carrying these products, manufacturers sell fewer units. RPM can prevent price drops and secure a range of sales channels, thereby increasing sales volume. In the 1920s, Shiseido reintroduced products that it had used as loss leaders at their list prices alongside a wide selection of other products after creating a series of chains. This strategy enabled the company to achieve rapid growth and success.

4.2.3.3 Summary of the economic effects of RPM

In principle, RPM is illegal in Japan and, with the exception of certain exclusions (described in detail in Sect. 4.2.6), RPM has not been approved in any cases. However, from an economics perspective, RPM has the potential to promote competition and improve economic welfare. RPM restricts intra-brand competition, but it can also promote inter-brand competition, in which manufacturers compete to sell different products. Whether RPM is treated as legal with certain illegal cases banned or treated as illegal with certain legal cases allowed, it is reasonable to believe that expanding RPM's application from its current one is suitable given the functions and benefits that it accrues. However, few previous cases of RPM can be used to justify this argument. Further empirical studies and research of case law are required.

4.2.4 Supreme Court Decision on RPM: The Wakodo Case

As described in Sect. 4.1, as a rule, the Antimonopoly Act treats RPM as illegal in principle. This treatment is based on the precedent set in the Supreme Court decision described below. First, we summarize that case:

The opinion in a July 10, 1975, decision by the First Petty Bench of the Supreme Court on the litigation appealing the trial decision in the *Wakodo* case reads:

> The appellant [Wakodo], the principal vendor of infant formula manufactured by Sankyo Milk KK, in the pursuit of sales of ... the aforementioned formula, specified the wholesale and retail prices of the product in advance to maintain a fixed price and forced retailers to comply with this price by 1) creating a registry of retailers and revoking the membership of those failing to comply with the pricing; 2) forcing wholesalers to pay a specific wholesale price to the appellant, with the appellant paying any returns to the wholesaler in the form of a separate bonus such that if the wholesaler failed to observe the wholesale price or transacted with retailers that were not in the appellant's retailer registry, the bonus amount was adjusted to the wholesaler's disadvantage; and 3) employing sales strategies used to individually establish distribution channels for each product, thereby confirming the retail prices and destinations of the products sold by wholesalers, notifying retailers of these sales strategies, and employing these strategies. The appellant clearly engaged in retail price maintenance.

The appellant made the following statement:

> The Court's interpretation that the aforementioned sales strategies were intended to restrain wholesalers and retailers is unreasonable, as the most important point for determining whether restraints were employed, namely, the extent of the market dominance of the appellant's infant milk formula, was not taken into account. This error is serious, and rendering a decision in the absence of this consideration is illegal.

The Supreme Court began by defining the term "restraint" as "taking fair competition into account, the selection of prices and transaction partners should be made on an individual and free basis by those parties to the transaction with consideration to economic efficiency. For this reason, restraint to this transaction by a third party represents a clear restraint on what is herein defined as a transaction." The court then noted the unique circumstances surrounding powdered milk:

> The hearing decision determined that consumers commonly select a specific brand of infant milk formula and purchase it even if different brands have different prices, given the particularities of this product. As a rule, consumers do not switch brands after using one brand, meaning that the demand for a given brand will not decrease. Thus, retailers are under special conditions in which they must permanently stock inventory of the aforementioned brand

> regardless of its quantity. Given that these conditions apply to the appellant's brand of infant formula and given that the wholesalers with which the appellant transacts carry not only the aforementioned infant formula but also a range of infant products and baby preparations manufactured or sold by the appellant, the hearing decision's foregoing acknowledgment is clearly based on substantive facts.

The court then stated that the market share held by a party engaging in resale was irrelevant. In other words:

> Based on these facts, even when, according to the appellant's opinion, its share of the market for infant formula is low and retailers stock small quantities of its product, wholesalers receiving orders from retailers cannot rescind their dealings with the appellant for the aforementioned milk product. If they continue to transact with the appellant, they clearly must abide by the retail pricing and restrictions imposed by the appellant to obtain the aforementioned returns in the form of a bonus. Thus, this Court finds that, irrespective of the appellant's market share, the sales strategies employed restrain the wholesalers and retailers with which the appellant transacts, and the decision is therefore entirely reasonable.

Finally, with respect to the meaning of "justifiable grounds," the court stated:

> [The] term "justifiable grounds," as used herein, refers to the idea of maintaining fair and free competition and situations in which the terms of such restraints do not impede other business operators' abilities to freely compete. In other words, cases in which rationality or necessity only arises from the perspective of business management or transactions that are not directly related to the maintenance of competitive order, among others, cannot be regarded as having "justifiable grounds" as described here.

Based on the above discussion, the Supreme Court stated that even if the market share held by those engaging in RPM is small (in this case, 5–7%), RPM is still illegal. It also stated that RPM restricts so-called intra-brand competition (though it does not restrict inter-brand competition) but results in prices being maintained at a fixed point. The court described the reason for this outcome as so-called "product differentiation," that is, the need to have all brands permanently available on shelves. Finally, it noted that "justifiable grounds" is limited to meaning the impediment of fair competition and is not incorporated into the concept of reasonable cause for business and management reasons.

This Supreme Court decision was made in 1975 and, thus, is an old precedent. The attorneys for the plaintiff did not describe the economic arguments of the prevention of free riders and the avoidance of double marginalization as justifiable grounds, and we can surmise that they lacked knowledge of these ideas at the time. However, we also note that neither the avoidance of double marginalization nor free riders are relevant to this case.

Furthermore, it is possible that the RPM in this case was operated as a manufacturers' cartel, concerted practices, or a pricing cartel among retailers (i.e., a dealers' cartel). The rationale for this assertion is that Morinaga and Meiji, Japan's other two major milk producers, were also subject to legal measures by the JTFC at that time.

Following this Supreme Court decision, the JTFC enacted the precursor to Article 2, paragraph 9, item 4 of the current Antimonopoly Act through a formal notice. That notice stated that RPM is illegal in principle irrespective of the actor's market share (i.e., even if a clearly minuscule actor engages in RPM). In other words, RPM activities contravene the Antimonopoly Act except in the case of justifiable grounds (Art. 2(9)(iv)). Further, as the Supreme Court stated, justifiable grounds can only be invoked from the perspective of the impediment of fair competition and do not take into account any reasonable cause or need for business or transactional reasons. This position clarified that RPM is legal in very few cases, with justifiable reasons as an exception.

Although a range of economic theories seem to justify RPM, it is illegal in principle at this time based on the above discussion. Thus, it is illegal, for example, for an appliance manufacturer to restrain retailers' ability to set the price of liquid-crystal display televisions and to stop shipping products to retailers who offer them at a discount. It is also illegal for a beverage manufacturer to restrain retailers' abilities to set prices on its bottled tea drinks sold in supermarkets.

However, this rule has two types of exceptions. The first type is exceptions provided by law, which are referred to as "exemptions." These exceptions are defined in Article 23 of the Antimonopoly Act and are described later in this chapter. The second type is cases of justifiable grounds. The prevention of free riders and the avoidance of double marginalization ostensibly seem to fit into this category, but the prevailing view is that these cases do not apply as exceptions.

The JTFC publishes a document called "Guidelines Concerning Distribution Systems and Business Practice under the Antimonopoly Act" ("Distribution & Business Practice Guidelines" for short), which explains why RPM is illegal:

> One of the most basic aspects of an enterprise's business activities is independently determining a sales price in keeping with market conditions and securing competition among enterprises and consumer choice. If an enterprise restricts the sales price of distributors as part of marketing activities or upon a distributor's request, this action is in principle illegal as an unfair trade practice because it reduces or eliminates price competition among distributors.

The JFTC's basis for treating RPM as illegal in principle includes two arguments: independently setting retail prices is the most fundamental aspect of business practices and RPM diminishes and eliminates price competition among distributors. Of these arguments, the latter can be explained from an economic perspective, and the former fits into the framework of a legalistic perspective. We describe these arguments in more detail later in the text.

4.2.5 Justifiable Cause for RPM: The Economic Case

First, free riders are rarely discussed in legal textbooks. The following description by Kawahama et al. (2020, p. 264) is likely the only coverage of the subject:

> Products for which this issue arises are limited to those that require an explanation prior to purchase but do not require further interaction between the consumer and the retailer after purchase. If C [a customer] has an acquaintance who is familiar with computers, C will simply buy a computer at a discount shop in the first place. For a computer amateur, however, problems are likely to occur post-purchase, and such a customer will frequently return to the shop after buying a computer. In that case, although it may be more expensive, C is

likely to purchase a computer from a shop that offers post-purchase assistance. Additionally, some operators of standalone businesses likely provide pre- and post-purchase advice that customers can obtain without going to a retailer. In such cases, the issue of free riding likely occurs for very few products.

Kawahama et al. (2020, p. 264) also discuss double margins:

> Is resale price maintenance permissible if double monopoly [double margins] can be avoided? First, this discussion is limited to cases in which double monopoly occurs and the restriction on prices takes the form of maximum price resale price maintenance, whereby the maximum price is set. This logic cannot be used to justify restrictions in the form of minimum price resale price maintenance, whereby the minimum price is set, or resale price maintenance in general.

They add:

> Can we say that this resale price maintenance diminishes free competition? This process clearly sets the maximum price and restricts free price setting. This resale price maintenance was achievable because of the low level of market control in this situation, and maximum price resale price maintenance is simply the exercise of that power. However, whereas resale price maintenance ordinarily promotes the exercise of market control, raises prices, and decreases production output, maximum price resale price maintenance reduces the extent to which existing market control is exercised, lowers prices, and increases production output. Further, maximum price resale price maintenance neither newly creates, maintains, nor strengthens market control, and it does not promote the exercise of market power; if anything, it restricts the exercise of such power. To date, no court decision has rendered maximum price resale price maintenance as a means of avoiding double monopolies legal, but we interpret it as an exception that does not impede fair competition.

In this way, they state that double margins can represent justifiable grounds. However, Kanai et al. (2020, pp. 330–331) raise an objection to this argument:

> In theory, this logic is sound, but in practice, allowing the maximum sale price to be determined by manufacturers replaces the notion of a sale price that is properly determined by market competition and treats prices that are artificially set by manufacturers as sale prices. This outcome conflicts with the fundamental idea of the Antimonopoly Act and would be difficult to put into practice.

This explanation is similar to first argument offered by the JTFC and effectively represents a negation of the above discussion.

Franchise stores (e.g., McDonald's and Kentucky Fried Chicken) offer products at the same price at all establishments. Opinions on whether this pricing is a form of RPM placed on franchisees by the franchise headquarters state that this uniform pricing is intended to prevent franchisees from free-riding quality inspection of franchisors. Thus, we can treat this situation as an exception that proves the rule. However, JFTC documentation on this subject (i.e., "Franchise Guidelines: Interpretation of the Antimonopoly Act in the Context of Franchise Systems") does not treat this reasoning as fair. Nevertheless, this pricing scheme is still allowed. The interpretation of this situation seems to be that franchisees merely observe the suggested pricing presented by the company headquarters at their own discretion and are not engaging in RPM.

4.2.6 Exemptions to RPM Laws

Article 23 of the Antimonopoly Act defines exemptions to RPM laws. The first exemption is Article 23, paragraph 1, which describes products designated as excluded by the JFTC. Previously, numerous products were specified, but the JTFC no longer exercises this right to designate. The second is Article 23, paragraph 4, referred to as "resale price maintenance of published works," which states: "Paragraph 1 also applies to legitimate acts engaged in by an enterprise that publishes works or an enterprise that sells such published works in order to fix and maintain the resale price thereof with another enterprise that purchases such works."

In Japan, many books, magazines, newspapers, and music CDs have a fixed price. This pricing is a form of RPM under Article 23, paragraph 4; in the case of books, publishers effectively restrict bookshops' ability to set prices. The theoretical reasoning for this restriction dates back to 1953: when the Antimonopoly Act was amended to make RPM illegal in principle, books, magazines, and music records were sold at a fixed price; the Antimonopoly Act reflected this practice. Music CDs are effectively equivalent to music records and, thus, are treated in the same fashion.

Article 23, paragraph 4 treats published works as excluded. However, the JFTC interprets the term "published works" in paragraph 4 to mean only books, magazines, newspapers, phonograms, music tapes, and music CDs. The JFTC provides as the basis for this decision the fact that the above items are additions to the practices defined in the Act and that "published works" as described in Article 23, paragraph 4 and "published works" as described in the Copyright Act are different concepts. The JFTC has also regularly expressed its interest in repealing this exclusion on the grounds that no reasonable basis for its inclusion exist and that few countries incorporate such an exemption (see Sect. 4.2.7). The publishing and newspaper industries emphasize that books, magazines, and so forth are sold at the same price in rural regions and cities to protect the culture of publication, and they oppose a repeal of the exemption system. For postal and telephone services, a certain amount of money is collected from subscribers by law to cover the high costs of providing services in remote areas, thereby maintaining uniform rates throughout the country. This principle is referred to as "universal service." Various opinions on applying universal service to printed matter and magazines have been expressed, but no consensus has been reached.

In spite of the above clause, university cooperative associations sell books and magazines below the list price. It is interesting to ask why this pricing is possible.

One possible reason is that university cooperative associations have entered into RPM contracts (which publishers and booksellers enter to maintain a certain list price) per Article 23, paragraph 4, but do not abide by these contracts. Such contracts must be kept, but even if they are breached, no problem arises if the publisher does not mind and does not claim default. However, this reasoning is not accurate. Consider paragraph 5, which states: "Organizations formed pursuant to the provisions of any of the following Acts may not be included in another enterprise who purchases goods or works provided in paragraph 1 or the preceding paragraph." The Consumer

Cooperatives Act is one of the acts referenced by this paragraph. Thus, university cooperatives represent a special exemption and, returning to the underlying rule, imposing resale restrictions on cooperatives is an infringement of the Antimonopoly Act. The organizations listed in Article 23 (e.g., university cooperatives, cooperative societies, etc.) include consumers, small and medium businesses, and employees that serve the public welfare by providing everyday necessities to their constituents. It is held that if cooperatives were obligated to enter into a resale contract, their recognized functions (i.e., jointly buying products to enable constituents with lesser purchasing power to transact evenly with others) would fail to operate.

Column 8. Regulations on RPM in the United States and Europe

In the United States, RPM is regulated by Article 1 of the Sherman Act and Article 5 of the Federal Trade Commission Act. RPM had been deemed illegal per se in the United States following a 1911 Supreme Court ruling (*Dr. Miles Med. Co. v. John D. Park & Sons, Co.*), but a 2007 Supreme Court ruling (*Leegin Creative Leather Products v. PSKS, Inc.*) known as the *Leegin Decision* deemed that RPM could be regulated based on the rule of reason. Like RPM, non-price restrictions, such as a territory system restricting business areas, have been illegal per se in the United States, but the Supreme Court's 1977 *Sylvania* ruling (*Continental TV, Inc. v. GTE Sylvania, Inc.*) deemed that the rule of reason applied because the restrictions promoted inter-brand competition even if intra-brand competition was limited.

In the European Union, Article 101 of the Treaty of the Functioning of the European Union regulates collusive activity, and Article 102 prevents those holding dominant positions in the market from abusing that position. RPM is listed among the vertical restraints regulated by Article 101.

The European Commission has published guidelines on vertical restraints (May 19, 2010) that distinguish between hardcore and non-hardcore restraints. Price floor and fixed-price RPM are deemed hardcore restraints and are therefore illegal in principle and are not subject to block exemptions. However, defendants have room to claim individual exemptions based on efficiency, as the guidelines stipulate that the free rider issues of advertising and investments to enter a market should be given consideration. In contrast, maximum price limits are non-hardcore restraints, and, thus, if the relevant market share is less than 30%, block exemptions apply, and they are deemed legal.

4.2.7 RPM of Books Overseas

Of the six types of media described in Sect. 4.2.6, RPM of music records and CDs is largely barred in most countries with the exception of Japan. In the United States,

RPM is likely to be legal in these cases because RPM is based on the principle of the rule of reason, which states that legality is determined by considering various factors. However, in practice, RPM is not carried out. German domestic law allows RPM for books. In this way, books published in Germany can legally be resold to the extent that they are sold within the country. In Germany, RPM of books is described as lawful because it enables the publication of expensive academic literature and, thus, supports the maintenance of culture. Libraries and universities purchase academic literature even if it is expensive, meaning that its publication is enabled by offsetting the costs of production. However, the European Commission does not authorize RPM across borders; thus, the distribution of a book from Germany into Austria, another German-speaking region, for RPM is illegal. If, for example an Austrian consumer purchases a book from a German Internet shop, it is considered illegal for the publisher to enforce the retail price.

4.3 Tie-In Sales

4.3.1 What is Tying?

We now take a look at tying. Tying is the act of compelling somebody who wants to purchase a product to also buy another product or products and is regulated according to Article 2, paragraph 9 of the Antimonopoly Act. Tying is also known as "bundling" and "tie-in sales."

We start by examining the text of the Act. The text of Article 2, paragraph 9 of the Antimonopoly Act states "the term 'unfair trade practices' as used in this Act means an act falling under any of the following items," and item (6) designates "any act falling under any of the following items, which tends to impede fair competition and which is designated by the Fair Trade Commission, other than the acts listed in the preceding items," and "unjustly inducing or coercing the customers of a competitor to deal with oneself." Of particular importance in relation to the phrase "designated by the Fair Trade Commission [JFTC]" is The Fair Trade Commission Public Notice No. 15 of June 18, 1982. This public notice is referred to as the "General Designation." Item (10) of the General Designation defines tying as "unjustly causing another party to purchase goods or services from oneself or from an entrepreneur designated by oneself by tying it to the supply of other goods or services, or otherwise coercing the said party to trade with oneself or with an entrepreneur designated by oneself." The Antimonopoly Act defines tying in this way.

We also describe a precedent known as the *Fujitaya* case (JFTC Hearing Decision, February 28, 1992). A wholesaler, Y (Fujitaya), decided that because the newest game in the *Dragon Quest* video game series (IV) was popular, it would not sell it to retailers unless the retailers agreed to simultaneously purchase three other, less popular games from its inventory. In this case, Y required retailers to purchase the game (*Dragon Quest*) by tying it to the supply of other goods or services (the three unpopular games), which constitutes an act of tying. If this act was considered unjust (i.e., if it impeded fair competition), then it would meet the requirements detailed in item (10) of the General Designation. In this case, the tying product (i.e., *Dragon Quest*) is referred to as the "primary product," and the tied products sold along with it (i.e., the three unpopular games) are referred to as the "secondary products."

In the remainder of this section, we discuss an economic assessment of tying and the application of the law.

4.3.2 An Economic Assessment of Tying

4.3.2.1 Reasons for Tying

Tying may be used for a variety of reasons. In the case of products that are assembled from a larger number of smaller parts, such as cars, the assembly costs are lower and the process is more efficient if a single manufacturer produces a car than if consumers buy and assemble all of the individual parts themselves. Such products are considered as single items in their entirety and pose no problems with regard to the Antimonopoly Act. Additionally, products that are used in conjunction with consumable goods, as in the case of printers and ink cartridges, are often made only to be used with so-called "genuine," or officially licensed, consumables. Even if unlicensed goods can be used with these products, their use is often not covered by the products' guarantees, and if a product is damaged through the use of unlicensed consumable goods, then the consumer may not be entitled to free repairs. In this way, when a consumer purchases a product and is compelled to purchase consumable goods or warranty services from the product's manufacturer, that consumer is said to be "locked in."

It is also common that consumers are unable to receive free repairs if they use unofficial parts to repair or enhance certain products, such as personal computers. Such cases may be thought of as tie-in sales of products with consumable goods and repairs, but this practice is undoubtedly necessary to maintain products' functionality and safety in some cases. In other cases, however, it has been decided that companies operating under these pretenses were actually aiming to increase their profits through price discrimination or the exclusion of their competitors. Thus, the ideal level of regulation remains a point of contention. In the following discussion, we take a detailed look at tying for the purpose of price discrimination and tying for the purpose of excluding competitors from the market.

4.3.2.2 Tying for the Purpose of Price Discrimination

First, we consider tying for the purpose of price discrimination. Price discrimination is the act of trying to increase profits by setting prices in a more complex way, rather than simply assigning a price per unit sold. Examples include telephone fees composed of base fees and separately collected usage fees and discounts for purchasing in bulk,

Table 4.1 An example of tying

	Primary product (yen)	Secondary product (yen)
Consumer A	9,000	2,000
Consumer B	4,000 (9,000)	5,000

as explained in Chap. 1. Tying, in which two different products are sold together in a set, is also a form of price discrimination.

Bearing the *Fujitaya* case in mind, we consider the following examples. Suppose that a consumer intends to pay up to 10,000 JPY for a certain primary product and has no intention of paying anything at all for any secondary products. We also ignore marginal costs in this example. The manufacturer's suggested retail price of 5,000 JPY is written on each product in this scenario, and the retailer believes that it will be difficult to sell the products above that price. Alternatively, we may suppose that the products' prices are fixed by governmental pricing regulations or illegal RPM. If the retailer could set prices freely, it would undoubtedly sell the primary product for 10,000 JPY with no tying. If the retailer is unable to tie the products, then it will have to sell them for 5,000 JPY each, but if it can tie two products together, then it can sell them for 10,000 JPY and increase its profits. If tying is not possible, then a consumer surplus of 5,000 JPY is produced, but if tying is possible, then the producer captures that surplus. In this way, tying transfers the surplus from consumers to producers. This kind of tying is not problematic from a total surplus perspective but is a bigger issue from a consumer surplus perspective.

Conversely, we should also point out that in cases of price discrimination due to tying, the consumer surplus may increase in addition to companies' profits increasing. Suppose that Consumer A intends to pay up to 9,000 JPY for a primary product and up to 2,000 JPY for a secondary product and that Consumer B is willing to pay up to 4,000 JPY for the primary product and up to 5,000 JPY for the secondary product (Table 4.1). We again ignore the issue of marginal costs. If a retailer with a monopoly in the market for the two products does not tie them, then it earns a profit (i.e., producer surplus) of 14,000 JPY by selling the primary product for 9,000 JPY and the secondary product for 5,000 JPY, and there is no consumer surplus (Consumer A only buys the primary product and Consumer B only buys the secondary product). In contrast, if the retailer ties the two products and sells them for 9,000 JPY, then the producer surplus increases to 18,000 JPY and the consumer surplus grows to 2,000 JPY. Thus, both the producer and consumer surpluses are greater with tying. Consumers A and B both buy the tied products, and Consumer A receives a consumer surplus of 2,000 JPY.

We also note that tying does not always increase the producer surplus. If, for example, Consumer B values the primary product at 9,000 JPY instead of 4,000 JPY, then the primary product can be sold for 9,000 JPY and the secondary product for 5,000 JPY if the products are not tied, resulting in a producer surplus of 23,000 JPY. However, if the products are tied and sold for 11,000 JPY, then the producer surplus is only 22,000 JPY.

It is useful to understand the circumstances under which the consumer surplus actually increases with tying. For example, it may increase when the price of a base product is low but prices for usage fees or consumable goods are high, as in the cases of tying cell phones with call time and printers with ink cartridges. If it is not possible to tie these products and consumers can purchase cheap calls or ink separately from the devices at a different retailer, then the company selling the devices is obliged to set the price high enough to make a profit on the devices alone. In this case, consumers who make only a few calls or print only rarely will be unlikely to buy the expensive devices. However, if tying is possible such that consumers buying cell phones from cell phone carriers can only make calls through the same carrier or printers can only be used with ink produced by the same company, then by setting low prices for devices and high prices for consumable goods or usage, the company can sell to consumers with lower usage rates as well. In these cases, the losses made from selling devices cheaply are regained through the usage fees or the prices of consumable goods. This kind of tying makes it easier to sell products with expensive base prices, and, although the result ultimately depends on the change in the surplus for consumers with high usage rates, it is possible for both the consumer and the producer surplus to rise. If the products with high base costs are new and use new technology, tying can also hasten the diffusion of and promote innovation in new technologies.

4.3.2.3 Tying for the Purpose of Gaining Power in a Competitive Secondary Product Market

Next, we consider the use of tying to exclude competing businesses. Suppose that the market for the primary product is monopolistic and the market for the secondary product is competitive. Now, consider the two products in two separate scenarios: one in which the two products are consumed independently (i.e., it is reasonable to only consume one or the other) and one in which the two products are consumed complementarily (i.e., if they are consumed, they are consumed as a set). The case of *Microsoft Japan* (JFTC Hearing Decision, December 14, 1998) is a fitting example. At the time of the case, Excel held a large share of the market for spreadsheet software, and Ichitaro, a product of JustSystems Corporation, held a large share of the market for word processors; thus, computer manufacturers wished to combine Excel and Ichitaro. Microsoft compelled computer manufacturers to tie Excel (the primary product) with Word (the secondary product). As a result, Word's market share rose, and Ichitaro's share fell.

Suppose that a consumer is willing to pay up to 10,000 JPY for a primary product and a secondary product. The marginal costs of the primary product and the secondary product are both 1,000 JPY, which is also the market price of the secondary product. In this case, a company with a monopoly in the primary product market cannot increase its producer surplus through tying. Even if the products are tied, the company can only sell them for 11,000 JPY, and the producer surplus remains 9,000 JPY. This result is because if, for example, the company tries to tie the items and sell them for 12,000 JPY, the consumer surplus of 9,000 JPY (10,000–1,000 JPY) when a consumer buys only the secondary product from a different company is greater than the consumer surplus of 8,000 JPY (20,000–12,000 JPY) when the consumer buys the tied products.

Next, we consider cases involving two complementary products. Here, the secondary product becomes useful when it is purchased in a set with the primary product, as in the case of elevator maintenance parts and services (see the *Toshiba Elevator* case in Sect. 4.3.3) and an operating system (OS) and the software that can be used with it (see the *Microsoft US* case in Sect. 4.3.2.5). We again consider a scenario in which the market for the secondary product is competitive, the consumer is willing to pay 10,000 JPY for each of the two products, and the marginal cost of each product is 1,000 JPY. Unlike in the *Microsoft Japan* case, in this case, if the two products are tied and sold together, it is pointless to purchase only the secondary product from another business. If the price is 20,000 JPY or less, the consumer will buy the products in a set, and the producer surplus is up to 18,000 JPY. Interestingly, however, even in this case, a monopoly producer can obtain the same profits without tying. In short, the consumer is willing to pay 20,000 JPY for the two products combined and can purchase the secondary product for 1,000 JPY; thus, the consumer will purchase the primary product if it costs up to 19,000 JPY. Accordingly, it is possible to obtain a producer surplus of 18,000 JPY even without tying the products.

In this way, if the market for a secondary product is competitive and unprofitable, then a business with a monopoly in the market for the primary product has no incentive to tie the two products. However, if products are tied in these cases, we can imagine that tying may reduce the company's production expenses, and so on.

4.3.2.4 Tying for the Purpose of Gaining Power in a Noncompetitive Secondary Product Market

It may appear that a business with a monopoly in a market has no incentive to tie products regardless of the circumstances. Thus far, we have considered only situations in which the market for the secondary product is competitive. However, it is possible to increase profits through tying if the market for the secondary product is profitable and not entirely competitive (i.e., if the market price exceeds the marginal costs).

First, with regard to the example of the two complementary products at the end of Sect. 4.3.2.3, a business with a monopoly on the primary product can increase its profits through tying. If this business ties the two products and sells them for 20,000 JPY, then consumers buy this tied set of products, and the producer can obtain a producer surplus of 18,000 JPY each from every consumer. The business cannot obtain this producer surplus without tying. For example, suppose that a secondary product with a marginal cost of 1,000 JPY is sold in an oligopolistic market by some businesses for 5,000 JPY. Without tying, the price of the primary product cannot be higher than 15,000 JPY. Furthermore, although the primary product provides the monopolist with a producer surplus of 14,000 JPY from every consumer, the monopolist receives a producer surplus of 4,000 JPY only from consumers who also purchase the secondary product from the monopolist. In this case, the business obtaining the producer surplus through tying changes, but the consumer and total surpluses do not change.

Now, we consider the case of two independently consumed products described at the beginning of Sect. 4.3.2.3. In this case, profits are increased through tying. For example, suppose that a secondary product with a marginal cost of 1,000 JPY is sold in an oligopolistic market for 5,000 JPY. If the monopolist in the primary product market sells the products without tying and sets the price of the primary product to 10,000 JPY and that of the secondary product to 5,000 JPY, then it can obtain profits of 9,000 JPY and 4,000 JPY from the primary and secondary products, respectively. However, whereas the primary product is bought by every consumer, the company only makes a profit on the secondary product from the consumers who purchase it. In contrast, if the products are tied and sold as a set for a little less than 15,000 JPY, the company can obtain a profit of 13,000 JPY from every consumer.

In this way, when the secondary product market is profitable because it is oligopolistic (or for other reasons) rather than being competitive or otherwise unprofitable, a business with a monopoly on the primary product can increase its profits by excluding competing businesses from the market for secondary products through tying.

4.3.2.5 Tying for the Purpose of Maintaining Market Power in Markets for Primary Products

We now discuss the *Microsoft US* case. This case is an example of a company attempting to maintain its monopolistic position in the market for a primary product (i.e., OSs) by using tying to exclude a prominent business from the market for a secondary product (i.e., Internet browsers). At the time of the case, Netscape's Navigator program was a prominent product in the Internet browser market. By tying its own browser, Internet Explorer, to its Windows OS, Microsoft caused Navigator's market share to rapidly decrease, and Netscape could no longer sell its program for a fee. The dominance of Windows OS was partly supported by the wide variety of software that could be used with it (i.e., word processors, spreadsheet software, etc.), and this abundance of software was also supported by the high market share of Windows OS. Netscape's Navigator was said to function as so-called "middleware" between an OS and other software, meaning that the software could be used regardless of the OS. This functionality would allow cheaper OSs to enter the market, and Microsoft could have lost its monopoly over the OS market as a result. It is said that Microsoft therefore tried to exclude Navigator from the market. This exclusion through tying clearly had a negative influence on economic welfare. One can conclude that if it were possible to use a variety of software on different OSs, the OS market would become more competitive. This competition would bring about the emergence of cheap and highly useful software, raising consumer surplus, and production levels of OSs and personal computers would also increase.

From an economics perspective, opinions differ on whether tying for the purpose of price discrimination and tying that excludes competing businesses to gain power in secondary product markets should be regulated depending on whether the Antimonopoly Act's standards are assumed to apply to the consumer surplus or the total surplus. However, tying for the purpose of excluding competing businesses from a secondary product market to maintain power in the primary product market should be regulated.

That being said, an additional point applies in this case. Because the unification of Microsoft's OS and browser improved convenience for consumers, Microsoft argued that it was not tying two different products but rather unifying two products. It is true that OSs have developed by expanding the variety of features that they offer, and, thus, it is difficult to make an economic judgment when considering the situation from a technological standpoint. We investigate the outcome of Microsoft's argument in the following section.

4.3.3 Explanations and Precedents of the Antimonopoly Act: Acts that Constitute Tying

We now discuss the actual application of the Antimonopoly Act with regard to tying. First, we check the requirements for an act to constitute illegal tying. Many acts may be thought of as illegal tying. Consider the following six examples and assess whether they count as illegal tying.

Examples

(1) A consumer's right shoe broke, so she went to a shoe store and tried to buy only a right shoe. She was told that she could only by shoes in pairs that included both left and right shoes.

(2) A consumer went to eat lunch, but the meal came with a salad containing a vegetable that he disliked. He said that he did not need the salad and asked for the meal's price to be reduced to account for the missing salad, but he was denied.

(3) A consumer wanted to buy a car, but it had air conditioning installed. The consumer said that she did not need an air conditioner because she wants to be kind to the environment and asked for the car's price to be reduced accordingly, but she was denied.

(4) When a consumer joined a sports club, he realized that he did not require (and would never use) many of the services attached to his membership. The consumer said that he wanted to exclude these services from his membership and pay lower sign-up and monthly fees as a result, but he was denied.

(5) A consumer wanted to buy a smartphone that was in short supply due to its popularity. When she finally found a shop that had the phone in stock, she was required to sign up for a plan for customers who make many calls despite making calls very rarely.

(6) A small business tried to obtain financing from a bank. Although no risk of fluctuating interest rates was anticipated in the short term, the business was told that it would not receive financing if it did not purchase an interest rate swap (a financial derivative instrument) for the purpose of risk hedging.

Item (10) of the General Designation (described above) explains that for an act to constitute tying it must be "unjust" and must involve "other goods or services," "coercion," and so on. Thus, for an act to constitute tying, it must meet the following requirements: it must involve other (separate) goods or services (in other words, the products must constitute two or more separate products), coercion must be involved, and there must be no justifiable grounds for tying the products. However, the question of whether the third requirement is necessary has been raised, as it could also fall under the requirements for an act to be classified as unjust.

First, with regard to the requirement of other (separate) goods or services (i.e., more than one product), an act does not constitute tying if the primary and secondary products can thought of as a single product when brought together. In the example of the left and right shoes, two shoes are generally considered as one product, as shoes are not usually sold individually. As in the example of the lunch, although such items as rice, meat, fish, salad, and so on can constitute individual products, a lunch can also be thought of as a single product. Determining whether something constitutes a single product or other (separate) goods or services may entail determining whether consumers recognize the items as separate products or whether the market treats them as separate products. Additionally, it is the norm for cars in Japan to come with air conditioning, but in Europe, for example, many cars do not come with air conditioning (coolers) attached, and, thus, the third example may be handled differently in Europe. Furthermore, consider the case of a built-in navigation system rather than the case of air conditioning. Many people buy and install commercially available navigation systems in their cars, whereas many others are content to use the navigational features built into their smartphones. Cars and navigation systems may therefore count as other (separate) goods or services. In many cases, it is difficult to make a determination. In the aforementioned *Microsoft US* case, which embroiled Microsoft in litigation for much of the 1990s, the question of whether Windows OS and Internet Explorer constituted other (separate) goods or services or a single product became a large point of contention. In many similar cases, it is difficult to pass judgment on the tying of features (called "functional tying"). In the *Microsoft US* case, the court determined that the products had been unified and offered new functionality that was not available when they were sold separately, and, thus, Windows and Internet Explorer were a single product. However, the Microsoft case was also litigated in the EU, and the European Commission and the European Court of Justice determined that Windows and the Media Player application were other (separate) goods or services.

Next, we skip over "coercion" and consider the definition of "without justifiable grounds." The *Toshiba Elevator* case (Decision of Osaka High Court, July 30, 1993) played out as follows. Toshiba was an elevator manufacturer that ranked third in the industry. The law required that elevators be inspected several times a year. Toshiba Elevator Service (which we refer to as Toshiba Elevator) monopolistically provided parts for elevators made by Toshiba and had contractual maintenance agreements with around 80% of the users of Toshiba-made elevators. However, the owner of a building equipped with a Toshiba-made elevator, A, entered into a maintenance contract with an independent maintenance company that had lower maintenance fees. One day, one of A's elevators malfunctioned, and it became necessary to replace its computer panel. When A and the independent maintenance company, I, asked Toshiba Elevator to supply them with the necessary parts, Toshiba Elevator responded that it would provide the parts three months later and would not provide the parts at all unless it performed the replacement. As this state of affairs continued, A unwillingly broke its contract with I and signed a maintenance contract with Toshiba Elevator.

In this case, Toshiba Elevator asserted that it needed to perform the replacement itself to guarantee safety, as there was a risk that the elevator could fall if a mistake was made during the replacement. It was determined that the former Ministry of Construction had created a qualification system for elevator maintenance and that the employees at the independent maintenance company also possessed the necessary qualification. Although safety can be a justifiable ground, the court decided that because safety could be guaranteed through a less restrictive alternative (LRA; this term is occasionally used in constitutional law), it did not constitute a justifiable ground in this case. The term "unjustly" is also an important issue in this example, and, thus, we will investigate it further in the following section.

4.3.4 *Explanations and Precedents of the Antimonopoly Act: (Unjustly) Impeding Fair Competition*

We now consider the term "unjustly." Item (10) in the General Designation specifies that tying must be unjust to be illegal. "Unjustly" means "likely to impede fair competition" (refer to the Supreme Court judgment in the *Wakodo* case in Sect. 4.2.4). This requirement can also be called "harm to competition." It is important to understand the circumstances in which tying is unjust.

In the aforementioned *Microsoft Japan* case, Microsoft expanded its share of the word processing market through tying, overtaking Ichitaro for the top position.

In the *Toshiba Elevator* case, the primary product was elevator parts, and the secondary product was their installation (or even an elevator maintenance contract). As a result, the independent maintenance company was excluded, Toshiba Elevator gained a monopoly over the maintenance of Toshiba-made elevators, and customers were obliged to pay expensive maintenance fees.

In the *Fujitaya* case, *Dragon Quest IV* was the primary product, and the three other games in stock were the secondary products. Accordingly, buyers were coerced into purchasing unnecessary software, and consumers were coerced into paying excessive amounts.

In the *Mitsui Sumitomo Bank* case (JFTC Hearing Decision, December 26, 2005), the Mitsui Sumitomo Bank encouraged the companies that it financed to purchase interest rate swaps when performing certain transactions, such as renewing existing loans, implying that if the companies did not purchase these swaps, then their loans would be treated unfavorably. JFTC determined that the bank was abusing its superior bargaining position by making these purchases unavoidable (Art. 2(9)(v)). Furthermore, interest rates were stable at the time, with little need for risk hedging, and the bank was also engaging in inexplicable overhedging of risk. It was said that the bank aimed to obtain revenue from commissions by forcing its customers to purchase interest rate swaps. This case qualified as abuse of a superior bargaining position, but it was also said to constitute tying.

To what extent are the actions in these cases unjust? In the judgment on the *Toshiba Elevator* case, because Toshiba Elevator's acts impeded fair competition, the court decided that "the tying and trading of these kinds of products and services should be said to be unjust, as it causes buyers to lose the freedom to select products and impedes fair and effective competition between businesses." In other words, the issues of infringement on the freedom to choose services and impeding fair and effective competition were both raised in the decision. The decision on the *Fujitaya* case stated:

> [The term] "unjust" refers to the act of preventing the free choice of products by enforcing the purchase of tied products, impeding effective competition [providing high-quality or low-price products to acquire customers] and resulting in acts that are likely to adversely affect the system of competition [...] Dragon Quest IV is a popular product, and [the company] used its market power to tie and sell other games regardless of their price and quality, preventing buyers from freely choosing products and impeding fairness by infringing upon effective competition between wholesalers.

The issues raised include infringement on the free choice of products, infringement of effective competition (i.e., providing high-quality or low-price products to acquire customers), and unjust methods of competition.

In the *Microsoft Japan* case, although the judgment did not say so directly, it seems that Microsoft Japan gained the market power to raise prices and reduce production in the Japanese language word processor market through tying, allowing it to eventually raise prices. Similarly, in the *Toshiba Elevator* case, given that there is a market for the maintenance of Toshiba-made elevators, then surely gaining power in that market enabled Toshiba to increase the price of maintenance. In these examples, companies raised the prices of secondary products and maintained their positions in these products' markets. In the Antimonopoly Act, this action is called the impediment of competition, or the impediment of free competition (according to economic theory, however, a company with a monopoly in the market for a main product may not always be able to increase its profits), and it meets the requirement of "tendency to impede fair competition."

Manufacturers of printers for household use that do not allow the use of unlicensed toners and reclaimed goods, for example, may also meet this criterion. However, these cases constitute so-called price discrimination, and the improvement of economic welfare and the increased consumer surplus can be considered justifiable grounds for this pricing.

In contrast, in the *Fujitaya* case, it is unclear whether Fujitaya obtained market power in the secondary products' market (i.e., the market for unpopular games), as Microsoft Japan did. Similarly, in the *Mitsui Sumitomo Bank* case, it is unclear whether the bank gained power in the market for interest rate swaps. Unpopular games and interest rate swaps are sold by many businesses, securities companies, and so on, meaning that it is difficult to draw such an conclusion. However, even if a company does not gain power in the secondary product market (i.e., impede free competition), tying is regulated. The grounds for this argument may be found in the judgment on the *Fujitaya* case, which states that "preventing buyers from the free choice of products," that is, dispossessing buyers of the freedom to choose products freely, is grounds for criticism. The judgment on the *Toshiba Elevator* case determined that the case could be explained by the impediment of free competition and constituted "the prevention of the free choice of products" and "unjust competitive methods." Opinions as to whether this judgement is appropriate may vary between economists or lawyers, and even lawyers' opinions may differ.

Incidentally, with regard to the *Toshiba Elevator* case, the following issues also arise. Toshiba Elevator excluded independent maintenance companies through its actions, and its customers should have been well aware that its maintenance fees were high. Thus, customers who disliked expensive maintenance fees should have stopped choosing Toshiba-made elevators, as Toshiba was only the third-largest player in the elevator market. One may therefore question the necessity of restricting Toshiba Elevator's acts through the law. Perhaps the people who bought Toshiba-made elevators despite their expensive maintenance fees believed that it was worth paying extra for Toshiba-made elevators. Similarly, in the case of printers for household use, if a company forces consumers to purchase its brand of toner and sets a high price for that toner, one can argue that consumers can simply switch to using printers from a different manufacturer (or stop buying printers). The argument about locking in is a useful reference for a counterargument. However, although judgments and decisions do not explicitly touch on such issues as locking in, in the *Toshiba Elevator* case, for example, opinions affirming that the company's acts constitute an impediment to fair competition (or free competition) from that perspective are prominent in legal theory as well (see Kawahama et al. 2020, p. 242).

4.4 Conclusion

This chapter discussed some key examples of RPM and tying as unfair business practices. Legal scholars' and economists' opinions on these topics are divided with regard to the Antimonopoly Act. We have seen that the two parties' differing opinions mainly stem from differences in the values that they consider most important; whereas economists determine whether actions are right or wrong based on their efficiency, legal scholars emphasize distributors' right to determine prices for themselves in the case of RPM and emphasize consumers' freedom of choice in the case of tying.

Unjustly low sale prices, the abuse of superior bargaining positions, and restrictions on mergers and acquisitions are other examples of areas where opinions vary. Setting an unjustly low sale price means pricing a product below its cost, and abuse of a superior bargaining position occurs when the party with a superior bargaining position unjustly puts the other party at a disadvantage. With regards to these issues, legal scholars tend to approve regulations that favor businesses that suffer from unjustly low prices and weaker businesses in transactions (in fact, political pressure is one reason that JFTC has so many law enforcement cases of unfair selling), although opinions are changing. In contrast, economists tend to emphasize businesses' freedom of conduct and oppose regulation. In the case of mergers, legal scholars focus on the anticompetitive effects on the market, whereas economists focus on the effect on efficiency, and this distinction can lead to differences in opinion between the two in specific cases.

In many other cases, however, legal scholars and economists cooperate to tackle issues related to the Antimonopoly Act. In some cases, jurists have made actual regulations based on economists' findings. For example, in disputes related to the regulation of corporate mergers, the definition of the market, which entails determining to what extent a group of products and the area in which a transaction takes place can be thought of as a relevant market, is often important. Economic expertise is increasingly being used as a method to determine the boundaries of markets. Furthermore, to regulate cartels and bid rigging, a system was introduced to the law in 2005 offering leniency to the company involved in a cartel or similar activity to admit its involvement. Under this system, a company that confesses its involvement in a cartel or bid rigging is exempted from surcharges or criminal prosecution or receives lower penalties. This system can be said to employ the prisoner's dilemma, a concept from game theory (see Sect. 4 of the Appendix). Although the role of economics is increasing in many areas of regulation related to the Antimonopoly Act, however, regulations are being preserved and strengthened in other areas, such as areas that prioritize other values besides efficiency (e.g., RPM and tying). An example is the introduction of new charges for the abuse of superior bargaining positions or RPM in the legal reforms of 2005. Needless to say, the majority of lawyers and regulatory bodies involved in actual law enforcement and conflict resolution have a background in law. Thus, one can conclude that the actors involved in the regulation of the Antimonopoly Act use the strengths of both economics and law.

Column 9. "Public" schools are actually private establishments: private and public law

Column 3 introduced the term "private law" as a counterpoint to the concept of "public law." Although the Japanese words *kō* and *shi* are often treated as equivalent to "public" and "private" in English (for example, a public company under Anglo-American law is a publicly traded company; that being said, many people find it confusing to learn that public schools in the United Kingdom are actually private schools, as the use of "public" in this case may have originally referred to students from all over the United Kingdom attending the school), possible errors can arise when trying to understand Japanese *kōhō* (if literally translated, public law) as equivalent to "public law" by extension. This issue is because the word "public" in English carries a three-dimensional or spatial nuance that one may term "openness," whereas "public law" in Japan can be described as the aggregate of all laws that regulate the relationships between citizens and state or administrative power and those that regulate state or administrative power itself. In other words, it can be described as a vertical relationship. Conversely, "private law" refers to a set of laws governing rights and obligations between citizens, which can be understood as horizontal relationships. Whereas private law typically falls under the Civil Code and Commercial Code in Japan, public law generally deals with the Constitution of Japan, the Administrative Procedures Act, the Social Security Act, the Penal Code, the Code of Civil Procedure, and the Code of Criminal Procedure. For some, it may be easier to think of Japanese public law as governmental law rather than public law.

Incidentally, Column 3 states that the Code of Civil Procedure is included under civil law. If the Code of Civil Procedure is also a public law, one may be curious about the relationship between private law (i.e., civil law) and public law. Essentially, civil law includes both regulations governing rights and obligations between citizens (i.e., private law) and procedural regulations related to the establishment and realization of those rights and obligations. The latter includes the Code of Civil Proceedings, which is considered public law, because it includes procedural regulations regarding the conduct of civil proceedings. Similarly, criminal law includes not only the criminal laws that stipulate crime and punishment but also the Criminal Procedure Code, which provides procedural regulations for confirming whether a crime has been committed and then deciding whether to impose punishment. As mentioned above, both are part of public law.

In practice, however, divisions between the concepts of public and private law are not always rigidly defined, and, thus, it is not always clear whether specific laws or regulations fall under public or private law. For example, consider whether the Antimonopoly Act is a private or public law according to these definitions. Additionally, given that it stipulates penalties under Article 89, with the maximum penalty listed as imprisonment, consider whether the Antimonopoly Act is a civil or criminal law. Regarding the first question, it is commonly assumed in law that economic laws, including the Antimonopoly Act, are a mix of private and public law (social laws, such as labor laws and social security laws, are similar) and do not belong exclusively to either category. Regarding the second question, it is better to consider each provision individually rather than categorizing the entire Antimonopoly Act as civil or criminal law.

Study Questions

1. Briefly explain the possible procompetitive effects of RPM. Then, explain the possible reasons that RPM is illegal in Japan despite its potential benefits.
2. Explain why Japan's regulations on tie-in sales are stricter than those of the United States and other countries.
3. Why do companies conduct tie-in sales? Explain the meaning of the one monopoly profit theorem in relation to tie-ins.
4. Explain the meanings of intra- and inter-brand competition. Then, explain how RPM and tying affect both types of competition.

References

Kanai T, Kawahama N, Sensui F (2020) Dokusen kinshi hō (Antimonopoly law), 6th edn. Koubundou, Tokyo [publication in Japanese]

Kawahama N, Seryo S, Sensui F, Wakui M (2020) Basic keizai hō: dokusen kinshi hō nyūmon (The basic economic law: introduction of antimonopoly law), 5th edn. Yuhikaku, Tokyo [publication in Japanese]

Chapter 5
Determining the Desirable Rules for the Labor Market: Labor Law

Shinya Ouchi and Kazufumi Yugami

Contents

5.1 Introduction 102
5.1.1 What is Labor Law? 102
5.1.2 Labor Law Systems 104
5.1.3 The Need for Rules Governing the Labor Market 105
5.2 Minimum Wage Systems as Measures to Address Poverty 108
5.2.1 The Minimum Wage Act 108
5.2.2 Law and Economics of the Minimum Wage System 109
5.2.3 Why Does the Minimum Wage Exist? 111
5.3 Employment Protection Legislation and the Labor Market 112
5.3.1 Definition of Dismissal 112
5.3.2 Impact of Dismissal Regulations 114
5.3.3 Why Do Dismissal Regulations Exist? 116
5.4 Conclusion 118
References 118

This chapter aims to introduce the views of law and economics on the rationale for the existence and function of rules governing the labor market and to understand the differences between the two views. In the labor market, labor services and the compensation for these services, known as wages, are determined through transactions between firms and workers. Some of these transactions occur on a daily basis within a firm's organization, and others occur when a worker enters or exits the firm's organization, as when starting to work or retiring from work. In both economics and law, measures to intervene in these markets and correct a distribution between the

S. Ouchi
Graduate School of Law, Kobe University, 2-1 Rokkodai-cho, Nada-ku, Kobe 657-8501, Hyogo, Japan
e-mail: souchi@kobe-u.ac.jp

K. Yugami (✉)
Graduate School of Economics, Kobe University, 2-1 Rokkodai-cho, Nada-ku, Kobe 657- 8501, Hyogo, Japan
e-mail: yugami@econ.kobe-u.ac.jp

T. Yanagawa et al. (eds.), *Econo-Legal Studies*,
https://doi.org/10.1007/978-981-16-5145-8_5

parties to a transaction are sometimes justified, but the two disciplines' perspectives differ greatly. In law, the objective is to achieve justice between the parties, focusing on asymmetries in the bargaining power of the parties to each transaction. Conversely, economists argue that the market's functioning should be corrected to realize desirable transactions from the perspective of overall labor market efficiency. In this chapter, we discuss the most important topics related to the labor market, namely, wages and job security, and we study the approaches taken by law and economics.

5.1 Introduction

5.1.1 What is Labor Law?

A company can procure the necessary labor to run its business in one of two main ways. It can include labor providers in the organization and use their labor under a system of command, or it can procure labor providers from the market as needed. Workers who provide labor by the former and latter methods are usually called regular and non-regular employees, respectively. In addition, a non-regular employee may have an employment contractor another type of contract, such as an outsourcing contract or a business contracting contract. Furthermore, a company can utilize workers from other companies; this arrangement is called indirect employment because the company using a worker does not directly enter into a contract with that worker, and it is distinct from other types of direct employment. Examples of indirect employment include dispatching and outsourcing.

Labor law defines a "worker" as a person who provides labor services to a company in the form of an employment contract and is subject to legal protection. In terms of the above classification, regular and non-regular employees are workers. In the indirect employment framework, an employee who has an employment contract with a sending company, such as a staffing agency, is also a worker.

Some people who provide labor to a company are not defined as workers and are not protected by the law. This situation raises the question of why only workers are protected.

The Japanese Civil Code states that employment contracts are contracts in which "one of the parties promises to the other party that he/she will engage in work and the other party promises to pay remuneration for the same" (Art. 623). Thus, the key point of an employment contract is engaging in work, which implies that the employer provides instructions regarding the content of the work in which the employee engages. Compensation (i.e., wages) is then paid when a worker engages in the work as instructed by the employer.

Conversely, the Civil Code defines a contract for work as "a contract in which one of the parties promises to complete work and the other party promises to pay remuneration for the outcome of the work" (Art. 632). The contractor's (worker's) obligation is to complete the work, and remuneration is paid for the result of the work. The point of this kind of contract is that as long as the work is completed properly, the contractor has fulfilled his or her obligation.

The difference between employment contracts and contracts for work corresponds to the difference in the way of working under each type of contract. In other words, the difference lies in whether the worker receives specific instructions from the other party regarding when, where, what, and how to work or only receives specific instructions as to what work to do, with the worker determining how the work is done. The former situation describes an employment contract, which is a subordinate way of working in that the worker works under orders; in contrast, contractors have an independent way of working in that they work at their own discretion.

The need for protection arises from the subordination of those who work under an employment contract. In contrast, those with a contract for work do not need protection owing to their independence (they work at their own discretion and responsibility). Thus, people who work under employment contracts are considered workers and are covered by labor law (see Art. 9 of the Labor Standards Law and Art. 2(1) of the Labor Contract Act, among others).

Employment contracts are also governed by the Civil Code, but the Civil Code does not include any provisions protecting workers. For example Article 627, paragraph 1 of the Civil Code states: "If the parties have not stipulated the term of employment, each party may request termination at any time. In this case, the employment shall be terminated on the expiration of two weeks from the date of the request for termination."

In other words, in the case of indefinite employment, either party (i.e., not only the worker but also the employer) can terminate employment at any time with two weeks' notice; this provision guarantees not only the worker's freedom to resign but also the employer's freedom to dismiss. This provision is based on the liberal concept that if either party does not wish to continue the contract, the contract should not be enforced against that party's will. In addition, the Civil Code treats both parties as equals, as evidenced by the fact that it equates workers and employers. As shown here, the contract theory of the Civil Code (more precisely, classical contract theory) is built on the idea that parties are free to enter into contracts on equal footing. Even if the employment contractincludes the subordination of command and order, no particular problem arises as long as the worker also agrees to it and enters into the contract from a free and equal standpoint.

However, in practice, workers do not enter into contracts on free and equal footing. Thus, the contents of a contract may be unfairly favorable to the employer and, in fact, social problems, such as poor working conditions and poverty among workers, have arisen. Labor law was created for this reason. It focuses on the inequality between workers and employers, which is called the subordination of workers (denying or restricting the principle of freedom of contract in the Civil Code and broadly regulating contracts by law). Contracts protected by labor law are called labor contracts, which are distinct from employment contracts in the Civil Code.

Labor law is a set of legal rules designed to protect workers in weak positions (i.e., subordinate workers) by focusing on the fact that labor contracts are concluded by unequal parties.

5.1.2 Labor Law Systems

Labor law is divided into two main areas. One of these areas is called individual labor relations law. This type of law is characterized by the fact that it directly intervenes to impose certain obligations on employers to protect subordinate workers. Some of these laws, such as the Labor Standards Act, provide strong regulations, including imposing penal sanctions on employers who violate the law, supervising the law's implementation by administrative authorities, and granting workers rights that can be enforced by courts. Other laws, such as the Labor Contract Act, provide for neither penal sanctions nor administrative supervision. In addition, other types of legal provisions attempt to realize the content of the law through administrative guidance in the form of imposing a duty of effort on employers.

Individual labor relations laws include not only the abovementioned Labor Standards Act and Labor Contract Act but also the Minimum Wage Act; the Industrial Safety and Health Act; the Industrial Accident Compensation Insurance Act; the Act on Ensuring Wage Payment; the Act on Ensuring Equal Opportunities for and Treatment of Men and Women in Employment; the Act on Childcare Leave, Caregiver Leave, and Other Measures for the Welfare of Workers Caring for Children or Other Family Members; the Act on the Succession to Labor Contracts upon Firm Split; and the Whistleblower Protection Act. Furthermore, laws that aim to protect some specified categories of workers include the Act on Improvement of Personnel Management and Conversion of Employment Status for Part-Time Workers and Fixed-Term Workers, the Act for Securing the Proper Operation of Worker Dispatching Undertakings and Improved Working Conditions for Dispatched Workers, and the Act on Stabilization of Employment of Elderly Persons.

Another area of labor law is collective labor relations law. This area of law supports subordinate workers in improving their economic status and working conditions by forming labor unions and bargaining collectively with employers and employers' organizations. The Labor Union Act and the Labor Relations Adjustment Act are the main laws in this area. In particular, in Japan, the Constitution (Art. 28) guarantees workers' rights to organize, bargain collectively, and take collective action, and the Labor Union Act provides a special system of unfair labor practice remedies to certain anti-union acts by employers (Arts. 7, 27, etc.).

This explanation describes the statutory law, but fully understanding the legal rules concerning individual and collective labor relations also requires an understanding of case law. For example, until a 2003 amendment to the Labor Standards Act codified the rules restricting dismissal, the content of these rules was determined exclusively by case law (this principle is called the doctrine of the abusive exercise of the right of dismissal and now is a codified rule in Art. 16 of the Labor Contract Act). The legal principle restricting suspension after the repeated renewal of a fixed-term labor contract was also governed by case law until a 2012 amendment to the Labor Contract Act, and the legal principle that enables employers to unilaterally make disadvantageous revisions to work rules if they are reasonable was also covered by case law until the Labor Contract Act was enacted in 2007. The law that allows employers to lock out against trade union strikes was made by a judge, is not stipulated in either the Constitution or the Trade Union Act, and remains subject to case law. As in other fields of law, many of the legal rules in labor law are formed by case law.

In a broader sense, labor law includes not only individual and collective labor relation law but also labor market law and national or local public service law.

Labor market law deals with the legal system for the matching supply and demand for labor in the labor market; representative laws include the Employment Security Act, the Employment Insurance Act, and the Act on Comprehensive Promotion of Labor Measures, and Stabilization of Employment of Employees, and Enrichment of Their Working Lives. In addition, legislation related to the supply side of the labor force includes the Human Resources Development Promotion Act. Furthermore, legislation addresses dispatched, part-time, elderly, and disabled workers.

In terms of legislation on public services, because public servants do not work under a contractual relationship but rather have a special service relationship under public law, the Labor Contract Act does not apply to public employees (Art. 21(1)). Public servants are also subject to a special provision preventing them from taking direct action (i.e., strikes). However, many academics argue that this provision is unconstitutional because the Constitution guarantees the right to collective action regardless of worker type.

5.1.3 The Need for Rules Governing the Labor Market

As described above, labor law is a set of legal rules designed to protect subordinate workers. From an economics perspective, however, this law can be interpreted as an attempt to control the labor market, in which labor services are exchanged. As in other markets, a transaction between a firm and a worker in the labor services market determines the price (i.e., wage) and quantity (i.e., amount of employment and working hours) of labor. However, unlike ordinary consumer and capital goods, such as machinery, labor services are inseparable from the person who sells them.

For example, workers are concerned not only with wages but also with their working environments. Furthermore, firms hiring workers do not have ownership rights to their labor services, and, thus, the quantity and quality of labor services depends on a worker's effort. However, it is generally financially or technically difficult for firms to directly monitor or measure workers' efforts, meaning that some mechanism must be set up to ensure that workers exercise their full potential. In addition, each worker has different abilities and skills, and the value of these skills can be enhanced by education and training within a firm. These factors all encourage the distribution of information about the quality of labor services and foster stable business relationships in transactions between workers and firms. In fact, these factors have led to firm practices for workers concerning promotions, raises, relocations or transfers, retirements, and dismissals. Thus, the functions of allocating work and pricing labor services exist both within a firm and in the labor market outside the firm. We call this function within a firm the "internal labor market," and we distinguish it from the "external labor market," in which people move between firms or enter and exit the labor market. Although labor legislation takes a limited view of labor market law, as described above, the field of economics views labor law as a whole as rules governing the labor market (in the case of labor market law, the labor market corresponds only to the external labor market in economics).

This discrepancy in the basic approaches of law and economics regarding this issue stems from these fields' different interpretations of whether respecting the principle of freedom of contract and leaving market transactions to the involved parties creates desirable outcomes for both parties. We consider the basic principles and consequences of the behavior of economic agents in the market from an economics perspective.

Workers obtain satisfaction not only from buying and consuming various goods using the income that they earn from their work but also from enjoying leisure time for hobbies and family gatherings (in economics, satisfaction is called "utility"). As a worker spends more time working, the worker's income (and consumption realized by that income) and utility increase. At the same time, however, the worker must sacrifice leisure time to work more, and, thus, there is a trade-off between income and leisure time. Workers therefore choose the number of hours to work to maximize their utility given the wages offered by the firms in the labor market. In this case, the wage determined in the market represents the monetary value that a worker loses by giving up leisure time. For example, if the hourly wage at a part-time job is 1,000 JPY, then enjoying one hour of leisure time is equivalent to giving up 1,000 JPY of income. Thus, if the market wage is even slightly higher than the monetary value of enjoying leisure time at the expense of consumption (e.g., 800 JPY/h), workers will choose to supply labor by cutting back on their leisure time. Firms, in contrast, demand labor services as a necessary production factor to make products or provide services. When a firm hires a new worker, it receives monetary value in terms of increased production and sales, but it also incurs the cost of paying the worker the market wage. In the end, a profit-maximizing firm chooses its demand for labor services such that the monetary value of a newly hired worker, that is, the monetary value of the worker's productivity, is equal to the market wage.

Now, suppose that neither workers nor firms have any influence on the wage, the price at which labor services are traded, but rather treat it as given and can enter or exit the labor market at will (we call this market a perfectly competitive market). In this case, the number of workers whose wages exceed the value of their leisure time is greater when the market wage is higher, and, thus, the overall labor supply in the market is greater. From a firm's perspective, the wage must equal the monetary value of the productivity of a worker being hired at that wage. If the market wage increases, the overall demand for labor in the market decreases because workers with low productivity cannot be hired at that wage. If the market wage equals both the value of the leisure time and the productivity of the additional workers, then all of the workers who supply labor services are employed by the firms that demand them. Thus, the equilibrium wage is determined by the equilibrium employment, at which the supply and demand of labor in the market are equal. In this case, for the many workers who are employed by firms at a higher market wage but who value their leisure time below the equilibrium wage, the difference between their wage and the monetary value of their leisure time is their profit. Similarly, for the many firms that employ workers whose productivity has a monetary value above the equilibrium wage, the difference between the productivity of these workers and the wage is these firms' profit. In other words, the equilibrium of a perfectly competitive labor market efficiently allocates labor resources to maximize the profits of the market participants.

Thus, from an economics perspective, the free trade of labor services in the labor market is desirable because it maximizes the respective interests of the economic agents, namely, firms and workers.

Conversely, in labor law, as mentioned above, the parties to a labor relationship are not considered to be on equal footing, and the principle of freedom of contract is denied. Thus, from a legal perspective, the market mechanism is not expected to function in the labor market; instead, government regulations (i.e., labor laws) are needed to regulate it. Then, the question arises of how to evaluate such regulations from an economics perspective.

As mentioned above, perfectly competitive markets have desirable characteristics in that they achieve an efficient allocation of resources. However, for this allocation to be realized, labor market participants must have instantaneous and cost-free access to complete information on wages and labor services, and the choices of each market participant cannot affect market wages. These assumptions are all extreme and often do not hold in real labor markets. We can consider a few examples.

In the first case, one (or both) of the participants in the transaction has control over wages. For example, it is known that when a firm has a monopoly position as a buyer of labor services in a regional labor market, it sets wages below the equilibrium wage in a perfectly competitive market to control labor costs and, thus, the employment level is also less than the equilibrium employment (Stigler 1946). Even in a market with a large number of firms, if information about job openings, job seekers, and wages is not instantaneous and the market actors must spend time and incur other costs to search for one another, firms' employment will depend on their own wage decisions, and wages and employment will still be lower than in a perfectly competitive market.

The latter source of wage dominance is due to incomplete information about job offers, job seekers, and wages, which is a problem with labor markets in general. For example, when a worker seeks a job, the employer and the job seeker have asymmetric information about the work environment. In this context, the standards for working hours and workplace safety set by the Labor Standards Act and the Industrial Safety and Health Act can help to improve efficiency by improving the matching of jobs and workers. Asymmetric information also provides a rationale for policies compensating workers for risks that reduce their earnings capacity or cause them to lose earnings opportunities, such as industrial accidents or unemployment. In general, insurance providers do not have a full understanding of their subscribers' risks. In this case, an insurance market is not viable because most of the individuals who would purchase this kind of insurance face a high risk of work-related accidents or job loss (i.e., adverse selection) or would repeatedly leave their jobs to collect insurance (i.e., moral hazard) (see Chap. 6). Labor laws that require most establishments that employ a wide range of workers (with some exceptions) to purchase insurance through the Industrial Accident Compensation Insurance Act and the Employment Insurance Act play a role in correcting these insurance market failures.

In practice, the labor market is more or less imperfect, and it cannot achieve the efficient allocation of resources that perfect competition achieves owing to market failures. We can consider that labor laws are established because most real-world labor markets are imperfect and, thus, these laws serve to correct these markets. However, the necessary interventions may differ depending on whether the market being regulated is competitive or imperfect and the cause of the imperfection. Moreover, laws and regulations targeting individual labor markets may distort the behavior of participants in other labor markets. In the following sections, we discuss the Minimum Wage Act and dismissal regulations as representative regulations that address wages and employment, respectively, among the laws that regulate economic agents' behavior in the labor market, and we introduce the perspectives of law and economics.

5.2 Minimum Wage Systems as Measures to Address Poverty

5.2.1 The Minimum Wage Act

The Minimum Wage Act was established in 1959 as an independent law. Before then, the minimum wage was governed by Article 28 and subsequent articles of the Labor Standards Act. The Minimum Wage Act was substantially amended in 1968 and again in 2007 to address the issue of the working poor, which has attracted considerable public attention.

The contents of the Minimum Wage Act are as follows. First, employers must pay wages that are no lower than the minimum wage (Art. 4(1)). If an employer concludes a labor contract that stipulates a wage below the minimum wage, then that part of the labor contract is invalid, and the minimum wage is directly applied (Art. 4(2)). Thus, the minimum wage provisions are mandatory and cannot be lowered by the agreement of the parties to a contract. Furthermore, employers who pay wages below the minimum wage are subject to penal sanctions in the form of fines (Arts. 4(1), and 40). The 2007 amendment raised the maximum amount of this fine from 20,000 to 500,000 JPY.

Japan has two types of minimum wages: regional minimum wages and specific minimum wages. The latter were known as industry-specific minimum wages before the 2007 amendment. Japan also had a system of regional minimum wages based on collective agreements before the 2007 amendment, but this system was abolished by that amendment.

A minimum wage must be determined for each region of Japan (Art. 9(1)), and these minimum wages have been determined by each prefecture. Each regional minimum wage "shall be determined by taking into consideration the cost of living and wages of workers in the region and the ability of ordinary businesses to pay wages" (Art. 9(2)). Furthermore, the 2007 amendment added the provision that "in consideration of the living expenses of workers set forth in the preceding paragraph, the consistency between regional minimum wages and public assistance policies shall be considered to ensure that workers can lead a healthy and cultured minimum life" (Art. 9(3)). This provision was added to address the issue that people earning the minimum wage received less income than those receiving public assistance in some prefectures.

A reduction of the minimum wage may be granted to certain workers, including those with extremely low working capacities owing to mental or physical disabilities, those in probationary periods, those receiving accredited vocational training under the Human Resources Development Promotion Act, those with particularly few prescribed working hours, those engaged in light work, and those engaged in intermittent work, as long as they receive permission from the head of the Prefectural Labor Bureau (Art. 7 and Minimum Wage Act Enforcement Regulations, Art. 3).

5.2.2 *Law and Economics of the Minimum Wage System*

In Article 1, the current Minimum Wage Act stipulates, "The purpose of this Law is to improve working conditions for low-wage workers by guaranteeing them a minimum wage, thereby contributing to the stabilization of their livelihoods, improving the quality of the labor force, ensuring fair competition in business, and contributing to the sound development of the national economy." It also stipulates that the minimum wage is determined by the government. The minimum wage's purposes and the criteria for determining the minimum wage are to stabilize workers' lives, improve the quality of the labor force, ensure fair competition in business, and promote the sound development of the national economy. Here, we focus particularly on the first and third objectives.

Workers' livelihood is the main legislative objective. As mentioned above, the 2007 amendment to the Minimum Wage Act requires accounting for consistency with public assistance in determining regional minimum wages, and the perspective that a minimum wage should guarantee a healthy and culturally appropriate minimum standard of living is strongly reflected in the law. This understanding is based on the perspective that wages should not just be compensation for labor (Art. 11 of the Labor Standards Act) agreed upon by the parties to the labor relationship through a free contract but rather should also be used to stabilize workers' lives.

In contrast, economics considers wages to represent the monetary value of labor services for both workers and firms; as we discussed in Sect. 5.1.3, the market wage offered to workers equals the monetary value of the leisure time that the workers forgo to spend more time working. At the same time, this market wage also equals the monetary value of the firm's productivity increase when its input of labor services increases by one worker. Under these circumstances, it is worth considering what may happen if the hourly minimum wage rate is raised, taking into account the cost of living. Firms will reduce their demand for workers whose value is below the new minimum wage, that is, workers whose productivity is lower, or they will replace lower-productivity workers with more productive workers or machinery and equipment. Conversely, workers for whom the new minimum wage exceeds the monetary value of their leisure time will choose to supply labor services and remain in the labor market, thereby resulting in unemployment. In addition, if the increase in the minimum wage renders firms that provide many low-productivity jobs unviable, employment opportunities will decrease further as these firms go out of business. Ultimately, as long as the wages of low-income earners reflect their productivity, raising the minimum wage to combat poverty will help to stabilize the lives of workers who remain employed after the minimum wage is increased. However, some low-income earners will lose their income opportunities and become unemployed, which may unintentionally increase income inequality.

In addition to these side effects on the labor market, the minimum wage system as an anti-poverty measure has long been criticized because low-income workers who receive the minimum wage do not necessarily belong to poor households. In fact, according to a Japanese study that examined the attributes of workers who earn close to the minimum wage, the typical minimum-wage worker is a woman working for a small business or a young part-time worker (Tachibanaki and Urakawa 2006). The majority of these workers are non-household heads and have annual household incomes of 5 million JPY or more (Kawaguchi and Mori 2009). In other words, the minimum wage supports households in the upper half of the income distribution rather than low-income households that truly need relief. Considering the aforementioned side effects on employment, the effectiveness of the minimum wage as an anti-poverty measure is questionable.

This discussion assumes that wages reflect workers' productivity. However, if workers' wages are less than the monetary value of their productivity owing to market failure, the introduction of a minimum wage may be justified to improve the efficiency of resource allocation. This rationale is also in line with the third objective of the Minimum Wage Act, that is, to ensure fair competition in business.

For example, as mentioned earlier, if a region has only a few firms that buy labor services (monopsony) or if the labor market contains frictions and obtaining information about job openings, job seekers, and wages incurs time and other costs, then the number of the firm's employees, new hires, and worker turnover all depend on the firm's wage decision. The firm pays a wage that equals the monetary value of a worker's leisure time but is less than the monetary value of a worker's productivity, resulting in underemployment relative to a competitive labor market. In this case, if the government can successfully set the minimum wage above the current wage but below workers' productivity, firms will be able to increase their demand for labor, leading to higher wages and more employment. Thus, in an imperfect labor market, a minimum wage may be justified depending on the actual labor market conditions of low-income workers. According to an empirical analysis, most jobs with wages close to the minimum wage are offered by small and medium-sized firms that employ part-time workers (Tachibanaki and Urakawa 2006), and it is difficult to argue that these firms hold monopsonies in their regions. In addition, many jobs that pay close to the minimum wage are also unskilled jobs and, given that wages remain low and stable in a competitive market, it is difficult to make the assumption that these workers will spend money to search for wage information (Ohashi 2009). Furthermore, many empirical studies in Japan find that an increase in the minimum wage reduces the employment of workers earning close to the minimum wage, especially young people and married middle-aged women (Kambayashi et al. 2013; Kawaguchi and Mori 2009). From an economics perspective, it is difficult to argue that minimum wage systems are justified from the perspective of correcting labor market imperfections and improving the efficiency of resource allocation.

5.2.3 Why Does the Minimum Wage Exist?

As mentioned above, the minimum wage system, which guarantees a minimum wage level, has two objectives: to improve efficiency by correcting market failures caused by monopsony and imperfect information and to achieve fairness by guaranteeing a certain wage for low-income groups and reducing income inequality. In other words, this policy intervention is based on the premise that without a minimum wage, inefficiency will occur because wages will be less than workers' contributions and, furthermore, workers will be unable to sustain a reasonable livelihood owing to low wages. In recent years, Japan's minimum wage system has drawn attention to the existence of the working poor, who hold jobs but earn less than the welfare level. After the law's 2007 amendment, more emphasis has been placed on the minimum wage's role in ensuring fairness. The 2007 amendment raised the minimum wage substantially, especially in areas where the minimum wage was less than the level of public assistance.

However, even with the assumption of an incomplete labor market, which justifies a minimum wage from the perspective of correcting market failures, a high minimum wage may reduce employment opportunities for low-wage workers and further widen the income disparity, which goes against the policy goal of achieving fairness. Recent studies examining the impact of the increased minimum wage due to the 2007 amendment report that it negatively impacted teenage employment (Kawaguchi and Mori 2013), suggesting that the appropriate minimum wage level should be determined carefully. Furthermore, the reality is that many workers who earn close to the minimum wage are auxiliary household workers, such as young people and housewives who work part-time. The minimum wage policy therefore does not necessarily target the poor. Thus, because the minimum wage system can affect the target population's employment to some extent and has diverse policy targets, it is preferable to directly support low-income workers who truly need relief through income redistribution and social security policies targeting low-income groups rather than intervening in the labor market.

5.3 Employment Protection Legislation and the Labor Market

5.3.1 Definition of Dismissal

In economics, the term "dismissal" may broadly include the termination of a fixed-term labor contract by agreement or resignation. However, the legal concept of dismissal is limited to the unillateral resolution of a labor contract by an employer.

Under the Civil Code, dismissal is freely permitted in the case of an employment contract with no fixed term as long as two weeks' notice is given (Art. 627(1)). In the case of a fixed-term contract, dismissal during the fixed term is not allowed in principle, but a contract can be terminated immediately if so-called "unavoidable reasons" arise (Art. 628). This provision also applies to a resignation, that is, a unilateral termination by a worker.

The Labor Standards Act established provisions on dismissal to modify the provisions of the Civil Code. The main provision is setting the notice period to 30 days and obliging the employer to pay an alternative notice allowance if the notice period is shortened (Art. 20). In addition, this act established provisions prohibiting the dismissal of workers on leave for medical treatment owing to industrial accidents and workers on leave before and after childbirth (Art. 19). Workers who are hired on a daily basis are exempted from the application of Article 20 (Art. 21). However, some provisions restrict or prohibit dismissals in some specific cases, such as sex discrimination.

However, as mentioned above, case law based on the general clause of the Civil Code (Art. 1(3)) that "abuse of rights is not permitted" established the legal principle that if a dismissal lacks an objectively reasonable explanation and is not deemed appropriate from a socially accepted viewpoint, then this dismissal shall be invalidated as an abuse of the right. This legal principle has been incorporated into law since 2003 (currently Art. 16 of the Labor Contract Act).

In this way, although Civil Code considers the dismissal of regular permanent employees to be unrestricted, the doctrine of abuse of the right to dismiss restricts employers' ability to exercise this right, and this restriction, combined with the establishment of long-term employment practices, is applied very strictly. Thus, in practice, the rule that dismissal is not possible without just cause has been diffused and is now established.

Typically, the following reasons are interpreted as justifiable grounds for dismissal according to judicial and academic opinions: the worker's ability or eligibility is significantly lacking, the worker has committed a serious breach of discipline, it is necessary to reduce the workforce for managerial reasons, or the dismissal is based on a union shop agreement (i.e., the worker is no longer a member of the union).

However, even though all four situations can be considered legitimate reasons for dismissal in the abstract, courts have not judged dismissals to be effective if only these reasons are present. For example, in cases in which a regular employee is dismissed owing to a lack of ability, courts have argued that the company should try to maintain employment as much as possible. Dismissals for disciplinary reasons may be treated as disciplinary or ordinary dismissals. In the latter case, many companies agree to provide severance pay, whereas they do not provide severance pay in the former case. Thus, the former case is more disadvantageous for workers than the latter case is. In any case, the response must be proportional to the degree of the disciplinary violation, and if this balance is not achieved, the dismissal is considered an abuse of rights.

In the case of dismissals based on union shop agreements, case law states that dismissing an employee who leaves or is expelled from a union and then joins or forms a new one is unlawful. As a result, it is rare for dismissals to be deemed valid for this reason.

In addition, dismissals for managerial reasons are called adjustment dismissals or dismissals for the purpose of restructuring, and case law clarifies that the validity of these dismissals can be judged according to the four factors of adjustment dismissals. These factors are the extent to which the workforce needs to be reduced, whether the company has made every effort to avoid dismissals, whether the criteria for selecting workers to be dismissed are reasonable, and whether the company has fully consulted with the workers or their labor union. Under these rules, it is not easy for companies to carry out valid layoffs (in particular, efforts to avoid dismissals place a heavy burden on companies), and the business community believes that it is very difficult to carry out adjustment dismissals. For this reason, companies try to avoid dismissals as much as possible and instead seek consensual terminations (i.e., amicable retirements), such as, for example, increasing severance pay and soliciting voluntary retirements (as mentioned above, consensual terminations are not dismissals, meaning that the four factors of adjustment dismissals do not apply).

Additionally, the Labor Contract Act, in response to the aforementioned Article 628 of the Civil Code, provides that an employer may not dismiss an employee in the middle of a fixed-term labor contract except for unavoidable reasons. Because mid-term dismissals are not otherwise permitted, it is understood that the requirements for mid-term dismissals are stricter than those for dismissals of labor contracts without fixed terms.

In addition, the doctrine of abuse of the right to dismiss (Art. 16 of the Labor Contract Act) applies not only to ordinary dismissals but also to suspensions of employment under a fixed-term labor contract by analogy (currently Art. 19 of the Labor Contract Act).

5.3.2 Impact of Dismissal Regulations

From an economics perspective, the rules regulating the unilateral termination of labor contracts by employers impose considerable employment adjustment costs on firms. Firms must bear not only the time costs associated with the notice period for dismissal but also the cost of procedures and lawyers if litigation occurs. Although Japanese law does not mandate severance pay in the event of a dismissal, large firms pay premium retirement allowances for voluntary retirements, which are carried out prior to dismissals for the purpose of reorganization. These allowances can be regarded as de facto severance payments. Thus, we can consider the impact of these dismissal regulations on the labor market based on some assumptions. Although the actual situation under Japanese law is somewhat different, we define a dismissal regulation as the imposition of a mandatory severance payment when a company dismisses a worker. We then examine the effects of these regulations on the labor market by changing the assumptions in turn (Boeri and van Ours 2008).

The first prediction is that if a dismissal regulation forces an income transfer from firms to workers in the form of severance pay, then introducing variable wage contracts can eliminate the effects of this regulation on employment and firm profits (Lazear 1990). Suppose that a firm offers a wage contract that pays a constant wage throughout the employment period in the absence of the dismissal regulation and that under the dismissal regulation, the firm is obliged to pay a certain amount of severance pay when dismissing a worker in the future. In this case, the firm offers the worker a wage contract in which the wage in the earlier part of the contract period (e.g., when the worker is young) is reduced by an equivalent amount to the severance payment under the dismissal regulation, and any worker who is not dismissed in the later part of the contract period (e.g., when the worker is middle-aged or older) is paid a higher wage, including an equivalent amount to the severance payment. In this way, the discounted present value of the amount that the firm pays to a worker remains unchanged regardless of the dismissal regulation, and, thus, labor supply and demand do not change in any way. Of course, workers who are dismissed late in the contract period receive an equivalent amount to the pay deducted in the earlier part of the contract period as severance pay.

However, the neutrality of such a dismissal regulation holds only if all of the following conditions are met. First, workers must be risk-neutral and must not care about the risk of wage changes over time (in this case, between the first and second periods of the contract), and their utility must depend only on the expected value of wages. Second, wages must not exhibit downward rigidity, and it must be possible to reduce wages in the first half of the contract by an equivalent amount to the severance pay. Third, all of the costs of the dismissal regulation borne by firms must take the form of transfers from firms to workers. However, these conditions are often not met, and, thus, the neutrality of a dismissal regulation cannot be established.

The first condition does not hold for risk-averse workers. Even if a worker's lifetime wage is constant, a wage contract that fluctuates throughout the employment period lowers the worker's utility, and, thus, the dismissal regulation is not neutral.

Furthermore, it is impossible for firms to offer wage contracts that include severance pay if wages are downwardly rigid. In this case, it is rational for a profit-maximizing firm to keep the amount of employment constant regardless of economic conditions to avoid paying severance for dismissals. However, because firms cannot maximize their profits in response to business cycle fluctuations, their profits are lower than they would be in the absence of dismissal regulations, and labor market inefficiencies arise. The third condition has more important implications when considering the real labor market. Japanese law requires a just cause (i.e., objective rationality and social acceptability) for dismissal. Moreover, the law does not allow companies to terminate employment relationships through monetary compensation if the dismissal is deemed illegal or invalid owing to a lack of rationality or fairness. In other words, the principle is for a dismissed worker to return to his or her original position. In this case, the dismissal cost borne by the firm is regarded as a tax paid to a third party in the form of litigation costs rather than a transfer to the worker (Boeri and van Ours 2008). Because firms can escape this burden by not reducing their employment, they are discouraged not only from firing workers but also from hiring and recruiting new workers owing to the possibility of future dismissal costs. As a result, firms create and lose fewer jobs when dismissal regulations are stricter, and fewer workers transition between unemployment and employment. Thus, once a worker is unemployed, he or she may not become employed for a long time. It follows that although insider workers who are already employed by firms enjoy future job protection owing to the dismissal regulation, firms' profits decline, and unemployed workers experience long-term unemployment. These consequences create income distribution issues among labor market participants.

Furthermore, the dismissal regulations are not applied uniformly to all workers, which also creates distributional problems. As mentioned earlier, the doctrine of abuse of the right to dismiss for permanent employees with indefinite labor contracts also applies to the termination of employment at the end of a fixed-term labor contract under certain requirements (Art. 19 of the Labor Contract Law). However, the protections for dismissals of fixed-term contract workers are inferior to those for dismissals of permanent contract workers. Thus, when employers make employment adjustments, they are allowed to distinguish fixed-term workers from permanent employees and treat them as a workforce in need of redundancy. In fact, during recessions, firms can adjust employment by declining to re-sign fixed-term contracts before laying off permanent workers. After the financial crisis of 2008, the suspension of temporary workers' employment became a social problem. This asymmetry in employment protections leads to a dual structure in the labor market, as the employment of workers with high dismissal costs (i.e., permanent workers) declines mainly owing to natural attrition, whereas the employment of workers with low employment adjustment costs and unstable employment (i.e., fixed-term contract workers) expands (Boeri and Garibaldi 2007; Kahn 2010).

5.3.3 Why Do Dismissal Regulations Exist?

Thus far, we have discussed the effects of dismissal regulations related to permanent employment on the overall labor market mainly from a distributional perspective. However, we have not discussed the rationale and justification for the dismissal regulations related to permanent employment. We now introduce the views of law and economics on this rationale.

In economics, the rationality of long-term employment contracts is based on the incompleteness of labor contracts. In a labor contract, the parties to the contract, that is, the employer and the worker, transact labor services by stipulating various matters, such as the duties in which the worker will engage and the remuneration that the employer will pay, in the contract. In this case, to guarantee that the contractual obligations are carried out, it is necessary to identify all possible contingencies before concluding the contract in a manner that is clear to a third-party court and to specify the responses to these contingencies. However, the future is generally uncertain, and it is either impossible or very costly to specify all possible contingencies in a contract. In addition, it is often difficult to specify the duties required of workers and the necessary quality of those duties in advance. Thus, the details of the contractual matters cannot be specified in a labor contract, rendering it incomplete.

In an incomplete labor contract, the parties to the contract have incentives to act opportunistically by withholding or changing their contractual obligations. In particular, labor services are inseparable from the workers providing them. This opportunism becomes a serious problem when employers and workers jointly invest in enhancing workers' capabilities or when employers cannot observe workers' levels of effort. For example, employers can improve the quality of workers' labor services by enhancing the workers embodied knowledge and skills (i.e., human capital) through training inside and outside of the workplace. However, workers can acquire two types of skills: general skills that are useful in all firms and firm-specific skills that are useful only in specific firms. In the case of general skills, workers can utilize their abilities at any firm after receiving the training. A firm therefore has no incentive to bear the cost of general skills training because its workers may leave after training, and, thus, workers must bear all of the costs. In contrast, firm-specific skills improve workers' productivity primarily in the firm in which they are trained. In this case, neither a worker nor a firm has an incentive to bear the entire cost of training. The rationale for this conclusion is as follows. If a worker bears all the costs of firm-specific training, the worker will not be able to recover them if he or she is laid off after receiving the training. If the firm bears all the costs, it cannot recover them if the worker leaves the firm. In this case, it is rational for the worker and the firm to conclude a wage contract such that the worker and the firm share both the costs of training and the benefits of the higher productivity after training. In this way, training leads to the accumulation of firm-specific skills. In addition, because the firm and the worker have no incentive to sever the relationship after training, a long-term employment relationship is created. In the second case, if firms cannot observe workers' effort levels, which determine the quality and quantity of labor services, or if doing so is very costly, then they need to address workers' opportunistic behavior of shirking. In this case, firms can elicit workers' efforts by concluding a deferred compensation contract (Lazear 1979). In this type of contract, wages are initially set below the value of labor services (i.e., productivity) but are later set above that level. From the worker's perspective, he or she makes a type of deposit with the firm at the beginning of the employment period and later receives it back and, thus, can recover the cost of the deposit within a long-term employment relationship through devotion to his or her work. Thus, a long-term employment relationship is rational for workers who expect to improve their abilities and effort levels. It is thought that the background for the prevalence of long-term employment practices in Japan, especially among large firms, is firms' implementation and adoption of firm-specific training and mechanisms to draw out workers' efforts.

In jurisprudence, various arguments have been made to justify the restrictions on dismissals (Araki and Otake 2008). Many past arguments sought to leverage the right to life (Art. 25) provided by the Constitution as the principle for protecting workers from unemployment and justifying employment security. Recent discussions have focused on the continuous nature of labor contracts, and a new argument has been made that the continuity principle proposed for continuous contractual relationships in civil legal theory is a universal legal norm and that this principle underpins employment security in labor contracts (Tsuchida 2004). Furthermore, some have argued that if long-term employment is established as a practice and is agreed upon as an implicit contract of employment security, a worker's reasonable expectation of long-term employment can be infringed upon only in limited circumstances (Ouchi 2004). Dismissal regulations that emphasize long-term employment imply that actual long-term employment practices are deeply related to dismissal regulations. Economists also raise the theoretical argument that dismissal regulations serve to increase workers' incentives to acquire firm-specific skills by stabilizing the employment of skilled workers after they receive training (Chuma 1998).

However, the extent to which legal guarantees of long-term employment actually contribute to the formation of firm-specific skills has not been clearly evaluated. Even if employment security improves efficiency by encouraging permanent employees to acquire skills, it also creates inefficiency in the labor market by increasing firms' dismissal costs, thereby reducing their profits. In addition, as mentioned above, it can widen the gap between regular employees and other workers by reducing entries and exits in the labor market. Traditionally, Japan's employment system has been characterized by a well-developed internal labor market, and various legal systems have developed accordingly. In the future, it will be necessary to examine the effects of laws on the overall labor market and their effectiveness while also accounting for the advantages of the Japanese employment system.

5.4 Conclusion

Labor law has focused on the inequality between the parties to labor contracts, and the law intervenes to achieve equality. Legal disputes are ultimately settled in courts, and it is natural for the system to seek justice in the relationship between the company and the workers (or labor union) who are parties to a dispute. However, when considering the overall labor market, the realization of justice between two specific parties may not always mean justice for all workers.

In contrast, the field of economics addresses the issue of justice for workers in aggregate from an efficiency perspective, taking the entire labor market into account. An efficient labor market reduces unemployment and other disparities among workers. Thus, economists believe that relaxing dismissal or minimum wage regulations to restore efficiency may inevitably harm the interests of currently employed workers. Of course, it is necessary to address the poverty that arises as a result of these changes. However, this task should be undertaken not by intervening in the labor market but rather by supporting the target population through public systems, such as social security and taxation (i.e., income redistribution policies).

The different views of jurisprudence and economics regarding the labor market ultimately stem from different perceptions of the raison d'etre of labor law. Specifically, these views depend on whether labor law is simply a means of correcting market failures or whether market failures are fatal to the labor market and legal intervention is necessary to directly achieve redistribution.

Study Questions

1. Explain the rationale for government intervention in the labor market, touching on the particularities of labor services.
2. Explain the advantages and disadvantages of minimum wage regulations.
3. Discuss the possible effects of one of the recent labor policies. In doing so, refer to the perspective of improving labor market imperfections (efficiency) and the perspective of achieving a fair distribution among market participants (equity).

References

Araki T, Otake F (2008) Kaiko kisei (Dismissal regulations). In: Araki T, Ouchi S, Otake F, Kambayashi R (eds) Koyō shakai no hō to keizai (Law and economics in an employment society). Yuhikaku, Tokyo, pp 1–28 [publication in Japanese]

Boeri T, Garibaldi P (2007) Two tier reforms of employment protection: a honeymoon effect? Econ J 117:357–385

Boeri T, van Ours J (2008) The economics of imperfect labor markets. Princeton University Press, Princeton

Chuma H (1998) "Kaikoken ran'yō hōri" no keizai bunseki: koyō keiyaku hōri no shiten kara (An economic analysis of "the law of abuse of the right to dismiss": from the perspective of employment contract theory). In: Miwa Y, Kanda H, Yanagawa N (eds) Kaishahō no keizaigaku

(The economics of corporate law). University of Tokyo Press, Tokyo, pp 425–451 [publication in Japanese]
Kahn LM (2010) Employment protection reforms, employment and the incidence of temporary jobs in Europe: 1996–2001. Labour Econ 17:1–15
Kambayashi R, Kawaguchi D, Yamada K (2013) The minimum wage in a deflationary economy: the Japanese experience 1994–2003. Labour Econ 24:264–276
Kawaguchi D, Mori Y (2009) Saitei chingin rōdōsha no zokusei to saitei chingin hikiage no koyō he no eikyō (Socioeconomic background of minimum wage workers and the effect of minimum wage hike on employment in Japan). Jpn J Labour Stud 593:41–54 [publication in Japanese]
Kawaguchi D, Mori Y (2013) Saitei chingin to jakunen koyō: 2007 nen saitei chingin hō kaisei no eikyō (Minimum wages and youth employment: the impact of the 2007 amendments to the minimum wage law). In: Otake F, Kawaguchi D, Tsuru K (eds) Saitei chingin kaikaku: Nihon no hatarakikata wo ikani kaeru ka [Minimum wage reform: changing the way people work]. Nippon Hyoron Sha, Tokyo, pp 39–64 [publication in Japanese]
Lazear EP (1979) Why is there mandatory retirement? J Political Econ 87:1261–1284
Lazear EP (1990) Job security provisions and employment. Q J Econ 105:699–726
Ohashi I (2009) Nihon no saitei chingin seido ni tsuite: ōbei no jittai to giron wo fumaete (The minimum wage system in Japan: based on experiences in Europe and the U.S.). Jpn J Labour Stud 593:4–15 [publication in Japanese]
Ouchi S (2004) Kaiko hōsei no "pro veritate" (The "Pro Veritate" of dismissal legislation). In: Otake F, Ouchi S, Yamakawa R (eds) Kaiko hōsei wo kangaeru: hōgaku to keizaigaku no shiten (zōhoban) (Thinking about dismissal legislation: perspectives from law and economics (expanded edition)). Keiso Shobo, Tokyo, pp 241–264 [publication in Japanese]
Stigler GJ (1946) The economics of minimum wage legislation. Am Econ Rev 36:535–543
Tachibanaki T, Urakawa K (2006) Nihon no hinkon kenkyū (Study on poverty in Japan). University of Tokyo Press, Tokyo [publication in Japanese]
Tsuchida M (2004) Kaikoken ran'yō hōri no seitōsei: "kaiko ni wa gōriteki riyū ga hitsuyō" ni gōriteki riyū wa aru ka? (Legitimacy of the law of abuse of the right to dismiss: is there a rational reason for "dismissal requires a rational reason"?). In: Otake F, Ouchi S, Yamakawa R (eds) Kaiko hōsei wo kangaeru: hōgaku to keizaigaku no shiten (zōhoban) (Thinking about dismissal legislation: perspectives from law and economics (expanded edition)). Keiso Shobo, Tokyo, pp 91–121 [publication in Japanese]

Chapter 6
Equity and Efficiency in the Safety Net: Social Security Law

Yuki Sekine and Takashi Oshio

Contents

6.1 An Outline of the Social Security System and Its Significance 122
6.1.1 Why is Social Security Necessary? 122
6.1.2 Risk Diversification and Risk Mitigation 123
6.1.3 Minimum Living Standard 124
6.1.4 The Social Security System 125
6.1.5 The Administrative Bodies that Implement Social Security: The Distribution of Competences Between National and Local Governments 126
6.1.6 Social Security Benefits and Financial Resources 127
6.1.7 The Insurance and Welfare Principles 128
6.1.8 Social Security and Income Redistribution 129
6.1.9 Legal Nature of Social Security Benefits and the Settlement of Disputes 130
6.2 Principles and Roles of Social Insurance 131
6.2.1 Risk-Averse Individuals and Expected Utility 131
6.2.2 The Significance of Social Insurance 132
6.2.3 Principles of Social Insurance 133
6.2.4 Justifications for Compulsory Enrollment 134
6.2.5 The Issues of Forced Enrollment and Moral Hazard 135
6.3 Structure of and Issues with the Current System 136
6.3.1 Structure of Public Pensions 136
6.3.2 Public Pension Sustainability and Intergenerational Inequality 137
6.3.3 Generational Accounting 138
6.3.4 Structures of Medical and Long-Term (Old-Age Dependency) Care Insurance 139
6.3.5 Problems with Health and Long-Term Care Insurance 141
6.3.6 The Structure of Public Assistance (or Livelihood Protection) 142

Y. Sekine (✉)
Graduate School of Law, Kobe University, 2-1 Rokkodai-cho, Nada-ku, Kobe 657-8501, Hyogo, Japan
e-mail: Sekiney@kobe-u.ac.jp

T. Oshio
Institute of Economic Research, Hitotsubashi University, 2-1 Naka, Kunitachi, Tokyo, Japan
e-mail: oshio@ier.hit-u.ac.jp

T. Yanagawa et al. (eds.), *Econo-Legal Studies*,
https://doi.org/10.1007/978-981-16-5145-8_6

6.3.7 Problems with Public Assistance and Optimal Low-Income Support Measures from an Economics Perspective 143
6.4 Conclusion 145
References 148

Because the pursuit of equity is an important theme, social security is a field in which law and economics have a high affinity. Based on the principles of Article 25 of the Constitution of Japan on the provisions of the right to life, the legal approach to social security considers the way that the system should be set up so that it is accurate and fair, or just, even if the implementation of fairness is imperfect, and it still conforms to the other constitutional provisions. An economic analysis can be helpful when determining equity or fairness. Additionally, economics emphasizes efficiency in system design and operation in the context of social security, as it does in other fields. However, maximum consideration is also given to equity. Social security is closely related to income redistribution, and supporting people who are socially in need is the key issue. Legal thinking plays a complementary role in considering this issue. The desirable form of social security depends on the surrounding socioeconomic context and value judgments. These aspects change over time and in different contexts, but taking a multifaceted approach using law and economics is particularly useful in the context of social security.

6.1 An Outline of the Social Security System and Its Significance

6.1.1 Why is Social Security Necessary?

People's daily lives are deeply connected to social security programs, such as public pensions, medical and nursing insurance, employment insurance, and public assistance. This chapter considers social security from legal and economic perspectives. First, we discuss why social security is necessary.

In daily life, people face various risks that cannot be attributed to personal responsibility. Examples include becoming ill or needing nursing care, losing work or having to quit, aging, and having a reduced ability to work. People want to avoid such risks as much as possible, that is, they tend to be risk averse. However, it is difficult for an individual to prepare for these risks. Many people's savings may not be sufficient to cover treatment for illnesses or the cost of living once they become too old to work.

In the past, it was not uncommon for families and community members to support one another in such circumstances, but many individuals do not have family members or acquaintances that they can rely on. People find comfort in a system that prepares for risks in society as a whole and enables members of society to help one another when those risks come to fruition. Moreover, if such a system is in place, society is prepared to bear the costs of its operation.

Thus, the social security system is set up so that people, being risk-averse in nature, can prepare for various risks as a society, and it is operated by national and local governments for that purpose. Of course, other systems besides social security can help to prepare for risks. As mentioned above, families and local communities were once typical examples of social support, as were self-help groups created among members of an occupation or region. However, as society modernizes, individuals are becoming its main building blocks, ways of living are becoming freer and more diverse, and small self-help groups are becoming unsustainable. As the individual becomes the primary societal unit, preparation for social risks must be taken on individually instead of being provided by families or regional communities. The system created for that purpose is social security. The functions performed by the social security system are often called "safety nets."

6.1.2 Risk Diversification and Risk Mitigation

When considering social security's role, it is useful to refer to the "Recommendation Concerning the Social Security System" published in 1950 by the Social Security System Council of Experts, which was established within the government in 1949 and which deliberated on social security in Japan after the war. This recommendation proposes the ideal social security system for Japan using the basic concepts of social security presented in the Beveridge Report, published in 1942 by Sir William Beveridge of the United Kingdom, and "The Way to Social Security," published in the same year by the International Labour Organization.

This recommendation states:

> The social security system is a means of providing economic protection in an insurable manner or directly at the expense of the public against illness, injury, childbirth, disability, death, old age, unemployment, multiparity, and other causes of poverty. It guarantees the minimum living standard through state assistance for those in poverty, improves public health and social welfare, and ensures that all citizens live a life deserving of a member of civilized society.

As this explanation shows, social security has two purposes. The first is preparing for various economic risks arising for reasons that cannot be attributed to an individual in a statewide manner and, in some cases, at public cost, and the second is reducing the likelihood that such risks occur as a matter of national responsibility. We can call the former the "risk diversification" function (i.e., the "risk pooling" function) and the latter the "risk mitigation"" function.

At the beginning of this chapter, we explained the need for a social security system from a risk diversification perspective. However, in designing a social security system, the risk mitigation function is equally important. Taking public health as an example, risk mitigation at the state level can be justified as follows. If people take care of their health on a daily basis, such as by paying attention to their hygiene, they will not only maintain their own health but will also benefit others. For example, a worker with healthy colleagues will make faster progress. Conversely, a worker whose colleagues are ill will not be able to do any work. From an economics perspective, taking care of one's own health has external economic effects (i.e., positive externalities).

Additionally, jurisprudence considers health to be a citizen's obligation that corresponds to the right to life security. In daily life, people may not pay attention to their health because they are aiming for this external effect or because they are constantly aware of this connection between rights and obligations, and, thus, people's attention to their health is always below the optimal level for society as a whole. In this sense, it is desirable to create a public health system that raises people's awareness of their roles as constitutive members of society and drives them to pay attention to their health on a societal level to mitigate the risks of illness.

6.1.3 Minimum Living Standard

The most important goal for social security, which performs risk diversification and mitigation functions, is ensuring that "all citizens live a life deserving of a member of civilized society," as explained in the 1950 Recommendation Concerning the Social Security System. In other words, the state is required to guarantee a national minimum living standard to all citizens. Each person's right to a minimum living standard is called the "right to subsistence."

Article 25 of the Constitution of Japan stipulates that all people have a right to subsistence and that the government has the obligation to guarantee this right. In other words, the first paragraph of Article 25 stipulates that "all people shall have the right to maintain a minimum standards of wholesome and cultured living," and the second paragraph states that "in all spheres of life, the State shall use its endeavors for the promotion and extension of social welfare and security, and of public health."

This constitutional stipulation of the right to subsistence is the basic legal foundation for all social security plans in Japan. Specific social security laws provide the legal foundations for these social security plans, determine matters relating to their operation, and regulate the relationships between parties pertaining to social security.

Here, the specific content of the phrase "the minimum standards of wholesome and cultured living" is debatable. Setting the income level needed to achieve a minimum standard of living is a difficult issue. In economics, some practitioners consider the absolute income level, which determines in some way the contents and quantity of goods and services necessary to maintain a minimum standard of living and guarantees a sufficient living to obtain those goods and services. Others argue that the minimum standard of living should be set in comparison with the average income level of the society in question. Historically, the Japanese public assistance system determined the minimum cost of living based on an absolute standard until the 1960s. Since then, the minimum income level has been calculated with the aim of not widening the income gap based on trends in the living standards of the general public.

In jurisprudence, if the state specifically defines "minimum standards of wholesome and cultured living" and creates a system that guarantees these standards, it must make sure that the methods it uses are appropriate and that the system is in line with Article 25 of the Constitution when it is actually implemented. It is not unusual for policymakers to set policies that drastically reduce social security owing to their political inclinations at the time, even though they should not do so. In principle, the Constitution should prevent such reductions, but the situation is not that simple.

The Constitution only makes an abstract statement in this regard, and this issue has arisen frequently. The stipulation on the right to subsistence has three theoretical interpretations, as follows:

(1) Article 25 merely expresses the state's political and moral obligations (the "stipulations as a political program" theory).
(2) The right to subsistence takes shape only when specific legislation is enacted, giving people concrete rights; only then can the court examine whether the rights conform to the Constitution (the "abstract rights" theory).
(3) Article 25 itself directly gives citizens a specific right to "minimum standards of wholesome and cultured living," and the unconstitutionality of a legislative inaction or omission can be examined even if no specific legislation has been enacted (the "concrete rights" theory).

The most commonly accepted interpretation is the second one, that is, the "abstract rights" theory.

6.1.4 The Social Security System

Social security in Japan can be defined broadly or narrowly. In its narrower sense, social security consists of the following.

(1) *Social insurance*: systems whose benefits are in principle conditional on the prior payment of an insurance fee (or contribution) by their members. Pensions, health insurance, unemployment and occupational hazard insurance, and old-age dependency or long-term care insurance belong to this category.
(2) *Social welfare*: public services provided by the national and local governments to assist citizens with specific needs. These comprise disability, childcare, and elderly care services, among others.
(3) *Public assistance or livelihood protection*: income benefits provided by the government to households whose incomes do not meet the defined minimum standards of wholesome and cultured living along with administrative guidance to support their paths to independent livelihoods.
(4) *Social allowances*: income benefits that are provided universally under defined circumstances, such as children's allowances. Social security in its broader sense also includes the following.

(5) *Public health*: public services aimed at maintaining and improving people's general health.
(6) Support for war victims

Among the components of the Japanese social security system, social insurance and public assistance are risk diversification tools. However, they have significant differences. Social insurance is a contributory system in which people pay insurance fees in advance to prepare for risks, whereas public assistance is financed by taxes. In terms of benefits, social insurance provides relief almost automatically if the need arises provided that the insured person's contributions have been properly paid. In the case of public assistance, in contrast, people are strictly questioned on whether and why they need relief. This difference in how benefits are financed therefore has significant legal consequences for the recipients. In other words, the nature of the benefits' entitlement rights (i.e., whether they can be legally claimed) is much more clearly defined in the case of social insurance and, thus, is easier to defend in front of a court.

In contrast, social welfare, social allowances, and public health can basically be seen as risk mitigation tools. For example, child welfare and child allowances are expected to reduce the social risks that children may face throughout their development, and pursuing the promotion of public health has the straightforward effect of reducing the overall risk of disease.

6.1.5 The Administrative Bodies that Implement Social Security: The Distribution of Competences Between National and Local Governments

National and local governments play a central role in the operation of social security systems. Roughly speaking, the national government (i.e., the Ministry of Health, Labor and Welfare) is responsibile for the overall system design and income security in the form of cash benefits, whereas local governments are responsible for regulating benefits in kind, such as health, medical care, and welfare.

In concrete terms, the national government is responsible for managing public pensions, namely, the national pension *(kokumin nenkin)* and employees' pensions *(kōsei nenkin)*, and forms of workers' compensation insurance, such as unemployment and occupational hazards insurance. Conversely, local governments implement national health and old-age dependency insurance and social welfare. In addition, as government functions have decentralized, the role of local governments has increased, with a general aim of meeting the specific needs of local citizens.

Social security is essentially operated by public institutions. However, the government has been outsourcing some of these operations to private companies over a certain size, leveraging their pre-existing management infrastructures to provide social benefits to their employees. When these private companies perform these services, they are legally regarded as administrative agencies, and disputes are handled under administrative law. For example, large companies (i.e., those with 700 or more employees) may operate public health insurance and pensions (i.e., employees' pension funds and defined contribution pensions), and they may add their own benefits on top of these programs under conditions defined by the law. Companies otherwise fulfill their usual roles of collecting their employees' social insurance fees for government agencies.

Although public institutions, such as national and local governments, play the most important roles in social security, informal and atypical providers of social security should not be overlooked. The family, for example, is an important provider of social security, as are local connections, such as neighborhood networks and associations. Non-profit organizations also play a major role in diversifying social risks. Empirical analyses have recently shown that areas with more social capital, such as areas with more connections between neighbors, generally have better health conditions.

6.1.6 Social Security Benefits and Financial Resources

We now consider the size and nature of social security benefits in Japan. In terms of budget size, the total amount of social security benefits paid to citizens was 121.5 trillion JPY in fiscal year 2018 (30.1% of the total national income, or 961,200 JPY per person). International comparisons generally consider total social expenditures, including those that are not directly paid to individuals, such as hospital costs and preschool education expenses. From that perspective, benefits amounted to 125.2 trillion JPY in fiscal year 2018.

Breaking down the content of these social security benefits by category, pensions, healthcare, and welfare and others account for 45.5%, 32.7%, and 21.8%. of benefits, respectively. All of the pensions and a large portion of healthcare benefits are operated by social insurance programs, showing that social insurance plays an extremely important role in Japan's overall social security system.

Benefits aimed specifically at the elderly accounted for 66.5% of social security costs in fiscal year 2018. This proportion was only 32.8% in 1975, demonstrating the drastic impact of population aging on social security.

In terms of financing, approximately 54.7% of the costs were financed by social insurance contributions in fiscal year 2018. This finding again demonstrates the importance of social insurance in Japan. In the case of employees' social insurance plans, social insurance fees are usually split between the employee and the employer. However, all other insured individuals (i.e., the self-employed, sole proprietors, and the unemployed) pay their own insurance fees. For this reason, the calculation of insurance contributions differs significantly for employees' plans and national plans.

It is worth noting that taxes (i.e., public expenditures) account for a very high proportion (38.0%) of social security financing. Thus, social insurance is not funded solely by social insurance contributions, and taxes from the national treasury largely make up the difference. The question of whether it is better to finance social security from taxes or social insurance contributions is difficult to answer, and it is related to the design of the social security system itself, as we will describe later.

6.1.7 *The Insurance and Welfare Principles*

The relationship between social security benefits and funding is not simple. This complexity reflects the fact that the social security system's operations are based not on a unified policy or even its historical evolution but rather on a mixture of different, diverging ideas. The two interrelated approaches to implementing social security systems are the insurance-driven approach and the welfare-driven approach.

In the insurance-driven approach, members pay insurance fees and pool them to prepare for potential economic risks, eventually using those resources to help members who actually are affected by the risks. In this case, social security benefits are only offered to those who have paid the insurance fees, and the benefits decreases if the payments are insufficient. This concept is called the principle of exclusion. If an individual has made the proper insurance contributions, he or she receives benefits regardless of income. As we explain above, social insurance is based on an insurance principle, which is a contribution-based system, and, thus, the right to receive benefits is, to some extent, compensation for prior payments of insurance fees.

Conversely, the welfare-driven approach aims to help those affected by economic risks regardless of their prior payments of insurance fees, using taxes when necessary. In this case, the recipients of social security benefits are those who can prove that they are in need. As an example, under the entirely welfare-driven livelihood protection plan, people who claim benefits must submit to a means test that scrutinizes their income and assets in detail. This concept of benefits is called the principle of selection (as opposed to the principle of exclusion).

The insurance and welfare principles have different historical backgrounds. The insurance principle (or approach) was developed in Germany, where social insurance was emphasized after the Bismarck era in the late nineteenth century. The welfare principle (or approach), in contrast, originated in England with the 1601 Act for the Relief of the Poor and was developed later in the nineteenth century with the Factory Acts and the New Poor Law. Both are reasonable ways of thinking about risk diversification mechanisms. Social insurance is often connected with the insurance principle, whereas public assistance is usually connected with the welfare principle.

However, as in many modern societies, the Japanese social security system mixes elements of these two approaches without specific arrangements. A typical example is social insurance, which receives significant financing from taxes, as we mentioned earlier. This system makes social security complicated and difficult for people to properly understand.

In 1997, Japan's approach to social welfare was fundamentally revised (recall that, unlike in the case of social insurance, entitlement to social welfare benefits is not conditional on prior payments of insurance fees, which is why they are called "non-contributory benefits"). Behind this reform was a societal need to respond to new demand created by changes in Japanese people's lifestyles driven by increased incomes, population aging, and the evolution of nuclear families.

The reforms introduced in 1997 transformed the initial approach to social welfare. Whereas social welfare was previously designed as a poverty-prevention policy, the reforms now defined a recipient as any citizen with a defined common need, such as childcare or disability support. Services were now provided by private companies, with the state retaining a supervisory role. The recipient, now called the "user" of the services, was to select the provider and content of the services up to a threshold determined by the welfare administration under contractual terms. The user would bear a fraction of the cost, and the remaining costs would be paid through taxes. This reform defined the recipients of both social insurance and social welfare as the entire population, and more in-depth debates arose as to whether certain benefits should be provided as insurance or welfare. The differences in financing methods (i.e., insurance fees for social insurance and public expenditures for social welfare) raised questions of benefits entitlement, as we explained above. Long-term care insurance, created in 1997 and implemented starting in 2000, is typically a mixture of social welfare and social insurance, as it was created in the spirit of the 1997 welfare reform. As such, although it provides services that were originally offered as welfare for the elderly, it has become a form of social insurance and thereby exhibits characteristics of both social insurance and social welfare.

As a result of these important and widespread reforms, the relationships between the administration and citizens have been profoundly modified, giving rise to new types of disputes and leading to the revision of the law on dispute resolution in 2004 (i.e., the Administrative Case Litigation Act). The revised act expanded the mechanisms by which recipients can claim their benefits from the national and local governments.

6.1.8 Social Security and Income Redistribution

The distinction between the insurance and welfare principles leads to debate not only about whether social security should be financed by insurance fees or taxes but also about the extent to which social security should be expected to function as an income redistribution mechanism.

As mentioned earlier, social security is expected to perform both risk diversification and risk mitigation functions. Furthermore, judging from the importance of social insurance to actual social security benefits in Japan, its risk diversification function has become extremely important. Moreover, as the description in the 1950 Recommendation Concerning the Social Security System shows, social security was not originally required to serve as an income redistribution mechanism in which people with high incomes support those with low incomes. Of course, as we explain in Sect. 6.2, social insurance mechanisms do entail ex post income transfers from people who have not been subjected to a risk to people who have. However, it remains controversial whether social security should serve as a mechanism to support people with low incomes beyond such ex post income transfers.

Regarding this debate, it is important to note that another policy instrument can effectively provide income redistribution: taxes. A desired income distribution cannot be achieved solely by social security without utilizing the tax system. In fact, the Dutch economist Nikolaas Tinbergen showed that *n* independent policy instruments are needed to achieve *n* independent policy goals (Tinbergen's theorem). Furthermore, the Canadian economist Robert Mundell showed that policy instruments should be assigned to the policy objectives for which they are relatively most effective (Mundell's theorem).

Social security includes the social insurance mechanism, which is an effective device for risk diversification. Considering that a progressive tax burden can be set up within the tax system, it seems that holding social security responsible for risk diversification and taxes responsible for income redistribution is a natural method of organization based on Tinbergen's and Mundell's theorems. However, many experts argue that social security should also perform an income redistribution function. Furthermore, among the various social security systems, public assistance is expected to have an income redistribution effect because it substantially supports low-income groups from the outset.

In addition, income redistribution through taxes also serves an insurance-like function, as the tax burden increases and decreases along with income, reducing the risk of income fluctuation (additionally, the benefits from the government services financed by tax revenues provide some insurance). Thus, the attribution of risk diversification to social security and income redistribution to taxes both face some ambiguities.

6.1.9 Legal Nature of Social Security Benefits and the Settlement of Disputes

Social security benefits are provided by the government and, as such, have fundamentally different characteristics from benefits provided by the private sector.

The first characteristic of the legal nature of social security benefits is their "non-transferability." The right to receive social security cannot be transferred or provided as a guarantee even among family members or relatives (an exception is that old-age and retirement pensions may be seized for national tax collection). The purpose of this disposition is to protect beneficiaries from their own actions or the actions of others that prevent the beneficiary from receiving benefits.

The second characteristic is their "personal exclusivity." The right to receive benefits is exclusive to the beneficiary and expires upon his or her death; it cannot be inherited. This characteristic is easily explained by the purpose of social security, which is to guarantee a stable living to each member of society; thus, it does not constitute assets.

The third characteristic is the "obligation to return unjust gains." If benefits are paid incorrectly, the social insurance administration can cancel them ex officio, and the beneficiary is legally obliged to return any unjustly received benefits regardless of who was responsible for the error. As an exception, if it is deemed that returning the benefits would significantly impact the recipient's livelihood or that the recipient's trust in the government should be protected, the obligation to return the benefits cannot be exercised, and the government's claim becomes illegal.

Most social security disputes take the form of ex post remedies for administrative dispositions determining amounts of benefits. It is a legal requirement in the context of social security to first make a claim for examination within social security administration services, which is a faster and simpler dispute resolution procedure, prior to engaging in administrative litigation in front of the court.

6.2 Principles and Roles of Social Insurance

6.2.1 Risk-Averse Individuals and Expected Utility

In the previous section, we highlighted risk diversification as an important function of social security. The basic mechanism for risk diversification is social insurance. Social insurance has economically interesting characteristics and brings up important issues from a jurisprudence perspective as well, and, thus, we revisit it in this section.

First, we assume that utility, represented by U, is determined only by income, represented by Y. This relationship is expressed as U = U(Y). Utility is increasing in income. Furthermore, we assume that people are risk-averse. Risk aversion means that, for example, if a person initially has an income of 1 million JPY, the decrease in utility when that person's income falls by 50,000 JPY is greater than the increase in utility when it rises by 50,000 JPY. In other words, we assume that even though the change in income (50,000 JPY) is the same, the shock when income falls is greater than the joy when it rises. Thus, if utility is plotted on a graph with income on the horizontal axis and utility on the vertical axis, the utility function rises from left to right, but the slope of the curve declines as income rises (Fig. 6.1).

Now, suppose that someone has an income of 1 million JPY and a 10% chance of getting sick, in which case he or she must pay 500,000 JPY in medical expenses. Without health insurance coverage, this person's remaining income is 500,000 JPY if he or she gets sick and 1 million JPY otherwise. We can calculate this person's so-called "expected utility" by weighting his or her utilities in the cases of sickness and health by the probability of each case occurring. Based on the above assumptions, the expected utility, EU_0, can be expressed as

$$EU_0 = 0.9U(100) + 00.1U(50),$$

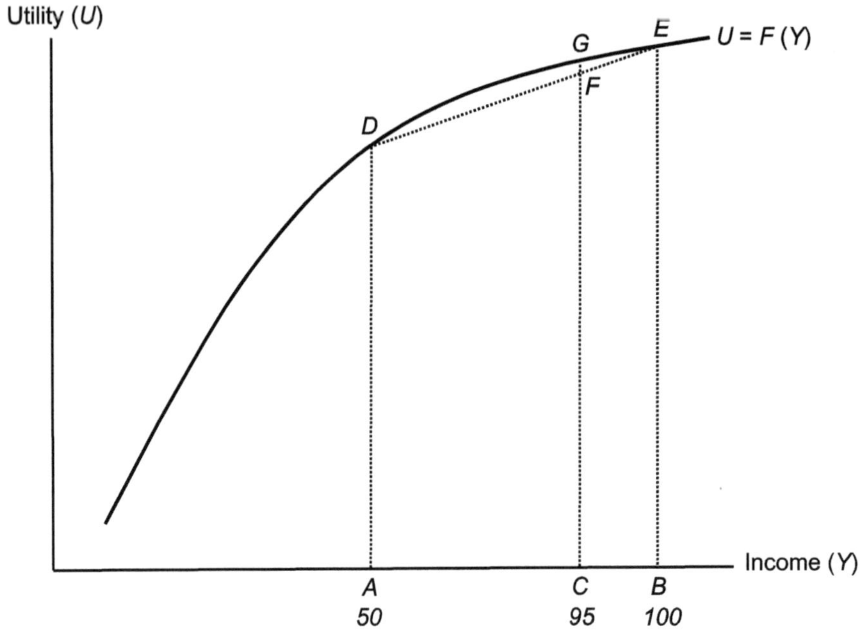

Fig. 6.1 Risk diversification by medical insurance

where income is given in units of 10,000 JPY. This value corresponds to the length of the line segment CF in Fig. 6.1.

6.2.2 *The Significance of Social Insurance*

Here, we consider the impact of health insurance in this scenario. In general, the entity providing insurance is called the insurer, and the entity whose risk is covered by the insurance is called the insured. The chance of getting sick is 10%, and medical expenses in the case of sickness are 500,000 JPY, meaning that the insured must pay at least 50,000 JPY (= 500,000 JPY × 10%) as an insurance premium to maintain health insurance that covers the full medical expenses.

A person who is covered by this health insurance pays a premium of 50,000. If he or she gets sick, however, the medical expenses of 500,000 JPY are covered by the insurance, and he or she still has 950,000 JPY. If this person does not get sick, he or she still pays the insurance premium and is left with 950,000 JPY. Thus, in either case, the remaining income is 950,000 JPY. In other words, the expected utility for enrolling in health insurance, EU_1, is

$$EU_1 = 0.9U(95) + 00.1U(95) = U(95),$$

which corresponds to the length of the line segment CG in Fig. 6.1. In this case, the expected utility is free from the risk of a lower income due to illness. This example illustrates why health insurance is a risk diversification mechanism.

We now compare the utility EU_0 (the case of no health insurance coverage) and the utility EU_1 (the case with health insurance coverage). The line segment CG is longer than the line segment CF, meaning that $EU_1 > EU_0$, that is, it is more desirable to enroll in health insurance. This result comes from the assumption that the utility curve's slope declines as income rises, that is, the assumption that this individual is risk-averse. If the utility curve were a straight line that increased to the right, utility would be the same with or without health insurance. If the utility curve's slope increased as it rose to the right, this individual would not want to purchase health insurance at all.

The sustainability of health insurance is also important to consider. For health insurance to be financially sustainable, each individual must pay an insurance premium of at least 50,000 JPY. This premium is acceptable because expected utility increases when this individual pays it. Thus, health insurance is financially sustainable.

6.2.3 Principles of Social Insurance

Social security law and theory both state that social insurance is a risk diversification mechanism. Two characteristics are often highlighted as the basic principles of social insurance.

The first is the principle of benefits and counter-benefits. Here, the benefits are the insurance benefits, and the counter-benefits are the insurance premiums. It is necessary for the value of the benefits evaluated by risk to roughly equal that of the counter-benefits. A state in which insurance benefits and premiums are commensurate with each other from a risk perspective is described as "actuarially fair." However, as already explained, a risk-averse individual is willing to pay insurance premiums that are slightly higher than the value that corresponds to the risk.

The second is the principle of equivalence. This principle states that the total amount of insurance premiums collected from an insured individual must equal the total amount of insurance benefits, and this principle is necessary to sustain insurance. The principle of benefits and counter-benefits operates at the individual level, and the principle of equivalence operates at the level of the insurer. This principle of equivalence is automatically achieved if the principle of benefits and counter-benefits is achieved. However, the principle of benefits and counter-benefits may not necessarily be achieved even if the principle of equivalence is achieved.

It should be noted, however, that social insurance achieves neither of these two principles in practice. First, regarding the principle of benefits and counter-benefits, health insurance premiums are not necessarily linked to the risk of illness at the individual level. For example, the premiums for the health insurance programs in which employees are enrolled are calculated in proportion to employees' remuneration.

This mechanism is not consistent with the principle of benefits and counter-benefits unless remuneration is also proportional to the risk of illness, which is clearly not typically the case.

In addition, social insurance does not actually achieve the principle of equivalence. As we mentioned earlier, a large proportion of social insurance benefits are financed not only by insurance premiums but also by taxes. In this regard, social insurance differs from private insurance in that it represents society as a whole helping those in need of support (i.e., it achieves the principle of assistance and national solidarity). Thus, it is often explained that the general principle of insurance should be modified. Many countries do not finance social insurance using taxes. The idea has also been put forth that social insurance should use the insurance principle as much as possible, with those who cannot be helped by the insurance principle being supported via a different mechanism, such as income redistribution through the tax system.

6.2.4 *Justifications for Compulsory Enrollment*

In actual practice, people do not enroll in social insurance voluntarily; instead, it is a compulsory scheme. Why is social insurance compulsory? Economists argue that one reason for compulsory social insurance is that asymmetric information on various social risks covered by social security causes adverse selection, as stated below.

In the case of health insurance, information is assumed to be asymmetric, as individuals know more about their risk of illness than the insurer does. For example, if the risk of illness in society as a whole is known to be 10% and medical expenses are 500,000 JPY, the insurance company sells insurance at a premium of 50,000 JPY (= 500,000 JPY × 10%) based on the principle of equivalence. Each individual considers whether enrolling in this insurance plan is beneficial. People who believe that their risk of illness is lower than 10% do not enroll in this plan because they would end up losing money. Only those who are aware that their risk of illness is greater than 10% enroll. In this way, if only high-risk individuals obtain insurance, the insurer's initial prediction is incorrect, and it ends up with a deficit.

Suppose that the insurer then raises the insurance premium to 70,000 JPY to earn a profit. However, the only people who are willing to pay this higher premium are those at an even higher risk of illness (i.e., 14% or more). Then, the insurer again ends up with a deficit and raises the premium further, but the population who chooses to buy insurance continues to shrink to only individuals with higher risks. This adjustment process continues until only those at the highest risk of illness in society remain insured. Eventually, only one person remains insured and is left to face the risk of illness alone, and the system cannot be called social insurance anymore. Thus, if health insurance is left to the private sector, the insured population will continue to narrow to those at a high risk of illness, and the insurance business fails. Adverse selection explains that because of this issue, mechanisms for mandatory enrollment regardless of risk should be introduced.

However, this explanation is not entirely correct. The premise that insured people (i.e., individuals) know more about their risk of illness than insurers do is not realistic. It is hard to assume that people really know their risk of illness well. Furthermore, because private insurance companies pursue profitability, they should want to avoid insuring those with a high risk of illness as much as possible. To this end, insurance companies assess the health of each applicant and reject those with a high risk of illness. At this stage of assessment, the information asymmetry around the risk of illness is significantly reduced. Insurance companies actually have more specialized knowledge of risks than individuals do, and they may be able to assess them more accurately.

Thus, private sector health insurance may exclude people with a high risk of illness, contrary to the explanation of adverse selection. This situation is called "risk selection." Risk selection may be a better description of actual insurance practice than adverse selection is. Although the explanations are complete opposites, the consequences of adverse selection and risk selection are the same in that both of them provide a rationale for compulsory enrollment in social insurance.

Social security law says that the social security system is based on a fundamental right to subsistence (Art. 25 of the Constitution), which covers Japanese citizens or, rather, all residents (i.e., pension coverage and health insurance are universal). Thus, the state does not have the freedom to accommodate those with high incomes or low risks enrolling in insurance to prevent adverse selection, as explained in economics. That is, the state has a constitutional requirement not to perform risk selection, as private insurance companies do, which in principle severely weakens its risk diversification function. From this requirement arises the need for compulsory enrollment, which automatically establishes an insurance relationship when conditions stipulated by the law are met.

6.2.5 The Issues of Forced Enrollment and Moral Hazard

We now understand that social insurance uses a compulsory enrollment mechanism because of adverse selection and risk selection. However, from an economics perspective, these issues only justify compulsory enrollment in social insurance and do not justify the government's monopoly over the operation of social insurance. Alternatively, the government could oblige residents to enroll in social insurance but entrust the system's operation to private or legal entities that are independent from the government.

Some countries' public health insurance systems do give people the freedom to choose an insurance company while still maintaining a system of compulsory enrollment. This system forces insurers to compete, requiring them to strive for efficiency. Of course, a criticism of this system is that it cannot guarantee the public character of social insurance. However, it is possible and efficient to support this system using taxes after objectively evaluating whether it is being operated appropriately based on the characteristics of the insured. For example, if many of the insured are elderly, health insurance costs will be unavoidably higher because this population has a high risk of illness.

However, even if social insurance is compulsory, it is impossible to prevent changes in people's behavior due to their enrollment in insurance, namely, the moral hazard effect of insurance. People who are covered by health insurance normally pay attention to their health, but they are less willing to promote their health actively because they only need to pay a fraction of the costs of medical care. In addition, both doctors and patients may become unwilling to reduce costs for the insured, and, thus, unnecessary and sometimes costly treatments and medications may be provided. A system that requires patients to bear some of the costs of receiving medical services even though they are covered by insurance may partially prevent moral hazard from occurring.

Moral hazard occurs not only in health insurance but also in public pensions. Public pensions are a form of social insurance designed to prepare for the risk of struggling to earn an income as one ages. However, in practice, the age at which pension payments start is fixed regardless of a person's ability and intention to work, enabling people to start receiving their pensions once they reach that age. People may want to live only on their pensions once they can receive them even if they are still able to work. A problem with the public pension system may be that it reduces the elderly's willingness to work, even though it is intended as a provision for old age.

6.3 Structure of and Issues with the Current System

6.3.1 Structure of Public Pensions

In this section, we outline the current social security system and identify its issues and the challenges to be addressed. Public pensions in Japan have a universal coverage structure, as all citizens (or residents, as foreigners residing in Japan are also covered) are covered by some type of pension scheme. Japan's public pensions are unified under the National Pension Insurance scheme. The enrolled population is divided into three categories: Category I (the default category, namely, all people not included in categories II and III), Category II (private and public sector employees), and Category III (dependent spouses of people in Category II). In this way, all citizens are enrolled in a basic, common first pension layer. Employees, that is, people in Category II, are also enrolled in the employees' pension (EPI), a wage-proportional pension plan.

The method for calculating insurance contributions also differs by category. Whereas people in Category I pay a fixed monthly insurance fee to the National Pension, people in Category II, who are covered by the EPI, pay an insurance fee in proportion to their wages that also includes their basic pension insurance fee and that of those in Category III (i.e., their dependent spouses, as a separate group). People in Category III do not contribute to the system because, theoretically, their working spouses' contributions cover theirs. This structure was originally designed to alleviate the income gap between single- and dual-income households, but in practice, it provides a comparative financial advantage to housewives over working spouses, who are generally women and who must contribute from their salaries. This practice has long been the subject of criticism because it obstructs women's participation in the labor market. In addition to this core public pension, other voluntary pension plans can be joined on a corporate or individual basis.

Notably, although public pensions are called social insurance, participants cannot claim their old-age pension benefits until they reach the legal age of eligibility (currently 65). Before reaching that age, individuals can only contribute to the insurance and cannot usually benefit from it unless they qualify for a survival spouse or a disability pension. For that reason, a public pension can be viewed for all practical purposes as a mechanism for redistributing income from the young to the elderly.

6.3.2 Public Pension Sustainability and Intergenerational Inequality

There are two main types of public pension system management (i.e., financing methods). The first is the pay-as-you-go method, in which the pension benefits paid to the elderly are financed by the insurance fees paid by the young at that moment in time. Because this type of pension successively alternates the supporting generation and the supported generation, it can be described as an intergenerational support structure (i.e., mutual aid from generation to generation).

The second method is the funded method, in which individuals accumulate insurance contributions when they are younger and receive pensions by withdrawing those funds once they are old. Requiring individuals to prepare for old age creates a risk of insufficient savings. Additionally, moral hazards, such as insufficient preparation for old age, can arise. Public pensions that use the funded method include an aspect of compulsory savings to avoid such problems.

Although Japan's public pensions have reserve funds, they fundamentally use the pay-as-you-go method. If the population continues to grow well, the pay-as-you-go and funded methods are not very different. With the pay-as-you-go method, insurance fees are not invested in the market to generate profits. However, when the population increases, the number of young people making insurance contributions increases, and, thus, the effect is the same as if insurance contributions were being invested in the market. When the population starts to decline, however, the number of young people making insurance contributions decreases. If older citizens have already been promised a level of benefits based on their earlier contributions, then the only option is to increase the insurance fees borne by the young.

In this manner, as the population decreases and society ages, public pensions using the pay-as-you-go method are disadvantageous to younger generations. This situation is a typical example of the problem of intergenerational inequality. In contrast, the funded method is less susceptible to demographic changes, such as population declines, because it does not transfer income between generations. Accordingly, people often argue that as a country's population declines, it should transition to a funded method.

However, transitioning to a funded method is not easy. If a country wants to transition to a funded system, it must find a way to finance the pensions that were already promised to the current elderly population. The working generation at the time of the transition must therefore bear the burden of insurance contributions to cover the pensions of the elderly as well as insurance contributions for their own old age. This problem is called the "double burden" problem. Of the two burdens, the insurance premium paid for one's own pension is not a burden from a lifetime perspective because it is repaid later. However, the insurance premium paid to fund pensions for the current elderly is certainly a burden. Given this additional burden, one may ask why transitioning to a funded system makes sense.

However, although this point is often misunderstood, even if transitioning to a funded method cannot mitigate intergenerational inequality, the pay-as-you-go method is not necessarily better. Even if the current pay-as-you-go system is maintained, it will not eliminate intergenerational inequality. Moreover, if the elderly oppose a reduction in benefits and the young oppose an increase in insurance fees, finding a solution for this inequality can only be postponed as a burden on future generations. If the population is growing sufficiently, this postponed burden can be handled without difficulty, but if not, the system will cease to function at some point.

6.3.3 Generational Accounting

As the above discussion shows, social security reform is closely related to intergenerational conflicts of interest. The concept of generational accounting, which considers the flow of money related to financing for each generation, highlights this relationship. The total amount of this financing, including both the total amount of services that the government provides to infinite future generations funded the current generation (in other words, the government benefits received by infinite future generations that are funded by the current generation) and the net debt (i.e., debt minus assets) that the government already currently holds, always corresponds to the total amount of taxes and insurance contributions borne by the current generation and infinite future generations. However, the total amount discussed here is the discounted current value of everything in the future. The discounted current value is calculated by discounting an amount at a future point in time by the interest. For example, at an interest rate of 3%, the discounted current value of 1,000,000 JPY acquired ten years later is calculated to be approximately 744,000 JPY (1,000,000 JPY/$(1 + 0.03)^{10}$).

Thus, the identity (not equation)

$$\text{Governmentnetdebt}+\text{thetotalbenefitsforeachgeneration}$$

$$= \text{thetotalburdenforeachgeneration}$$

holds. The left side of this identity is government debt, and the right side is government assets.

After some rearranging, this identity can be expressed as

$$\text{Netgovernmentdebt} = \text{totalnetburdenofeachgeneration}$$

(net burden = burden – benefits). Here, because the value on the left side of this identity is fixed, this identity indicates that system reforms that reduce the net burden of one generation must increase the net burden of some other generation, creating an intergenerational zero-sum game. The pension reform situation is exactly the same. Reforms that increase future generations' benefits also increase the current generation's losses (and vice versa). However, pension reform is not the only example of this situation. Every kind of social security reform is an intergenerational zero-sum game in some way. It is extremely difficult to devise reforms that increase benefits for all generations at the same time.

6.3.4 Structures of Medical and Long-Term (Old-Age Dependency) Care Insurance

Next, we discuss the structures of health and long-term care insurance. First, health insurance in Japan provides universal health coverage, meaning that all citizens are covered by some form of public health insurance. This structure generally takes one of the following three forms. The first form is health insurance to which employees subscribe, which can take the form of employees' health insurance (private sector employees) or a mutual aid association (public servants). Employees' health insurance consists of corporate health insurance (i.e., union health insurance), to which the employees of large companies that have established such plans subscribe, and the Health Insurance Association, to which the employees of all other companies subscribe. The second form is National Health Insurance (NHI), in which anyone who is not enrolled in employees' health insurance (and who is not a dependent family member of an employee) enrolls. These people are usually self-employed, unemployed, or agricultural workers. The third form of health insurance is insurance for senior citizens, in which people aged 75 and above must enroll.

Insurance fees for employees are calculated in proportion to their wages and are split equally between an employer and its employees. Both employees and their dependent family members are insured, and the benefits cover 70% of their medical costs. The remaining 30% of any medical costs are borne by the patient up to a certain monthly threshold. This proportion is the same for all public health insurance plans. A tax that equals approximately 16% of the benefit expenses is invested in the Health Insurance Association.

NHI is mainly local, municipality-controlled insurance that is implemented by municipalities, with the exceptions of some remaining profession-based mutual aid associations that are organized by trade and prefecture. Insurance fees vary by municipality, and four types of calculation methods are used: income-based rates, flat rates per household, per capita rates based on the number of persons in a household, and asset rates. Notably, under municipality-controlled NHI, insurance fees include a per capita contribution, meaning that they increase when the number of members of a household increases. Additionally, 50% of NHI's healthcare costs are financed by taxes.

Healthcare insurance for senior citizens is managed by entities called elder senior citizen healthcare regional unions, which are organized by prefectures.

As people grow older and retire, their income decreases, but their propensity to need healthcare increases. As such, to cover their medical expenses, financial adjustments have traditionally been made using contributions from the insurance fees of "active" generations, namely, employees' health insurance and NHI. The elder senior citizen healthcare system launched in 2008 also benefits from financial transfers from the insurance programs for active generations, as discussed below.

The elder senior citizen healthcare system is financed by insurance fees from the elder senior citizens who are insured (10%), public expenditures (50%), and elder senior citizen support funds from the health insurance plans that cover the active generations (40%). The insurance fees are a combination of income-based and per capita rates. In principle, the percent of medical expenses covered by the patient is limited to 10%, which is, of course, lower than the 30% applied to the other two insurance types. However, this percent is increased to 30% for elderly people with sufficient incomes. Additionally, in the financial adjustment system for younger senior citizens, each medical insurer pays an amount based on the amount of medical care benefits provided to younger senior citizens, calculated based on the assumption that the younger senior citizen enrollment rate is same as the national average. Copayments for those aged 65 to 69 are the same as those for the current workforce, and, in principle, copayments for those aged 70 to 74 are 20% (30% for those with incomes comparable to working people's incomes).

In addition to health insurance, long-term care insurance, which is equally important to senior citizens, was introduced in 2000. This type of social insurance provides long-term care services when a person becomes dependent. The insurers are municipalities. The enrolled population is grouped into Category I (persons aged 65 and above) and Category II (persons aged 40 to 65 who are enrolled in health insurance). The benefits are financed equally by insurance fees and taxes. Insurance fees are determined by municipalities for Category I and by the national government for Category II. Benefits are basically only provided to persons in Category I (persons in Category II only receive benefits when they need long-term care owing to old-age specific illnesses) and are divided into long-term care and prevention benefits. To receive benefits, a person must undergo an evaluation and then receive an official certification of the needs for long-term care and support. The copayment for these benefits is 10%.

6.3.5 Problems with Health and Long-Term Care Insurance

Health and long-term care insurance face many important issues. Among these, from an economics perspective, the most important issue in terms of system management is that, although these programs are referred to as insurance, the insurance-driven principle is insufficiently implemented. This problem is most apparent for NHI. This program was originally structured on the assumption that its participants would be people who could not access employees' health insurance, such as agricultural or self-employed workers. In recent years, however, with increases in irregular employment and job cuts, the percentage of NHI subscribers who are senior citizens, unemployed, or non-regular employees who cannot access employees' health insurance has dramatically increased.

For this reason, NHI is increasingly serving as a last resort in the medical field, but the proportion of insured people with low incomes is growing, and, thus, NHI cannot expect to collect insurance fees. Further, because the insurers for municipality-controlled NHI are municipalities, the financial situation is becoming severe in more than a few locations owing to the small scale of the plans and the aging population. Under NHI's current structure, municipalities are no longer able to fulfill their functions required as insurers. Thus, the medical safety net is weakening.

Further, the healthcare system for senior citizens is also facing major problems. Health insurance is essentially a structure for decentralizing the risk of illness, but this risk increases with age. Thus, it is naturally impossible for all age groups to be insured by the same health insurance under the same conditions. The money flows from the young, who have a low risk of illness, to the elderly, who have a high risk of illness. This situation is the same as that of public pensions using the pay-as-you-go method. Health insurance in which the working generation is enrolled functions as both insurance for the working generation's risk of illness and financial support for the elderly, reducing the system's sustainability.

In legal terms, the purpose of the Law Concerning the Security of Healthcare Treatment for Senior Citizens is as follows:

> to plan for the security of adequate healthcare treatment for citizens of an advanced age, [...] based on the ideals of cooperation and national solidarity with regard to the healthcare treatment of senior citizens, the purpose is to plan for the improvement of national health and increase the welfare of senior citizens through establishment of the systems necessary to carry out adjustments in the burden of costs between insurers in regard to younger senior citizens and to achieve adequate medical care benefits for elder senior citizens (Art. 1)

As a basic principle, "citizens of this nation will, based on an attitude of self-help and solidarity, …bear a fair share of the burden of the costs required for the healthcare treatment of senior citizens" (Art. 2). The cooperation and solidarity of Japan's citizens and sharing the burden of medical expenses fairly are provided as the basis for financial transfers from the young to the elderly. Here, the degree of financial burden on the young for the medical expenses of the elderly that can be called a fair share of the burden is debatable. An economic analysis like that described earlier can serve as the foundation for this evaluation.

Long-term care insurance, like health insurance, faces the challenge of improving its financial sustainability within an aging society. Because the probability of needing long-term care increases rapidly with age, this challenge is only natural. Furthermore, as in the case of NHI, long-term care insurers are municipalities, and they may not be able to sufficiently carry out their functions as insurers in terms of economic power and scale.

6.3.6 The Structure of Public Assistance (or Livelihood Protection)

As economic stagnation continues, interest in the public assistance (i.e., livelihood protection) system, the last resort in securing a minimum standard of living, is growing. The structure of public assistance is based on the ideals stipulated in Article 25 of the Constitution, whereby, with regard to all of the nation's citizens living in financial need, the state's purpose is to provide the necessary protection to respond to that need and to promote a path to independence while providing a minimum standard of living (Art. 1 of the Public Assistance Act). This program's funding is not supplied by contributions but rather is entirely covered by taxes (i.e., public expenditures).

The foundation of the public assistance system is the minimum cost of living, which is calculated according to a standard determined by the national government. The minimum cost of living corresponds to the income required to secure a minimum standard of living, and it is determined relative to a standard household's income. Various adjustments to this standard are made according to family structure and area of residence. The benefits are the difference between the calculated standard minimum income and the actual cumulated income of a given household.

An important principle of this system is that it has a complementary nature. Article 4, paragraph 1 of the Public Assistance Act stipulates that "protection is provided as a necessity for those living in need, to make use of their available assets, abilities, and everything else in order to maintain a minimum standard of living." In other words, public assistance benefits are structured such that payments are provided in a complementary form to households that cannot reach the minimum standard of living after using of all of their assets (e.g., savings and real estate), all of their abilities (e.g., capacity to work), and any other form of aid and assistance provided by other laws. Thus, for a household to receive benefits, its assets, income, and any potential support from other benefits or relatives will be examined and scrutinized.

6.3.7 Problems with Public Assistance and Optimal Low-Income Support Measures from an Economics Perspective

A structure in which public assistance payments are provided based on the principle that they should be complementary is reasonable in that the nation is making up for an inability to achieve a minimum standard of living. Because public assistance is financed by taxes rather than insurance fees, this principle is easy to understand. However, public assistance is not necessarily structured to "promote self-reliance" in its current form (Art. 1 of the Public Assistance Act). Rather, economists often point out in that, contrary to the system's original purpose, it can keep recipients of public assistance payments trapped in poverty.

The idea is that receiving public assistance payments potentially lowers a person's desire to work. We can explain this point using the concept of marginal tax rates. The marginal tax rate is the increase in the amount of tax to be paid when income marginally (i.e., slightly) increases (in contrast, the average tax rate is the ratio of tax to income). For example, when a person's income increases by 10,000 JPY and the tax to be paid increases by 2,000 JPY, the marginal tax rate is said to be 20% (=2,000/10,000 JPY). When the marginal tax rate is high, the incentive to work to increase income is weaker.

Because public assistance payments are provided to cover the difference between a household's income and the minimum cost of living, if a household's income increases by 10,000 JPY, public assistance payments decrease by 10,000 JPY. Thus, the marginal tax rate is 100% (because the structure deducts labor, the reduction in payments is slightly less than 10,000 JPY in practice, but the marginal tax rate is still greater than 80%). Hence, some people prefer to continue receiving public assistance payments rather than making an effort to increase their work hours and increase their income from wages. This situation is a typical form of moral hazard, but the current public assistance system does not adequately anticipate it. The principle that this system has a supplementary nature certainly leads to a fair and impartial structure, but economic analyses, which emphasize efficiency, have long shown that this system also has the serious problem of reducing people's desire to work.

A few solutions have been proposed for these problems with public assistance. A typical example is a negative income tax. Under this structure, although a minimum cost of living is provided, income tax is borne in proportion to income. Because low-income households receive more payments for living expenses from the government than they pay in income tax, their income tax can be thought of as negative. In terms of support for low-income households, a negative income tax is the same as public assistance, but because the marginal tax rate is much lower than 100% with a negative income tax, it does not hinder the desire to work as much as public assistance does.

For example, consider a structure in which the government unconditionally provides payments of 100,000 JPY to cover the minimum cost of living but taxes earned income at a rate of 20%. In this case, a person with earned income of 50,000 JPY pays 10,000 JPY (= 50,000 JPY × 20%) in income taxes. Additionally, because this person also receives 100,000 JPY from the government to cover the cost of living, he or she obtains 90,000 JPY on net from the government. In other words, this person pays a negative income tax. Now, suppose that this person is considering whether to work more hours and increase his or her earned income by 10,000 JPY to 60,000 JPY. The income tax increases by 2,000 JPY to 12,000 JPY (i.e., the negative income tax decreases to 88,000 JPY). In this case, the marginal tax rate is 20% (2,000 JPY /10,000 JPY), which is much lower than in the case of public assistance. As a result, the effect of reducing the desire to work is considerably reduced.

Recently, many have advocated for a structure of tax deductions with benefits, which is a similar concept to this kind of negative income tax. If a fixed sum is deducted from income (i.e., an income tax deduction is made) and taxes are imposed only on the remaining income after the deduction, low-income households will be exempt from the burden of taxes. However, this income deduction cannot provide additional support to low-income households, and high-income households also benefit from a lower tax burden. In contrast, tax reduction is a system in which low-income households also pay income tax and a fixed amount is deducted from their taxes. Here, low-income earners whose original taxes to be paid exceed the tax exemption are provided with the difference. In this structure's name, the phrase "with benefits" refers to this system. In this way, low-income earners pay negative taxes, and support can be obtained through a policy that goes beyond the case of income deduction.

In comparison with public assistance, a negative income tax and tax deductions with benefits hinder the desire to work to a lesser extent and are more efficient. In comparison with income deductions, they are superior in terms of equity in that they provide more support to low-income households, but they are inferior in terms of efficiency because the marginal tax rate is still positive. Another key feature of a negative income tax and tax deductions with benefits is that they render the means tests used for public assistance unnecessary.

Regarding the relationship between public assistance and the desire to work, problems with the minimum wage system have also been pointed out, as we touched upon in Chap. 5. In Japan, the minimum wage is determined by each prefecture. It is reexamined annually in relation to economic factors, such as industry circumstances, the cost of living, average wages, and so forth, but it has been pointed out that several prefectures experience a reverse phenomenon in which people who work full-time at the minimum wage fall short of the standard minimum income set by the livelihood protection administration. Consequently, the minimum wage system has been revised since 2007 so that consideration must be given to the livelihood protection standard when setting the minimum wage. In other words, a person working for the minimum wage should not earn less than a person receiving public assistance does in practice. It has been pointed out that, even though the system of livelihood protection, which aims to promote self-reliance, helps to strengthen aspects of the recipients that will promote their employment, the system is inconsistent if people still receive public assistance even when working full-time. Additionally, wages, which are compensation for labor, and public assistance benefits, which are social security benefits, have different objectives; it is an inappropriate oversimplification to merely compare the two. In relation to the problem of the working poor, it has also been pointed out that instead of raising the minimum wage, it is more appropriate to help them secure a living that is substantially above the standards of public assistance by making the most of other social security benefits (e.g., benefits connected to childcare and housing and social insurance coverage) (see Chap. 4). Although economic policy arguments, such as growth strategies emphasizing that increasing wages, including the minimum wage, is connected to the strengthening the competitive power of small to medium-sized enterprises, and arguments on securing a minimum standard of living through social security, including public assistance, are clearly connected, care must be taken to avoid conflating them.

6.4 Conclusion

This chapter has discussed a variety of points related to social security by separately considering both legal and economic approaches. To conclude, we summarize the characteristics of both approaches.

First, the legal approach to social security considers the way that a system should theoretically be set up based on the principles of Article 25 of the Constitution of Japan on the provisions of the right to life, as explained at the beginning of this chapter. This system should be fair and socially acceptable even though fairness is essentially vague, and it should conform to the relevant other constitutional provisions, especially provisions related to basic rights. The definition of "fairness" differs with current mentalities and societal circumstances, the political and economic situation, and people's beliefs and lifestyles. However, economic analyses of efficiency and equity can provide an indication of fairness. A system that can embody the right to life in a rationally efficient way and conforms to other constitutional ideals, such as solidarity and equality, can provide elements for evaluating the fairness of a system.

For a system to be fair, it should be managed consistently, and the establishment of rules to manage the system should also be subject to jurisprudential analysis. This subjection to analysis applies not only to the settlement of disputes during implementation but also to the court's decisions related to disputes that were not anticipated when the law was enacted. Case law can prepare grounds for these disputes until the law is revised. Social security jurisprudence can also insure that the system is implemented according to the legislator's intentions.

Additionally, economics takes a similar approach to social security as it does to other fields by emphasizing efficiency. In designing a social security system, it also emphasizes its effects on people's behavior. For example, economists often argue that public assistance, which should support the self-reliance of low-income households, provides a disincentive to work, and they argue that social and health insurance programs tend to induce behavior (i.e., moral hazards) that goes against the intent of the system. Furthermore, an economics approach, which emphasizes efficient resource allocation, focuses on financial constraints from the perspective of the system's sustainability.

However, economic analysis considers not only efficiency but also equity. Social security is closely related to income redistribution, and the optimal way of offering assistance to those living in social poverty is an important policy issue. Thus, the perspective of equity is emphasized when analyzing social security issues from an economic standpoint. Further, as the population continues to shrink and society ages, the problem of achieving intergenerational equity in social security, which originally involved income transfers between different generations or age brackets, is also becoming an important concern.

As we have seen, although law and economics take different approaches to social security, they may be more compatible with each other in this context than in other areas because they both consider equity to be an important theme. Law and economics also are complementary to each other in that the problems that are not highlighted by one approach are fully discussed by the other. Further, as in the problem of establishing a minimum wage, the desirable form of social security evolves over time and is largely determined by the socioeconomic context and value judgements regarding the type of society that is considered desirable. Owing to the nature of the themes addressed by social security, it is particularly useful to consider this system using a multifaceted approach that jointly applies the views of both law and economics.

Because the pursuit of fairness is considered an important theme, social security is a field in which law and economics have a high affinity. The legal approach to social security considers ways of setting up an accurate and fair, or just, system, even if its implementation of fairness is imperfect, based on the principles of Article 25 of the Constitution of Japan on the provisions of the right to life and conforming to other constitutional provisions. An economic analysis can be helpful when determining what is fair. Conversely, economics emphasizes efficiency in system design and operation in the context of social security, as it does in other fields. However, it also gives maximum consideration to fairness. Social security is closely related to income redistribution, and determining how to support people who are socially in need is an important issue. Legal thinking plays a complementary role in considering this question. The desirable form of social security ultimately depends on the context of socioeconomic situations and value judgments. Although these factors can change over time, social security is a field in which a multifaceted approach of law and economics is particularly useful.

Column 10. "Law Like Love:" law and interpretation (1)

Several years ago, a student of mine brought up the poem "Law Like Love" by W.H. Auden. "Oh, do you like poetry?" I asked. "No," the student replied, "I came across it in a manga. The story was about a leader who put a tax on all people in love because he had lost his beloved fiancée long ago. He kept on using the tax money to build monuments to his deceased lover."

The reason that so many people have been attracted to this tragically beautiful poem and it has been transmitted through generations and across linguistic lines is perhaps the poet's truthful portrayal of the inscrutable yet mysteriously powerful nature of the words "love" and "law." As this poem so beautifully expresses, the word "law" has many potential meanings, just as the meaning of the word "love" can vary widely depending on the narrator's influence and the reader's interpretation. A translator once explained that the idea of machine translation is ridiculous because the word "love" has almost infinite meanings: "*Ai* in Japanese is not *love* or *l'amour* or *Liebe*. Time and place transform love into infinite forms."[1]

Thus, we can see that words are spun together through strands of interpretation. As long as words remain words, interpretation is inescapable. The scientific mentality sometimes denounces this characteristic as ambiguous and subjective; if objective meaning cannot be properly determined with consensus, then there is no reliable basis for new ideas or discoveries. This criticism may be logical in the case of the law, if the law is interpreted by readers of laws. However, this interpretation is not necessary only an act of randomness. The aforementioned translator explains, "It is the attempt to grasp the true meaning that gives translation such endless enjoyment and eternal despair. To do so with a machine is to wash away the blood stains that humans have accumulated on our skins over tens of thousands of years...it's not even worth a discussion."[2]. Yes, interpretation is more than simply determining some sort of inherent true meaning of words; it is a constant struggle to identify facts and reality in the face of historical and societal change. That is and will always be the nature of words. Does this explanation also apply to interpretations of the law? A judge once explained that although interpretations and applications of the law are certainly subjective, the litigation system has been created with the aim of making subjective evaluations and decisions by judges as fair and consistent as possible: "Of course there should be one right choice, one right answer to the question [...] this viewpoint is very attractive."[3]

Study Questions

1. Explain the difference between the welfare and insurance principles.
2. Explain why social insurance should be compulsory.
3. Explain the legal nature of the entitlement to social security benefits and the underlying concepts therein.

---

[1] Taken from Inoue I (2010) Hon'yaku no hanashi (On Translation). In: Takahashi R et al. (eds) Tōkyō sōgensha bunko kaisetsu sōmokuroku: shiryō hen. Tokyo Sogensha, Tokyo, pp 226–228 (original text appeared in 1958).

[2] Ibid.

[3] Taken from Nakamura J (1989) "Saiban" ni tsuite kangaeru (Thinking about "adjudication"). In: Nakamura J, Saiban no sekai wo ikite. Hanrei Taimuzusha, Tokyo, pp 397–432 (original text appeared in 1984).

4. Discuss how social security reform should be carried out in the context of declining fertility and an aging population from the perspectives of law, economics, public finance, and entitlement protection.

References

Hiroi Y (1999) Nihon no shakai hoshō (Social security in Japan). Iwanami Shoten, Tokyo [publication in Japanese]

Japan Association of Social Security Law (2012) National minimum no saikōchiku (Reconstructing national minimums). Horitsu Bunka Sha, Kyoto [publication in Japanese]

Mukuno M, Tanaka K (2006) Hajimete no shakai hoshō (An introduction to social security), 11th edn. Yuhikaku, Tokyo [publication in Japanese]

Nishimura K (2003) Shakai hoshō hō (Social security law). Yuhikaku, Tokyo [publication in Japanese]

Oshio T (2013) Shakai hoshō no keizaigaku (Social security and economics), 4th edn. Nippon Hyoron Sha, Tokyo [publication in Japanese]

Chapter 7
When is Breaking a Promise Allowed? Contract Law

Akira Saito, Hiroshi Tanaka, and Yoshinobu Zasu

Contents

7.1 Introduction 150
7.2 Legal Theories of Remedies for Breaches of Contract: A Comparative Study of Japanese and English Law 152
7.2.1 A Breach and Its Remedies 152
7.2.2 Right to Demand Performance 153
7.2.3 Right to Claim Damages 155
7.2.4 Right to Avoid Contracts 157
7.2.5 Underlying Concepts of Contract Law: The Grounds and Scope of Binding Power 159
7.3 Suitability of Remedy Methods: Analysis of Two Cases 160
7.3.1 Two Typical Cases of Buying and Selling 162
7.3.2 Obligation of a Buyer Who Can Use the Market to Purchase a Substitute Product 163
7.3.3 Logic for Legitimizing the Substitute Transaction Obligation 163
7.3.4 Obligation to Mitigate Damages as the Market Use Norm 169
7.3.5 Explanation from Historical Examples 170
7.4 Contract Law: An Economic Approach 171
7.4.1 Role of Contract Law 171
7.4.2 Example 1: Vehicle Contract 171
7.4.3 Example 2: The Painting Contract 177
7.5 Conclusion 181
References 183

A. Saito · H. Tanaka (✉)
Graduate School of Law, Kobe University, 2-1 Rokkodai-cho, Nada-ku, Kobe 657-8501, Hyogo, Japan
e-mail: tanaka@diamond.kobe-u.ac.jp

A. Saito
e-mail: asaito@kobe-u.ac.jp

Y. Zasu
Faculty of Economics, Kansai University, 3-3-35 Yamate-cho, Suita 564-8680, Osaka, Japan
e-mail: zasu@kansai-u.ac.jp

T. Yanagawa et al. (eds.), *Econo-Legal Studies*,
https://doi.org/10.1007/978-981-16-5145-8_7

A contract is a tool for social and economic cooperation, and adhering to contracts is a universal rule dictated by society. Contracts enable people to coexist and live better and happier lives through voluntary, mutually beneficial economic exchanges. From this perspective, the legal system supporting contracts is desirable from both economics and law perspectives. However, each country's laws vary greatly, including their methods for addressing and remedying contract breaches. In this chapter, we attempt to clarify why Japanese and English laws differ greatly in their approaches to obligations to mitigate damages (i.e., the other party's obligation to cooperate to reduce the liability of the breaching contractor) despite having almost identical rules regarding the scope of damages. This chapter also investigates which method is superior from the perspectives of economics and law.

7.1 Introduction

Living in modern society means exchanging money for goods and services. Such transactions are legally called contracts. In other words, contracts is are tools for social and economic cooperation that enable people to coexist and live better and happier lives through voluntary, mutually beneficial economic exchanges. Most parties only enter a contract after determining what they stand to gain. Thus, one can say that the majority of contracts can be successfully concluded without any legal involvement. For example, when a Japanese person purchases a product (i.e., concludes a sales contract) overseas, he or she is unlikely to notice any differences from buying the item locally. Thus, contracts and economics have a shared goal of creating mutual benefits for both parties and a shared need for a legal system that promotes more efficient exchanges.

Executing a contract based on true free will is more challenging if one party is in a weaker position in terms of financial resources, information, and so forth. In such situations, the law provides measures to protect disadvantaged parties to a certain extent. However, as we discuss in this chapter, the law (i.e., contract law) governs contracts in which both parties are deemed to be on equal footing. The legal system's treatment of contract breaches is a matter of great significance. Furthermore, the laws for addressing and remedying such breaches vary greatly by country. These differences are unavoidable because they stem from the fact that each country has an independent legal system. However, if the involved contracts have the same fundamental purpose, it should be possible to examine which systems are superior.

From an economic perspective on contract law, it is ideal (i.e., most efficient) for all involved parties to anticipate all future events before entering into a contract, thereby forming a complete contract. The role of contract law is to define the rules governing the involved parties if an existing contract is breached, aiming for completeness (i.e., increased efficiency). Thus, greater efficiency implies superiority.

In this chapter, we compare Japanese and English law from this perspective. Monetary compensation is the most widely accepted remedy for a contract breach offered by the law, and it is recognized by many legal systems worldwide. Countries with a civil law tradition (originating from the study of Roman law) stipulate many rules concerning contracts in their civil codes. Japan is no exception to this principle, and its Civil Code is strongly influenced by French and German law (which also follow the civil law tradition). It is also widely accepted that Article 416 of the Japanese Civil Code (a key provision that sets the scope of damages for breaches of contract) is based on English case law. Nobushige Hozumi, one of the drafting committee members of the Japanese Civil Code, obtained his qualifications as a barrister after studying in England in the early Meiji era (i.e., the late 1800s). Article 416 was almost undoubtedly introduced by Hozumi. He was also proficient in German law and is regarded as an excellent comparative law researcher even today. In summary, it is highly likely that Article 416 underwent much discussion and many comparisons with other countries' provisions before it was adopted in the Japanese Civil Code.

Although Japanese and English laws share these major rules, they nevertheless handle specific cases of breaches very differently. English law focuses on exchanging commodities that can be purchased in the market, with the exception of certain contract items that cannot be purchased in the market (e.g., artwork) because their individuality is crucial to their value. In contrast, the Japanese Civil Code focuses on transactions of specific goods, which are not standardized like commodities in the modern market.

In this regard, Morton Horwitz, a renowned researcher in the history of English and American law, states that a large commodity market was developed in England only in the late eighteenth century (Horwitz 1977). Current English contract law treats market goods as substitutes owing to the prevalence of currency and the establishment of such markets. As a result of these factors, market prices were formed, transforming contracts from merely a means of transferring ownership of goods to a method of securing the economic benefits realized by transactions. This idea illustrates the influence of England's economic history on contract law.

In Sect. 7.2, we first review the theory of Japanese contract law by comparing it with that of English law. The study of law is based on words and language. Thus, we must first clarify the direction of the theory from such language. Next, in Sect. 7.3, we apply Japanese law along with legal theories of remedies for contract breaches in English law. We then assign specific numerical values to cases involving transactions of substitutes and specific products and examine their differences. Finally, in Sect. 7.4, we evaluate both systems from an economics perspective based on the preceding examinations and discussions.

7.2 Legal Theories of Remedies for Breaches of Contract: A Comparative Study of Japanese and English Law

The following two examples are used throughout this chapter:

Example 1: Car transaction (alternatives available)

B enters into a contract to purchase a new car from A. The contract is concluded, but A runs out of stock due to a sudden spike in the car's popularity. Because there is a shortage of the contracted model, A's emergency restock expenses exceed her selling price to B.

Example 2: Painting transaction (no alternatives)

B enters into a contract to purchase a painting from A. Obtaining this painting is B's longtime dream, and he is willing to buy it even if it requires selling off all his assets. Thus, B is overjoyed to be able to enter into a sales contract for this painting. However, C then offers A a higher buying price than B does.

In this example, B wants to purchase this specific painting by this specific painter and will not be satisfied with a similar painting. Thus, unlike in Example 1, buying a replacement in the market is not an option in this case.

7.2.1 A Breach and Its Remedies

We first compare the responses of Japanese and English contract law to these breaches of contract. The first salient point is that Japanese law addresses both examples using a common legal framework, whereas English law treats them distinctly. The key to this distinction is whether a similar object (i.e., an alternative) can be purchased in the market (e.g., a new car) or whether the buyer will only be satisfied with a specific item (e.g., a specific painting). This section focuses on remedies for breaches of contract but also provides explanations of contract law's underlying framework.

In Example 1, suppose that B signed a sales contract with A but did not receive the car by the due date. Both Japanese and English law explain this situation in almost the same manner, as follows. When a sales contract is concluded, the seller (A) has an obligation to deliver the contracted object (a car) to the buyer (B), and, in response, the buyer has a right to require the seller to deliver that object. Conversely, the buyer has an obligation to pay the contracted price to the seller, and, in response, the seller has a right to enforce the payment of the purchase price. In such cases, the person bearing the obligation is called the debtor, and the person with the right is called the creditor. If the debtor fails to fulfill his obligation, then the situation is referred to as a breach of contract (mainly referred to as a "breach" hereinafter). In Example 1, the seller breaches the contract if she fails to deliver the contracted object to the buyer by the due date.

The buyer has some options if the seller does not deliver the contracted object to him, as the contract is useless if the buyer cannot take any action against the seller. The law provides certain rights (remedies) for the prejudiced party, and three remedies are provided under both Japanese and English law. These rights also apply to most contract laws worldwide.

(1) *Right to demand performance*. A party has the right to demand performance of the obligation from the other party. In Example 1, the buyer can require the seller to deliver the car, which is the contracted object.
(2) *Right to claim damages*. A party has the right to demand compensation (i.e., money) from the other party for damages caused by the breach. In Example 1, the buyer can compel the seller to compensate him for damages arising from the undelivered car.
(3) *Right to avoid contracts*. A party has the right to avoid the contract with the other party. In Example 1, this right eliminates the buyer's obligation to pay the seller the purchase price.

Importantly, different legal systems handle these the three remedies differently. Japanese and English law have contrasting approaches despite sharing the same rules regarding the scope of damages. Next, we examine these three remedies in detail by comparing the ways in which the two legal systems handle them.

7.2.2 *Right to Demand Performance*

7.2.2.1 Right to Demand Performance Under Japanese Law

In Japanese law, the involved parties are generally entitled to the right to demand performance when a contract is concluded. As long as the parties are bound by the contract, they are legally required to fulfill it. Japanese Civil Code Article 414, paragraph 1 enforces the execution of contracts as outlined below, and it establishes the natural premise that the right to demand performance is granted to the involved parties:

> If an obligor voluntarily fails to perform an obligation, the obligee may request the court to enforce the obligor to perform through methods such as direct compulsion, execution by substitution, or indirect compulsion, in accordance with the provisions of the Civil Execution Act and other laws and regulations concerning the procedure for compulsory execution; provided, however, that this does not apply if the nature of the obligation does not permit the enforcement.

For example, when a sales contract is concluded, the buyer is granted the right to demand that the seller deliver the contracted object (i.e., the right to claim the contracted object), and the seller is granted the right to demand that the buyer pay the purchase price (i.e., the right to payment). Japanese contract law considers the right to demand performance as the primary remedy for breaches.

However, the right to demand performance not is granted under Japanese law without exception. These rights are not granted in certain cases, as follows.

The first case is when the contract becomes impossible to fulfill (i.e., impossibility of performance). This situation can occur because of physical impossibility, which arises when execution is impossible for physical reasons, such as the loss of the contracted object, or impossibility under normal social conventions, which arises when fulfillment is deemed legally impossible even if it is physically possible. An example of the latter type of impossibility is when an object (e.g., a ring) sinks to the bottom of a lake or is transferred to another person and cannot be reclaimed.

If the debtor acquires a right or profit as a substitute for the subject of the obligation for the same reason that the performance of the obligation became impossible, the creditor may demand the transfer of that right or the reimbursement of that profit from the debtor up to the amount of damage sustained (Civil Code Art. 422-2). This right is called the right to demand substitute goods. For example, if fulfilling a contract becomes impossible because a third party committed arson, the buyer cannot demand that the seller fulfill it. However, the seller has the right to claim damages against the third party who committed arson based on torts (Civil Code Art. 709). In this situation, the buyer's right to demand substitute goods may compel the seller to transfer any damage compensation from the third party to the buyer to the extent of the buyer's damages.

The second case is when the doctrine of change of circumstances becomes applicable. Under this doctrine, when the circumstances on which the contract was based at the time of its signing change owing to the emergence of a factor that the involved parties could not foresee and if the contractual obligation becomes excessively onerous, then both parties are granted the opportunity to be released from the contract's binding power.

An example is when a contracted object's market price suddenly spikes owing to inflation based on a completely unexpected situation, disrupting the balance between the original trading value agreed upon in the original contract and the contracted object. However, this doctrine only applies in very exceptional cases and does not apply simply because a seller suffers damages when the market price of an object increases. If this doctrine is applied, then the seller can petition to revise or avoid the contract. In this case, the right to demand performance as originally agreed upon is not granted.

7.2.2.2 Right to Demand Performance Under English Law

In contrast with Japanese law, under English law, the principal remedy for a breach of contract is a claim for damages, and the right to demand (specific) performance is only granted as an exception. This right is only granted if the object's individuality is significant to the contracting party, as in Example 1. Furthermore, whether such an exceptional remedy is granted is at the judge's discretion after taking the case's specific circumstances into account.

7.2.3 Right to Claim Damages

The right to claim damages is the right to seek compensation (money) from the other party to a contract based on damages caused by a breach. This right is granted under Japanese Civil Code Article 415, paragraph 1, whereas English law treats it as a fundamental remedy for breaches. Japanese and English law are largely similar with regard to damages, meaning that the following explanation applies almost entirely to English law as well.

> If an obligor fails to perform consistent with the purpose of the obligation or the performance of an obligation is impossible, the obligee may claim compensation for loss or damage arising from the failure; provided, however, that this does not apply if the failure to perform the obligation is due to grounds not attributable to the obligor in light of the contract or other sources of obligation and the common sense in the transaction.

7.2.3.1 Right to Claim Damages: Requirements

In legal terms, the requirements for a certain right to be granted are called requisites. A claim for damages is only granted if four requisites are present, and it is not granted if any of them is missing. These requisites are as follows: there is a breach of contract, the creditor has suffered damage, the breach is related to the damage, and the breach is not due to grounds that are not attributable to the debtor. For example, if a breach of contract occurs because of an unexpected catastrophe, the debtor is not liable for damages because the fourth requisite is not present.

Japanese law classifies damages as one of two types, related to the fact that the right to claim performance is generally recognized. These types of damages are compensation for a loss in lieu of performance and compensation for other losses caused by delays and other such issues. Among these, the former is intended to compensate for the value of the contract's performance (e.g., the value of the object) and is not compatible with the right to request performance. In Example 1, the buyer would be doubly compensated if he could claim both the car and its monetary value. In circumstances in which the right to request performance is granted (i.e., when there is no impossibility of performance or avoidance), a special requisite must be present, in addition to the four requisites already mentioned, for compensation for loss in lieu of performance to be recognized. Such requisites may include the debtor not taking any action even after considerable time has passed since he or she received a notice from the creditor demanding performance or the debtor outright refusing to comply (Civil Code Art. 415(2)). Such legal action stems from the value judgment that fulfilling the contract (original purpose) is more desirable than providing monetary compensation (damages). In other words, a remedy via a claim for performance is preferred. If a special requisite is satisfied, however, both the right to request performance and the right to claim damages are recognized as remedies for the creditor. However, the creditor may exercise only one of these rights. Conversely, compensation for other losses is intended to compensate for damages that persist even if the debtor's obligations are fulfilled, such as damages caused by delays in performance (e.g., damages caused by a car's unavailability due to the seller's late delivery). This compensation is compatible with the right to request performance, meaning that the creditor can demand the debtor for both performance and compensation for damages caused by a delay.

7.2.3.2 Scope of Damages

Even if the right to claim damages is granted because the above requisites are present, the creditor will not necessarily be compensated for all damages suffered owing to a breach. Japanese Civil Code Article 416 limits the compensable damages to within a reasonable scope:

(1) The purpose of the claim for compensation for the loss or damage for failure to perform an obligation is to have the obligor to pay the compensation for loss or damage which would ordinarily arise from the failure.
(2) The obligee may also claim the compensation for damage which has arisen from any special circumstances if the party did foresee, or should have foreseen, the circumstances.

This article indicates that the scope of the damages to be compensated is determined by certain rules, as follows. In principle, compensable damages are damages resulting from a breach of contract that arise from the usual course of events (i.e., ordinary damages). In this case, the amount of damages is generally calculated based on the contracted object's market value, which can be determined by appraisal if the market value is unclear. In addition, if the buyer procures a substitute through a third party because the seller did not deliver the object, then the costs of this transaction (i.e., the price of the replacement) are included in ordinary damages and, thus, in compensable damages.

In contrast, damages caused by special circumstances (i.e., special damages) are, in principle, outside of the scope of compensable damages. These damages are only considered compensable if they are deemed to have been foreseeable by the involved parties. For example, if the buyer resold the contracted object to a third party and that resale was counted as a special circumstance, the buyer's profits from the resale are only counted as compensable damages if the resale was deemed foreseeable by the involved parties. In any case, not all damages linked to breaches are compensable.

As previously mentioned, the drafting of Article 416 of the Japanese Civil Code was heavily influenced by English law. The description of the scope of damages is also almost identical to that defined in English law.

7.2.3.3 Possibility of Compensation Reduction

As stated above, even if the debtor is liable for damages, if the creditor neglected to prevent the damage from occurring or spreading, the debtor's liability may be denied, or the compensable amount may be reduced. In Japanese law, this situation is called comparative negligence (Civil Code Art. 418).

> If the obligee is negligent regarding the failure to perform the obligation or the occurrence or spreading of a damage caused thereby, the court determines the liability for compensation for loss or damage and the amount thereof by taking these elements into consideration.

Here, a creditor is assumed to have certain obligations to avoid damages or bear the duty to mitigate them. The creditor's non-observance of these obligations may be taken into account when determining the amount of damages. In English law, creditors clearly bear a duty to mitigate damages. However, Japanese law differs significantly from English law in terms of which creditors are obliged to take measures to prevent the spread of damages. English law clearly affirms the buyer's obligation to avoid escalating damages by procuring substitutes from third parties (i.e., the alternative transaction obligation). In contrast, Japanese law is cautious about imposing such an obligation on buyers. A few commentators have asserted that alternative transaction obligations should be recognized in Japanese law, as they are in English law. This debate is discussed in more detail in Sect. 7.3.

7.2.4 *Right to Avoid Contracts*

7.2.4.1 Right to Avoid Contracts Under Japanese Law

The right to avoid contracts, as its name suggests, is the right to avoid one's contractual relationship with another party. This right is granted under Japanese Civil Code Articles 541 and 542, paragraph 1.

> **541** If one of the parties does not perform that party's obligation, and the other party demands performance of that obligation, specifying a reasonable period of time, but no performance is completed during that period, the other party may avoid the contract; provided, however, that this does not apply if the non-performance of the obligations upon the passage of the period is minor in light of the contract and the common sense in the transaction.
>
> **542**(1) In the following cases, the obligee may immediately avoid the contract without making the demand referred to in the preceding Article:
>
> (i) if the performance of the whole of the obligation is impossible;
>
> (ii) if the obligor unequivocally manifests the intention to refuse to perform the obligation in whole;
>
> (iii) if the performance of part of the obligation is impossible, or if the obligor clearly manifests the intention to refuse to perform part of the obligation and the purpose of the contract cannot be achieved by the performance of the remaining part of the obligation;
>
> (iv) if, due to the nature of the contract or a manifestation of intention by the parties, the purpose of the contract cannot be achieved unless the obligation is performed at a specific time on a specific date or within a certain period of time, and the obligor fails to perform the obligation at that time or before that period of time expires; or
>
> (v) beyond the cases set forth in the preceding items, if the obligor does not perform the obligation and it is obvious that the obligor is unlikely to perform the obligation to the

extent necessary to achieve the purpose of the contract even if the obligee makes the demand referred to in the preceding Article.

The right to avoid contracts to be granted under Japanese Civil Code Article 541 has three requisites: a breach of contract has occurred, a considerable period has elapsed since the creditor's notice, and the breach is not minor.

Of these, the second requisite is intended to provide the debtor with an opportunity to perform the obligation before the contract is avoided. Again, this requisite is based on the notion that it is more desirable to maintain contractual relationships as much as possible and fulfill them in their original forms. Thus, a contract cannot be avoided if the debtor performs in response to the creditor's notice. However, it is unnecessary to give the debtor a chance to fulfill the contract if it is ultimately impossible. Hence, this requisite is deemed unnecessary for impossible contracts (Civil Code Art. 542(1)).

A contract is avoided via a display of intention toward the other party (Civil Code Art. 540(1)). As such, the contractual relationship is only avoided when the creditor displays such an intention to the breaching party:

If one of the parties has the right to avoid pursuant to the provisions of the contract or the law, the avoidance is effected by manifestation of intention to the other party.

Thus, a breach of contract does not automatically avoid the contractual relationship but rather gives the creditor the choice to do so. A prejudiced creditor can either maintain the contractual relationship and demand that the other party fulfill it or avoid the contractual relationship with the other party.

Avoiding the contract ends the contractual relationship with the other party, resulting in the termination of debts borne by the other party, the termination of the right to demand performance from the other party, the termination of the duty to receive performance from the other party, and the obligation to return any fulfilled benefits (Civil Code Art. 545(1)). However, the right to claim damages based on a breach of contract still remains (Civil Code Art. 545(4)).

(1) If one of the parties exercises the right to avoid, each party assumes an obligation to restore the other party to that other party's original state; provided, however, that this may not prejudice the rights of a third party.

(4) The exercise of the right to avoid does not preclude claims for compensation for loss or damage.

As a result, if the buyer avoids the contract owing to the seller's failure to deliver the contracted object, the following outcomes occur in both examples. First, the buyer is no longer obliged to pay the seller the purchase price. Second, the buyer can no longer demand that the seller deliver the object. Third, the buyer can refuse to accept the object even if the seller subsequently delivers it. Fourth, if the buyer has already paid the seller, the payment must be refunded to the buyer. Fifth, the buyer can still claim damages from the seller owing to the breach of contract.

7.2.4.2 Avoidance of Contracts Under English Law

In contrast with Japanese law, English law states that, in principle, a contract is automatically avoided if the seller does not deliver the contracted object by the due date. Unlike in Japanese law, in English law, the creditor does not need to state an intention to avoid a contract for it to be avoided. This stipulation is based on the concept that, in English law, contractual provisions are essentially classified as conditions and warranties. If a condition is is violated, the contract's execution loses its meaning, and the contract is naturally avoided. In sales contracts, an arrangement regarding the date of performance is a classic example of a condition. As a result, the contractual relationship is automatically avoided if the due date passes without performance, meaning that the creditor has no option to maintain the demand for performance without avoiding the contract, unlike in Japanese law.

Thus, despite having almost identical rules regarding the scope of damages, Japanese and English law vary greatly in terms of avoiding contracts.

7.2.5 Underlying Concepts of Contract Law: The Grounds and Scope of Binding Power

The admissibility of these remedies for breaches means that a contract exerts a certain legally binding force (i.e., the binding force of the contract) on its parties. Japanese and English law are similar in this respect. However, a wide variety of approaches can be used to understand the grounds and scope of a contract's binding power. Both Japanese and English law can assume these diverse underlying concepts. In this section, however, we examine just two of the more prominent approaches and determine which approach is more compatible with both laws.

The first approach is to recognize the important ethical value of complying with an agreement and to affirm the binding power of a contract for that reason. Once a contract has been enacted based on free will, the parties are bound by the contract and must fulfill it. This principle is the foundation for *pacta sunt servanda*. With this approach, even if a breach results in greater overall profits, it is not necessarily justified. This approach also places importance on claims for performance for the purpose of fulfilling the original contract. Japanese law emphasizes the right to demand performance as the primary remedy for contract breaches and prioritizes the fulfillment of original contracts. This approach is therefore more compatible with Japanese law.

An alternative approach is the view that contracts are binding because there is value to be gained from complying with the agreement. In other words, the binding power of a contract is respected not because complying with an agreement has direct significance but because doing so allows people to enjoy the benefits of exchanging goods, thereby resulting in a more efficient allocation of goods (i.e., economic efficiency). With this approach, binding contracts are a tool for achieving economic efficiency and should be recognized to the extent that they achieve this objective. For example, a contract should only be fulfilled if it contributes to economic efficiency. If a contract is breached, an economically efficient solution is sought, meaning that it is usually sufficient to avoid the contract and settle damages. In this case, it is not always necessary to grant the right to claim performance, and doing so may instead reduce economic efficiency. This approach may also lead to the affirmation of "efficient breach of contract," by which breaching a contract may be considered acceptable if economic efficiency is improved. In English law, contracts are automatically terminated when they are breached, with damages generally serving as the remedy, and claims for performance are not typically recognized. Thus, this approach is more compatible with English law.

As previously mentioned, Japan's rules on the scope of damages were developed in England and adopted into Japanese Civil Code Article 416 with the objective of protecting expected profits. As a result, the relationship between claims for performance and damages is undeniably unclear in Japanese contract law. However, this lack of clarity is not just present in the Japanese Civil Code. The same issue persists in the Vienna Convention, also known as the Contracts for the International Sale of Goods (CISG), which is currently the global standard for sales contract law. This treaty has the same provisions as Article 416 of the Japanese Civil Code along with provisions for non-performing parties to conduct alternative transactions (CISG Arts 74, 75, 76). Furthermore, it acknowledges the buyer's right to claim performance (CISG Art. 46(1)) and entrusts its use to the judgment of the court of the contracting state (CISG Art. 28). This half-hearted response demonstrates the difficulty of forming an international consensus on the issue.

7.3 Suitability of Remedy Methods: Analysis of Two Cases

We can investigate whether Japanese or English law is more desirable from a legal standpoint. This discussions thus far show that the difference in abstract values is very large. Debating them further will not lead to any conclusions. However, researchers have recently praised the obligation to mitigate damages from a legal standpoint using the related agreement theory (Campbell 2007). Because such thinking is heavily influenced by transaction cost economics, which was established by Oliver E. Williamson, it also contains a tinge of economic thought. However, even among law researchers, this argument is just one possible position within orthodox legal studies. This question can be regarded as an inherent debate in law. From this standpoint, a contract is a way to obtain mutual profits from an economic exchange. The parties to a contract can be thought of as joint cooperative parties working toward the fulfillment of the contract. As in Example 1, many contract breaches are due to events that could not be foreseen when the contract was concluded. In these circumstances, following the original contract may not be profitable. Under such conditions, the original project plan (i.e., the contract) is already flawed. Thus, when contract breaches occur, both parties must cooperate to minimize their mutual damages. As a result, to reduce the damages for the buyer and seller, they must cooperate to acquire a substitute product from the market (i.e., there is a substitute transaction obligation based on the obligation to mitigate damages).

We can make numerical assumptions for the two examples below and observe the results when different rules are applied. A typical case should lead to a result that many people can accept. Otherwise, the respective legal theory cannot be used to resolve a dispute even if the theory seems correct. Many lawyers think this way. Even in traditional legal studies, it is not unusual to use numerical calculations to evaluate whether a rule is good or bad. Categorizing example court solutions for past incidents into types and adjusting a rule's settings are also typical methods in legal studies. Below, we provide specific numbers for the two examples outlined earlier in this chapter and observe the different results under Japanese and English law.

Column 11. "My objection then was overruled by Mr. Justice Swindon. As yours is now, by me:" Anglo-American and continental law

"I suppose that it is the first time on record that anyone has ever been driven to commit suicide by a quotation from the Law Reports." These words from a barrister conclude *Tragedy at Law*, a quintessential British legal mystery novel by Cyril Hare in which the murder does not occur until the very end of the story. This character's words are derived from the actual necessity for lawyers working within Anglo-American law to regularly review law reports. Agatha Christie's famous play *The Witness for the Prosecution* (and Billy Wilder's outstanding film adaptation of the play) concludes with a scene in which a lawyer seeks a seemingly unusual resumption of argument for which multiple concrete judgments are provided as grounds. The prosecution's objections are dismissed, and the lawyer's petition is granted (as is shown by the title of this column). Thus, it goes without saying that judicial precedent is crucial in winning this case.

It is often stated that Anglo-American law is characterized by the principle of judicial precedent. Conversely, continental legal systems, such as the German and French systems (as well as the Japanese system) are defined by their basis in statutory legal principles. These terms refer to differences in the primary legal basis used to justify judicial decisions, but they are also closely linked to fundamental differences in the two systems regarding legal thought. Under the principle of legal precedent, a vast history of past cases is available for premises, including previous cases that are similar to a current case in terms of either the facts themselves or the legal issues involved. Thus, one of the most important tasks for any lawyer is to search through past judgments to determine whether similar cases have been heard previously. This thought process is known as an inductive (or "scanned") approach to reasoning. An intrinsic principle guiding fairness within this legal sphere is that similar cases should be treated similarly. Thus, it is not surprising that the word "just," meaning "fair," is the root of the word "justice," which has the dual meaning of "judiciary" and "justice" (i.e., "fairness" in the abstract). Conversely, under the statutory principle, a system of statutes serves as the premise from which lawyers can identify laws and regulations that relate to a current case. They can then interpret these laws, apply them to the specific case, and draw conclusions. In contrast with the system of judicial precedent, this reasoning can be described as deductive and linear. Hence, *recht* and *droit*, which are both synonyms for "just" or "right" in continental law, have the etymological meaning of "straight." This comparison is somewhat awkward however, because English also uses the word "right" to mean "just" or "rights," as in "human rights" (additionally, the etymological meaning of the word "straight" can encompass the word "right").

That being said, statutes have been incredibly prominent within the realm of Anglo-American law, and judicial precedent is not without significance in the courts of continental law. As a result, some have stated that the differences between judicial precedent and statutory law are not as great now as they were in the past, and the two seem to be integrating somewhat alongside the development of the Council of Europe and the European Union (e.g., owing to the dynamic activity of the European Court of Human Rights).

7.3.1 Two Typical Cases of Buying and Selling

We now provided fixed numbers for the examples laid out earlier in this chapter. Based on these numbers, we review the consequences of the remedy system for contract breaches.

Example 1: B signed a contract to purchase a new car from A for 1 million JPY. Normally, A obtains this car model for 700,000 JPY. However, D sells the same car model for 1.35 million JPY. After A signed the contract with B, buyer interest in this car model rose, and A ran out of stock. Because this car model is in short supply, A tried to procure more cars. However, the wholesale price increased to 1.4 million JPY. Furthermore, we can assume that A and D are rival sellers, and, thus, it is impossible for A to buy only one car from D for 1.35 million JPY. When A breaches the contract, the car's market price is 1.5 million JPY.

Example 2: B signed a contract to buy a particular painting from A for 1 million JPY. A paid 800,000 JPY to procure the painting. Buying this painting has been B's longtime dream, and he was willing to spend all of his assets to buy it. Thus, B was very happy to sign a purchase contract to buy the painting for 1 million JPY.

In this case, we assume that B wants to buy a certain painting by a specific artist and will not be happy with a similar painting. Thus, unlike in Example 1, it is not possible to buy a substitute painting in the market. However, C unexpectedly tells A that she wants to buy the painting for 1.8 million JPY. C is thinking of selling the painting to E for 2 million JPY. Suppose that the painting is valued at 1.7 million JPY.

7.3.2 *Obligation of a Buyer Who Can Use the Market to Purchase a Substitute Product*

Under English law, if the buyer can purchase a substitute product on the market, the substitute transaction obligation requires him or her to do so. Because the fulfillment deadline is stipulated by a condition in the contract, if the product is not delivered, most of the purchase contract is automatically avoided. As a result, in these examples, B must mitigate his own damages and must promptly purchase a substitute product from the market. Legally, because of the important role of the obligation to mitigate damages in the case of a contract breach, purchasing a substitute product is required.

In Example 1, B can make a substitute purchase from D for 1.35 million JPY. As a result, B's damages are 350,000 JPY, which is the difference between the purchase price of 1.35 million JPY and the contracted price with A of 1 million JPY. Demanding these damages from A is sufficient to secure the expected profit for B. Of course, any incidental damages, such as the cost of transportation to D's store and the communication costs for conducting negotiations, can also be demanded as foreseeable damages.

In a nutshell, English law on the obligation to mitigate damages utilizes the substitute transaction obligation. However, many people may intuitively feel uneasy with this obligation. If this rule is easily accepted, it may appear to encourage A to breach the contract.

In Japan, the adoption of the substitute transaction obligation was deliberated. However, even today, this position does not represent the majority view. The basic principle of *pacta sunt servanda* in civil law on contracts and the obligation to mitigate damages are clearly at odds. In modern society, if a buyer can make a substitute transaction, there are arguments for limiting the demand for execution (Uchida 1990). To make this argument more persuasive, however, an adequate rationale must be presented to explain why the buyer should have mitigated the damages even though the Civil Code provides the right to request performance.

7.3.3 *Logic for Legitimizing the Substitute Transaction Obligation*

To borrow terminology from economics, we can say that the substitute transaction obligation is a way to reduce the ex post facto inefficiency inflicted on A by procuring a substitute product from the market upon the agreement of the contract's parties. A contract is signed so that both parties can gain profits. However, if a contract causes one of the parties to suffer damages after it is signed, legal systems differ as to whether the contract's original stipulations must be realized. Under Japanese law, the demand for execution is regarded as the first remedy to consider for any contract breach. However, under English law, only the difference between the contract's original price and the substitute product's purchase price is specified as the amount of compensation for damages.

In Example 1, from A's perspective, an event that could not be foreseen when the contract was signed occurred. The 300,000 JPY profit that was expected from the transaction with B became a 400,000 JPY loss after the contract was signed. This swing was due to A's incorrect forecast, and, thus, A can be held liable. However, it is useful to consider why A signed such a contract with B. Because people cannot rationally foresee every possible future outcome (i.e., they have only bounded rationality), they cannot completely avoid signing incomplete contracts in modern society. Herbert A. Simon, who received the Nobel Prize in Economics, advocated that the standard used to describe real humans' abilities in decision-making models should be shifted from complete to bounded rationality. People tend to think rationally within their range of perception. However, because this range of perception is limited, complete rationality cannot be achieved. In the real world, risk-free transactions mostly do not exist. If a set percentage of the risk facing A exists in the world, it may be desirable to incorporate this risk into contract law from the system design stage. Based on this idea, instead of strictly upholding the individual articles in a contract, it may be possible to achieve greater social value by using a law that better emphasizes the economic objectives that both parties are pursuing via contract.

The idea used to justify the obligation for the mitigation of damages is that if a seller has an ex post facto inefficiency, the parties must cooperate to resolve this inefficiency as long as it does not lower the profit sought by the buyer from the contract. Bringing out this legal standard is not difficult. In other words, the seller and buyer recognize that by signing a purchase contract, they become joint parties cooperating to attain a mutual gain, which is the original economic objective.

In most actual contract breaches, one of the parties to the contract has an ex post facto inefficiency. Even in such cases, the parties to the contract should cooperate to minimize the unforeseen loss after the contract is signed. From this standpoint, we present a detailed analysis of various remedy methods. We calculate the respective profits to be gained by A and B and compare them to determine which remedy is more rational.

Example 1: This contract's expected interests if the initial objectives are attained are as follows. For A, the difference between the expected selling and procurement prices is 300,000 JPY. Because B expects to purchase a car valued at 1.5 million JPY for 1 million JPY, his expected profit is 500,000 JPY. If the purchase contract's objectives bring these profits to both parties, the total expected interest is 800,000 JPY. However, because the procurement price increased, A does not sell the car to B.

When B faces this ex post facto inefficiency, Japanese law provides two choices. B can demand fulfillment, or the contract can be avoided and B can claim compensation

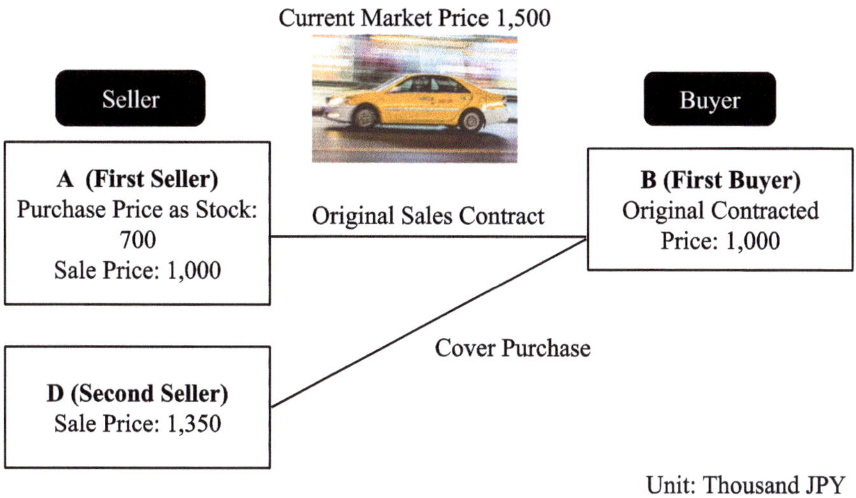

Fig. 7.1 Case 1 (sale of a new car)

for the loss of expected profit. Under English law, the only option is avoidance of the original contract, which is automatic. Once a substitute product is purchased, B can claim compensation for the difference from his expected profit (Fig. 7.1).

In part (1) of Table 7.1, Japanese law applies, and B demands fulfillment. Thus, B pays 1 million JPY to A, and A is required to give the car to B. However, because A must spend 1.4 million JPY to procure the car, A suffers a loss of 400,000 JPY. Conversely, because B pays 1 million JPY to purchase a car worth 1.5 million, B's profit is +500,000 JPY. Consequently, the total profit for both parties is +100,000 JPY.

Next, in part (2) of the table, Japanese law applies, and B chooses to avoid the contract and claim damages. Then, if the substitute transaction obligation is not imposed, A compensates B for damages of 500,000 JPY (1.5 million JPY [car's market value] − 1 million JPY [car's price]).

In addition, because B was not able to use the car, A must compensate B for the foreseeable damages, defined as α. In other words, A's profit is −500,000 JPY − α, and B's profit is +500,000 JPY + α. As a result, the total profit for both parties is 0.

When English law is applied, as in part (3) of the table, B can claim compensation based on the loss of the profit that he would have earned if the contract were fulfilled successfully (Japanese law calls this amount "performance interest," and English law calls it "expectation interest"). However, in accordance with the obligation to mitigate damages, B must purchase a substitute product in the market. In this case, B can demand that A pay compensation of 350,000 JPY, which is the difference between the purchase price of the substitute product (i.e., the car obtained from D for 1.35 JPY million) and the contract price of 1 million JPY. As a result, A's profit is −350,000 JPY, and B's profit is +500,000 JPY (B pays 1.35 million JPY to D but receives compensation of 350,000 JPY from A; thus, in effect, B pays the original

Table 7.1 Profits of both parties resulting from each remedy (Example 1)

Expected profits from the successful completion of the original contract: • A: +300 • B: +500 Total Profit: +800 (Unit: Thousand JPY)
(1) Specific performance (English law: not possible. Japanese law: possible)
A is to deliver the car to B in exchange for 1,000
• A's Profit: −400 (+300)* • B's Profit: +500 (+500)* A and B's Total Profit: +100 [−700]*
(2) Expectation damages without the duty of cover purchase (English law: not possible. Japanese law: possible)
A is to pay 500 to B as damages (the current market price of 1,500 less the original contract price of 1,000). In addition, A is to provide monetary compensation for the foreseeable loss resulting from the inability to use the car
• A's Profit: −500 − α (+300) • B's Profit: +500 + α (+500) A and B's Total Profit: 0 [−800]
(3) Expectation damages with the duty of cover purchase (best case) (English law: possible; Japanese law: sometimes possible)
A is to pay 350 to B to compensate for the difference between the repurchase price and the original contract price
• A's Profit: −350 (+300) • B's Profit: +500 (+500) A and B's Total Profit: +150 [−650]

*The numbers in round brackets () are the expected profits at the conclusion of the contract. The numbers in square brackets [] show the gap between expected and actual profits

contract price of 1 million JPY to obtain a car worth 1.5 million JPY). Thus, the total profit for both parties is +150,000 JPY. Of course, B normally bears a small transaction fee for doing business with D. Because this fee can also be foreseen, B can seek compensation for this fee from A. However, it is not large in most cases.

Thus, based on the calculation above, the parties achieve the maximum total profit in the third case, which reflects English law. A and B are regarded as joint cooperative parties who work together to reap a profit. From that perspective, the third case is the most desirable outcome. In this case, excluding any extra inconvenience of buying the car from D, B can ultimately acquire the car for 1 million JPY (1.35 million JPY – 350,000 JPY), as originally stipulated by the contract. Thus, the remedy results in essentially the same outcome as in the other two cases. Moreover, if the cost of the additional transaction between B and D is borne by A, A can be relieved from the original obligation through B purchasing a substitute product. Thus, the burden on A is prevented from being excessive. English law sets the obligation to mitigate damages, and, thus, the buyer is obligated to utilize the market, reducing the total damages for both parties.

Example 2: When the buyer is willing to buy only the specified item, as in the case of paintings and other artwork, English law recognizes specific performance as a special remedy based on equity. This remedy is equivalent to Japanese law's demand for execution and is written into England's statutory law by the Sale of Goods Act 1979, section 52.

First, in the case in which the contract is successfully fulfilled, A obtains a profit of +200,000 JPY, whereas B's expectation interest is $+\beta$. This value is the priceless happiness gained from owning the painting by buying it for 1 million JPY.

Even in this case, Japanese law allows B to choose one of two remedies. He can implement the demand for execution, or he claim compensation for damages based on the performance interest. If B chooses demand for execution as a remedy, A gives the painting to B in exchange for 1 million JPY. In this case, A's profit is +200,000 JPY, and B's profit is $+\beta$. Thus, the total profit is 200,000 JPY $+\beta$. This result is the same as when the contract is fulfilled as originally expected. In the case described by Example 2, specific performance is possible even under English law. Thus, this choice can probably be made under English law as well (Fig. 7.2).

If B selects compensation for damages for the performance interest, as in the second case in Table 7.2, A only pays B 700,000 JPY, the difference between the market value and the contract price. Under contract law, the damages for B's emotional distress are usually not considered. Thus, A's profit is +300,000 JPY, and B's profit is +700,000 JPY $-\ \beta$. The total profit for both parties is +1 million JPY $-\ \beta$. We can compare this result with the original objective of +200,000 JPY $+\ \beta$. B gains +700,000 JPY in monetary compensation in this setting. However, B thought that the painting was his and then unexpectedly lost it, causing him great mental distress.

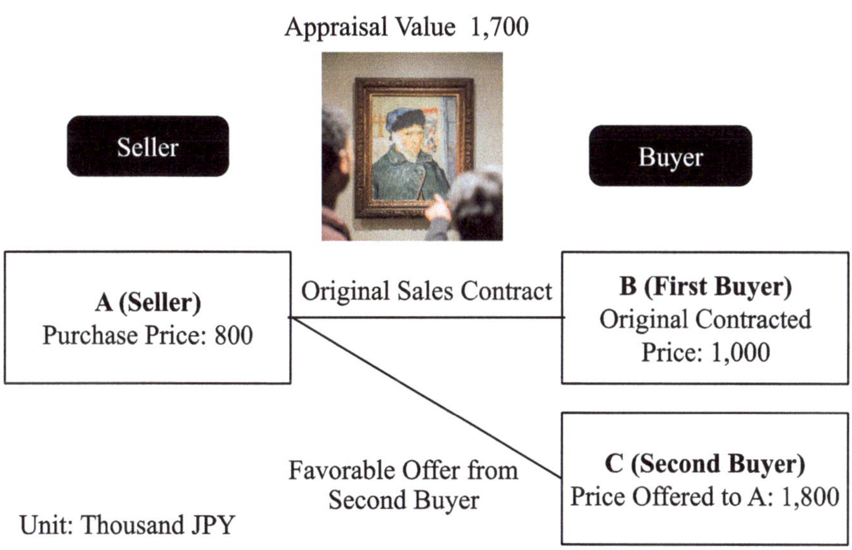

Fig. 7.2 Case 2 (sale of a painting)

Table 7.2 Profits of both parties as a result of each remedy (Example 2)

Expected profits from the successful completion of the original contract: • A: +200 • B: +β Total Profit: + 200 + β (Unit: Thousand JPY)
(1) Specific performance (English law: possible. Japanese law: possible)
A is required to deliver the painting to B in exchange for 1,000 • A's Profit: +200 (+200) • B's Profit: +β* (+β) A and B's Total Profit: +200 + β [0]
(2) Expectation damages (painting is sold to C) (English law: possible. Japanese law: possible)
A pays 700 to B (in most cases, any other loss derived from mental distress is not taken into account)
• A's Profit: +300 (+200) • B's Profit: +700 − β (+β) A and B's Total Profit: +1,000 − β [+800 − 2β]
(3) A proposes renegotiating with B to increase the price to 1,700 (best case)
B must accept the renegotiation if he still wants the painting (a typical "hold up" case)
• A's Profit: +900 (+200) • B's Profit: +β − 700 (+β) A and B's Total Profit: + 200 + β [0]

+β is the profit derived from B's happiness from owning the painting, which cannot be assigned a monetary value

Assume that after the contract with B is signed, another buyer appears who wants to buy the painting for 1.8 million JPY, which reflects a typical scenario in breach of contract cases. In this case, if A tells B that there is a new buyer, she may be able to sell the painting to B if B pays the higher price of 1.7 million JPY. If B really wants the painting, as in Example 2, he will have to accept A's new proposal. In this case, A's profit is +900,000 JPY, and B's profit is +β − 700,000 JPY. The total profit for both parties is +200,000 JPY + β. At first glance, this result looks like it attains the original contract's objectives. However, a closer look shows that some of the + 700,000 JPY profit that was supposed to go to B went to A instead. Thus, A is just quibbling.

Regarding the three choices described above for Example 2, if B's happiness with owning the painting is so large that it cannot be priced, giving B the right to implement the demand for execution is the most desirable option for protecting both parties' profits.

7.3.4 Obligation to Mitigate Damages as the Market Use Norm

If the market can be used and the buyer can choose the demand for execution or damages for performance interest as a remedy method, the choice of remedy does not lead to markedly different outcomes for the buyer. Thus, the choice is greatly affected by the actual conditions and tiny differences in the legal system (e.g., whether the price increases or decreases after the contract is signed, criteria for the calculation of damage compensation, whether the buyer has an obligation to mitigate damages, demand for an easy execution application process and court costs), and the seller is likely to be put in an unstable position.

If the obligation to mitigate damages requires purchasing a substitute product, the costs of the new transaction are transferred to the buyer, who did not violate the contract. However, if the system ensures that this cost can be retransferred to the seller, it can either secure the buyer's performance interest or reduce the seller's damages. Thus, if both parties are considered as one entity, the possibility of Pareto reform is high, as economic analysis shows. If one party's projected profits are taken away (i.e., one party has an ex post facto inefficiency) for reasons arising after the contract was signed, the opposite party should cooperate to reduce the loss to the extent that it does not affect that party's profit. Imposing this obligation is justified when the contracted parties are seen as a joint party and there are no major legal qualms.

Obligating the buyer to purchase a substitute product from the market owing to the obligation to mitigate damages essentially imposes an obligation to use the market to resolve the ex post facto inefficiency. Thus, the regulation to maintain a healthy, competitive market intersects with the regulations governing contracts between parties in this context. Furthermore, the obligation to purchase a substitute product is a system for adapting to ex post facto changes after a contract is signed. In this respect, we can think of it as a remedy method that includes the same objectives as the principles of changing conditions, the obligation for renegotiation, hardships, and so forth as systems for handling incomplete contracts and parties' bounded rationality.

However, both parties can expect to profit when a contract is concluded even in the case of products for which the market cannot be used (e.g., artworks). Additionally, this condition is unlikely to change during the fulfillment time period. In most such cases, A has already procured the product in most cases (i.e., the procurement price is set).

After the contract is signed, if C makes a separate request to purchase the same product at a higher price, it is thought to cause a breach of contract in many cases. This case is a typical "efficient breach of contract" presented by Richard Posner as an example of increasing one's own profit. However, if the painting's assessed value does not change greatly and the performance interest compensation is approved, this contract breach is unlikely to be efficient unless the proposed price increases substantially. Ultimately, this lack of efficiency is because A must pay B a large amount in damages. Moreover, if contract law neglects such opportunism, the artwork buyer's values and satisfaction, which are difficult to price, will be greatly reduced. Moreover, even if the contract in Example 1 is valid, the original profitable conditions are basically maintained, and the right to overturn the contract ex post facto is easily recognized, the transaction's basic principle may still collapse.

7.3.5 Explanation from Historical Examples

However, because English law is case law, even if a lawyer (usually a judge) can give a judgement in a case, it is difficult to present a general theory from first principles. It is interesting to ask how the contract parties become regarded as joint cooperative parties in England. The answer to this question probably involves a convincing historical explanation with a slightly skewed ideological angle. In other words, rather than seeing the differences in Japanese and English law as a clash of basic ideas, it is possible to explain them as differences created amid different stages of economic system development. As mentioned earlier, the contract law system in civil law originating from Roman law cannot easily be separated from the theoretical system configured mainly around transactions of specific things. In contrast, England contract law, which was formulated to handle market transactions during the latter half of the eighteenth century, directly reflects the characteristics of market transactions. Depending on the market, the price of a similar (i.e., substitute) product is indicated by the market price. That value does not directly indicate the product's abstract and inherent price. It is determined by the balance of the occasional demand and supply. In other words, by signing a sales contract, a buyer is economically positioned to acquire a certain type of product at the market price when the contract was signed. The importance of obtaining ownership of the product falls into the background (Horwitz 1977) because as long as the market continues to exist and function, there is no risk of not being able to obtain the same type of product.

This theory can still be applied today, as in Example 1, when a substitute car can be sold. However, this explanation cannot be applied when selling a specific painting, as in Example 2. Even under English law, a remedy based on the *pacta sunt servanda* value judgment, that is, the specific performance remedy under equity, may be approved as an exception in Example 2. Based on a request by the parties, a judge can take into consideration the incident's specific conditions and approve this remedy at his or her discretion as an exception. Example 2 is a typical situation in which this remedy may be approved.

The explanation above has already incorporated several perspectives from economics. Many of them can be explained based on the experience and intuition of justice. Even traditional legal methods have no major disagreements in accepting this explanation. However, from the perspective of orthodox economics, which values more scientific analyses, this thought process is simply a case-by-case explanation. We may not be able to call it a strictly theoretical evaluation. Thus, we evaluate the same examples below using a more orthodox economic analysis as much as possible.

7.4 Contract Law: An Economic Approach

In this section, we consider the effects of contract breach remedies on the contracting parties from an economic perspective. We consider the aforementioned examples with numerical values.

7.4.1 *Role of Contract Law*

Insofar as law and economics are concerned, the most crucial role of contract law is to compensate for the incompleteness that exists in contracts and render the eventual situation identical (or as close as possible) to the eventual result that would have arisen if the contract were complete. Here, a complete contract is one that stipulates all actions to be taken by all involved parties for all possible events after the conclusion of the contract. The actions to be taken in different situations are stated in detail in a complete contract, and, thus, such contracts are in the best interest of all contracting parties. However, in practice, as we noted in the previous section on bounded rationality or transaction costs, it is impossible for the parties to a contract to predict all future events. In addition, it is difficult to describe all possible situations in a contract, and it is difficult for a court to accurately evaluate the description of a contract. Concrete examples show that contract law plays an important role when contracts are incomplete. Thus, for incomplete contracts, we focus on whether the total payoffs (i.e., contract surpluses) of the parties involved, expressed in monetary terms, are the same as (or similar to) those under a complete contract when certain remedies are applied. In a sales contract, both parties can increase their respective payoffs by setting the contract price appropriately. Thus, both parties can improve their situations by increasing the surplus created by a contract. From this perspective, we will determine the desirability of various remedies based on the surplus from each contract.

7.4.2 *Example 1: Vehicle Contract*

We use the examples from Sect. 7.3 wherever possible in this section, although we make minor modifications owing to the nature of economic analysis. First, we again consider the vehicle sales contract. This example includes car dealer A and buyer B. Here, we also suppose that B considers the car to be worth 1.3 million JPY. In other words, the buyer is willing to pay up to 1.3 million JPY for this vehicle. Conversely, we assume that the car dealer purchases vehicles at fluctuating prices. Thus, although it normally costs only 0.7 million JPY for the car dealer to purchase a vehicle, the cost may occasionally rise to 1.4 million JPY owing to vehicle shortages. If the contract were concluded when the purchase price is 1.4 million JPY, it would yield a loss (i.e., a negative payoff) for the dealer. In addition, it would be inefficient ex post facto because the sum of the payoffs to the dealer and the buyer (i.e., the surplus from the contract) would be negative. Specifically, the cost to perform the contract would be 1.4 million JPY, whereas the sum of the profits that the dealer stands to receive would only be 1.3 million JPY.

We now examine the timeline of the contract. First, the buyer and the car dealer conclude the contract, and the buyer pays the car dealer 1 million JPY. In this analysis, to remain focused on whether the car dealer carries out the contract, we assume that payment is made when the contract is concluded. If we instead assume that the buyer pays once the car dealer has carried out the contract, the analysis remains the same. The only change is in the 0.3 million JPY difference between the profit and the payment, which is the expectation interest. Second, the car dealer determines whether it will cost 0.7 million JPY or 1.4 million JPY to acquire the vehicle. Third, based on this determination, the car dealer decides whether to carry out the contract by delivering the vehicle to the buyer or violate the contract by failing to deliver the vehicle to the buyer. Finally, if the contract is breached, the buyer sues and seek legal remedies (i.e., a claim for damages or specific performance). If the contract is carried out, the buyer does not need to consider remedies.

In the above scenario, we can observe that the key decision-making issue for both parties is whether the car dealer decides to carry out the contract. It is easy to imagine that this decision may be influenced by the possible legal remedies for breach of contract. In addition, this decision affects the payoffs (i.e., contract surpluses) of the buyer and the car dealer.

7.4.2.1 Complete Contract

First, as a benchmark, let us consider the situation in which no transaction costs are involved and the parties can conclude a complete contract. A complete contract maximizes the total payoff of the parties, whereas the total payoff under an incomplete contract is always less than the maximum payoff. We focus on how to establish remedies in the real world, where parties can only make incomplete contracts, so that the remedies can complement insufficient contracts.

If the contract in the above example were complete, it is unlikely that the car dealer would agree to sell the vehicle for 1 million JPY when its purchase cost is 1.4 million JPY. Thus, the buyer has no choice but to allow the car dealer to not purchase the new vehicle in this case. In other words, the dealer only purchases the vehicle when the contract surplus for the two parties is positive (rendering the contract efficient) if she purchases the car, and the dealer does not purchase the car when the contract is inefficient. Thus, a complete contract would read as follows.

When the vehicle's purchase cost is 0.7 million JPY, the car dealer purchases the vehicle and delivers it to the buyer. When the vehicle's purchase cost is 1.4 million JPY, the car dealer does not purchase it.

When the vehicle's purchase cost is 1.4 million JPY, the payment is refunded to the buyer.

Under this contract, the car dealer buys the vehicle when it costs 0.7 million JPY and does not buy when it costs 1.4 million JPY. Thus, the buyer obtains the car that he wants when the purchase cost is 0.7 million JPY but obtains nothing when the purchase cost is 1.4 million JPY. Thus, the payoffs of the buyer and the car dealer are as follows.

[When the dealer's cost is 0.7 million JPY]
Buyer's payoff: 1.3 m − 1 m = 0.3 m JPY
Car dealer's payoff: 1 m − 0.7 m = 0.3 m JPY
Contract surplus (total payoff): 0.6 m JPY
[When the dealer's cost is 1.4 million JPY]
Buyer's payoff: −1 m + 1 m = 0 JPY
Car dealer's payoff: 1 m − 1 m = 0 JPY
Contract surplus (total payoff): 0 JPY.

Based on this analysis, we can see that the contract payment (in this case, 1 million JPY) is simply a transfer of earnings between the parties and does not affect the size of the contract surplus. In other words, we need to subtract the car dealer's costs from the buyer's profits to calculate the surplus from the contract. In this discussion, however, we assume that the contract is complete. In practice, transaction costs are likely to arise, and contracts are bound to be incomplete. In the following sections, we examine both parties' decisions in cases of incomplete contracts.

7.4.2.2 Incomplete Contract (With Specific Performance as the Remedy)

If the transaction costs cannot be ignored, it is difficult (or impossible) to conclude a complete contract that can respond to situational changes. In this case, the involved parties must conclude the contract as follows.

The seller performs the contract regardless of the circumstances and delivers the product to the buyer.

When the contract is incomplete, as in this particular analysis, the seller may be more likely to violate the contract. As a result, the available legal remedies for a breach of contract may affect the seller's decisions regarding payoffs. We first consider the case in which specific performance is requested as the remedy, and we then consider the case in which compensation for specific performance is sought.

If specific performance is requested as the remedy, the seller must purchase the contracted product (in this case, the car dealer must purchase the new vehicle) regardless of its cost because even if she violates the contract by failing to deliver the promised product, she will eventually receive an order from the court requiring her to deliver the product to the buyer according to the contract.

[At 0.7 million JPY]
Buyer's payoff: 1.3 m − 1 m = 0.3 m JPY
Car dealer's payoff: 1 m – 0.7 m = 0.3 m JPY

Contract surplus (total payoff): 0.6 m JPY
[At 1.4 million JPY]
Buyer's payoff: 1.3 m − 1 m = 0.3 m JPY
Car dealer's payoff: 1 m − 1.4 m = − 0.4 m JPY
Contract surplus (total payoff): −0.1 m JPY.

If the purchase price is 0.7 million JPY, the profits under complete and incomplete contracts are the same. However, when the purchase price increases to 1.4 million JPY, the total profit for both parties (that is, the contract surplus) is greater under a complete contract. In other words, changing the current incomplete contract to a complete contract is Pareto improving. In this example, the buyer's payoff is the same regardless of the purchase cost, and, thus, it appears that only the seller suffers a loss when the purchase cost of the vehicle is 1.4 million JPY. In practice, however, a seller who anticipates this possibility will sell the car to the buyer for 1.2 million JPY, for example, instead of 1 million JPY to reduce her loss when the vehicle's purchase cost is 1.4 million JPY and, accordingly, increase her profit when the purchase cost is only 0.7 million JPY. As a result, the buyer's payoff in this example is 0.1 million JPY regardless of whether the car costs the dealer 0.7 million JPY or 1.4 million JPY. This result shows that both parties are more likely to earn lower profits under an incomplete contract than under a complete contract.

7.4.2.3 Incomplete Contract (With Compensation for Expectation Interest as the Remedy)

Next, we consider the case in which the remedy is compensation for expectation interest. Under this contract, the buyer's expectation interest is 1.3 million JPY, as are the expectation damages. In practice, it is often difficult for outsiders to evaluate expectation interests. Here, as a benchmark for analysis, we consider the effects of damages to expectation interests on the involved parties when the expectation interests are correctly evaluated. This analysis will demonstrate the importance of correctly assessing expectation interests wherever possible.

When the remedy is expectation damages, the seller's decision when the vehicle's purchase cost is 1.4 million JPY may be different from that when it is 0.7 million JPY. We therefore must examine these cases separately. When the vehicle's purchase price is 1.4 million JPY, the seller compares this price with the 1.3 million JPY that she will have to pay as damages to the buyer if she fails to deliver the vehicle and logically chooses the latter. Thus, we can conclude that the seller will choose to pay the 1.3 million JPY damages for breaching the contract.

If the cost of purchasing the vehicle is 0.7 million JPY, the seller still weighs the options of carrying out the contract by delivering the vehicle to the buyer or violating the contract and compensating the buyer and chooses the more beneficial option. In this case, we can infer that the seller will pay 0.7 million JPY and carry out the contract.

The above analysis shows that the seller will purchase the vehicle when the purchase cost is 0.7 million JPY and will violate the contract and pay damages when the purchase cost is 1.4 million JPY. Thus, we can infer that the buyer receives the vehicle when the purchase cost is 0.7 million JPY and is compensated when the purchase cost is 1.4 million JPY. Thus, each party's payoff and the contract surpluses are as follows.

[At 0.7 million JPY]
Buyer's payoff: 1.3. − 1 m = 0.3 m JPY
Car dealer's payoff: 1 m – 0.7 m = 0.3 m JPY
Contract surplus (total payoff): 0.6 m JPY
[At 1.4 million JPY]
Buyer's payoff: 1.3 m − 1 m = 0.3 m JPY
Car dealer's payoff: 1 m − 1.3 m = − 0.3 m JPY
Contract surplus (total payoff): 0 JPY.

When the purchase cost is 1.4 million JPY, the total contract surplus for both parties is greater when the remedy is expectation damages than when it is specific performance. This result is the same as that under a complete contract. Although the seller's payoff is negative, it is still greater than when specific performance is requested. That is, the remedy of expectation damages is more advantageous to the seller. Furthermore, at least in this case, compensation for expectation interests (expectation damages) is a more socially desirable (i.e., more efficient) remedy for a contract violation than specific performance is based on the contract surplus.

7.4.2.4 Compensation for Damages When the Court Cannot Make an Accurate Judgement

To this point, we have examined cases based on the assumption that a system with complete information allows the court to accurately observe the buyer's expectation interests and reflect them as compensation. Now, we investigate the potential outcomes in a system with incomplete information, which makes it impossible for the court to accurately determine the buyer's expectation interests. We now assume that judges have limited abilities to accurately assess buyers' expectation interests. We suppose that the vehicle's market price is 1.5 million JPY. We consider the scenario in which that market price (i.e., 1.5 million JPY) is used as a proxy for the buyer's true expectation interests because the judge cannot observe the buyer's expectation interests directly.

When the seller compares the vehicle's purchase cost of 1.4 million JPY with the 1.5 million JPY that she would have to pay the buyer if she fails to deliver the vehicle, the seller logically chooses to purchase the vehicle and carry out the contract. When the purchase cost is 0.7 million JPY, the seller similarly compares the purchase cost to the 1.5 million JPY that she would have to pay to the vehicle buyer if she fails to deliver the vehicle and again chooses to carry out the contract.

As a result, the contract is carried out regardless of the purchase cost, as in the previous case when specific performance is the remedy. Again, each party's payoffs and the contract surpluses are as follows.

[At 0.7 million JPY]
Buyer's payoff: 1.3 m − 1 m = 0.3 m JPY
Car dealer's payoff: 1 m – 0.7 m = 0.3 m JPY
Contract surplus (total payoff): 0.6 m JPY
[At 1.4 million JPY]
Buyer's payoff: 1.3 m − 1 m = 0.3 m JPY
Car dealer's payoff: 1 m − 1.4 m = − 0.4 m JPY
Contract surplus (total payoff): −0.1 m JPY.

This analysis shows that if the amount of compensation is too high, the contract is "over-executed," that is, it is carried out even if it would be more efficient not to execute it.

7.4.2.5 Inaccurate Expectation Damages and Obligations to Mitigate Damages

Next, suppose that the expectation interests are still calculated inaccurately and that the buyer has an obligation to mitigate damages, as in Sect. 7.3.4. We set the following additional conditions for this particular analysis.

Suppose that another dealer sells the same vehicle for 1.35 million JPY. Because of the obligation to mitigate damages, the buyer must purchase the vehicle from this other dealer when the original seller cannot carry out the contract. If the buyer chooses to not purchase a substitute vehicle, the amount of damages is reduced to 1.35 million JPY. In either case, the damages are only 1.35 million JPY.

The seller compares the vehicle's purchase cost of 1.4 million JPY with the 1.35 million JPY that she must pay the vehicle buyer if she fails to deliver the vehicle to the buyer and logically chooses the latter option. In other words, the seller violates the contract and pays 1.35 million JPY to the buyer.

If the buyer purchases the vehicle from the other dealer, he receives a benefit of 1.3 million JPY. However, the compensation if he does not purchase a vehicle is 1.35 million JPY. Comparing these benefits, the buyer chooses to not buy the vehicle and receive damages. In this example, the buyer does not purchase a substitute. However, if the price of the substitute were lower than the buyer's expectation interests (e.g., 1.25 million JPY versus 1.3 million JPY in this example), then the buyer would purchase the substitute.

When the vehicle's purchase cost is 0.7 million JPY, the seller compares it with the 1.35 million JPY that she will have to pay the buyer if she fails to deliver the vehicle and logically chooses the option with the lower cost. Thus, in this case, the seller chooses to carry out the contract. The parties' payoffs and the surplus from this particular contract are as follows.

[At 0.7 million JPY]
Buyer's payoff: 1.3 m − 1 m = 0.3 m JPY
Car dealer's payoff: 1 m – 0.7 m = 0.3 m JPY
Contract surplus (total payoff): 0.6 m JPY
[At 1.4 million JPY]
Buyer's payoff: 1.35 m − 1 m = 0.35 m JPY
Car dealer's payoff: 1 m − 1.35 m = −0.35 m JPY
Contract surplus (total payoff): 0 JPY.

When the dealer's cost is 1.4 million JPY, the contract surplus is greater than when information on compensation damages is incomplete or when specific performance is requested. A policy implication of this analysis is that if the court cannot accurately assess the buyer's expectation interests, then it can be more efficient for the court to impose the obligation to mitigate damages on the buyer. In other words, the obligation to mitigate damages is a supplementary measure that can be used when information on expectation interests is incomplete.

7.4.3 *Example 2: The Painting Contract*

Next, we analyze the previous example of a contract for a painting that has no substitutes available for purchase in the market. This example focuses on seller A, buyer B, and a (potential) second buyer referred to as C. Recall that A owns a painting that costs 0.8 million JPY and previously concluded a contract for the painting with B, who values the painting very highly. Now, for the purpose of this analysis, we consider two scenarios, one in which B values the painting at 1.6 million JPY and another in which B values the painting at 2.2 million JPY. C plans on reselling the painting for 2 million JPY. In other words, C values the painting at 2 million JPY. Finally, we assume that the painting has an appraised value of 1.7 million JPY in the market.

We now consider the timeline of the contract. First, A and B conclude a sales contract for the painting in question, and B pays 1 million JPY for the painting. Then, C may appear and ask to purchase the painting from A for 1.8 million JPY. Now, A has two choices; she can either carry out the contract and sell the painting to B or violate the contract and sell the painting to C. If the contract is violated, B will go to trial, and the court will provide a remedy (i.e., a claim for specific performance or compensation damages for expectation interests). The remedies are not an issue if C is not involved or if the contract is carried out.

7.4.3.1 Complete Contract

As before, we first analyze this example under a complete contract. The contents of the contract differ depending on whether B considers the painting to be worth 2.2

million JPY or 1.6 million JPY. In the former case, when C tries to buy the painting that B values at 2.2 million JPY, it makes more sense for A to sell the painting to B, as C values the painting at only 2 million JPY. Thus, when B values the painting at 2.2 million JPY, the parties can conclude the following complete contract.

A delivers the painting to B (regardless of whether C is involved).
Under this contract, each party's payoff is:
Seller A's payoff: 1 m – 0.8 m = 0.2 m JPY
Buyer's B's payoff: 2.2 m − 1 m = 1.2 m JPY
Contract surplus: 1.4 m JPY
Buyer C's payoff: 0 JPY.

Note that if the painting is sold to C when B values the painting at 2.2 million JPY, the contract surplus is 1 million JPY, which is less than the aforementioned 1.4 million JPY even if we include C's payoff.

Next, we investigate a scenario with a complete contract when B values the painting at 1.6 million JPY. In this case, because C values the painting more highly than B does, the contract surplus is larger if A sells the painting to C when C tries to purchase it. In this case, a complete contract can be written as follows, for example.

A delivers the painting to B if C does not appear.
A delivers the painting to C if he does appear.
A pays B 0.7 m JPY in addition to a refund of 1 m JPY.

The 0.7 million JPY is a substantial change in the cost of the painting in the likely event that the painting is sold to C. We can see that this change improves both A's and B's situations. Under this contract, if C appears to buy the painting, the payoffs for A and B and the total contract surplus are as follows.

Seller A's payoff: 1 m – 0.8 m + 1.8 m − 1 m – 0.7 m = 0.3 m JPY
Buyer B's payoff: −1 m + 1 m + 0.7 m = 0.7 m JPY
Contract surplus: 1 m JPY

Under this complete contract, selling the painting to C yields greater profits for A and B than not selling it to C does.

Depending on B's valuation of the painting, we may consider a remedy such that the incomplete contract may approach the ideal complete contract scenario. Because the seller's behavior may change depending on the remedy, we particularly focus on the seller's decision. One may wonder why the contract surplus does not include C's payoff. When we consider the situation in conjunction with the analysis in which B values the painting at 2.2 million JPY, we can see that maximizing the total payoffs of A and B and maximizing the total payoffs of all parties including C are two sides of the same coin. In other words, the payoffs for all parties increase when the payoffs of both A and B increase, and we need only focus on the contract surplus. In other words, using the contract surplus as a criterion for policy evaluation leads to the maximization of profits, including those of third parties. In the following analyses, we perform policy evaluations based on the contract surplus, as before.

7.4.3.2 Incomplete Contract (With Specific Performance as a Remedy)

In the following analyses, we consider the effects of various remedies on the surplus in the case of an incomplete contract, as we did in the discussion of Example 1. First, we consider the case in which the right to request specific performance is granted as a remedy.[1] Under this system, the seller, who anticipates this remedy, carries out the contract rather than violating it. The seller therefore always reliably carries out the contract, and B always receives the painting. C does not receive the painting. Thus, the payoffs of A, B, and C and the contract surplus (i.e., the sum of A's and B's payoffs) for valuations of 1.6 million JPY and 2.2 million JPY are as follows.

A's payoff: 1 m – 0.8 m = 0.2 m JPY
B's payoff (when the painting is valued at 1.6 m JPY): 1.6 m – 1 m = 0.6 m JPY
B's payoff (when the painting is valued at 2.2 m JPY): 2.2 m – 1 m = 1.2 m JPY
C's payoff: 0 JPY
Contract surplus (when the painting is valued at 1.6 m JPY): 0.8 m JPY
Contract surplus (when the painting is valued at 2.2 m JPY): 1.4 m JPY.

These results show that when B values the painting at 2.2 million JPY, the right to request specific performance yields the same surplus as a complete contract does. However, when B values the painting at 1.6 million JPY, the contract surplus is less than that under a complete contract.

7.4.3.3 Incomplete Contract (with Compensation for the Expectation Interest as the Remedy)

In this scenario, we first examine the case in which B values the painting at 1.6 million JPY and then examine the case in which he values the painting at 2.2 million JPY. When B considers the painting to be worth 1.6 million JPY, the compensation for the expectation interest is 1.6 million JPY. The seller's cost of carrying out the contract is 0.8 million JPY. The actual cost of a breach when C appears is 0.8 m + 1.6 m – 1.8 m = 0.6 m JPY because C's payment of 1.8 million JPY can be subtracted from the total purchase and compensation costs. Thus, A's payoff in the event of a breach is 1 m – 0.6 m = 0.4 m JPY. Conversely, the seller stands to gain 1 m – 0.8 m = 0.2 m JPY if she chooses to carry out the contract. Comparing the two options, the seller logically chooses the former. That is, if C appears, the seller violates the contract and delivers the painting to C.

[When C does not appear]
A's payoff: 1 m – 0.8 m = 0.2 m JPY
B's payoff (when the painting is valued at 1.6 m JPY): 1.6 m – 1 m = 0.6 m JPY
C's payoff: 0 JPY

[1] In Japanese law, if the painting is transferred to C and cannot be reclaimed, damages become the remedy for the breach owing to the impossibility of performance (see also Sect. 7.2.1). The analysis of this case is the same as that of compensation for the expectation interest.

Contract surplus (when the painting is valued at 1.6 m JPY): 0.8 m JPY
[When C appears]
A's payoff: 1 m – 0.6 m = 0.4 m JPY
B's payoff (when the painting is valued at 1.6 m JPY): 1.6 m – 1 m = 0.6 m JPY
C's payoff: 2 m – 1.8 m = 0.2 m JPY
Contract surplus: 1 m JPY.

In this scenario, A always reliably carries out the contract and B always reliably receives the painting if C does not appear. Thus, we focus on the potential outcomes when C does appear. If C appears, the total payoff is greater in this case than if specific performance is requested. Note that this result is true even if C's payoff is excluded from the total surplus.

Next, suppose that B values the painting at 2.2 million JPY. The compensation for the expectation interest is therefore 2.2 million JPY. If C appears, the seller's actual default cost for violating the contract is 0.8 m + 2.2 m – 1.8 m = 1.2 m JPY. Thus, the payoff in the event of a default is 1 m – 1.2 m = −0.2 m JPY, which is lower than the payoff if specific performance is requested (1 m – 0.8 m = 0.2 m JPY). Thus, the seller always carries out the contract in this case. As a result, when C appears, the payoff of each party and the contract surplus are as follows.

[When C appears]
Seller A's payoff: 1 m – 0.8 m = 0.2 m JPY
Buyer B's payoff (when the painting is valued at 2.2 m JPY): 2.2 m – 1 m = 1.2 m JPY
Buyer C's payoff: 0 JPY
Contract surplus: 1.4 m JPY.

This result also holds when specific performance is requested.

7.4.3.4 Inaccurate Expectation Interests as the Remedy

Until now, we have examined scenarios under the assumption that the court can accurately observe expectation interests. In practice, expectation interests are personal information and, thus, it is unnatural to assume that they can be known by other people. Thus, in this section, we assume that the court cannot observe expectation interests and can only evaluate them based on appraised values from the market. In this case, the damages are 1.7 million JPY. Again, as before, we first examine the case in which B considers the painting to be worth 1.6 million JPY and then consider the case in which he considers the painting to be worth 2.2 million JPY.

First, when B values the painting at 1.6 million JPY, the actual cost that A must pay for violating the contract if C appears is 0.8 m + 1.7 m – 1.8 m = 0.7 m JPY. A's cost of carrying out the contract is 0.8 m JPY. Thus, A stands to receive 1 m – 0.7 m = 0.3 m JPY if she violates the contract and 1 m – 0.8 m = 0.2 m JPY if she carries out the contract. As such, if C appears, A logically chooses to violate the contract.

[When C appears]

A's payoff: 1 m – 0.7 m = 0.3 m JPY
B's payoff (when the painting is valued at 1.6 m JPY): 1.7 m – 1 m = 0.7 m JPY
C's payoff: 2 m – 1.8 m = 0.2 m JPY
Contract surplus: 1 m JPY.

When C appears, the result is the same as that yielded by an accurate assessment of compensation for expectation interests and is more desirable than that when specific performance is requested.

Next, when B values the painting at 2.2 million JPY, A's cost of violating the contract when C appears is 0.8 m + 1.7 m – 1.8 m = 0.7 m JPY. Thus, A chooses to violate the contract when C appears, as in the previous case. This result is different from that when expectation interests can be accurately assessed.

This result is inferior those when compensation for expectation interests is accurate and when specific performance is requested.

As remedies for contract breaches, expectation damages are preferable to specific performance requests if the court can correctly evaluate the expectation interests. In an imperfect system that uses a market price (in this case, an appraised value) as a proxy variable for an individual's expectation interests, expectation interests may or may not be preferable to specific performance requests if a contract is breached. As this example shows, when the actual interests are greater than those evaluated by the court (e.g., when the buyer values the painting at 2.2 million JPY), a request for specific performance is a more desirable remedy.

If B values the painting very highly, then a specific performance request is very likely to be an efficient remedy. In such cases, the buyer can choose specific performance as a remedy under English law. Thus, in terms of efficiency, English and Japanese law are equal.

7.5 Conclusion

This chapter examined legal remedies for breaches of contract based on Japanese and English contract law and verified their legal (Sect. 7.2) and specific validity (Sect. 7.3) using actual numerical values in various examples. We also analyzed these examples based on three perspectives using numerical analyses from traditional economics (Sect. 7.4).

English law's obligations to carry out alternative transactions based on the obligation to mitigate damages seem to provide some benefits in terms of economic efficiency. However, it is not always ideal to determine the validity of legal obligations using only their efficiency. The law is also important as a code of conduct for people in society. In that sense, the law must embody justice, and unless individual rules are compatible with people's natural sense of justice, the law will not be able to exercise enough power to provide discipline. Thus, it seems to be a serious problem for the law to encourage people to violate contracts if they can promote their interests by doing so.

However, given that the interests generated from contracts are the fundamental reason that people form contracts in the first place, it is only natural for people to want to protect themselves from contracts that would later bring them harm. As such, it is impossible to completely prevent people from doing so, and it may not always be ideal. A country's system of legal remedies operates upon a complex but subtle balance of interests. As such, it is difficult—if not impossible—to determine whether Japanese or English law is superior.

In Sect. 7.3, we examined the desirability of different remedies using numerical examples. This method examines the validity of Japanese and English law by applying them to examples with set numerical values, and lawyers often use such methods. The results of these methods, however, are still far from actual outcomes in practice. These discussions do not take into account legal costs and the psychological burdens that come with such lawsuits. In the real world, however, these are heavy burdens that the involved parties must consider. Thus, even with these analyses, we cannot view a complete picture of legal disputes. Nevertheless, these methods may still be used in theoretical legal studies because simple and clear logic must be presented when considering legal norms. In this sense, it is clear that the legal system itself simplifies and formalizes information differently from economics. In essence, Sect. 7.3 shows that contract law attempts to interpret the legal affirmation of the obligation to make an alternative transaction to face and adapt to the market economy. We have seen with some clarity that the type of value judgment made by economics is also operating within contract law.

Nevertheless, we need to recognize that law and economics are different. Complete contracts are the ideal form of contracts, and Sect. 7.4 tries to bring reality closer to that ideal from an economics perspective. In contrast, Sect. 7.3 assumes that real-world actors have only limited rationality and attempts to verify from a legal perspective whether the alternative trading obligations that have been created empirically in English contract law can be justified for products traded on the market. In addition, economic analysis is based on the premise that efficiency depends on the involved parties' valuation of a product. However, if a market price has actually been established for a product, that product can be obtained by paying the market price. As such, an individual's subjective valuation of an object may not be as important when considering remedies. An individual only buys an object if his or her valuation of the object is greater than its market price. Thus, the notion of alternative trading obligations seems persuasive as a legal system that can leverage the market's ability to provide alternatives.

Insofar as deepening understanding is concerned, there seems to be a rich potential in examining the socioeconomic phenomenon of contracts from different perspectives and comparing the results, even if these results do not lead to clear conclusions.

Study Questions

1. Explain the similarities and differences between the legal and traditional economic approaches to breaches of contract.

2. Compare the positions of both Japanese and English law on breaches of contract. Which do you think is preferable? Include the advantages and disadvantages of each position with your opinion.
3. Assuming that a competitive market exists, discuss whether the duty to mitigate damages, which imposes a duty to purchase substitute goods on a party who suffers damages owing to a contract's non-performance, is incompatible with Japanese contract law.

References

Campbell D (2007) Keiyaku ihan no kankeiteki keiyakuron ni yoru saikōsei: keiyaku ihan seido no daini genri to shite no kyōryoku no igi (Reconstructing breach of contract with relational contract theory: the meaning of cooperation as second principle of the breach of contract system). In: Saito A (ed) Ichiba to tekiō (Market and adaptation). Horitsu Bunka Sha. Kyoto, pp 38–55 [publication in Japanese]
Horwitz MJ (1977) The transformation of American law, 1780–1860. Harvard University Press, Cambridge
Uchida T (1990) Kyōsei shikkō to songai baishō: "songai keigen gimu" no kanten kara (Compulsory execution and compensation for damages: from the perspective of the "duty to mitigate damages"). Hōsō Jiho 42(10):1–29 [publication in Japanese]

Chapter 8
The Meaning of Compensating Damages: Tort Law

Takayuki Furutani and Shinjiro Miyazawa

Contents

8.1 Introduction 186
8.1.1 What is Tort Law? 186
8.1.2 This Chapter's Objective 186
8.2 Summary of the Tort System 187
8.3 Legal and Economic Perspectives on Tort Law 189
8.3.1 Legal Perspectives 189
8.3.2 Perspective of Economics 192
8.3.3 Legal and Economic Perspectives 197
8.4 Principle of Negligence Liability 198
8.4.1 What is Negligence? 199
8.4.2 Why is Liability for Negligence a Principle? 200
8.5 Conclusion 204
Appendix: Optimal Deterrence in the Case of Bilateral Precaution 205
References 208

In law, when an individual case is under dispute, the key question to consider is how to resolve the case. In this situation, the interpretation of the purpose of tort law is actively debated using judicial precedents and theories. Traditionally, the purpose of tort law is thought to be the pursuit of its endemic function, that is, providing remedies for the victim (i.e., compensation for damages).

Conversely, in the study of economics, the main issues are the functions of tort law and ways to evaluate each of those functions. Moreover, rather than prioritizing the functional purpose of providing remedies for the victim (i.e., compensation for

T. Furutani
Faculty of Law, Kyoto Sangyo University, Motoyama, Kamigamo, Kita-ku, 603-8555 Kyoto, Japan
e-mail: tfurutani@cc.kyoto-su.ac.jp

S. Miyazawa (✉)
Faculty of Business Administration, Hosei University, 2-17-1 Fujimi, Chiyoda-ku, 102-8160 Tokyo, Japan
e-mail: miyazawa@hosei.ac.jp

T. Yanagawa et al. (eds.), *Econo-Legal Studies*,
https://doi.org/10.1007/978-981-16-5145-8_8

damages), economics prioritizes deterrence of the wrongful act, a function that is considered to be absolutely desirable above all else.

Although the basic perspectives of law and economics on tort law differ in this manner, the basic notion that in principle, the rules of negligence liability apply and, in exceptional cases, the rules of strict liability may apply, which has been established through legal discussions and debate, can be justified (through consideration of tort law's functions) from an economics perspective as well.

8.1 Introduction

8.1.1 What is Tort Law?

During the course of people's lives, countless accidents occur on a daily basis, generating various types of damages as a result. For example, a pedestrian may be hit by a car, a car may be damaged in an accident, or playground equipment in a park or school may break, injuring a child. In addition to these tangible types of damages involving a person's life, body, or property, intangible types of damage may occur as well. Examples include actions that damage a person's honor or invade a person's privacy, resulting in a loss in social standing or a disturbance in a person's life. In these cases, tort law helps to determine who is responsible for the damage caused to a victim in what situations and to what extent.

8.1.2 This Chapter's Objective

Although we are discussing tort law, there is not necessarily a specific law with that name. Many laws exist to compensate victims for damages that they have incurred, and the term "tort law" refers to the aggregation of all of such individual laws. In general, however, when we refer to tort law, we specifically mean the group of provisions (Arts. 709 to 724-2 of the Civil Code) regarding torts under the Civil Code, Part III, Chapter V. In this chapter, we examine Article 709 of the Civil Code (a general provision regarding tort law) to understand how it operates in real-world situations, and we consider and observe this rule from the perspectives of both law and economics.

Column 12. The position of tort law within civil law

Part III of the Civil Code provides for "claims." A claim is a right that allows a person to demand a certain action from another specific person. The causes of claims are divided into contracts (Chapter II) and other causes (Chapters III

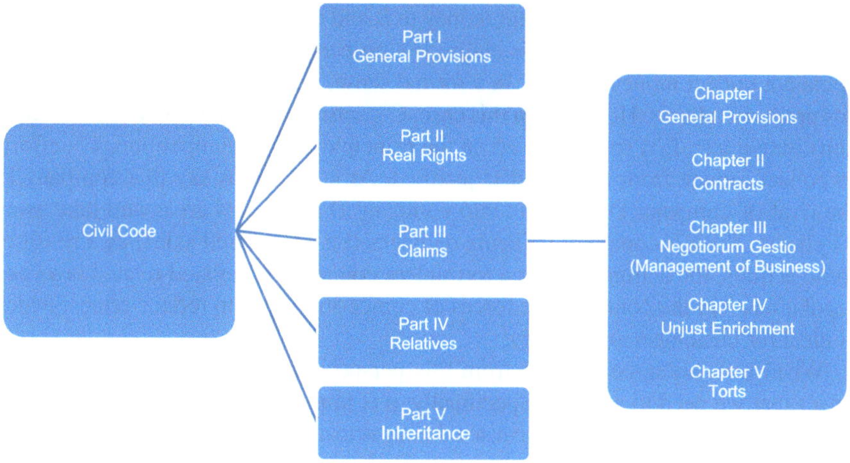

Fig. 8.1 The system of the Japanese Civil Code

to V), and torts are positioned within civil law as one of the causes of claims other than contracts (Chapter V), as Fig. 8.1 shows.

8.2 Summary of the Tort System

Tort law is a system in which a person (i.e., the victim) can seek compensation from another person (i.e., the perpetrator) for damages incurred as a result of the latter person's actions. It is necessary to keep in mind, however, that tort law is not a system for restituting a victim's damages under any circumstances. We begin by explaining this point in more detail.

For example, it is possible that although a person's actions caused damages to someone, it was inevitable that those damages would occur no matter how careful that person was. In such cases, the Civil Code, in principle, does not order the person who committed the wrongful act to compensate the victim for the damages. This lack of compensation may be highly disturbing for the victim who incurred the damages. However, if people were held liable in any situation in which they caused any damage to another person, then they would hesitate before taking any action and they would not be able to lead a smooth social life. To strike a balance between the two important values of remedies for victims and freedom of action, the law holds a perpetrator liable for an action only when the action amounts to social blame.

Furthermore, in certain cases, a victim may be expected to cover some damages caused by another person's actions. For example, assume that A lent money to B and wants to get it back, but C also lent money to B and collected money from B's assets first. Because C collected on this claim, B's property is now gone and, as a result, A cannot collect money from B. In a formal sense, one can say that C infringed on A's property (claim). However, in this case, C's actions are not usually considered to constitute a tort. In a society based on the principle of free competition, C's efforts to collect money from B are rather justified. As such, let us say that company E, the rival of company D, expands into company D's business areas and take away its clients. Even if company D incurs damages (i.e., decreased sales) as a result of these actions, the actions are not a tort unless company E violated related laws and regulations. On the contrary, the forces of competition tend to reduce prices, which is ideal for customers and society.

When tort law is considered from this perspective, a highly challenging issue arises that we need to address. Specifically, it is important to determine under what circumstances a person who has caused damages to a victim can be held legally liable for compensating those damages in a tort. A criterion for understanding this issue is Article 709 of the Civil Code, which states:

> A person that has intentionally or negligently infringed the rights or legally protected interests of another person is liable to compensate for damage resulting in consequence.

As a single reading shows, Article 709 is a very simple provision. In practice, however, this provision covers many tort issues that occur daily, and it is one of the most frequently used articles in the Civil Code.

This provision sets the ground for claims of compensation for damages. Moreover, it sets out the types of situations in which the perpetrator is liable to compensate for damages. We can clarify the content of this provision by examining the definition of each phrase.

First, for damages to be awarded based on a tort, the victim's rights or legally protected interests must be infringed. Rights include the rights to life, body, health, and property as well as other rights set out by the law. Legally protected interests are broader in interpretation than rights and refer to interests that should be protected legally. However, the scopes of these terms are not always clear. Some matters are already recognized by law, and the court also newly establishes rights and legally protected interests in some cases. These concepts are expected to change with the times. For example, the right to determine one's own way of being in society (i.e., the right of self-determination) is increasingly widely recognized as individuality in society is becoming more respected. New rights, such as privacy rights and environmental rights, are being recognized in similar ways. By creating and expanding rights and legally protected interests, tort law is required to protect victims within an appropriate scope.

Next, the perpetrator's actions must be performed intentionally or negligently. "Intentional" and "negligent" colloquially mean "on purpose" and "careless," respectively, but the legal definitions of these terms are slightly stricter. We describe this point in more detail later on. Here, we confirm that the Civil Code is based on the principle of negligence liability. As the phrase "no liability without negligence" shows, unless the perpetrator acted with negligence (i.e., carelessness), it is not possible to hold the perpetrator liable for compensation for damages.

Third, the victim must incur some kind of damage. Even when rights are infringed, if no "damage" has been incurred, tort law provides no protection. In this context, damage includes damages against life, body, or property (i.e., proprietary damages) and intangible damages, such as mental anguish (i.e., non-proprietary damages). Non-proprietary damages are evaluated monetarily in the form of consolation money.

Finally, the wrongful act and the damages must have a causal relationship. The phrase "resulting in consequence" in Article 709 indicates that a legal relevance between the wrongful act and the damages needs to be established. Consider the following case as an example. A driver of a car carelessly causes an accident involving a company worker, F. As a result, F loses a vital business opportunity, causing enormous damage to the company. In this case, the company incurs damages because of the driver's actions. In other words, the accident and the damages to the company have a genuine causal relationship. However, holding the perpetrator liable for the damages to the company would be too severe. Thus, one perspective is that the perpetrator is liable for compensation to the extent that protection is needed according to the law. A causal relationship is necessary within the limited scope of legal relevance. Thus, in the above case, the perpetrator is only liable to provide compensation for the treatment and medical fees that F pays at the hospital, F's mental anguish, and similar damages.

An understanding of these four essential points can help to determine who is liable to what degree and in what situations from a legal perspective. In the following sections, we also present an approach from an economics perspectives and analyze the tort law system in terms of both law and economics.

8.3 Legal and Economic Perspectives on Tort Law

We now consider the legal and economic perspectives on the tort law that was explained in Sect. 8.2. In law, the main point of discussion is the purpose of the tort law system. In contrast, economics mainly considers the functions of tort laws and whether those functions are desirable. This section explains the underlying thinking behind each of these questions and the processes of reaching conclusions and then compares the two.

8.3.1 Legal Perspectives

8.3.1.1 Purpose of the Tort Law System

Why does tort law exist? In law, discussions on the purpose of the tort law system generally focus on remedies for victims (i.e., compensation for damages). Here, we introduce a Supreme Court judgment in 1997 that clearly stated this purpose. The issue in the case, called the *Mansei Kogyo* case, was the validity of a foreign judgment in Japan. Based on the Civil Code of California regarding punitive compensation for damages, the foreign judgment ordered the defendant to pay compensation. Punitive compensation for damages in a claim litigation for compensation for damages based on a tort means that if the perpetrator's actions amount to substantial blame, the court orders the perpetrator to pay compensation beyond the actual damages. Punitive damages are mainly recognized in Anglo-American law. Thus, the issue in this case was the validity of punitive damages in Japan.

***Mansei Kogyo*case (Supreme Court Judgement, July, 11, 1997, 51 Minshū 2573)**

The case can be summarized as follows. When a lease contract was concluded, a Japanese company (Mansei Kogyo) conducted a fraudulent practice against plaintiff X. Based on the Civil Code of California, Mansei Kogyo was ordered to pay not only the actual damages but also punitive compensation for damages of 1,125,000 USD. X filed suit in the Tokyo District Court to enforce this foreign judgment. The Tokyo District court, however, ruled in a February 18, 1991, judgment that the foreign judgment's order to pay massive punitive compensation for damages was counter to public order. Thus, it ruled against enforcing the judgement. In an appeal to the Tokyo High Court, the court upheld the verdict of the first hearing in a June 28, 1993, judgment and did not recognize the enforcement of this foreign judgment in Japan. X then appealed the case.

The Supreme Court made the following statement:

> It is evident that the system of punitive damages as provided by the Civil Code of the State of California (hereinafter, 'punitive damages') is designed to impose sanctions on the culprit and prevent similar acts in the future by ordering the culprit who had effected malicious acts to pay additional damages on top of the damages for the actual loss and, judging from the purposes, is similar to criminal sanctions such as fines in Japan. In contrast, the system of damages based upon tort in Japan assesses the actual loss in a pecuniary manner, forces the culprit to compensate this amount, and thus enables the recovery of the disadvantage suffered by the victim and restores the status quo ante (Judgment of the Supreme Court, 1988 (O) Case No.1749, Judgment of the Grand Bench, March 24, 1993, Minshū 47–4–3039), and is not intended for sanctions on the culprit or prevention of similar acts in the future, i.e. general prevention.

Then, the Supreme Court stated that it is not necessary to consider sanctions and the deterrence of torts as the purpose of the tort law system for the following reason:

> In Japan, sanctioning of the culprit and general deterrence is left to criminal or administrative sanctions. Thus, the system in which in tort cases, the victim is paid damages for the purpose of imposing sanction on the culprit and general deterrence in addition to damages for the actual loss should be regarded as against the basic principles or basic ideas of the system of compensation based upon tort in Japan.

The philosophy of strictly separating civil compensation for damages from criminal or administrative sanctions is called the theory of distinction between civil and criminal liability. This philosophy places the satisfaction of revenge and retaliation through sanctions under the state's jurisdiction (as punishments or administrative sanctions) and distills the central role of civil liability to just compensation for damages. In this way, the purpose of the tort law system is separated from deterrence and sanctions, and tort law is viewed as providing remedies for victims (i.e., compensation for damages). Of course, this perspective does not mean that paying compensation does not have a deterrent or sanctioning effect. However, when considering the primary purpose of the system, the basic idea of the distinction between civil and criminal liability is to prioritize remedies for victims (i.e., compensation for damages).

8.3.1.2 Characteristics of Legal Approaches

The characteristics of legal approaches are clear from the traditional notion of distinguishing between civil and criminal liability, which views compensation for damages as the central function of tort law and deterrence and sanctions as secondary functions. Thus, when legal disputes occur, the laws are applied and interpreted with the primary purpose of achieving an appropriate solution for each case.

We consider in more detail the court's process for applying and interpreting the law and making a final judgment in an ex post situation. First, the application of the law is the process of applying the legal norms that are related to the case. As stated in Sect. 8.2, when there is a legal dispute, the court applies legal norms (in this case, Article 709 of the Civil Code) to the case and examines, in turn, whether an infringement of rights or legally protected interests has occurred, whether the requirement of intention or negligence is recognized, whether damages have occurred, and whether a causal relationship exists. When all of these criteria are met, the court decides to hold the perpetrator liable to pay compensation for damages.

Of course, many cases cannot be solved merely by applying laws. For example, for a perpetrator's liability for compensation for damages to be recognized, the victim's rights or legally protected interests must have been infringed. In practice, however, it may not be clear whether the disadvantages incurred by victims can be categorized as infringements of rights or legally protected interests. Example of this uncertainty include whether the right to enjoy a good view (the right to a view) or the right to be free from the cigarette smoke of others (the right to live free from smoke) is covered under "rights" (or "legally protected interests") in Article 709. If a building is constructed in front of an apartment building at a height that blocks residents' views, have the apartment residents' rights (or legally protected interests) been infringed? Smoke from a cigarette may annoy non-smokers, but does it infringe upon non-smokers' rights (or legally protected interests)? When the rights are not yet established and therefore it is not clear whether or not the perpetrator is liable for damages, it is necessary to interpret and judge whether the rights in question (e.g., the right to a view or the right to live free from smoke) should be considered rights (or legally protected interests) under Article 709. This process is called "legal interpretation" (here, the interpretation of the wording of Article 709). When the court interprets the terms "rights" or "legally protected interests" broadly, rights and interests that were not conventionally protected under the law gradually start to be recognized. For example, the issue of workplace sexual harassment was simply dealt with as an uncomfortable feeling in the past. Now, however, there is almost a consensus that it should be dealt with in courts as a tort for personal rights infringement. This evolution is an example of the court's legal interpretation creating a new category of rights infringement. Thus, through the trial process, tort law also has the function of creating new categories of torts.

8.3.2 Perspective of Economics

8.3.2.1 Characteristics of an Economics Approach

Evaluating a particular law from the perspective of economics means considering how the system regulated by that law affects the actions of members of society and the consequences of these actions and evaluating these outcomes. Analyses of the former type are called positive analyses, and those of the latter type are called normative analyses.

Positive analysis does not just analyze the effects on parties involved in disputes during dispute resolutions. Usually, it also analyzes the effects on pre-dispute behaviors by anyone who may be involved in the dispute. The first perspective is called the ex post perspective, and the second perspective is called the ex ante perspective.

In a normative analysis, the criterion for a decision is the desirability of the possible options for all members of society. The indicator of the degree of this desirability is generally called social welfare. Social welfare can be thought of in many different ways, but people typically consider that unless other people's personal satisfaction changes, social welfare is greater when individuals are more satisfied. Here, we call the degree of personal satisfaction "utility." Note that the term "social surplus" (or "total surplus") may be used as an indicator of social welfare depending on the purpose or needs of an analysis.

Next, we review the functions of the tort law system before and after certain disputes occur and how they can be evaluated from a social welfare standpoint.

8.3.2.2 Evaluating Ex Post Functions: Remedies, Sanctions, and Income Redistribution

As discussed in Sect. 8.2, the tort law system is designed to require a perpetrator to compensate a victim based on the value of the damages incurred by the victim to resolve a dispute if the case meets certain requirements. In this discussion, to simplify the explanation, we assume that the requirements set by Article 709 have been essentially fulfilled. We investigate the requirement of intention or negligence in somewhat more detail in Sect. 8.4.

This compensation mechanism can be divided into two aspects: the aspect of the victim receiving a payment and the aspect of the perpetrator making a payment.

As explained below, these two aspects of this mechanism actually have different functions. The aspect of the victim receiving a payment serves to compensate for damages and provide a remedy for the victim. By receiving this payment, the victim can recover from the utility reduction caused by the damages. For example, a victim of a traffic accident can collect the money spent to receive medical treatment and can be compensated for the lost salary caused by time in the hospital and doctor visits. Through these payments, the lost utility as a result of the accident can be recovered. Thus, a function of tort law is providing remedies for victims (i.e., compensation for damages).

Conversely, the aspect of the perpetrator making a payment serves to impose sanctions against a perpetrator regardless of the legal discussions. Making a payment decreases the perpetrator's utility by reducing his or her assets. Thus, it can be said that another function of tort law is imposing sanctions against perpetrators. The Supreme Court decision described earlier in this chapter seems to have stated that tort law has such a function only when punitive damages are applied. However, as we explain here, tort law can still have this function even when the standard compensation for damages is applied.

Remedies for victims have the effect of increasing victims' utilities, and they improve social welfare in that sense. However, the function of sanctioning perpetrators lowers perpetrator' utilities, decreasing social welfare. Thus, it is necessary to investigate in more detail whether tort law improves social welfare overall.

The tort law system, which requires a perpetrator to pay for the appraised damages incurred by a victim, has the overall function of decreasing the perpetrator's assets and simultaneously increasing the victim's assets. Thus, it simultaneously reduces the perpetrator's utility and improves the victim's utility. The tort law system can therefore be said to have an income redistribution function. This function has almost no effect on total social welfare if the perpetrator and the victim initially have similar amounts of assets and the amount of compensation is small relative to both parties' assets. The only change is that a high utility subject is replaced with a low utility subject. However, if one side has fewer assets than the other or if the compensation amount is large relative to both parties' assets, then the impact on social welfare may be significant. Usually, a person who owns fewer assets experiences a more significant utility improvement from an asset increase, and reducing inequality in assets translates into higher social welfare. Thus, if the victim has fewer assets, then tort law's income redistribution function can improve social welfare. However, if the perpetrator has fewer assets, then the income redistribution function may reduce social welfare. Because either the perpetrator or the victim may have more assets, it is possible to conclude that tort law's income redistribution function can either improve or reduce social welfare depending on the circumstances; in other words, the effect is indeterminate.

Tort law's function of sanctioning perpetrators may also serve to improve social welfare. When a person dies or become severely disabled owing to pollution, a medical injury, or a traffic accident, the victim and those related to the victim often have the desire to punish the perpetrator (i.e., the desire for revenge and retaliation). In these cases, fulfilling these desires improves these people's utility. In such cases, the function of sanctioning the perpetrator reduces the perpetrator's utility, thereby reducing social welfare, as mentioned before. However, it has the conflicting effect of improving social welfare by improving the utilities of the victim and the victim's relatives. Thus, it is again not clear whether this function improves overall social welfare.

8.3.2.3 Evaluating Ex Ante Functions: Deterrence and Risk Allocation

The tort law system's function is not only to resolve disputes ex post but also to influence decision-making of those who may be a perpetrator (i.e., a potential perpetrator) and those who may be a victim (i.e., a potential victim) before an incident occurs. For example, sanctioning a perpetrator may cause a potential perpetrator to rethink taking a wrongful action or be more careful to prevent a wrongful act. This effect is called the "wrongful act deterrence function." This function works even when punitive compensation for damages is not applied, as previously explained in the case of the function of sanctioning the perpetrator.

We consider this function in more detail using an economics approach. Typically, an economics perspective considers that people make decisions regarding their actions to maximize their utilities. If a potential perpetrator determines that conducting a wrongful act will increase his or her utility, then the perpetrator will decide to conduct the tort. Otherwise, the perpetrator will decide not to carry out the wrongful act. Furthermore, a perpetrator will only take care to prevent a wrongful act if doing so ultimately improves his or her utility; otherwise, the perpetrator will not try to prevent the act. When a wrongful act is committed to fulfill specific interests, not committing the act means forgoing an improvement in utility. Not taking care to avoid wrongful acts is less tiring and allows a potential perpetrator to focus on more enjoyable matters; thus, taking care to avoid wrongful acts also reduces utility. A potential perpetrator therefore chooses to commit wrongful acts or to not take care to avoid wrongful acts unless the adverse effects (or costs) cancel out the positive effects (or benefits).

Tort law provides the benefit that not conducting a wrongful act or taking care to deter wrongful acts allows a person to avoid utility reductions caused by having to pay compensation for damages. If this benefit exceeds the costs explained above, then a potential perpetrator chooses to not commit wrongful acts and chooses to take care to avoid wrongful acts. As a result, wrongful acts are prevented from occurring. For this reason, tort law has the function of deterring wrongful acts.

This function can be evaluated by investigating its impact on social welfare ex ante. We use the following hypothetical situation to explain the essence of the discussion clearly. This explanation is a prerequisite for understanding the explanations of negligence in Sect. 8.4, so please pay close attention when reading this discussion. In this example, potential perpetrator decides whether to take care. If the perpetrator takes care, no wrongful act ever occurs, and if the perpetrator does not take care, a wrongful act always occurs. Additionally, we define the utilities of potential perpetrators and victims as constant values from which the effective cost burden is subtracted. In addition, we determine social welfare by the social surplus, or the sum of the utilities of both parties.

In this hypothetical situation, we first check what results are desirable for society. When the utilities of the involved parties and the social welfare are determined as described above, the social welfare can be calculated by subtracting the social cost, or the sum of each involved party's effective cost burden, from a constant value. Additionally, if the potential perpetrator chooses to take care, then the social cost is the cost of taking care. If the potential perpetrator does not take care, then the social cost is the amount of damages. Thus, from a social welfare perspective, it is ideal to take care when the cost of taking care is less than the potential damages; otherwise, it is ideal not to take care. Thus, deterrence is preferable in the first case and not in the second case.

Next, we explain the results that actually occur. A potential perpetrator makes decisions to maximize his or her utility without considering whether the consequences of those decisions are desirable for society. In the current situation, because the perpetrator pays compensation for any damages caused to the victim, he or she either incurs the cost of taking care or chooses not to take care and pays the amount of damages. Thus, if the cost of taking care is less than the amount of damages, the perpetrator choses to take care. Otherwise, the perpetrator chooses not to take care.

The above discussion implies that tort law's function of deterring a wrongful act is desirable from a social welfare perspective. This implication is because when a potential perpetrator takes care and a wrongful act is deterred, social welfare improves. Additionally, this discussion shows that the tort law system does not always prevent wrongful acts. When the amount of damages is less than the cost of taking care, the potential perpetrator does not take care, and a wrongful act occurs. As stated before, however, this result is desirable from a social welfare perspective. Taking this fact into consideration, the function of deterring wrongful acts should be called "the function of optimally deterring wrongful acts."

Finally, we check the mechanism of how this function works. The social cost of taking care is the individual cost of taking care. This cost is incurred by a potential perpetrator. Conversely, the social benefit of taking care is the prevention of damages. This benefit, however, is enjoyed not by the potential perpetrator but rather by the potential victim. Potential perpetrators will not consider any benefits that they do not personally enjoy (i.e., benefits that others receive in the case of external economies, called external benefits) when making decisions. Thus, in the absence of tort law, perpetrators will choose not to take care even when it is socially desirable to do so. In these situations, tort law works to change an external benefit into a personal benefit for a potential perpetrator, that is, the ability to avoid paying compensation for damages. Such changes are generally called the "internalization of external benefits." By internalizing an external benefit, as in the above example, potential perpetrators both incur the social costs and receive the social benefits of taking care. As a result, the social benefit of taking care begins to match the potential perpetrator's benefit of taking care, and the perpetrator's decision on whether to take care becomes socially desirable (see Sect. 6 of the Appendix for details on externalities).

Notably, this explanation omits the possibility that the occurrence of the wrongful act may be uncertain and the fact that a person can take care to different degrees. Even when considering these possibilities, however, the same conclusions apply. We briefly explain this result in Sect. 8.4.

One additional point about the function of deterring wrongful acts is important to make. This point relates to the distinction between civil and criminal liability in Sect. 8.3.1. It is evident that criminal law has the function of deterring wrongful acts. However, this fact alone is not grounds to deny that tort law serves to deter wrongful acts, and this function is socially desirable.

Conversely, tort law may also affect a potential victim's ex ante decision-making based on the aspect that the victim receives compensation for damages. First, if in addition to a potential perpetrator taking care, a potential victim taking care can also affect whether damages occur, tort law also affects a potential victim's decision to take care. This effect has an important role when considering the significance of negligence, and, thus, we explain this point again in Sect. 8.4.

In other ways, tort law's function of providing remedies for victims can affect potential victims' decisions regarding the creation or maintenance of property. If the law restores a potential victim's property when a wrongful act damages it, then a potential victim will build property more assertively and try to maintain it more appropriately relative to the case in which no remedy is provided. As a result, social welfare improves. The content in Chap. 2 is also a useful reference for these effects.

As explained before, compensation for damages is an ex post system to shift the burden of damages caused by wrongful acts from victims to perpetrators. Here, considering a situation in which the occurrence of damages is uncertain from an ex ante perspective, compensation for damages can be seen as a system for transferring the risk of damages from potential victims to potential perpetrators. Thus, tort law can also be said to have a risk allocation function.

The existence and contents of risk affect the ex ante satisfaction levels (or expected utilities) of each subject, and the allocation of risk affects social welfare. This affect is because attitudes toward risk differ among subjects who could bear the burden of risk. If one subject strongly dislikes risks and the other subject does not care very much about (or even likes) risks, it is clear that having the latter subject take risks rather than the former subject improves social welfare (Sect. 2 of the Appendix provides more details on risk and risk preference). Thus, for example, if subjects with few assets tend to dislike risks more than subjects with more assets do, and if individuals dislike risks more than corporations do, then it is more desirable from a social welfare perspective to allocate risks to subjects with more assets rather than to subjects with few assets and to allocate risks to corporations rather than to individuals. Because the tort law system places the burden of risk on potential perpetrators, the risk allocation function improves social welfare if the potential perpetrators have more risk tolerance. However, social welfare decreases if the potential perpetrators are more risk averse. Because many different subjects can be either perpetrators or victims, it is not possible to make a general statement regarding whether potential perpetrators or potential victims are more risk averse. Thus, it is not clear if this function improves social welfare.

We also note two related discussion points regarding the risk allocation function. The first point is the relationship with the social security system (see Chap. 5 for more details on the social security system). Under a social security system in which the government uses tax (or social insurance) revenue as funds to provide payment to victims, the burden of risk is thinly and widely distributed across all taxpayers. On the contrary, in tort law, the burden of risk is placed solely on the perpetrator. If society is composed only of people who dislike risks, then the social security system's risk allocation is less likely to lower social welfare owing to risk than tort law's risk allocation is. Thus, from a risk allocation perspective, it would be more desirable for the social security system to provide remedies for victims than for tort law to do so. The second point is related to the existence of damage and liability insurance. When people anticipate the possibility of having to pay damages, they can prepare for the risk by joining an insurance plan. Potential victims can obtain damage insurance, and potential perpetrators can obtain liability insurance. When appropriate insurance is available, the risk is thinly and widely distributed among members, and the tort law system ceases to affect the risk allocation. Furthermore, the existence of insurance not only affects tort law's risk allocation functions but also affects its function of deterring wrongful acts. However, the explanation of this effect is beyond the scope of this book and is therefore omitted.

8.3.3 Legal and Economic Perspectives

Viewing tort law through the perspectives of law and economics leads to several conclusions. From a legal perspective, the critical aim is to determine the purpose of the tort law system. The answer is that the main purpose of tort law is to provide remedies to victims. In contrast, from an economics perspective, it is important to understand what functions tort law serves and whether each of these functions is desirable. The answer to this question is that the other conceivable functions of tort law each have their merits and demerits, but tort law's ability to deter wrongful acts is socially desirable. It is important to note here that this reasoning does not inherently lead to the conclusion that the purpose of tort law is to deter wrongful acts. Instead, it merely illustrates the differences in the subjects and themes discussed by law and economics, which naturally lead to contrasting conclusions.

In law, the issue of realistically applying the current system to individual and specific cases under dispute is unavoidable. In principle, law tries to derive a more universal understanding by examining the courts' solutions to this problem. A major key to this process is ways of comprehending the purpose of tort law. In law, people other than the two parties (the perpetrator and the victim) are basically excluded from consideration because any discussion starts from an individual and specific dispute. Furthermore, the law must resolve disputes in a way that is consistent with other existing laws (e.g., criminal law). As a result, the perspective of deterring wrongful acts, which is taken into account in criminal law, does not need to be taken into account in tort law (i.e., civil law).

In contrast, from an economics perspective, every discussion starts with the debate as to whether the current tort law system (or, perhaps, its very existence) is desirable to society. This debate comes before any argument about whether tort law should be used to resolve an individual and specific dispute. To answer this question, it is necessary to specify and evaluate tort law's functions. Examining whether the system itself is desirable for society necessarily brings not only the parties to an individual and specific dispute under scrutiny but also considers all subjects and constituents who could be perpetrators and victims, any possible effects that may result from a dispute, and any possible effects preceding that dispute as well. When making such considerations, the function of deterring torts is not excluded from the evaluation as a matter of course just because it should be the role of criminal law. Furthermore, as a supplementary note, although some people view the ex ante viewpoint as more important than the ex post viewpoint in economics, this way of thinking is not necessarily always correct. Nonetheless, the reason that the ex ante deterrence of torts is prioritized in discussions is simply because evaluating any other functions with certainty is very difficult.

The aforementioned issues illustrate the contrast between the fundamental perspectives of law and economics. As previously indicated, this discussion is not intended to suggest that the two disciplines are always in opposition over this issue, nor is this issue so contentious that the disciplines are completely unable to engage in discussion. In fact, without such distinct lines of thinking from both disciplines, it is more difficult to adequately comprehend tort law's actual role in society. So concludes the discussion of this issue in this chapter, but we recommend that readers interested in this discussion review the references.[1] Even in the legal field, in fact, the significance of emphasizing the deterrence aspect of tort law to eliminate the incentives for perpetrators to engage in wrongful acts has been discussed in relation to torts in which the perpetrator aims to gain profits (Kubota 2007). In addition, some argue that the main institutional purpose of tort law should be shifted from compensation for damages to deterrence of wrongful acts (Morita and Kozuka 2008).

Thus, we conclude the discussion in Sect. 8.3. In the next section, we examine perhaps the most controversial aspect of tort law, negligence.

8.4 Principle of Negligence Liability

The opening phrase of Article 709 states, "A person that has intentionally or negligently infringed …" Civil law is based on the idea that liability for damages cannot be imposed in a tort unless the perpetrator is at least negligent. This idea is called the "principle of negligence liability." In this context, the specific meanings of the words "intentionally" and "negligently" are controversial. The term "intentionally" is generally understood to mean acting in a way that causes an infringement of rights with an awareness of the consequences and a willingness to do so. Conversely, the

[1] See, for example, Morishima (1987), Hirai (1992), and Uchida (2011).

actual meaning of "negligently" has been hotly debated. In this section, we examine what negligence is and why negligence liability is a principle from the perspectives of both law and economics.

8.4.1 What is Negligence?

According to legal studies, negligence was traditionally understood as a psychological condition lacking in appropriate tension (i.e., a subjective psychological state) in which a subject could have foreseen a consequence but did not exercise appropriate caution or care to avoid it. However, with the rise in cases involving tort lawsuits in the 1960s and 1970s, the tendency to evaluate negligence based on the standards of objective acts (the so-called "objectifying of negligence") rather than based on a subjective psychological state became prominent. On this basis, negligence was no longer seen as a psychological state in which the person committing the act lacked appropriate psychological tension. Instead, perpetrators' acts were being judged from an objective standard according to whether these actions met the required standard of care. In recent years, it has become generally accepted that negligence is defined in these terms and that the criteria for negligence are specified according to the following formulation. Specifically, negligence is a violation of the duty to act (i.e., the duty to avoid consequences) even though the perpetrator could foresee the risk of damage (i.e., foreseeability) and was obligated to act to avoid the occurrence of this damage (i.e., the duty to avoid consequences).

Judicial precedents are traditionally based on the premise of objective negligence. In the case of a chemical company in Osaka (Great Court of Judicature Judgment, December 22, 1916 – "Osaka Alkali") that was accused of damaging the plaintiff's crops with the emissions produced by its factory, the court determined that if the chemical plant had carried out reasonable precautions according to the nature of its business to prevent the occurrence of damages arising from its normal business objectives, then it could not be found liable for damages. Thus, the court made its judgment based not on the presence or absence of a subjective psychological state of negligence on the part of the defendant (i.e., the Osaka Alkaline company) but rather on whether the company had made reasonable precautions in accordance with the nature of its business. In other words, the judgement was based on whether it had fulfilled its objective duty to act (i.e., the duty to avoid consequences).

Conversely, we can consider an economist's view of negligence. As we have already explained, the economics field evaluates social situations based on the standards of social welfare. Thus, the level of precaution that maximizes social welfare ex ante is considered to be due care, and perpetrators are considered to be negligent when their chosen precaution levels are below the due care level. Although this line of thinking is based on the premise of maximizing social welfare, which is unique to economics, it is not remiss to say that this perspective is practically identical to the legal viewpoint regarding objective negligence. As it stands, in practical terms, the legal perspective uses a formula known as the "Hand rule" to determine the presence or absence of negligence, which is similar to the approach taken by economics.

Three variables are said to be particularly important in determining the existence of negligence: the probability of breaking away, the gravity of the resulting injury, and the burden of adequate precautions (see United States v. Carroll Towing Co.—159 F.2d 169). Based on these determining variables, Judge Learned Hand created the following formula for negligence:

$$\text{the burden of taking precautions (B)} < \text{the probability of loss (P)} \times \text{the gravity of loss (L)}.$$

When the above relationship is established, then negligence exists. The burden of precaution in this formula corresponds to the cost of precaution in the explanation from an economics perspective.

For example, consider a situation in which a person (i.e., a victim) suffers damages of 100 million JPY with a probability of 15% if a different person (i.e., a perpetrator) performs a certain act. In this case, the important issue is how diligently the perpetrator committed to installing measures to prevent damages according to the expected amount of damages. In this example, if the perpetrator spends 10 million JPY to install measures to prevent damages, then those costs do not exceed the amount of expected damages of 15 million JPY (100 million JPY $\times$ 0.15). Thus, the measures taken by the perpetrator to prevent damages are insufficient, and the perpetrator is therefore negligent.

On the one hand, determining negligence according to the Hand rule does not necessarily entirely line up with the standard for negligence from an economics perspective, which aims to maximize social welfare (i.e., minimize social costs).[2] On the other hand, even in law, critics argue that this formula is not an all-purpose tool that can indiscriminately apply to any kind of case. The conclusion that the perpetrator is not liable simply because the costs of any precautions slightly exceed the expected cost of damages does not fit with the sense of justice. However, this formula is very important in that it enables a discussion from both law and economics perspectives.

8.4.2 *Why is Liability for Negligence a Principle?*

8.4.2.1 Principle of Negligence Liability and Its Exceptions: A Legal Perspective

The principle of negligence liability has been adopted with regard to tort law mainly for historical reasons. As stated at the beginning of Sect. 8.2, the various forms of economic activity include actions that inflict damages or losses on others. If people were held liable for any damages or losses to any victims that occurred as a result

[2] See, for example, Cooter and Ulen (2011) for more information on this issue.

of these economic activities, social activity would be hindered, and it would be impossible to smoothly carry out economic activities within society. Systematically introducing the principle of no liability without negligence into the Civil Code guarantees the freedom of movement and activity in social life. Accordingly, the principle of negligence liability is not self-evident but rather can be seen as being supported by the economic policy of developing one's own industry.

Moreover, this elementary proposition of tort law, which states that a perpetrator shall be held responsible for compensating a victim for damages only when the damage is caused by intentional or negligent behavior, was compelled to undergo modifications by virtue of social and economic development. In particular, a series of legislative acts have recognized a perpetrator's liability for damages without raising the question of the perpetrator's negligence (see, for example, Art. 25 of the Antimonopoly Law, Art. 3 of the Act on Compensation for Nuclear Damage, and Art. 3 of the Product Liability Act).

The development of the idea of strict liability raises a fundamental issue regarding the basis for the grounds of tort liability. Under the principle of negligence liability, the basis for attributing blame to the perpetrator is established when the perpetrator is found to have lacked appropriate psychological tension (the subjective negligence theory) or to have violated the duty to avoid consequences (the objective negligence theory). In any case, the notion of requiring the perpetrator pay for the costs of these damages is consistent with the ideals of fairness because the blameworthiness of the perpetrator's negligence is recognized. However, if a perpetrator is forced to bear responsibility for an action even in the absence of negligence, then the basis for attributing this responsibility cannot be explained from the perspective of negligence theory. It is therefore important to understand which perspective supports the standard of strict liability. The two general bases for assigning responsibility as it pertains to strict liability are risk liability (i.e., the person who creates, controls, or administrates a source of hazardous risk must be liable for any damages that arise from that risk) and profit liability (i.e., if the responsible party's actions generate profits for themselves, they are responsible for any damages arising from these actions).

8.4.2.2 Comparison of the Strict and Negligence Liability Rules: An Economics Perspective

One may ask whether the negligence liability rule, which is held as a guiding principle, is truly desirable from an economics perspective. Perhaps the strict liability rule, which is incorporated in the law as an exception, is more desirable. Because we did not consider the presence or absence of negligence in the analysis in Sect. 8.3, the results are the same if the strict liability rule is applied instead. Thus, we start by explaining how the results in Sect. 8.3 change when the negligence liability rule is applied.

First, we consider the matter from an ex post perspective. Under the negligence liability rule, if there is no evidence of negligence, then no income is redistributed from the perpetrator to the victim. Although this outcome may affect social welfare, it is impossible to say with certainty whether it would improve social welfare. For example, consider a tort case in which the perpetrator is a corporation with numerous assets and the victim is an individual with very few assets. In this case, the desirable outcome is for the law to find the corporation liable for compensating the victim even if it is not found to be negligent. Exceptions allowing the strict liability rule to be applied to certain types of tort laws, such as the product liability law, can be justified from an economics perspective for reasons like those in this example.

Furthermore, with regard to tort law's function of punishing perpetrators, under the negligence liability rule, no practical punishment is handed down against the perpetrator if no negligence is found. However, for the most part, the desire to punish the perpetrator is most likely to occur when the perpetrator is actually negligent. Thus, we can ignore any effect of this viewpoint on social welfare in almost all instances.

Next, we can consider the matter from an ex ante perspective. Here, unlike in Sect. 8.3, we assume that a potential perpetrator is able to select a level of precaution. Based on the aforementioned economics perspective on negligence, we define the level of precaution that maximizes social welfare as "due care." Perpetrators with a precaution level below due care are considered to be negligent, and those with a precaution level at or above due care are not negligent.

First, we explain that perpetrators choose to take due care under the strict liability rule. This explanation implies that optimal deterrence can be achieved even when a perpetrator has the ability to choose a precaution level, whereas we refrained from providing such an explanation in Sect. 8.3. As illustrated in Sect. 8.3, when the perpetrator bears responsibility, the costs borne by the perpetrator are identical to the social costs. Thus, a potential perpetrator's decision on whether to take additional precautions is in line with social desirability. For this reason, under the strict liability rule, the potential perpetrator necessarily chooses to take due care.

Now, we consider whether the level of due care is selected under the negligence liability rule. If the perpetrator choose a level of precaution below the due care level, then the perpetrator is liable for damages under either rule. As such, under the negligence liability rule, the costs borne by the perpetrator are the same as those for which they would be liable under the strict liability rule. If the perpetrator chooses the due care level, then the perpetrator is not liable for damages and, thus, the costs borne by the perpetrator under the negligence liability rule are lower than those under the strict liability rule. Considering that the potential perpetrator voluntarily chooses to take due care under the strict liability rule, the negligence liability rule, which lowers the cost burden of a perpetrator taking due care, never results in the perpetrator paying for a lower level of precaution than that of due care. Furthermore, because paying for any level of precaution at or above the level of due care ensures that a perpetrator will not be held liable for damages, paying for any levels of precaution beyond the due care level only increases the perpetrator's cost burden. For this reason, under the negligence liability rule, levels of precaution above due care are never selected. Thus, even under the negligence liability rule, due care is still chosen.

This result indicates that torts are optimally deterred under both the strict and negligence liability rules. This finding does not mean that the negligence liability rule should be held as the guiding principle from the perspective of deterring the occurrence of damages. However, the negligence liability rule provides benefits that the strict liability rule cannot provide, as follows. As mentioned in Sect. 8.3, the tort law system has the potential to affect the decision-making processes of not only potential perpetrators but also potential victims. These possible effects become an issue when both the potential perpetrators' and the potential victims' precaution levels affect the occurrence of damages. When the strict liability rule is applied in such situations, potential victims will likely choose to take only the minimal level of precautions among the choices available. Because victims are guaranteed to be compensated for any damages that occur, taking a higher level of precaution only results in higher costs for potential victims.

Conversely, if the negligence liability rule is applied to this situation, potential victims have an incentive to take some additional precautions. This result is because even if a potential victim suffers damages, he or she will not receive any compensation as long as the perpetrator has paid due care. Thus, potential victims prefer to voluntarily take some precautions to prevent the occurrence of damages. Explaining this result in detail is complicated, and, thus, we refer readers to the appendix at the end of this chapter for more details. In brief, under the negligence liability rule, both the potential perpetrator and the potential victim end up choosing levels of precaution that maximize social welfare because for both parties, this choice is the best response to the other party's choice (this situation is called a Nash equilibrium, as described in Sect. 8.4 of the Appendix).

As this comparison shows, if the level of precaution selected by the potential victim affects the occurrence of damages, the negligence liability rule can be considered the more desirable option because it incentivizes potential victims to choose the optimal deterrence level. Normally, from a legal perspective, the deterrence of a tort is not the systematic objective of tort law. However, from an economics perspective, the negligence liability rule's deterrence function is an important justification for the principle of negligence liability, which is one of the pillars of the tort law system.

Next, we compare the negligence and strict liability rules from the perspective of risk allocation. As mentioned earlier, because potential perpetrators voluntarily choose to take due care under the negligence liability rule, perpetrators are not liable to pay any compensation even if damages do occur. For this reason, potential victims end up bearing the risks of any possible damages. Conversely, when damages occur under the strict liability rule, the responsibility for compensation always rests with the perpetrator, meaning that the risk is borne by potential perpetrators. Consequently, the allocation of risk differs depending on which rule is adopted. However, because we cannot determine with certainty whether potential victims or potential perpetrators should bear the risk, we cannot determine which rule is more desirable based on their different risk allocations. However, in a tort in which a corporation is the perpetrator and an individual person is the victim, for example, rules that compel the perpetrator to bear the risks are preferable from a risk allocation perspective. Furthermore, the application of the strict liability rule to such laws as the product liability law are justifiable based on the risk allocation function in addition to the income redistribution function.

8.5 Conclusion

In this chapter, we discussed Article 709 of the Civil Code, which is a general rule regarding tort law. We first explained the system, and we then discussed the basic lines of thinking about tort law from both law and economics perspectives and compared the two perspectives.

Tort law serves the functions of providing a remedy to victims (i.e., compensation for damages), imposing sanctions on perpetrators, redistributing income, deterring damages, and allocating risks, among others. The function of providing a remedy to victims (i.e., compensation for damages) means that victims can receive compensation for their damages. The function of imposing sanctions on perpetrators means that perpetrators are compelled to pay for damages that they cause. The function of income redistribution is a comprehensive function in which compensation for damages is transferred from perpetrators to victims. All of these functions operate after a dispute, called a tort, arises. The function of deterring wrongful acts works by using the fear of paying compensation to induce potential perpetrators to avoid causing damages, and the function of risk allocation transfers the risk of damages occurring through a tort from potential victims to potential perpetrators. These functions operate before any such disputes arise. In addition, from a legal perspective, we can also identify other functions, such as the creation of previously unrecognized types of torts through court judgments.

Law examines what the main institutional purpose of tort law (among all these possible functions) is. It asks this question to gain an essential foothold in providing a universal solution that can be used to resolve individual and specific disputes involving torts. The answer to this question is that the major purpose of tort law is to provide remedies to victims. Conversely, economists start by debating whether the system (or perhaps the very existence) of tort law is desirable for society. To answer that question, they first examine the kinds of functions that tort law has and then examine whether each of those functions is desirable. The answer to this question is that setting aside the other functions, the function of deterring wrongful acts by perpetrators, which is part of tort law, is desirable for society.

As we can see here, although the legal and economics perspectives comprehend tort law fundamentally differently, both perspectives are important for adequately understanding its role in practical social settings. Furthermore, in many legal circles, the economics perspective has been incorporated into debates and discussions of tort law.

In this chapter, we further explained the topic of negligence, the most debated issue in all of tort law, in detail from both law and economics perspectives. From a legal perspective, the presence or absence of negligence is thought of as being objectively determined by whether the perpetrator's actions are consistent with taking the necessary level of precaution. Conversely, from an economics perspective, a perpetrator is considered to be negligent only when the perpetrator's precaution level is below the socially optimal precaution level. It is not remiss to say that both perspectives are fundamentally the same.

In general, tort law uses the principle of negligence liability, under which liability for damages occurs only when the perpetrator is found to be negligent. In law, this principle is thought to have been adopted in response to the needs to ensure people's freedom of action and to stimulate economic activity whenever possible. However, a growing trend in relatively recent history is the enactment of laws imposing liability for damages regardless of whether negligence is present.

From an economics perspective, when we consider tort law's function of deterring wrongful acts, potential perpetrators choose to take the socially optimal level of precaution to deter the occurrence of damages regardless of whether the negligence or strict liability rule is applied. However, when the aim is to incentivize potential victims to take socially optimal levels of precaution as well, the negligence liability rule is preferable to the strict liability rule. This result can justify the fact that the negligence liability rule is the guiding principle in tort law. Conversely, in specific cases of torts, the strict liability rule is more desirable from the perspectives of income redistribution and risk allocation. This result can justify the fact that product liability legislation adheres to the strict liability rule.

Appendix: Optimal Deterrence in the Case of Bilateral Precaution

When the levels of precaution of the potential perpetrator and the potential victim both influence the occurrence of damage, the situation is called a "bilateral precaution case." In this appendix, we explain in greater detail the contrast between the strict and negligence liability rules in the bilateral precaution case briefly mentioned in Sect. 8.4.2.2.

To simplify this discussion, we make a minor revision to the situation described in Sect. 8.4.2.2. In this situation, both the potential perpetrator and the potential victim can choose whether to take certain levels of precaution; absolutely no damage occurs when both parties take the precautions, but certain damage absolutely occurs otherwise.

First, we discuss the socially optimal result, that is, the pattern of precautions that minimizes the social cost. In this situation, the level of social cost is one of four levels depending on whether the related parties take the precautions. If neither party chooses to take precautions, then the social cost is just the amount of damages. If only one party takes precautions, then the social cost is the cost of the precautions taken by that party plus the amount of damages. We can immediately see that the social costs are not minimized if only one party takes precautions. Thus, the socially optimal result is either for both parties to take precautions, deterring the occurrence of damages, or for neither party to take precautions, in which case the damages are not deterred. If the total cost of the precautions taken by both parties is less than the amount of damages, then the former result is socially optimal. If the reverse is true (i.e., the total cost exceeds the amount of damages), then the latter result is socially optimal. We call the former situation "the situation in which deterrence is desirable" and the latter situation "the situation in which deterrence is not desirable." We examine each situation under the strict and negligence liability rules and determine whether potential perpetrators and victims choose to take precautions.

First, when the strict liability rule is applied, any damages that occur are always compensated by the perpetrator regardless of the potential perpetrator's decision. Thus, taking precautions only increases potential victims' cost burden. For this reason, potential victims choose not to take precautions. Potential perpetrators predict this behavior by potential victims and similarly choose not to take precautions. This result is because when damages occur, perpetrators are held liable for compensation regardless of whether they took precautions. Thus, taking precautions only increases their burden. We can see that in this situation, both parties choose not to take precautions.

Next, we discuss the situation in which the negligence liability rule is applied. If deterrence is desirable, perpetrators are not found negligent if they have taken precautions, but they are found negligent if they have not taken precautions. Thus, if potential perpetrators choose to take precautions, they bear the costs of these precaution, and if they do not take precautions, they bear the amount of damages. In this situation, because the amount of damages exceeds the costs of precautions, potential perpetrators choose to take precautions. The potential victims predict this behavior of the potential perpetrators and are faced with the choice of either paying the precaution costs or not paying the precaution costs and bearing the costs of the damages instead. In this case, because the amount of damages exceeds the precaution costs for potential victims, the potential victims choose to take the precautions. Thus, both parties will choose to take the precautions and, as a result, can deter the occurrence of damages.

Conversely, in a situation in which deterrence is not desirable, potential perpetrators are not found negligent even if they do not take precautions, and they are never found liable for compensation. Under this circumstance, taking precautions only increases their burden. For this reason, the potential perpetrators choose not to take precautions. The potential victims predict this behavior on the part of the potential perpetrators and also choose not to take precautions. This result is because the victims bear the costs of any damages regardless of whether they take precautions, meaning that taking precautions only increases their burden. Thus, both parties choose not to take precautions and, as a result, cannot deter the occurrence of damages.

As these results show, the optimal outcome cannot be achieved when deterrence is desirable and the strict liability rule is applied. Conversely, it can be achieved when the negligence liability rule is applied regardless of whether deterrence is desirable. These results hold even in situations in which levels of precaution can be chosen or the occurrence of damages is not entirely certain (concerning this result, see, for example, Shavell 1987).

Column 13. "How false and irresponsible a lawyer is": law and interpretation (2)

I admit that column 10 was written using some rather sentimental brushstrokes. Thus, I will settle down here and explain methods for interpreting the law in more detail.

In introductory texts on the study of law, the typical legal interpretation methods are often exemplified and enumerated as "literal interpretation" (following the wording of the law as literally as possible), "extended interpretation" (extending the meaning beyond the exact wording of the law), "analogical interpretation" (examining the effects of laws and regulations that stipulate certain facts and interpreting their effects on similar facts), and "contrary argument interpretation" (when multiple facts can be considered similar but the law provides only for specific facts, one may interpret that other similar facts do not have the effects stipulated by the relevant laws).

In practice, various factors, such as the positions of specific articles within each law, articles' relationships with other articles, the accumulation of judicial precedents and trends in academic debates, the status of discussions at the time of the legislation, and the aims and purposes of the law must all be narrowed down and considered comprehensively to arrive at interpretations (and conclusions). Thus, when faced with a specific concrete legal problem, legal practitioners and scholars do not always agree on which interpretation method is most appropriate. Additionally, if problems arise when a certain legal interpretation is actually provided, it may be that the logical process is not persuasively presented to readers of the interpretation. Certainly, it can be difficult to understand actual interpretations of the law through independent study because the technique of selecting the methods with which to interpret the law (and draw conclusions) requires extensive experience and awareness of new developments. Those within the legal world certainly hope that those outside of this world who encounter the realm of legal interpretation should understand how it is approached. However, if lawyers cannot persuasively explain why a certain interpretation or conclusion is reached, those outside the world of law, including the general public, will tend to view legal interpretation as arbitrary and unreliable (The title of this column is taken from page 82 of Kurusu S (2004) Hō no kaishaku to hōritsuka (Interpretation of law and lawyers). In: Kurusu S, *Kurusu Saburō chosakushū* I (Works of Saburo Kurusu I). Shinzansha Publisher, Tokyo (first published in 1954). The phrase "somehow trying to hide the subjective behind the objective" follows the quotation used in this title. Kurusu (1912–1998) was an outstanding legal scholar who worked on interpretations of civil law in the postwar era in Japan).

Study Questions

1. Explain the main institutional purpose of tort law from a legal perspective.

2. From an economics perspective, explain how tort law functions both ex post and ex ante.
3. Explain the basis for the principle of negligence liability from a legal perspective. Then, explain the criteria for judging negligence in detail.
4. How do the differences in the strict and negligence liability rules lead to different outcomes ex ante and ex post? How can these differences be evaluated?

References

Cooter R, Ulen T (2011) Law and economics, 4th edn. Pearson Education International, Boston
Hirai Y (1992) Saiken kakuron II: fuhōkōihō (The law of obligations II: torts). Koubundou, Tokyo [publication in Japanese]
Kubota A (2010) Fuhōkōihō (The law of torts). Yuhikaku, Tokyo [publication in Japanese]
Morishima A (1987) Fuhōkōihō kōgi (Tort law lectures). Yuhikaku, Tokyo [publication in Japanese]
Morita H, Kozuka S (2008) Fuhōkōihō no mokuteki (The purpose of tort law). New Bus Law 874:10–21. [publication in Japanese]
Shavell S (1987) Economic analysis of accident law. Harvard University Press, Cambridge
Uchida T (2011) Minpō II (Civil code II), 3rd edn. University of Tokyo Press, Tokyo [publication in Japanese]

Chapter 9
Appropriate Rules for Protecting the Environment: Environmental Law

Narufumi Kadomatsu, Takeshi Shimamura, and Kenji Takeuchi

Contents

9.1 Issues Discussed in This Chapter 210
9.2 Waste Management and Recycling 210
9.2.1 Economic Approach to Waste Management 211
9.2.2 Economic and Legal Approaches to Recycling: The Recycling of Home Appliances 215
9.2.3 Designing Recycling Law Systems 218
9.2.4 Evaluating the Home Appliance Recycling Law 219
9.3 Landscapes 223
9.3.1 An Economics Approach to Landscape Problems 223
9.3.2 Landscape Issues and the Legal System 225
9.3.3 The Law and Economics of Landscape Problems 232
9.4 Conclusion 235
References 237

Environmental problems are natural scientific phenomena related to the air, water, and soil. However, the causes of these problems are economic activities, such as industrial activities and household consumption. In addition, because laws regulate economic activity, the interplay between law and the economy has a tremendous effect on the environment and the severity of environmental problems. Considering the interplay between law and the economy related to environmental problems, it is most important for policymakers to incorporate incentives effectively to achieve

N. Kadomatsu · T. Shimamura (✉)
Graduate School of Law, Kobe University, 2-1 Rokkodai-cho, Nada-ku, Kobe 657-8501, Hyogo, Japan
e-mail: simamura@kobe-u.ac.jp

N. Kadomatsu
e-mail: kado@kobe-u.ac.jp

K. Takeuchi
Graduate School of Economics, Kobe University, Kobe 657-8501, Hyogo, Japan
e-mail: takeuchi@econ.kobe-u.ac.jp

T. Yanagawa et al. (eds.), *Econo-Legal Studies*,
https://doi.org/10.1007/978-981-16-5145-8_9

their policy goals. If a mechanism is created whereby people benefit by acting in an environmentally friendly way, their behavior can be changed. Another important point is to consider both costs and benefits. Although protecting the environment is undoubtedly important, the associated costs should not be ignored. It is necessary to carefully examine the extent to which the environment should be protected by factoring in both the costs and benefits to society.

9.1 Issues Discussed in This Chapter

Modern society is facing various kinds of environmental problems, of which climate change caused by greenhouse gas emissions is one of the most serious. When fossil fuels are burned, greenhouse gases are emitted and released into the atmosphere. However, because modern life depends so heavily on fossil fuels, such as oil, gas, and coal, it is not easy to reduce their consumption. Additionally, climate change is not a domestic problem but rather has a global impact. For this reason, it is crucial to promote cooperation among all countries worldwide.

To promote global initiatives to stabilize greenhouse gas concentrations, the United Nations Framework Convention on Climate Change was concluded, and the conferences of the parties have been held every year since then. In response to this agreement, the Act on the Promotion of Global Warming Countermeasures came into effect in Japan in 1998, and the government set a greenhouse gas reduction target and made an achievement plan under this law. In 2012, a tax for climate change mitigation was introduced. The tax rate corresponds to the amount of CO_2 emissions from all fossil fuels, and the tax creates economic incentives to reduce greenhouse gas emissions.

Although environmental problems are natural scientific phenomena related to the air and water, the causes of these problems are economic activities, such as industrial activities and household consumption. In addition, because laws regulate economic activity, the interplay between law and the economy significantly affects the severity of environmental problems. In this chapter, we discuss waste management, recycling policy, and landscape protection to analyze the relationship between law and the economy. In Sect. 9.2, we discuss waste management and recycling policy. Then, in Sect. 9.3, we discuss landscape policy. These two sections illustrate how these issues can be approached from legal and economic perspectives. Finally, the discussion is summarized in Sect. 9.4.

9.2 Waste Management and Recycling

Household consumption and industrial production generate large volumes of waste. Waste management and recycling is one of the major challenges of modern environmental policy. This section introduces the basics of environmental economics to help analyze waste and recycling policies. Then, we explore home appliance recycling to explain how economic and legal perspectives can help in designing better legislation and policies.

9.2.1 Economic Approach to Waste Management

9.2.1.1 External Diseconomies and Pigouvian Taxes

This subsection explains approaches to environmental issues from an economics perspective. These approaches can be traced back to the British economist Arthur Cecil Pigou, who authored *The Economics of Welfare* in 1920 (Pigou 1920). He extended the concept of externalities discussed by the English economist Alfred Marshall, and he advocated for governmental intervention as a remedy. Negative externalities occur when an economic activity generates a byproduct that affects third parties. Without government intervention, a market with external diseconomies results in a production level above the socially optimal level. Pigou illustrated this idea using the example of steam locomotives that scatter sparks and burn down forests near the train tracks. Despite the fact that these sparks inflict costs on society in the form of lost forests, they are not included in the railroad company's cost calculations. Thus, if the supply of trains is based solely on the demand for transportation and the costs of lost forests are not accounted for, more trains will run than is socially optimal. Although the free market appropriately adjusts demand and supply, it does not work very well when externalities are present.

Several points related to the above story are worth noting. First, even though markets with negative externalities fail to function properly, the market mechanisms themselves are not necessarily invalid. In fact, Pigou's solution to negative externalities actively utilizes the same market functions. He proposes imposing a tax on economic activities to provide an incentive to prevent negative externalities. This approach became known as a Pigouvian tax, and it forms the theoretical foundation for today's practice of environmental taxes. Second, this argument is based on the assumption that it is possible to measure the monetary value of negative externalities. If this value cannot be measured, it is impossible capture the extent of overproduction, let alone impose a Pigouvian tax. One may ask if the social costs of air pollution or deforestation can be measured This question is a major research challenge for environmental economics, and a variety of evaluation methods have been developed thus far to address this issue. Third, the economics perspective does not blame the economic agents who generate negative externalities from an ethical perspective. However, economics and ethics are not necessarily unrelated. People's values and ethics determine what is regarded as a negative externality. In addition, ethical judgements are incorporated in the argument that it is desirable to compare benefits and costs to determine optimal production quantities. However, it remains uncertain whether we can agree with the idea that economic decisions should be based solely on the results of societal cost–benefit calculations without paying any attention to distributional impacts.

9.2.1.2 Pigouvian Tax: Charging Garbage Disposal Fees

Fees for garbage disposal can be regarded as an example of a Pigouvian tax. Currently, residents of Kobe City can dispose of their waste free of charge. Provided that garbage is placed in plastic bags designated by the city and put out on designated days, people can produce as much garbage as they wish. These garbage bags are available at supermarkets and convenience stores, and ten 45-L bags for burnable garbage cost roughly 100 JPY. In contrast, garbage bags are sold at much higher prices in other municipalities. For example in Fukuoka City, ten 45-L bags for burnable garbage cost 450 JPY, which is more than four times higher than Kobe City's price. The difference arises because Fukuoka charges fees for garbage disposal services, whereas Kobe does not.

When people do not recognize the true costs associated with garbage, the amount of garbage is higher than the socially optimal level. This result is similar to Pigou's example, in which the railway does not consider deforestation risks and operates above the socially optimal level. If people recognize the costs of waste disposal, then they will have an incentive to reduce waste. Charging fees for garbage disposal services is a policy instrument for reducing waste disposal by creating such incentives.

Figure 9.1 illustrates an individual's demand for garbage disposal services. The horizontal axis represents the quantity of these services, measured in the number of

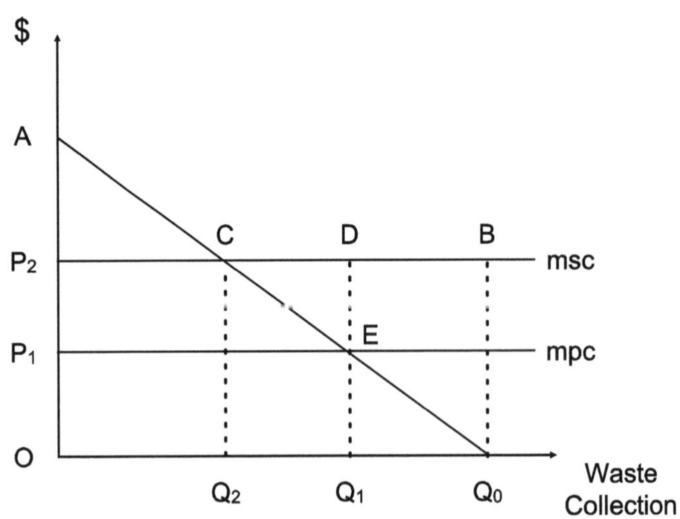

Fig. 9.1 Costs and benefits of waste management

garbage bags, and the vertical axis is the price. A demand curve shows the quantity of products or services that consumers will consume at a given price. Demand curves can indicate the marginal willingness to pay, that is, the amount that consumers are willing to pay for an additional unit of a good or service. The willingness to pay is measured by the vertical distance between the horizontal axis and the demand curve.

When the garbage disposal service is provided free of charge, the amount of garbage produced is Q_0. Because the price of this service is zero, people increase their consumption to the point where the additional willingness to pay is zero. For example, if the time frame for Fig. 9.1 is one month, this individual produces Q_0 bags of garbage each month. The area under the demand curve is called the total willingness to pay, and it is calculated simply by summing the marginal willingness to pay values. The total willingness to pay is the amount that an individual is willing to pay to enjoy a certain level of garbage disposal services relative to not having the service at all. For example, $\triangle AQ_0O$ is the total willingness to pay to dispose of Q_0 bags of garbage.

However, providing garbage disposal services also incurs costs. The line mpc in Fig. 9.1 represents the additional cost to provide disposal services for an additional garbage bag, which can include labor and energy costs. This cost is called the marginal private cost, and it is assumed to be constant in the figure regardless of how much garbage is produced. If garbage disposal is Q_0, then the total private cost is the rectangular area bounded by the mpc and Q_0. If garbage collection is free to an individual disposing garbage, then these costs are paid from the government budget. In addition, other costs are associated with garbage disposal services. When waste is incinerated, it can create air pollution. When it is buried in landfills, beaches may be lost. These outcomes are costs to society, although it is often difficult to recognize them. The sum of the marginal private costs and the costs of environmental damage are represented in Fig. 9.1 by the line msc. The costs imposed on society are called the marginal social costs.

To summarize, if garbage collection is free, then Q_0 bags of garbage are disposed, and the social benefit (i.e., the total willingness to pay) is the area corresponding to $\triangle A\ Q_0O$ in Fig. 9.1. Conversely, the costs associated with providing these services are $\square P_2B\ Q_0O$. The net social benefit (i.e., benefits minus costs) are $\triangle AQ_0O - \square P_2BQ_0O = \triangle ACP_2 - \triangle CBQ_0$ (Case 1). This value can be thought of as the net social benefit of providing free garbage disposal services for Q_0 bags. Although Fig. 9.1 illustrates an individual demand curve, a similar story holds for the entire population's demand curve (i.e., the aggregate demand curve).

Next, we consider the case in which a fee for garbage disposal services is partially introduced. Specifically, a disposal fee equivalent to the marginal private cost of providing garbage disposal services is imposed on each bag. This fee leads individuals to consider whether the marginal cost P_1 exceeds their willingness to pay each time they dispose bags of garbage. When the marginal cost is less than the willingness to pay, it is economically rational to dispose of an additional bag of garbage. If the marginal cost exceeds the willingness to pay, people will be unlikely to dispose of additional garbage. Thus, the number of garbage bags that an individual disposes of is Q_1, and the social benefit is the area $\square AEQ_1O$. The cost of providing this service is $\square P_2DQ_1O$, which comprises the technical cost of providing disposal services for Q_1 bags ($\square P_1EQ_1O$) and the environmental damage from disposing of Q_1 bags ($\square P_2DEP_1$). Thus, the net social benefit is $\square AEQ_1O - \square P_2DQ_1O = \triangle ACP_2 - \triangle CDE$ (Case 2).

Finally, we consider the case in which the optimal fee for garbage disposal services is introduced. This fee is set equal to the marginal social cost of providing garbage disposal services for each bag of garbage. Then, the number of bags disposed is Q_2, and the social benefit is the area $\square ACQ_2O$. The cost of providing this service is $\square$P2CQ2O. Thus, the net social benefit is $\square ACQ_2O - \square P_2CQ_2O = \triangle ACP_2$ (Case 3).

Comparing the net social benefits in the three cases shows that Case 3 > Case 2 > Case 1. In Case 3, garbage producers recognize the marginal social cost, and the net social benefit is maximized.

9.2.1.3 Two Ways to Impose Garbage Disposal Fees

Fees for garbage disposal can be imposed in two ways. The first is to collect fees when garbage is disposed, and the second is to collect fees when consumers purchase products that may later become garbage. For convenience, we call the first method the pay-as-you-throw method and the second method the advance disposal fee. The pay-as-you-throw system corresponds to the garbage collection fees introduced in many municipalities. These municipalities set a price for each designated garbage bag and will not collect garbage that is disposed in any container besides the designated garbage bags. The advance disposal fee is added to a product's price at the time of purchase. An example is Florida in the United States, which charges advance disposal fees of two cents per container.

The major difference between the pay-as-you-throw and advance disposal fee systems is the timing of fee collection, although the two systems have many other differences as well. For example, if fees are collected in the disposal stage, people have an incentive to dispose of garbage inappropriately, such as through illegal dumping. In contrast, an advance disposal fee effectively prevents illegal dumping. Moreover, advance disposal fees give manufacturers a direct incentive to design products that generate less waste, in line with the concept of extended producer responsibility (EPR).

According to the Organisation for Economic Co-operation and Development, EPR requires producers to bear a significant financial or physical responsibility for the treatment or disposal of post-consumer products (Otsuka 2020, p. 523). This approach was also introduced in Japan with the Basic Act on Establishing a Sound Material-Cycle Society. Firms' obligations to collect and recycle their products are stipulated in various laws, such as the Act on the Promotion of Sorted Collection and Recycling of Containers and Packaging (Containers and Packaging Recycling Law); the Act on Recycling of Specified Kinds of Home Appliances (Home Appliance Recycling Law); and the Act on Recycling, etc. of End-of-Life Vehicles (Automobile Recycling Law) (see Sect. 9.2.2). EPR is consistent with the design for the environment approach, which is the idea of environmentally conscious design. To effectively reduce products' environmental impact, it is necessary to reconsider their design. In other words, by imposing physical and financial obligations on producers, it is possible to provide incentives for them to change products' designs to reduce the volume of raw materials and waste or make products easily recyclable.

In practice, it is not easy to introduce an advance disposal fee. One reason for this difficulty is resistance from producers and consumers. Although the difference between the pay-as-you-throw and advance disposal fee methods lies in whether payment is made earlier or later in the process, both producers and consumers dislike advance disposal fees because they increase prices. Another reason is that setting an appropriate price level for an advance disposal fee is difficult. For example, the costs of collection, incineration, and landfill disposal vary significantly by location. If the pay-as-you-throw method is used, it is relatively easy for municipalities to reflect these differences. However, it is usually difficult to predict where a product will ultimately be thrown away at the time of purchase. Although the introduction of the pay-as-you-throw method was discussed in an amendment of the Home Appliance Recycling Law, it was not ultimately introduced.

9.2.2 Economic and Legal Approaches to Recycling: The Recycling of Home Appliances

9.2.2.1 Home Appliance Recycling

Based on the contents of Sect. 9.2.1, this chapter considers legislation on recycling to discuss potential legal issues when designing the system and analyze the legislation from an economics perspective. We focus on the issue of home appliance recycling.

When people move, they discard used appliances, such as air conditioners, televisions, and washing machines, that are no longer needed. Previously, used appliances were collected by municipalities and disposed in landfills. However, because landfill space is limited in Japan and these appliances are made up of components and materials that can be reused or recycled, simply throwing them away without recycling is not rational from the perspective of effective resource use. Thus, the Home Appliance Recycling Law, which obliges manufacturers to recycle specified home appliances, was introduced in 1998. Other laws, such as the 1995 Containers and Packaging Recycling Law and the 2002 Automobile Recycling Law, also require the recycling of end-of-life products.

It is worth asking who should be responsible for waste collection and recycling. Below, we refer to the responsibility for the collection and recycling of used appliances as the "physical responsibility." Similarly, it is worth asking who should be responsible for paying the costs of collection and recycling. We call the responsibility for these costs the "financial responsibility." The following discussion explores what approach should be taken according to an economics perspective. Furthermore, we discuss what points should be considered when a legislator establishes a law requiring the recycling of appliances.

9.2.2.2 Economic Approach to Recycling

9.2.2.2.1 Models

Who should be responsible for physical collection and recycling, and who should bear the cost? When designing a legal scheme for recycling, several options are available.

(i) *Municipal model.* As described above, municipalities once collected used appliances from households and disposed of them. Thus, the first option is a system in which municipalities are responsible for collection and recycling and bear the associated costs.

(ii) *Manufacturer responsibility model 1* (payment by manufacturers). Under the municipal model, the responsibility for collection and recycling is borne by municipalities, who do not have any knowledge about the materials and components of products. Thus, the municipal system does not work well to promote recycling. Instead, legislators can establish a system whereby manufacturers are responsible for collecting and recycling their own products once they are disposed and bearing the cost of doing so. This model is similar to the Container and Packaging Recycling Law, although under this law, municipalities rather than manufacturers are required to collect used appliances from households and bear the cost.

(iii) *Manufacturer responsibility model 2* (payment by users at disposal). The third model also requires manufacturers to collect and recycle end-of-use products. However, unlike in the second model, end users rather than manufacturers are responsible for paying the cost of recycling. The Home Appliance Recycling Law has adopted this model. Under this law, end users have to pay the costs of recycling to the manufacturers when disposing of their used appliances.

(iv) *Manufacturer responsibility model 3* (payment by users at purchase): The third model requires users to pay recycling costs when they dispose of an appliance, but these recycling costs are not necessarily always paid. Under the Home Appliance Recycling Law, a recycling fee must be paid when an appliance is disposed of, but in practice, many people who do not want to pay recycling fees unlawfully dump their used appliances. These problems will continue to occur as long as a payment-upon-disposal system is adopted. Taking this issue into account, we can consider a scheme in which users pay recycling costs at the time of purchase rather than at the time of disposal. The Automobile Recycling Law adopts this model.

9.2.2.2.2 Extended Producer Responsibility

One of the guiding principles of the debate about who should bear the responsibility for recycling and its costs is EPR. The concept of "product liability" may already be familiar. This concept concerns manufacturers' responsibility to pay compensation for damages to a user or a third party caused by defects in their products. EPR expands manufacturers' sphere of responsibility to all stages in the product life cycle, from production and use to post-use phases, such as recycling or disposal.

Manufacturers bear the responsibility of avoiding landfill disposals of used appliances and their components as much as possible in favor of using natural resources effectively and protecting the environment. Ways of fulfilling this responsibility include reusing (e.g., washing out a beer bottle and refilling it with beer) and recycling (e.g., melting down a used aluminum can and making another can).

One may ask why manufacturers should bear this responsibility. To reduce the burden on the environment after consumption, it is necessary to reuse or recycle products or their components so that as few components as possible are ultimate disposed. To do so, careful material selection and assembly design during manufacturing is vital. If manufacturers are obliged to collect and recycle the used appliances that they produced, then they will most likely design their products to be recycled at the lowest possible cost. In other words, the party in the position to recycle the product at the lowest cost (i.e., the party in a position to implement an environmentally friendly design; see Sect. 9.2.1) should be responsible for recycling. Considering this principle, the manufacturer responsibility models (ii)–(iv) are more suitable for promoting recycling than the municipal model (i) is.

9.2.2.2.3 Economics of Recycling

The Home Appliance Recycling Law requires manufacturers to collect and recycle used appliances. In this law, "recycling" means dismantling used home appliances and separating their parts and materials to be used as parts or raw materials for new products or transferring them, with or without charge, to entities who will reuse them. The standards for recycling are set out in the law. Specifically, the proportion of the gross weight of a product that should be recycled is established in the law (e.g., 80% of an air conditioner or 74% of a plasma television). Recycling helps to conserve natural resources and landfill capacity. However, the cost of recycling must be accounted for. Used appliances should be recycled to the point where the benefits of recycling equal the social cost of doing so (see Sect. 6 of the Appendix on social marginal costs) to achieve the most efficient amount of recycling (i.e., the optimal amount of recycling). In terms of efficiency, it is preferable for the recycling amount mandated by law to match the optimal amount of recycling.

Recycling costs vary depending on the recycling method, material, and product assembly method. Thus, it is preferable to impose the obligation of recycling on those who can reduce costs in the recycling and product design stages. For this reason, it is appropriate to require manufacturers to bear the burden of recycling. They can adjust their product materials and assembly methods and can be expected to reduce recycling costs over time through improved product design or further technological innovation. This logic is the basic idea of the EPR concept.

As for model (i), the municipal model, because municipalities can neither design products nor reduce recycling costs, they should not bear the responsibility of recycling. Thus, models (ii), (iii), and (iv) are all superior to model (i) in terms of efficiency.

We further examine the differences among models (ii), (iii), and (iv) later in this discussion.

9.2.3 Designing Recycling Law Systems

Here, we briefly describe the variation in Japanese recycling laws to understand how recycling laws are designed.

9.2.3.1 Containers and Packaging Recycling Law

After a consumer sorts and disposes of containers and packages, municipalities collect them. The responsibility for recycling the collected containers and packages is borne by business operators (in the law's terminology, "specified business operators" include the manufacturers of the containers and packages, the business operators producing the contents of the containers or packages, and the business operators that use the containers and packages to sell their merchandise).

In practice, these specified business operators entrust the responsibility for recycling the great majority of the waste containers and packages collected by municipalities to a designated body, the Japan Containers and Packaging Recycling Association (JCPRA). The JCPRA conducts a competitive bidding process and commissions the recycling companies with the lowest bids to carry out recycling. Waste containers and packages are transported from municipalities' storage facilities directly to the recyclers.

The recycling costs are allocated as follows. The municipalities are responsible for the costs of collecting the waste containers and packages disposed by households. However, the recycling costs are paid by the aforementioned specified business operators to the recyclers via the JCPRA. In short, the municipalities must pay the costs of collection, and the business operators bear the costs of recycling. Based on the models described above, although both the physical and financial responsibilities for recycling follow model (ii), the responsibility for collecting waste containers and packages follows model (i).

9.2.3.2 Home Appliance Recycling Law

When consumers dispose of air conditioners, refrigerators and freezers, washers and dryers, or televisions, they must bring them to a retailer or other agent. At this time, the consumer purchases an appliance recycling ticket. The retailer then transfers the discarded appliances to the manufacturer, and the manufacturer recycles them in an appropriate manner. The Appliance Recycling Law therefore follows model (iii).

9.2.3.3 Automobile Recycling Law

According to the Automobile Recycling Law, the owner of a used vehicle must transfer the vehicle to a registered collection operator to dispose of it. Then, fluorocarbons in the air conditioner and the airbags are removed and useful metal components and other materials are recovered before the car body is shredded. Under the Automobile Recycling Law, automobile manufacturers are not required to accept the entire bodies of end-of-life vehicles. Instead, they are obliged to accept and recycle only fluorocarbons, airbags, and automobile shredder residue. The reason that legislators did not require manufacturers to accept the entire bodies of end-of-life vehicles is as follows. Any vehicle components other than the above three items are traded in used parts markets, and, thus, it is not necessary to oblige manufacturers to accept them. The recycling costs of the three items that manufacturers must accept are covered by purchasers via an automobile recycling fee that is paid when a vehicle is purchased. The recycling fees paid by automobile purchasers are held in a pool operated by the deposit management entity (i.e., the Japan Automobile Recycling Promotion Center) until corresponding vehicles go out of service.

Thus, the Automobile Recycling Law adopts the aforementioned model (iv).

9.2.4 Evaluating the Home Appliance Recycling Law

9.2.4.1 Evaluation from the Perspective of EPR

9.2.4.1.1 Physical Responsibility to Collect and Recycle

We can compare the Home Appliance Recycling Law with the Container and Packaging Recycling Law and the Automobile Recycling Law in terms of the responsibility for collection and recycling. Whereas municipalities collect containers and packages under the Container and Packaging Recycling Law, manufacturers collect used appliances in the case of the Home Appliance Recycling Law. Thus, in terms of the responsibility for collecting end-of-life products, the latter law conforms more closely to the idea of EPR than the former law does.

Next, the Automobile Recycling Law does not require automobile manufacturers to accept and recycle the entire bodies of vehicles but rather only requires them to recycle the aforementioned three items. Because the Home Appliance Recycling Law obliges manufacturers to accept entire appliances, we can say the latter law conforms more closely to the idea of EPR than the former law does.

9.2.4.1.2 Financial Responsibility

Whereas the Container and Packaging Recycling Law requires business operators to pay recycling costs, the Home Appliance Recycling Law obliges a product's final user to pay recycling costs by purchasing a home appliance recycling ticket. From the perspective of EPR, financial responsibility under the Container and Packaging Recycling Law generally corresponds more closely to EPR than the Home Appliance Recycling law does, with the exception of the cost of collection under the former law, which is paid by municipalities.

The Automobile Recycling Law also places the responsibility for paying recycling costs on the final user. Although these recycling laws differ as to whether payment is due at the time of product purchase (as with automobiles) or at the time of disposal (as with home appliances), consumers are responsible for paying the recycling costs in both cases. Thus, neither the Automobile Recycling Law nor the Home Appliance Recycling Law corresponds to the EPR concept that requires manufactures to bear the financial responsibility for recycling.

9.2.4.1.3 Evaluation of the Home Appliance Recycling Law: Summary

As stated above, the concept of EPR covers both physical and financial responsibility. The Home Appliance Recycling Law conforms to the EPR concept in terms of the physical responsibility for recycling, but its imposition of recycling costs on consumers is problematic from the perspective that manufacturers should also bear the financial responsibility. It is claimed that a system in which users pay recycling fees at the time of disposal cannot promote design for the environment, which is the ultimate goal of EPR. We discuss this claim below.

9.2.4.2 Efficiency: Evaluation from an Economic Perspective

The previous discussion examined the issue of who bears financial responsibility for recycling and highlights that the Home Appliance Recycling Law and the Automobile Recycling Law are not in line with the concept of EPR because they place the responsibility for payment on consumers rather than manufacturers.

However, the issue of who should primarily pay the cost of recycling is distinct from the issue of who ultimately bears the financial burden of recycling costs. For example, even if business operators are legally required to pay recycling costs (as in model (ii)), those costs may be included in the price of a product and shifted onto consumers, depending on market conditions. Conversely, even if recycling costs are paid by consumers at the time of purchase, if the product is discounted by an amount equivalent to these costs, then retailers or manufacturers are ultimately bearing these costs.

Whereas models (ii), (iii), and (iv) differ on which party bears responsibility for the initial payment of recycling costs, they all place the physical responsibility for carrying out recycling on manufacturers. Thus, manufacturers are given an incentive to design their products to minimize recycling and waste management costs. Under models (iii) and (iv), manufacturers can collect recycling fees from consumers. However, these fees are little more than a bonus for the manufacturers. Because manufacturers bear the physical responsibility for recycling regardless of whether they receive these fees, they still have financial incentives to reduce recycling costs. Thus, models (ii), (iii), and (iv) do not differ from the perspective of providing incentives to reduce recycling costs; their only difference lies in the effect on income distribution, in case all of these products are legally recycled.

9.2.4.3 Rationality of Existing Recycling Laws

9.2.4.3.1 Illegal Waste Dumping (See Sect. 9.2.1)

If the physical responsibility for recycling is placed on manufacturers, then regardless of who primarily pays the recycling costs, manufacturers are incentivized to reduce them. It does not matter whether which model (ii), (iii), or (iv) is adopted.

However, the models have significant practical differences. One of them involves the issue of illegal waste dumping. The Home Appliance Recycling Law requires consumers to pay recycling costs at the time of disposal (model (iii)), meaning that consumers are tempted to dump products illegally to avoid this payment. Illegal dumping creates an externality in the form of environmental pollution and wastes resources, resulting in social inefficiency. Of course, an illegal dumper may be punished by the law (Art. 16 and Art. 25, item 14, of the Waste Management and Public Cleansing Law), but the government cannot enforce this law perfectly. After the Home Appliance Recycling Law was enacted, illegal dumping of home appliances increased, and municipalities were forced to deal with the problem. Theoretically, models (ii), (iii), and (iv) may be equally efficient. However, the lack of legal enforcement causes people to commit illegal dumping to avoid paying the costs under model (iii). If we take this issue into account, the choice of model does impact efficiency. Legislators must consider real-world issues, such as the lack of enforcement and human behavior, to establish an efficient legal system.

9.2.4.3.2 Arguments on a Revision of the Law

A revision of the Home Appliance Recycling Law was scheduled for 2008. At that time, the issue of illegal dumping was raised, and a proposal was made to revise the system requiring consumers to pay recycling fees upon disposal (model (iii)). However, this proposal was rejected for several reasons.

First, it is important to understand why the user payment-at-disposal model (model (iii)) was originally adopted. If manufacturers were required to accept home appliances that were sold before the recycling law was enacted (hereinafter "pre-purchased products") and to pay the recycling costs for these appliances (model (ii)), their burden would be too heavy. Manufacturers did not expect to be obliged to recycle at their own expense end-of-life products that they had sold, nor did they have a chance to consider the recycling costs when they set the prices of these products. Thus, it was thought that the retroactive imposition of such a burden should be avoided. To avoid this problem, manufacturers needed to at least be exempted from bearing the recycling costs for pre-purchased products. For these products, the recycling costs would be borne by consumers at the time of disposal (model (iii)). However, it is very difficult to handle products purchased before and after the enactment of the recycling law differently and to impose the financial responsibility for recycling only the latter products on manufacturers given the sheer number of home appliances involved. This kind of problem could be avoided by applying model (iii) to all end-of-life home appliances.

The Automobile Recycling Law adopts model (iv), and manufacturers are only responsible for paying recycling costs for vehicles sold after the law was enacted. The cost of recycling vehicles purchased before the law's enactment is paid by end users at the time of disposal. Because all new vehicles are registered with the government at the time of purchase, it is easy to distinguish vehicles sold before and after the law's enactment and adopt model (iii) for the former vehicles and model (iv) for the latter vehicles. However, this legislation raises other issues. First, it is assumed that the recycling fees collected at the time of purchase must be appropriated for recycling the corresponding product. This notion comes from the principle of self-responsibility and means in this context that consumers should bear the costs of recycling the products that they have bought, used, and disposed. The Automobile Recycling Law follows this concept by levying recycling fees at the time of purchase and keeping them in a pool managed by a deposit management entity until automobiles are disposed. This self-responsibility aspect of the Automobile Recycling Law has incurred massive administrative costs. In any case, given the large number of end-of-life home appliances and the lack of an administrative system for appliances that is equivalent to vehicle registration, it is not realistic to apply this model to home appliance recycling.

Another obstacle to revising the Home Appliance Recycling Law to impose financial responsibility on manufacturers is that many end-of-life appliances are not recycled even after the law's enactment. An investigation by the government showed that a large proportion of end-of-life appliances are not handled under the Home Appliance Recycling Law but rather are exported overseas as secondhand products or recycling materials (Shimamura et al. 2007). If recycling fees were collected from consumers at the time of purchase (model (iv)), consumers would be paying for recycling even though a large proportion of end-of-life products are not recycled. It is not realistic to monitor whether each of the over 22 million end-of-life home appliances generated each year is recycled. Given these circumstances, manufacturers would unjustly profit from recycling fees collected at the time of product purchase, as not every product would be recycled. This system would be unfair.

The Home Appliance Recycling Law, which obliges consumers to pay recycling fees when they dispose of products (model (iii)), does not seem efficient because it tempts people to dump end-of-life products illegally. Nevertheless, the law was not revised because of the normative and practical considerations explained above.

9.3 Landscapes

Cities are human-made. However, for city residents, the urban space is an environment. City residents enjoy a good landscape as part of their living environment. In this section, we focus on conflicts of interest and disputes related to landscapes and explore how law and economics can be applied to such problems.

9.3.1 An Economics Approach to Landscape Problems

This section first explains the key concepts for considering landscape problems from an economics perspective. The landscape, the air and water, and many other environmental resources can be regarded as commons. The term "commons" refers to shared land or resources that are not owned by a particular individual, corporation, or nation. Entire groups with loose associations, such as a local communities, own or are given usage rights to these scarce resources.

In 1968, an ecologist, Garrett Hardin, published an article about the tragedy of the commons (Hardin 1968). Suppose that there is a pasture that anyone may enter and use freely. Various farmers allow their livestock to graze on this pasture, and they determine the number of livestock to graze based on their own costs and benefits. However, by allowing their livestock to graze in the pasture, the farmers deplete the grass that feeds the livestock without considering the cost to other farmers. As a result, too many livestock are turned loose on the pasture, the farmers cannot maintain their own livestock, and no one ends up with their desired result. This situation is nothing short of a tragedy.

In fact, commons can be managed without becoming a tragedy by establishing rules regarding their usage. However, some conditions must hold for this result to occur. Two important conditions are that the benefits of breaching the rules must be small, and the penalties must be high. For example, suppose that the people of a village use a forest. They can collect nuts and firewood from the forest, making it a valuable resource for them. The collection of nuts and firewood can be restricted to a certain amount, allowing the forest to be used sustainably. Consider what would happen, however, if villagers are able to bring nuts to a city and sell them for a very high price or if there were no penalty for a villager using more than the predetermined

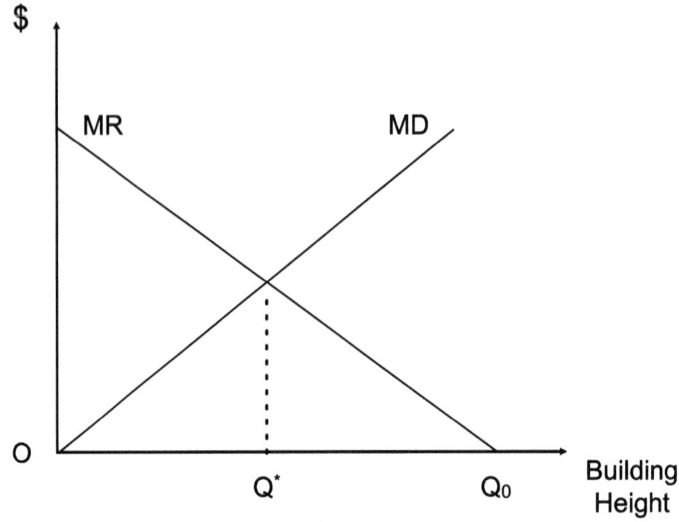

Fig. 9.2 Coase's solution to landscape problems

amount of firewood. Usage rights for commons are often distributed equally among members of the community, but it is necessary to make the details and responsibilities of the usage rights clear to manage them successfully.

An argument by Ronald Coase, called the Coase theorem (Coase 1960), illustrates the importance of establishing rights. However, Coase did not emphasize the Coase theorem per se; rather, he was interested in the concept of transaction costs.

The Coase theorem states that a Pigouvian tax is not necessary to correct external diseconomies. According to the Coase theorem, if it can be determined whether the polluters or the victims hold the rights, both parties can voluntarily negotiate with each other and achieve an efficient allocation of resources.

We explain the Coase theorem in Fig. 9.2. We plot the height of a building to be constructed on the horizontal access, and we plot the marginal damage and marginal revenue on the vertical axis. The downward sloping line is the real estate company's marginal revenue, which increases as the building's height increases. The upward sloping line is the marginal damage to local residents, which increases as the building's height increases. This damage is a negative externality.

Now, we consider two cases in which rights are established. In case 1, the local residents hold the environmental rights, and in case 2, the real estate company holds the right to freely determine the building's height. In case 1, the building's height starts at zero on the left side of the figure. The real estate company must compensate the local residents for the marginal damages caused by the deterioration of the landscape. The negotiation continues as long as the additional compensation to increase the height of the building does not exceed the real estate company's marginal revenue. As a result, the height of the building is Q*.

Next, we consider case 2. Because the real estate company can freely determine the building's height, it prefers to set the building's height at Q0, where the marginal revenue is zero. The negotiations therefore start here. Unlike in the previous case, the local residents must bribe the real estate company to reduce the building's height. The residents must compensate the company for the marginal revenue that it will lose by reducing the height of the building. The negotiation continues as long as the additional compensation to reduce the building's height does not exceed the marginal damage avoided. As a result, the height of the building is again Q*. In other words, no matter which party holds the rights, the building ends up being the same height.

In practice, it is difficult for local residents to unite and negotiate against a party causing negative externalities. Additionally, negotiations fail to reach an agreement in many cases because it is unclear which side holds the rights. Thus, the costs of negotiation (i.e., the transaction costs) must be small for the Coase theorem to apply.

9.3.2 *Landscape Issues and the Legal System*

9.3.2.1 Sample Case

In this section, we use a specific sample case to illustrate the legal system's operations related to landscape protection. Then, we attempt to implement the legal and economic approaches to landscape issues, considering the economics approach discussed in Sect. 9.3.1.

City A has a tradition of civic activity for town planning and is famous for its residents' awareness of landscape protection. In particular, B Street, which is lined with cherry blossom and ginkgo trees, is a symbol of the city's planning ability. Around B Street, no buildings are taller than 20 m, the height of the trees. Both the local residents' consensus and the city's landscape policy guidelines agree that buildings should be kept below that height. However, real estate company C planned to build a 44-m apartment building along B Street. At the time, the site for the apartment building was zoned as a category II mid/high-rise oriented residential zone under the City Planning Act. According to the city's zoning plan, the upper limit of the site's building coverage ratio (i.e., the ratio of the building's footprint area to the site area) was 60%, and the floor area ratio (i.e., the ratio of the building's total floor area to the site area) was 200%. In other words, constructing an apartment building of this height (44 m) was permitted under the zoning plan according to the City Planning Act and the Building Standard Act. City A attempted to provide administrative guidance, which did not have legal force, but the negotiations ultimately broke down. Thus, in response to local residents' requests, the city enacted a new district plan and building codes to limit the height of buildings in the zone to 20 m.

9.3.2.2 Land Ownership and Landscape: The Constitution and the Guarantee of the Right to Property

This example is taken from the Kunitachi condominium conflict, which resulted in several court cases in the 2000s, although it has been simplified and modified here (Kadomatsu 2017a). A dispute such as this one can be understood as a conflict between the interests of real estate company C, which wants to utilize the site based on its ownership of the land, and the interests of local residents, who want to enjoy a good landscape. Below, we attempt to address the issue from a legal standpoint based on the nature of land ownership rights.

First, Article 29 of the Japanese Constitution makes the following stipulations and guarantees the constitutional right to property:

(1)The right to own or to hold property is inviolable.

(2)Property rights shall be defined by law, in conformity with the public welfare.

(3)Private property may be taken for public use upon just compensation therefor.

The property rights referred to in Article 29 can be classified as a type of economic freedom. However, insofar as this right refers to the ownership of certain tangible objects, it is significantly different from other freedoms. If one person owns a particular piece of land, then other people do not own it. The owner can exclude others from using it (excludability; see Sect. 7 of the Appendix). In other words, one person's freedom excludes others from that freedom. In contrast, the freedom of expression is also a freedom, and although the exercise of that right has the potential to impinge upon the rights of others (e.g., in the case of defamation), affording the freedom of expression to one person does not necessarily mean denying it to others, making it a guaranteed freedom for the general citizenry.

In this way, the right to property is not a guaranteed freedom to the general citizenry (i.e., equally afforded to all) but rather is essentially an allocation of limited resources. Furthermore, there is no guarantee that the specific societal allocation of these resources will be reasonable or just. One may ask why the right to property is nevertheless guaranteed by the Constitution. Two arguments may justify it.

The first argument focuses on property rights' function in guaranteeing personal freedom. Property rights guarantee the holder a stable existence, and they can form the physical conditions of personal freedom. Thus, the state's arbitrary interference with those rights may drastically destabilize trust in the economic system and the stability of civic life. Even if the distribution of resources is not just and reasonable, it is important to be wary of the forced redistribution of those rights.

The second argument justifies property rights based on the fact that distributing resources by allocating property rights to individuals increases the efficiency of resource usage and improves society's overall welfare. The tragedy of the commons discussed in Sect. 9.3.1 is one such explanation. This situation shows that establishing some form of excludability rights on the use of resources can increase social benefits. It should be noted that such justifications for property rights do not necessarily apply to non-competitive assets and services, that is, those for which one person's consumption does not reduce another person's consumption. Intellectual property rights are one such right, and the justification them can be found in Chap. 2.

9.3.2.3 Private Law Restrictions on Land Ownership

The property rights in Article 29, paragraph 2 of the Constitution listed earlier are defined by law. The details of property rights are prescribed in statutory laws established by the Diet, Cabinet orders and ministerial ordinances delegated by statutory laws, and local government ordinances.

How does the law define the right to own land? Unlike personal property, such as furniture or a computer, land (or real estate) requires a legal mechanism for ownership. Land is ultimately continuous, meaning that it is not possible to possess land unless it is artificially divided up. The law divides up the land, assigns each parcel a lot number, and records it in the land registry, making it subject to ownership and transactions. In addition, the Civil Code establishes land ownership of the ground below and the air space above a property, stating in Article 207 that "Ownership in land shall extend to above and below the surface of the land, subject to the restrictions prescribed by laws and regulations." In other words, land ownership is created through a legal "dual partition of common space" (Kadomatsu 2017b, p. 498; Rousseau 1984, p. 109: "The first man who, having enclosed a piece of land, thought of saying 'This is mine' and found people simple enough to believe him, was the true founder of civil society").

However, such land ownership rights are also subject to private and administrative legal restrictions. First, we consider private legal restrictions.

9.3.2.3.1 Usufruct

First, a property right called "usufruct" (the right to use and profit from land owned by others for certain purposes) restricts the established land ownership rights in many cases with the consent of the parties involved. Servitudes (Civil Code Art. 280) are an example of this right. For example, if an electric company wants to run electrical wires over property owned by someone else, a servitude can be established whereby the company signs a contract with the land's owner to run the lines. However, the "right of common" (*iriai ken*), which is part of usufruct, is established by convention and not by the parties to an agreement.

Applying this concept to the case in Sect. 9.3.2.1, the local residents can enter into a contract with real estate company C to conserve their good views of the landscape by, for example, establishing a servitude whereby buildings over 20 m tall cannot be built. This method is one way to preserve the landscape. In this case, should C sell the land to a third party, the residents can assert their servitude against the third party.

9.3.2.3.2 Restrictions Based on Neighboring Relations

The Civil Code also establishes limitations on land rights derived from neighboring relations (i.e., the legal relationship between owners of adjacent land). Examples include Civil Code Article 209, which provides a landowner the right to request the use of neighboring land to the extent necessary to build or repair walls or buildings on or in the vicinity of the boundary, and Civil Code Article 210, which provides the owner of land that is surrounded by other land and has no access to public roads the right to pass through the other land to reach a public road. As noted above, land rights are inherently created by a dual partition of common space, but the continuous nature of space necessitates these restrictions.

9.3.2.3.3 Torts/Injunctions

As in the case of neighboring relationship restrictions, restrictions may be placed on ownership based on the continuity of space. For example, if a person causes damage to neighboring land by using his or her own land according to the ownership rights, that person is obligated to compensate the neighbor for any tortious damages (Civil Code Art. 709). The classic case law referred to as the *Shingen Kō Hata Kakematsu* case (Great Court of Judicature Judgment, March 3, 1919) is one such example. In this case, smoke from a national railway locomotive caused the death of an ancient pine tree along its route. The railway company argued that smoke is unavoidably generated regardless of how a train is driven or if coal is used as fuel. Thus, it believed that it was naturally within its rights as a railway operator. However, the Great Court of Judicature found that equipment could have been used to prevent the soot, established that this case was a tortious abuse of rights, and ordered the operator to pay damages to the country. This decision accurately illustrates the concept of negative externalities that arise through the exercise of rights (see Sect. 9.2.1). However, Japanese civil law scholars currently tend to believe that a tort can be established without involving the concept of the abuse of rights (Kubota 2018, p. 62).

A high-rise building interfering with local residents' sunlight and ventilation is also an issue of negative externalities that arise when land ownership rights are exercised, in this case for the act of construction. In determining whether a tort is established, the concept of a "tolerable limit" has come to be an almost universally accepted standard. In this case, in addition to the damages caused by tortious action, another problem is that the local residents may request an injunction against the construction. This legal structure and the different elements that should be considered for compensation of damages or injunctions are widely discussed (see Supreme Court Judgment, July 7, 1995). Theories based on personal rights are compelling, but tort theory, environmental rights theory, and illegal infringement theory may also be asserted.

9.3.2.4 Administrative Legal Limitations on Land Ownership: City Planning

In addition to the limitations in private law noted above, land ownership rights face administrative legal restrictions based on laws and regulations. Typically, administrative legal restrictions on land ownership are related to city planning. In addition to land use restrictions, city planning also comprises plans for the development of the urban infrastructure.

The core of the legal system surrounding city planning in Japan is the City Planning Act and the Building Standards Act. The concepts of a district plan and a category II mid/high-rise oriented residential zone introduced in the case described above are both aspects of city planning based on the City Planning Act. Local government building ordinances are also prescribed to enforce the content of the district plan under the authority delegated by the Building Standards Act. These provisions are understood to be part of the definition of the content of the right to property, as prescribed by Article 29, paragraph 2 of the Constitution. However, in actual legislative and administrative practice, this definition of the content does not mean that the content of property rights is created by law out of thin air. As mentioned before, land use regulation in practice is dominated by the idea that the land ownership exists first (notwithstanding the fact that land ownership is an artificial creation through the dual partition of common space) and is then restricted by law to the extent necessary (i.e., the minimum intervention principle).

9.3.2.4.1 Zoning

The need for administrative legal restrictions for city planning is also related to space's inherently continuous nature. The zoning system (City Planning Act 8 Art. 1(1)) is a typical restriction on usage in city planning. The category II mid/high-rise oriented residential zone mentioned in the case described above is one such example.

There are 12 types of zones, as Fig. 9.3 illustrates. Restrictions on the purpose for which land is used (i.e., usage restrictions) and restrictions on building configurations, such as density and height, (i.e., form restrictions) are established for each zone. These restrictions are set forth by the Building Standards Act. If these restrictions are violated, a builder may not receive the necessary permission to construct a building, and a building constructed in violation of these restrictions may be ordered to be demolished.

For example, in a category II mid/high-rise oriented residential zone described in the above case, such buildings as nightclubs, mahjong parlors, pachinko parlors, karaoke boxes, factories, and hotels may not be constructed. These usage restrictions can be thought of as addressing externalities. For example, if residential housing is next to a factory, the residents will be disturbed by the noise and vibrations from the factory, resulting in a poor living environment. Conversely, if the factory were to instead restrict its operations so as not to disturb nearby residents, the efficiency of its economic activity would be reduced (i.e., a negative externality). In addition,

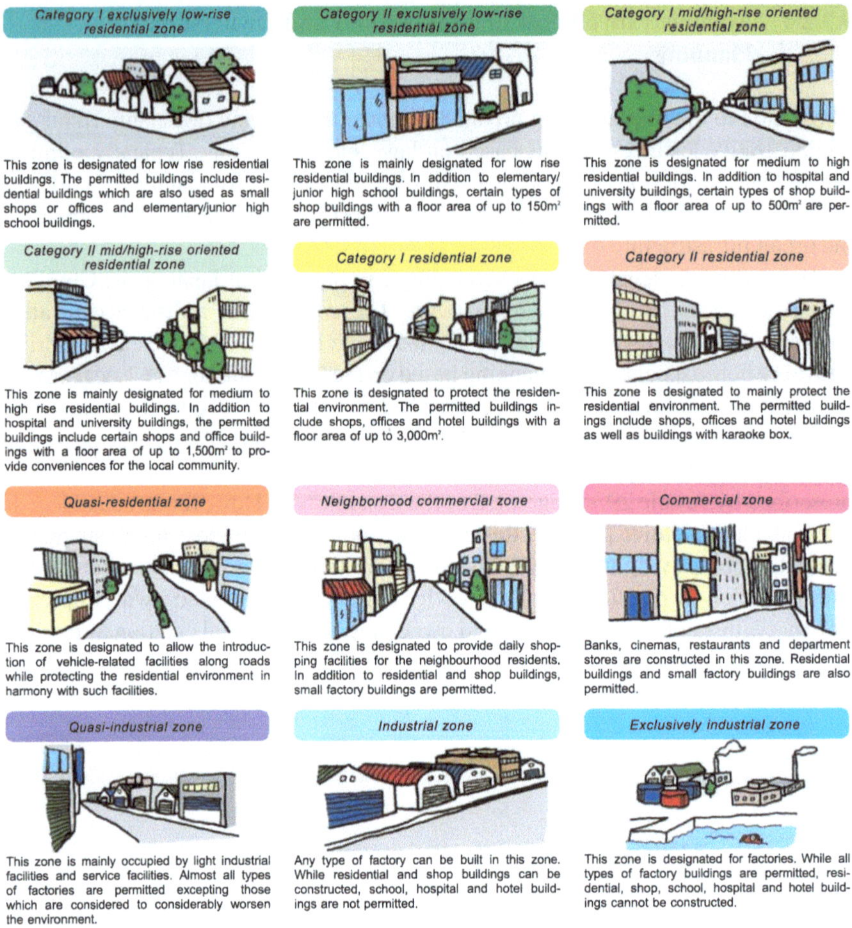

Fig. 9.3 Land use zones. *Source* Japanese Ministry of Land, Infrastructure, Transport and Tourism brochure (https://www.mlit.go.jp/crd/city/plan/tochiriyou/)

keeping factories close to each other may provide other benefits, such as improved logistics and the ability to exchange information and labor (i.e., positive externalities). Separating different spaces based on their functions may be beneficial not only to the different economic actors involved but also to society as a whole. However, Japanese zoning regulations are relatively loose, and buildings with a variety of functions commonly coexist.

Zoning also place form restrictions on buildings concerning their density and height. Density restrictions focus on building coverage and floor area ratios. The idea behind a building coverage ratio is that local environmental factors, such as sunlight and ventilation, can be maintained by ensuring that some open space remains on a site. The idea behind a floor area ratio is to exercise a minimal amount of control over vertical density and control the number of residents and scale of industrial activity

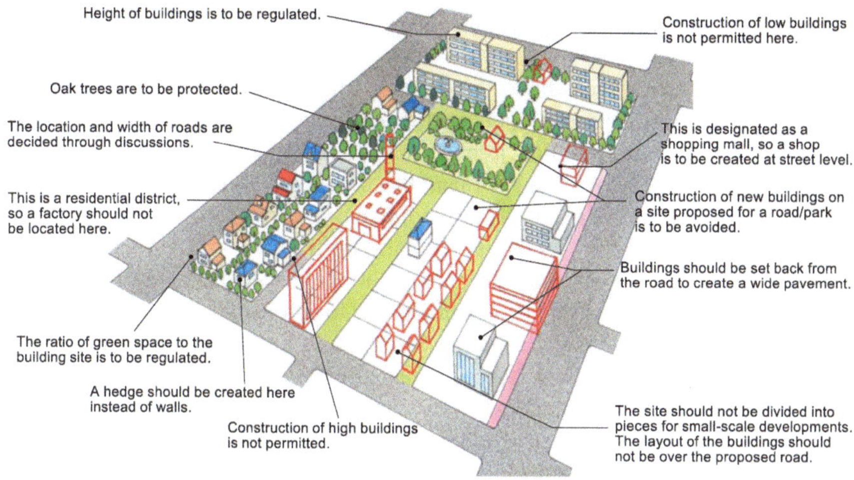

Fig. 9.4 District plan. *Source* Ministry of Land, Infrastructure, Transport and Tourism brochure (https://www.mlit.go.jp/crd/city/plan/tochiriyou/)

to maintain a balance and a standard level of urban infrastructure. The proposed apartment building in the example described above has a building coverage ratio of 60% and a floor area ratio of 200%, making it possible to construct an apartment building over 40 m tall by maintaining a low building coverage ratio. Restrictions on height can include setback regulations to preserve sunshine, lighting, and ventilation for neighboring properties and roads and height zones that establish maximum and minimum heights for buildings.

In this manner, the zoning system is designed to impose the minimum necessary regulations while still respecting architectural freedom in terms of form. This aim is a reflection of the minimum intervention principle. From the perspective of builders, this system offers a high degree of freedom and predictability. From the perspective of local residents, however, the zoning system alone does not offer predictability, as buildings of a scale that did not previously exist in an area may suddenly be constructed, changing the nature of that space. This style of regulation is somewhat rough and does not account for the specific characteristics of individual spaces.

9.3.2.4.2 District Plan

In the case described above, city A responded to the request of the residents and quickly enacted a city plan, known as a district plan (City Planning Act Art. 12(5)). Whereas zoning regulations are more roughly defined, a district plan is a detailed regulation on a relatively small district. District plans and district development plans are established as a set, allowing cities to impose extremely detailed rules on planning for roads and parks; limitations on the use of buildings; limitations on floor area ratios, building area ratios, and heights; and regulations on buildings' form, color, and design, among others.

In the example described above, city A established a maximum height restriction of 20 m in its district plan and district development plan, thereby making it impermissible to construct a 44-m building, as had been allowed under the zoning regulations. It is also possible to restrict usages of land that would otherwise be permitted under zoning regulations, by, for example, forbidding the construction of studio apartment buildings or karaoke boxes. Such district plans are typically enacted with a certain degree of consensus among residents, but unanimous consent is not legally required.

Local ordinances prescribed by a municipality to enforce its district development plan are enforceable under the Building Standards Act, and buildings that violate them can be ordered to be demolished. In the case described above, city A enacted a new ordinance, but a dispute arose over whether the date that the ordinance came into effect or the date that construction on the apartment building began was earlier. This dispute matters because if a law or ordinance is enacted or amended to change the building codes, buildings that already existed at that time or were being built at the time of the change are not subject to the new rules (Building Standards Act Art. 3(2), "Existing Non-Conforming Buildings"). Although this district plan system was modeled on the German B-Plan System, the two plans have an important difference. In Germany, a building cannot be constructed in a region that is not already built up unless a B-plan is established. In other words, the B-plan serves to relax existing regulations. Conversely, Japanese district plans serve to strengthen the building regulations imposed by zoning. Under this system, the incentive to enact a district plan is not strong enough.

In addition to these systems, the Landscape Act was established in 2004 to provide for landscape planning and landscape district systems, but we do not discuss this law here.

9.3.3 The Law and Economics of Landscape Problems

We now discuss the possible legal and economic approaches to landscape problems based on the economic approaches presented in Sect. 9.3.1 and the land rights and legal systems restricting them presented in Sect. 9.3.2.

9.3.3.1 Landscapes as Commons

As Sect. 9.3.1 describes, a landscape has the properties of a commons. A good landscape is shared among local residents and many other stakeholders. It is unignorable that a person living near a landscape benefits from the landscape, and one person's enjoyment of a landscape's benefits does not detract from another person's enjoyment of those benefits. The shared and public nature of landscapes is derived from the inherent continuity of space.

Some rulings related to the Kunitachi condominium conflict offer examples illuminating the nature of landscapes (Kadomatsu 2017b, p. 499):

> Building owners or residents can enjoy the landscape only when they themselves strive to maintain their beauty. In addition, the landscape can easily be destroyed if any of the users does not observe the rules necessary for its maintenance. One can enjoy the interest in the landscape continuously only when all users of the space form a relationship in which they mutually maintain and respect the landscape. Landscape can be maintained only when all the users of the space observe its rules. It is highly dependent on a consciousness of community of the users of the space. (Tokyo District Court Judgment, December 4, 2001.)

> There are cases in which the property-right holders establish certain standards on height, color or design for the buildings within the area and thus a certain landscape evolves. When not only the residents but also the society at large considers it to be a good landscape, it gives added value to the lot. Such added value of urban landscape is by its nature different from enjoyment of the natural landscape of mountains or coast, or from enjoyment of historical buildings which are preserved at a cost to their owners. It is the property-right holders who enjoy the added value of the landscape themselves that have brought forth the value by their continuous effort. It required their mutual understanding, solidarity and self-sacrifice. In order to maintain such added value, the above standards must be observed by all the property-right holders. Just one property-right holder can immediately destroy the uniformity of the landscape by a building that violates the standard and deprives other property-right holders of the above added value. (Tokyo District Court Judgment, December 18, 2002.)

As Sect. 9.3.1 shows, a tragedy of the commons can occur within a common space. To avoid this tragedy arising from the fact that space is continuous, the law artificially creates a land ownership mechanism through the dual partition of space. However, land that is thought to have been legally divided into private tracts can appear to have a commons-like nature when viewed as a landscape. Thus, it is possible for a tragedy of the commons to occur if individual owners destroy the landscape in the pursuit of their own interests.

9.3.3.2 Social Dilemmas

A social dilemma arises when individual rationality is at odds with social rationality. Consider the following example (see Ito 2006). Two people build one-story houses in a particular location and enjoy a pleasant landscape. They are both considering expanding their houses vertically because they have outgrown them, but if one person constructs a two-story house, the other person will be prevented from seeing the view, ruining the landscape.

Let us assume that the residents each receives a benefit equal to 3 for each story of their houses. Thus, the benefit from owning a two-story house equals 6. We also assume that the benefit obtained from the landscape equals 5. If both residents have one-story houses, each resident's benefit is equal to $5 + 3 = 8$. If only one resident expands his or her house, then that resident's benefit increases to $5 + (3 \times 2) = 11$. However, the other resident loses the benefit of the view and is left with a benefit of 3. If both residents expand their houses, then they both lose the benefit of the landscape and have a total benefit of $3 \times 2 = 6$.

In this case, the socially optimal outcome (i.e., the maximum total of both people's benefits) is for neither resident to expand his or her house, and the worst case is when both of them expand their houses. However, if we assume that the residents do not cooperate, then it is in each resident's best interest to add a second story, regardless of whether the other resident does so. Ultimately, the equilibrium is reached when both residents expand their houses, which the worst outcome for society.

What can be done to avoid this outcome? The ideal solution involves appropriately applying one of three methods: resolving the problem by establishing official rules, resolving the problem through a mutual transaction (Coase theorem), or resolving the problem through voluntary cooperation.

As shown above, the first solution, that is, establishing detailed rules using administrative legal regulations, such as a district plan, can effectively preserve the environment. However, mutual cooperation by the parties (the third solution) is essential for setting the rules and effectively implementing them. Because the rules are detailed, it is difficult to ensure that they are being observed using only legal enforcement.

9.3.3.3 Coase Theorem

One may ask if it is possible to employ the Coase theorem, as in Sect. 9.3.1. As described above, when transaction costs are low, the resulting building was the same height regardless of whether the real estate company or the local residents held the rights. If the real estate company held the rights, the local residents could still buy the real estate company's rights to keep the building's height lower. This possibility may seem somewhat unrealistic. However, as the section on private legal restrictions (Sect. 9.3.2.3) explains, it is possible in some cases to use a servitude (view easement) to conserve a landscape through private trading. However, the transaction costs are quite large in practice, and they may change depending on whether the rights are held by the builder or the residents (Mishan 1971).

Furthermore, achieving Coase-type solutions through purely private transactions can be very difficult in practice for several reasons. First, it is often hard to clearly establish the content of rights and conduct transactions based on these rights. In the case described above, a clear standard for height could be set, but such cases are rare in landscape issues. In many cases, vague standards, such as "harmony with the community and local area," are used. Second, in many cases, the damaged parties may be numerous and widespread, making mutual transactions difficult. Even if all of the local residents reach a consensus, many other parties have interests in the landscape, and those interests are often multi-layered (Kadomatsu 2017b, p. 499 (note 4)).

9.3.3.4 Discussion and Coordination-Oriented City Planning

From this perspective, a valuable option is a discussion-oriented city planning mechanism whereby the builder, residents, and administrative third parties discuss and coordinate with each other before construction begins to reach a desirable conclusion. This solution is a variation on the solution of resolving the problem by establishing official rules. If a win–win building plan that is acceptable to both businesspeople and residents can be established through early-stage discussions (Okata 2002, p. 32), they can reach a desirable solution together.

Discussion-oriented city planning systems set up a forum for quasi-Coase negotiations that can be difficult to create in their pure form, thereby making these negotiations somewhat feasible. In addition, by institutionalizing discussions, elements of resolving the problem through mutual cooperation can be incorporated, which can prevent the social dilemmas that may occur in the absence of mutual negotiations.

9.4 Conclusion

We have discussed environmental issues from law and economics perspectives. Law and economics can highlight the nature and extent of environmental problems and provide some important ideas for resolving them. Much can be learned from law and economics, but we would like to conclude by emphasizing the following two points.

First, it is better to use incentives. It is easy to ask people to improve the environment or recycle. However, it is difficult to change their behavior simply by asking. It is very difficult to change people's thinking. However, a mechanism whereby people benefit from improving the environment can change not only their way of thinking but also their behavior. Policies that do not consider incentives often fail. For example, the grand experiment with socialism ended in failure. The major reason for this failure was that ingenuity and effort were not rewarded in the system.

Column 14. "The world is not divisible without excess by reason": the purpose of law

The introduction explained that a distinctive feature of the law is the notion of respecting the purposes of individual laws and regulations and bringing about justice in individual transactions. Along with this idea, it is believed that the law as a whole has broader purposes beyond the purposes of individual statutes, such as the Japanese Constitution or the Civil Code. One of these purposes is to provide stable rules that provide guidelines for the actions of members of society, that is, legal stability. However, trying to satisfy this aim of legal stability can be an obstacle to the purposes of individual laws and constitutional values, such as freedom and equality, in some cases. These cases can be addressed by creating new statutes for future problems, but to solve past problems, it may be necessary to make judgments with specific validity. From this conclusion, the question arises of how to reconcile legal stability and specific validity. Additional questions arise, include what the other purposes of the law should be besides stability and how to achieve harmony between these various purposes

With these ideas in mind, one legal theorist advocates legal stability, justice, and fitness-for-purpose as the key principles of law, although he also states:

It must be said that the three principles of the legal philosophy of justice, fitness-for-purpose, and legal stability, despite slipping into sharp contradictions with one another at times, govern the law in its entirety. .... We just pointed to such contradictions and were unable to find solutions. We do not recognize it as a flaw in the philosophy... Do not think that the world was created through reason with purpose, and therefore, think how suspicious it would be if there was a philosophy that explained that world consistently within one rational system! And if the world is just consistent without contradictions, how useless it would be to exist if life were not a decision![1]

This explanation shows that the realm of law is not easily divided and categorized by any single principle or theory; indeed, this difficulty is one of the reasons for the existence of the legal system. The field of economics tends to emphasize theoretical uniformity, and, of course, law has this tendency to a degree as well. However, it is also possible for legal thought to simultaneously affirm such contradictions. This discussion is not intended merely to justify the fact that things were not always neatly divisible when we explained some of the concepts and ideas of law in the series of columns in this book

Study Questions

1. Explain the meaning of the term "tragedy of the commons."
2. Can you identify an example in which the Coase theorem holds? If not, why not?
3. Identify an example of unit-based pricing of household waste collection and examine the details of this pricing system.
4. Answer the following questions by referring to the description of a social dilemma in this textbook.

(1) Fill in the following payoff matrix by defining the benefit obtained from using one floor of a house as "a" and the benefit from the surrounding landscape as "e."

[1] Gustav Radbruch (2011) *Rechtsphilosophie: Studienausgabe*, 2 Auflage. C.F. Müller, Heidelberg, p 77 (original edn. 1932).

		Resident 2	
		Conservation (one floor)	Expansion (two floors)
Resident 1	Conservation		
	Expansion		

(2) Using the above payoff matrix, explain the relationship between a and e that must hold for the worst outcome from the perspective of society (i.e., the social dilemma) to occur.

(3) Suppose that a rule is established in the area to limit houses to one floor, and penalties are set. Fill in the following payoff matrix, where "p" represents the damage that the inhabitants suffer if they receive are penalized.

		Resident 2	
		Conservation (one floor)	Expansion (two floors)
Resident 1	Conservation		
	Expansion		

(4) Using the above payoff matrix, explain the relationship between a, e, and p that holds when a rule limiting houses to one floor is established.

(5) Explain the idea of extended producer responsibility. Then, consider an example of a system in your country that is built on that idea. Is this system economically efficient?

References

Coase RH (1960) The problem of social cost. J Law Econ 3:1–44

Hardin G (1968) The tragedy of the commons. Science 162:1243–1248

Ito S (2006) Jichitai hatsu no seisaku kakushin (Policy innovation from local governments). Bokutakusha, Tokyo [publication in Japanese]

Kadomatsu N (2017a) A misinterpretation or a productive diversion? The rise and fall of the "relationship of reciprocal interchangeability" concept and the possibility of reception of a legal interpretation. In: Russel L Weaver et al (eds) Comparative perspectives on administrative procedure. Carolina Academic Press, Durham, USA, pp 105–127

Kadomatsu N (2017b) Legal management of urban space in Japan and the role of the judiciary. In: Rose-Ackerman S et al (eds) Comparative administrative law. Edward Elgar Publishing, Cheltenham, UK; Northhampton, USA, pp 497–512

Kubota A (2018) Fuhōkōi hō (The law of torts), 2nd edn. Yuhikaku, Tokyo [publication in Japanese]

Mishan EJ (1971) The postwar literature on externalities: an interpretative essay. J Econ Lit 9(1):1–28

Okata J (2002) Toshi saisei to toshi keikaku (Urban reconstruction and city planning). Toshi Mondai 93(3):17–36 [publication in Japanese]

Otsuka T (2020) Kankyōhō (Environmental law), 4th edn. Yuhikaku, Tokyo [publication in Japanese]
Pigou AC (1920) The economics of welfare, 1st edn. MacMillan, London
Rousseau J (1984) A discourse on inequality (trans: Cranston M). Penguin Books, London
Shimamura T et al. (2007) Kokusai shigen junkan no hōdōtaigaku (Legal dynamics of international resource circulation). In: Kashimura S (ed) Hōdōtaigaku sōsho daisankan: kisei to jiritsu (Legal dynamics series, vol. 3: regulation and autonomy). Horitsu Bunka Sha. Kyoto [publication in Japanese]

Chapter 10
Appendix: Elements of Economics

Noritsugu Nakanishi

Contents

10.1 Incentives and Rational Choice 239
10.2 Preferences, Expected Utility, and Attitudes Toward Risk 241
10.3 Demand and Supply and Market Efficiency 243
10.4 Strategic-Form Games and Nash Equilibria 248
10.5 Extensive-Form Games and Subgame Perfect Equilibria 250
10.6 Externalities 252
10.7 Public Goods and the Tragedy of the Commons 254
10.8 Monopolies and Oligopolies 257
10.9 Asymmetric Information: Adverse Selection, Moral Hazard, and the Hold-Up Problem 260
10.10 Discounted Present Value 262

10.1 Incentives and Rational Choice

In economics, social phenomena are considered to be the results of interactions between people's various activities. Thus, expressing the behavior of each actor (i.e., *economic agent*) in an appropriate way is the first step to understanding social phenomena. An economic agent can be a single individual or a group of individuals, such as a family, a company, a political party, or an entire country. In any case, as long as an agent can make a coherent and consistent decision, it is considered an independent economic unit.

Consider the behavior of a consumer, as in introductory economics. The consumer seeks benefits, or utility, from consuming goods and services (i.e., *the objective*) and chooses the combination of goods and services that offers the highest utility

N. Nakanishi (✉)
Graduate School of Economics, Kobe University, Kobe, Japan
e-mail: nakanishi@econ.kobe-u.ac.jp

T. Yanagawa et al. (eds.), *Econo-Legal Studies*,
https://doi.org/10.1007/978-981-16-5145-8_10

(i.e., *optimizes*) within the set of available consumption bundles that satisfy the budget constraint, which is determined by the consumer's income and prices (i.e., *constraints*). Thus, an economic agent's behavior is described as selecting the most appropriate action to achieve a desired objective from among all actions that meet the given constraints.

An action that conforms to an economic agent's intended objective, or an agent carrying out such an action, is said to be *rational*. However, the meaning of the term "rational" must be interpreted carefully here. In economics, even if an agent's purpose is completely ridiculous from the perspective of social principles and decency, and even if the outcome of the agent's actions may be inconvenient, annoying, harmful to other people, illegal, or immoral, as long as the chosen action is in line with the achievement of the agent's objective, it is regarded as rational.

Given an agent's objective, the nature of the constraints determines the agent's actual behavior. Some of the constraints to which economic agents must adhere are determined by natural and physical conditions, whereas others are defined somewhat artificially as social rules and systems. The relationship between the range of feasible options defined by the constraints and the degree to which objectives are achieved is called an *incentive structure*. Economic agents change their choices and actions depending on the structure of these incentives.

We can consider the problem of preventing litter of empty cans. In one case, if the fines for littering are large enough, people who fear the possible consequences will refrain from littering. In this way, the possibility of being sanctioned eliminates the incentive to litter. However, these measures are not effective against people who make light of such fines and presume that they will not be caught even if they litter. Alternatively, a deposit of 10 JPY per can may be collected when canned beverages are sold and then refunded in exchange for empty cans. Then, the number of people who opt to discard their cans will be significantly reduced. The reimbursement offers an incentive to cooperate in collecting empty cans. The penalty and deposit-refund systems affect people's incentive structures regarding littering, and society changes as a result. In the case of penalties for littering, the search for culprits is expensive, and they may not necessarily all be found. In contrast, with a deposit-refund system, people will voluntarily cooperate to collect empty cans at no extra cost; moreover, some people may even begin collecting empty cans spontaneously.

This example of littering prevention illustrates two conclusions. First, the agents envisaged in economics are not always good or bad actors. People who ordinarily comport themselves with good behavior may cut corners or take advantage of a situation if given the opportunity. This behavior is pejoratively described as *opportunistic*. In that sense, economic agents are always opportunistic; they are not unconditionally good nor unconditionally unscrupulous but rather act to fulfill their own objectives to the extent that the circumstances allow. Second, if appropriate social rules and institutions can be designed and operated, it may be possible to achieve a more favorable social state by directing people to take "good" actions. Comparing the penalty and deposit-refund systems for preventing littering can clarify which system better engages people's incentives and creates a more desirable social state.

People react to incentives. To elucidate the economic phenomena that arise as a result of economic agents' behavior and interactions, it is important to understand the incentive structures that they face and the rational choices taken as a result.

10.2 Preferences, Expected Utility, and Attitudes Toward Risk

Individuals (i.e., economic agents) are subject to a variety of choices across different situations. The nature of these choices varies depending on the situation. Economics assumes that individuals can evaluate all available choices and select the most valuable option from those that meet the given constraints. Given two choices x and y, if an individual rates x higher than y, then this individual is said to *prefer* x to y. If an individual values x and y equally, the individual is said to be *indifferent* between them. Being indifferent between two choices does not imply that the agent is unable to judge which is better. The system of evaluation that an individual uses for a range of available choices is referred to as that individual's *preference* or *preference relation*.

A real-valued function that assigns larger numbers to an agent's more preferred choices (according to that agent's preference) and assigns the same number to choices that the agent is indifferent between is called a *utility function*. These functions are frequently denoted by the symbol u (whether a given preference can be represented by a utility function is an important theoretical question). Given two choices x and y, if an individual prefers x to y, it follows that $u(x) > u(y)$; if the individual is indifferent between x and y, it follows that $u(x) = u(y)$. Naturally, the choice for which the utility function takes a higher value is a better option for the individual.

Individuals may have opportunities to choose between not only clear and reliable options but also between options whose outcomes may be unclear. Uncertain outcomes are usually expressed using the notion of *probability*. Assume that an agent faces an uncertain situation such that either x or y will occur but the agent does not know which will occur. Then, the agent assigns probabilities to x and y to evaluate the situation. Some researchers distinguish between two different kinds of uncertain situations: one is *risk*, which can be described using the notion of probability, and the other is true *uncertainty*, which cannot be described even with the notion of probability. However, we leave this discussion for another time. An agent may objectively know the probabilities of the outcomes for some empirical or theoretical reasons, or they may use subjective judgments to determine them.

Now, we consider the following example in which an individual faces an uncertain income opportunity. The individual's income is 1 million JPY if the economy is in a recession but 9 million JPY if the economy is strong. The state of the economy depends solely on economic trends and is independent of the individual's efforts. Suppose that the probability of a recession for some particular reason is forecast to be 5/8 (62.5%), and the probability of a booming economy is 3/8 (37.5%). How can the individual assess this uncertain situation?

For an individual, the nominal amount of income is not as important as what the individual can consume with that nominal income. We suppose that an income of 10,000 JPY allows the individual to purchase 1 unit of the consumption good. If the individual can earn an income of 1 million JPY with certainty, then he or she can purchase 100 units of the good (note that 100 = 1 million /10,000) and obtain $u(100)$ units of utility with certainty. Similarly, if the individual can earn an income of 9 million JPY with certainty, then he or she can obtain $u(900)$ units of utility with certainty. Because the amount of income obtained is probabilistic, however, the utility is also probabilistic. The average value of the utility that can be obtained is expressed as the sum of the possible utility levels multiplied by their probabilities: $[5/8] \times u(100) + [3/8] \times u(900)$. This value is referred to as the *expected utility* from an uncertain situation (i.e., the situation in which the agent can consume 100 units with probability 5/8 and 900 units with probability 3/8). It is well-recognized that under certain conditions, an individual's preference for uncertain objects can be expressed using this notion of expected utility; this principle is known as the *expected utility theorem*. The function that assigns expected utility values to uncertain objects is called an expected utility function, and the function defined on the set of certain objects that constitutes the basis for calculating expected utility is referred to as the *von Neumann-Morgenstern (vNM) utility function*, expressed as u above.

Incidentally, in the above example, the individual's *expected income* is expressed as the sum of 1 million JPY and 9 million JPY multiplied by their probabilities (i.e., a weighted average of the incomes based on their probabilities). In other words, the individual's expected income is 4 million JPY (= $[5/8] \times 1$ million + $[3/8] \times 9$ million). If an amount equal to the calculated expected income could be obtained with certainty, then the individual could purchase 400 units of the consumption good and obtain $u(400)$ units of utility. Now, consider whether an individual prefers an income of 4 million JPY with certainty or an uncertain expected income of 4 million JPY. Because this comparison uses the same income of 4 million JPY with differences in the level of uncertainty, it can be seen as a way of expressing an individual's *attitude toward risk*. If $u(400) > [5/8] \times u(100) + [3/8] \times u(900)$, then the individual avoids the uncertain 4 million JPY and prefers the certain 4 million JPY; in this case, he or she can be regarded as *risk-averse*. If the converse is true, then the individual is regarded as *risk-loving*. If the two expressions are equal, then individual is indifferent between the uncertain and certain outcomes and, thus, is *risk-neutral*.

Whether people are risk-averse, risk-loving, or risk-neutral depends on the specific form of vNM utility function. For example, suppose that the vNM utility function is expressed as the square root of the amount of the consumption good, that is, $u(x) \equiv \sqrt{x}$. In the previous example, because $u(100) = \sqrt{100} = 10$, $u(400) = \sqrt{400} = 20$, and $u(900) = \sqrt{900} = 30$, it follows that $u(400) = 20 > 17.5 = [5/8] \times u(100) + [3/8] \times u(400)$, indicating that this individual is risk-averse. Fig. A.1 illustrates this situation by plotting real income (in terms of the consumption good) on the horizontal axis and utility on the vertical axis. For ease of illustration, the scale has been adjusted appropriately. In the case of uncertainty, the expected income is 4 million JPY, which is obtained by dividing the interval of 1 million JPY and 9 million JPY on the horizontal axis using the probability ratio of 3:5 (i.e., 3/8 to 5/8).

In addition, the expected utility under uncertain income is the height of point e (i.e., 17.5), which is obtained by dividing the line segment connecting points a and b, which correspond to 1 million JPY and 9 million JPY, respectively, at a ratio of 3:5. The utility under uncertainty is less than the utility when 4 million JPY is a reliable outcome, indicating risk aversion. Of key importance here is that *if an individual's vNM utility function is increasing and upward-convex (i.e., not necessarily the square root of real income), then that individual is risk-averse.* This statement can be tested by sketching an increasing and upward-convex graph of a vNM utility function. Conversely, any vNM utility function with an increasing and downward-convex graph represent a risk-loving individual, and vNM utility functions that are straight lines represent risk-neutral preferences.

The amount of certain real income that achieves the same level of utility as the expected utility of uncertain income is called the *certainty equivalent* of that uncertain income. Given the expected utility of 17.5 in the previous example, we can solve $17.5 = \sqrt{x}$ for x and find that 3.0625 million JPY is the certainty equivalent. If an individual is risk-averse, then the certainty equivalent is less than the expected income. The difference between the expected income and the certainty equivalent is called the *risk premium.*

A risk-averse individual will choose uncertain income over reliable income if, at minimum, an expected income equal to the risk premium is guaranteed. Alternatively, a risk premium can be thought of as the largest premium that an individual will pay to avoid uncertain income. In that sense, the risk premium is an indicator of an individual's degree of risk aversion. For risk-loving individuals, the risk premium is negative, implying that they are willing to spend money to bet on uncertain income (i.e., take a risk).

10.3 Demand and Supply and Market Efficiency

Many economic phenomena are related to *exchanges* of tangible or intangible things that are mediated with *money*. In other words, goods and services are traded between economic agents in exchange for particular amounts of money (hereafter, we refer to goods and services simply as "goods"). The value of one unit of a good in terms of money is called the *price* of that good. A *market* is a place where supply and demand for a certain good meet, people's supply and demand choices are adjusted and coordinated through changes in price, and exchanges are carried out. Some markets, such as fresh fish, fruit, and stock markets, are visible in the sense that transactions of these goods are conducted in specific places or buildings, whereas other markets are not visible. The term "market" is generally used to refer to an entire framework or institution for trading goods.

Any society has mechanisms or systems for determining who can obtain what goods, how much of a good can be obtained, and to what extent it can be used. Such a system is called an *allocation*. Once an allocation is determined, people's well-being, that is, their *economic welfare*, is determined in turn. It is unknown whether

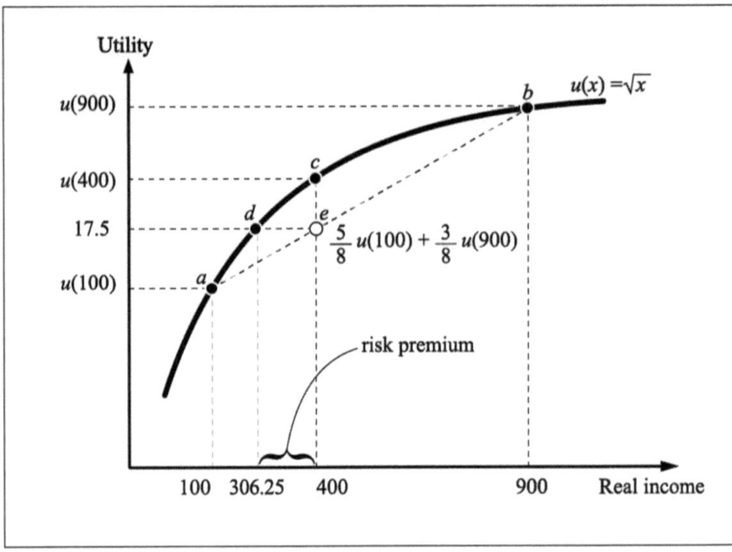

Fig. A.1 Risk-averse utility and risk premiums

a mechanism or system implemented in a society will necessarily produce socially desirable outcomes or allocations. Markets provide one mechanism for determining allocations, called the *market mechanism*. Can the market mechanism really bring about socially desirable allocations?

For the market mechanism to function as desired, certain conditions, such as the comprehensiveness of markets, perfect information, and perfect competition must be satisfied. The comprehensiveness of markets refers to the establishment of markets for all goods that can impact people's welfare. This characteristic is also called the completeness of markets. Because we are investigating how allocation mechanisms operate through markets, we can readily infer that the market mechanism will fail to work well if some goods fall outside of the scope of market transactions. Perfect information means that all relevant information about the nature and prices of goods is available at no (or very little) cost. Incomplete information can lead to the possibility of obtaining a defective product or missing an advantageous opportunity; clearly, such outcomes are not socially desirable.

When economic agents cannot manipulate market prices and instead determine their actions by taking market prices as given, then these agents are said to be *price takers* and the markets exhibit *perfect competition*. A market is perfectly competitive when it includes so many small sellers and buyers that the actions of individual agents do not have visible impacts on market prices. In this case, even if a single seller of a good tries to raise the price of that good independently, buyers can find other sellers who can offer cheaper prices, and, thus, the first seller cannot attract any buyers. Likewise, if a buyer tries to haggle one-sidedly, the seller can simply sell to other buyers. Ultimately, both sellers and buyers are forced to accept the street prices given in the marketplace.

We now consider the behavior of a *firm* that sells a good in a competitive market. When the firm supplies one unit of the good to the market, it earns income equivalent to the market price. However, the total production cost must increase to produce one additional unit of supply, and this incremental cost is referred to as the *marginal cost*. When its supply increases by one unit, the firm's profit increases by an amount equal to the difference between the price and the marginal cost. In other words, if the difference between the price and the marginal cost is positive, then the firm can increase its profit by increasing its supply; if the difference is negative, then it can do so by decreasing its supply. Thus, a firm that aims to maximize its profit should choose its quantity supplied such that the marginal cost equals the given price. The *supply curve*, which reflects firms' marginal costs, illustrates the relationship between market prices and the corresponding quantities supplied on a plane with the price of the good on the vertical axis and the quantity supplied on the horizontal axis. When the price increases, selling the good is advantageous, and firms increase their supplies. Thus, the supply curve is upward-sloping, as shown by curve S in Fig. A.2a.

Next, we consider the behavior of a *household* as a buyer of goods. When the price of a good increases, the household reduces its consumption of that good and increases its consumption of other goods (i.e., the *substitution effect*). Moreover, the household's real purchasing power decreases (i.e., the *income effect*). The demand for the first good decreases as a result of both effects (provided that the good is a *normal good* in the sense that an increase in income increases the demand for that good). This relationship is called the *law of demand*. The *demand curve* illustrates the relationship between market prices and the corresponding quantities demanded for a good. Reflecting the law of demand, the demand curve is downward-sloping, as shown by curve D in Fig. A.2b.

If the market price of a good is too high, then supply exceeds demand (i.e., *excess supply*); conversely, if the price is too low, then demand exceeds supply (i.e., *excess demand*). In either case, some economic agents cannot buy or sell the good as they intended. The price at which all economic agents can buy and sell the good as planned because total supply and demand are in balance is called the *equilibrium price*, and the volume of transactions at this price is called the *equilibrium quantity*. Taken together, the equilibrium price and quantity form the *market equilibrium*. The market equilibrium is depicted by the intersection of the demand and supply curves. In Fig. A.2c, the two curves intersect at point e^* (i.e., the *equilibrium point*), and the equilibrium price and quantity are p^* and q^*, respectively.

At the equilibrium price, both sellers and buyers can sell and purchase the good as planned. However, this point is merely a quantitative alignment of supply and demand and is not inherently socially desirable. To evaluate the social desirability of various allocations, we must introduce some criteria from the perspective of a society as a whole.

The supply curve reflects the marginal costs of firms. Thus, when the total quantity supplied is y, the trapezoidal area of $ycaO$ below the supply curve represents the *variable costs* required to produce y. When the price is p, the supply is y, and, thus, the revenue that accrues to the firms is represented by the rectangular area of *pcyO*. The difference between the total revenue and the variable costs, represented by the triangular area of *pca,* is referred to as the *producer surplus*. The producer surplus equals the sum of the profits and *fixed costs* of firms and is thought to represent the collective gain to the firms.

Next, the demand curve corresponds to the increase in benefits for households when consumption increases by one unit, that is, the *marginal benefits*. Thus, when the total quantity demanded is *x*, the trapezoidal area of *xdbO* below the demand curve represents the gross benefit that accrues to households from consuming that quantity. When the price is *p*, the total amount of expenditures required to purchase *x* is given by the rectangular area of *pdxO*. The net benefit to households after subtracting the purchasing costs from the gross benefits from purchasing *x* is represented by the triangular area of *pdb*, which is referred to as the *consumer surplus*. This value is thought to represent the gain to households.

If the gains that accrue to firms and households can be expressed as the producer and consumer surpluses, it is reasonable to conclude that outcomes with a greater *total surplus* (i.e., the sum of the producer and consumer surpluses) are more desirable for society as a whole. Based on the above criteria, we can say that the allocation with the greatest total surplus is the most desirable or socially optimal one.

The demand curve represents the marginal benefit of consuming goods, and the supply curve represents the marginal cost of producing goods. Thus, the vertical distance between the demand and supply curves represents the *marginal net benefit* to society of increasing the amount of goods by one unit. If the marginal net benefit is positive, then the social benefit increases when the quantity of goods increases; conversely, if the marginal net benefit is negative, then the social benefit increases when the quantity of goods decreases. Thus, the social benefit is maximized at the quantity for which the marginal net benefit is zero (i.e., the quantity at which the marginal benefit and marginal cost align). This observation leads to the following proposition:

> The total surplus is maximized in a perfectly competitive equilibrium.

This proposition is called the *first fundamental theorem of welfare economics*.

In the above discussion, we used the concept of the total surplus to illustrate the first fundamental theorem of welfare economics. However, some problems are associated with using the total surplus as a criterion for evaluating the social desirability of outcomes. For example, people's welfare may not be measurable by such a quantification in the first place (i.e., measurability), it may not make sense to compare the surpluses of different individuals even if they can be quantified (i.e., comparability), and it may not be reasonable to deem a large total surplus "good" in the presence of large biases or inequalities that are counter to people's interests (i.e., ignorance of the income distribution). It is more desirable to construct criteria for evaluating social welfare that do not depend on the measurability and comparability of welfare but are still based on the well-being of individual economic agents.

If a social situation or allocation changes, then the welfare of each economic agent changes accordingly. Some people may regard this allocation change as good, whereas others may think of it as bad. Such judgments by economic agents do not need to be expressed numerically at the level of each economic agent, but, at a minimum, each agent can determine whether an outcome is better, worse, or the same as before.

A change in allocation is called a *Pareto improvement* if it makes no one worse off and makes at least one agent better off. If a Pareto improvement is achieved by a change in allocation, we may conclude that this change in allocation is socially desirable in the sense of weak unanimity, as no one is likely to disagree with the change. This social value judgment is called the *Pareto criterion.* Given a certain allocation, if no Pareto improvement can be realized in any way, then this allocation is said to be *Pareto efficient* or *Pareto optimal.* Note that Pareto is the name of the scholar who developed these analytical concepts.

The first fundamental theorem of welfare economics relying on the Pareto criterion can be stated as follows:

> The perfectly competitive equilibrium allocation is Pareto efficient.

In a perfectly competitive equilibrium, an efficient state in which the potential for improving peoples' welfare is exhausted is realized.

Of course, the first fundamental theorem of welfare economics is established under such conditions as the comprehensiveness (or completeness) of markets, perfect information, and perfect competition. In other words, if these conditions are not met, the market mechanism fails to function as well as desired. This situation is called *market failure* (some market failures are discussed separately in subsequent sections).

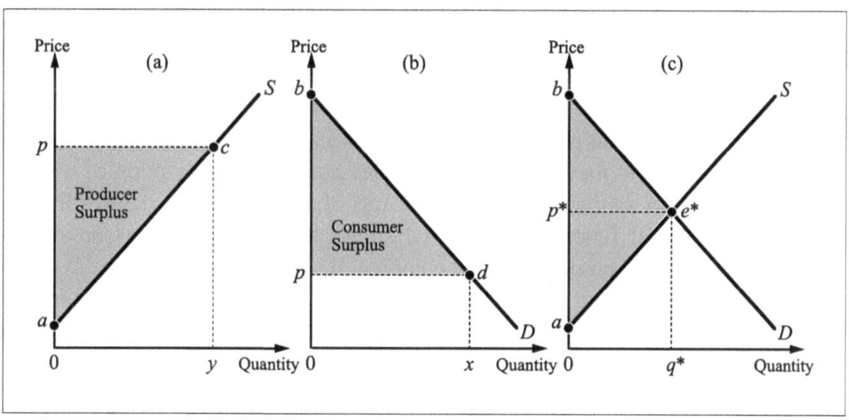

Fig. A.2 Supply curve, demand curve, market equilibrium, and surplus

10.4 Strategic-Form Games and Nash Equilibria

Consider a situation in which two competing companies, company A and company B, must decide whether to reduce their products' prices. If both companies leave their prices as is, then each can secure 100 units of profit. If only one company reduces its price, it can attract more customers and increase its profit to 120 units. However, if only the other company cuts its prices and the first company delays doing so, the latecomer loses customers, and its profit falls to 70 units. If both companies cut prices at the same time, each company's profit is 90 units. Table A.1 summarizes this situation. Each company must choose whether to keep or reduce its price. There are four possible combinations of choices, corresponding to the four cells in Table A.1. For each combination of the two companies' choices, company A gains the profit on the left in the corresponding cell, and company B gains the profit on the right. Will the companies opt to leave prices as they are or reduce them?

A situation in which parties must determine their own behavior while accounting for not only the impacts of their behavior on both their own interests and the interests of others but also the direct impacts of others' behavior on their own interests is referred to as a *game-like situation* or simply a *game*. The parties participating in a game are referred to as *players*, and they may be companies, consumers, governments, or other entities depending on the situation. In general, games do not need to have just two parties; in some games, more than two players must compete with many other rivals. Each player's plan (e.g., making or deferring price cuts as in the above example) for his or her actions is called a *strategy*. Typically, each player chooses one of several feasible plans. Once all players have made their decisions, a *combination of strategies* is determined. If all players takes actions according to their chosen strategies (i.e., play the game), one outcome is realized under the given strategy combination, and this outcome, in turn, determines the players' gains or losses. As players change their strategies, the resulting outcome changes, and the losses or gains change accordingly. A player's *payoff function* associates the combinations of players' choices with that player's gains or losses.

A *game in strategic form*, or a *strategic-form game*, is a description of a game-like situation in society that utilizes the concepts of a set of players, sets of feasible strategies, and payoff functions. Table A.1 shows the parties to the issue at hand (i.e., the set of players: company A and company B), the strategies that are available to each player (i.e., cutting prices or deferring), and their gains resulting from their strategy choices (i.e., the numbers in each cell). This kind of table is called a *payoff*

Table A.1 Price reduction competition between companies (prisoner's dilemma)

		Company B	
		Deferment	Price reduction
Company A	Deferment	100, 100	70, 120
	Price reduction	120, 70	90, 90

matrix. The payoff matrix depicts a simple case in which only two players participate in a strategic-form game.

A strategic-form game describes the various possible outcomes in a given game-like situation but does not actually indicate what happens in that situation. Thus, we can ask what we can reasonably assume each player will do and what outcomes we can expect to occur.

In the price reduction game depicted in Table A.1, we can consider the strategy combination whereby company A chooses to lower prices and company B chooses to defer price reductions. If company A were to change its strategy from price reduction to deferment, its profit would decrease from 120 to 100; thus, it has no incentive to unilaterally change its strategy. In contrast, if company B changes its strategy from deferment to price reduction (assuming that company A continues its strategy of price reduction), its profit will increase from 70 to 90; thus, company B is unlikely to continue deferring prices. In this way, a strategy combination in which one party has an incentive to unilaterally change its strategy does not last long. Conversely, if neither party has an incentive to change its chosen strategy unilaterally, then this combination of strategies will be permanent. In other words, *if no player has an incentive to deviate unilaterally from a given strategy combination, then that strategy combination can be deemed as coming to fruition.* A combination of strategies that meets this condition is called a *Nash equilibrium.*

In the price reduction game described earlier, we can show that the strategy combination whereby both companies reduce their prices constitutes a Nash equilibrium. Suppose that company B has selected price reduction. If company A changes its strategy from price reduction to deferment, then its profit falls from 90 to 70. The same logic holds for company B. Neither company has an incentive to independently alter its price reduction strategy. Thus, the strategy combination in which both parties implement price reductions is a Nash equilibrium of the price reduction game. When the companies choose this strategy combination, they each earn 90 units of profit.

In fact, the Nash equilibrium of the game in Table A.1 has a theoretically stronger property. Regardless of whether company B selects price reduction or deferment, company A enjoys greater profits if it selects price reduction. A strategy that is always the most advantageous strategy, regardless of the opponents' strategies, is called a *dominant strategy*. When every player has a dominant strategy, the combination of these dominant strategies is called the *dominant strategy equilibrium*. Although a dominant strategy equilibrium is necessarily a Nash equilibrium, the converse is not necessarily true. Because companies A and B are symmetric, the Nash equilibrium in the price reduction game in Table A.1 is also a dominant strategy equilibrium.

Note that if both companies choose to defer price reduction, they can both earn 100 units of profit. Both companies can therefore obtain higher profits than when they choose to cut prices. However, as long as its rival company is choosing to defer, it is more advantageous for a company to reduce its prices. Thus, the combination of strategies in which both companies defer price reduction does not constitute a Nash equilibrium. The pursuit of self-interest by each company prevents the realization of coexistence and co-prosperity (i.e., Pareto improvement) for both companies. This price reduction game has the same structure as a well-known example of the *prisoners' dilemma* that describes the potential for social and individual interests to diverge.

10.5 Extensive-Form Games and Subgame Perfect Equilibria

In the Nash equilibrium of a strategic-form game, each player chooses his or her own strategy without any knowledge of the actions that other players intend to take. However, in some cases, the players' actions occur in a certain order such that some players can choose their actions after observing the actions taken by other players.

Let us consider the following situation, known as the "chain store game." The food retail business of a town is monopolized by company B, but rumors are spreading that company A is planning to open a major chain store in town. Company B can compete by drastically cutting prices to protect its exclusive position against company A's opening, or it can conduct cooperative marketing. Of course, company A must consider these possibilities and decide whether to actually open a new store or abandon the plan.

The chain store game is represented by the diagram shown in Fig. A.3. This figure is called a *game tree*. First, company A decides whether to open a new store or abandon the plan; this stage is node 1, illustrated in the figure a circle with the number (1). If company A abandons the plan, then it can gain 200 units of profit in another town, company B gains 700 units of profit by maintaining the status quo, and the game ends. If company A opens a new store, however, the game enters the next stage. Now, company B must decide whether to cooperate or go on the offensive; this stage is node 2, illustrated in the figure by a circle with the number (2). If company B cooperates, the two companies can split the market and gain 350 units each. If company B competes, the companies both fail, each gains only 100 units of profit, and the game ends.

In a game tree, the stage in which each player makes a choice is represented by a single point, and branching occurs depending on the players' specific choices. The branches of the game tree illustrate the order and outcomes of the players' decisions, and the players' gains are represented by the combinations of numbers at the ends of the branches. In Fig. A.3, the gain of company A is shown on the left, and that of company B is shown on the right. A game represented by a game tree is called a *game in extensive form* or an *extensive-form game*.

Table A.2 shows the payoff matrix for the chain store game. This matrix is a copy

Table A.2 Payoff matrix of the chain store game

		Company B	
		Cooperation	Offensive
Company A	Open	350, 350	100, 100
	Abandon	200, 700	200, 700

of the game in extensive form shown in Fig. A.3 translated into strategic form. As can be readily seen, this game has two Nash equilibria. One is the combination of the abandonment and offensive strategies, and the other is the combination of the store opening and cooperation strategies. Which strategy combination do the players ultimately choose? The strategy combination of abandonment and offensive is a somewhat unconvincing equilibrium when the game plays out, as shown below.

When the equilibrium combination of abandonment and offensive is played, company A abandons the plan to launch a new store, and the game ends immediately. Accordingly, company B does not really have an opportunity to take action. The reason that the abandonment and offensive combination is an equilibrium is as follows. If company B chooses the offensive strategy, then if company A switches from the abandonment to the store opening strategy, its gains will decrease. In other words, company A abandons its plan out of fear that company B will launch an offensive price reduction campaign if company A opens a new store.

At node 2, however, when company A's decision to open a new store is revealed, it is not a good idea for company B to choose the offensive strategy because it gains 350 units if it cooperates but only 100 units if it competes. Company B therefore chooses to cooperate at node 2, and its offensive strategy is no more than an empty threat. If company A does open a new store, it is unlikely that company B will go on the offensive in equilibrium. Because a deviation by company A causes company B to rethink or change its strategy, the strategy combination of abandonment and offensive lacks stability as an equilibrium. In this way, if any player has an incentive to switch strategies at some stage, the original strategy combination is not a valid Nash equilibrium candidate in practice.

When no player has an incentive to change his or her initial strategy at any stage of the game, even when new information is received, then the strategy combination is referred to as a *subgame perfect equilibrium*. To determine whether a subgame perfect equilibrium exists, we must first consider the decision of the player in the last stage of the game. Then, we must consider the decision of the player in the penultimate stage, followed by that of the player in the preceding stage, and so on. The method of finding the solution of a game by working backwards from the game's outcome is referred to as *backward induction*.

In the chain store game, we first consider company B's selection stage (i.e., node 2). At this stage, company A has already chosen to open a new store. Thus, company B gains 100 units if it goes on the offensive but 350 units if it cooperates. Naturally, company B chooses to cooperate. Based on this result, we can inductively determine company A's decision at its selection stage (i.e., node 1). If company A chooses abandonment, then it gains 200 units, but if it chooses to open a new store, then it gains 350 units because company B will select cooperation in the subsequent stage. Thus, company A chooses to launch a new store at node 1. In this way, the strategy combination of store opening and cooperation constitutes a subgame perfect equilibrium.

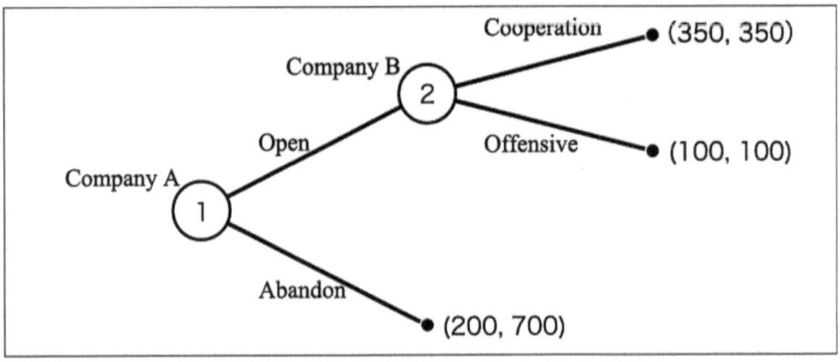

Fig. A.3 Game tree of the chain store game

10.6 Externalities

The waste liquid expelled from chemical factories pollutes the sea and causes damages to fisheries, which is a phenomenon known as environmental pollution. The production and sales of chemicals are the original market activities, and the resulting marine pollution and fishery damage are not part of the intended scope of those market transactions. In this way, certain events accompanying some market activities directly affect others outside of the market system; these events are called *external effects*or *externalities*. Outcomes that are desirable to the affected parties are referred to as *external economies* (i.e., positive externalities), whereas undesirable outcomes are referred to as *external diseconomies* (i.e., negative externalities). In the case of externalities, the main activities, which are subject to market transactions, and the secondary events, which are not subject to market transactions, appear together as a single phenomenon. The secondary events have no market, however, meaning that market failure occurs owing to the lack of complete markets.

In industries that produce externalities, the market equilibrium does not realize a socially optimum allocation even if the market is perfectly competitive. The key to this issue is that the agents performing the main activity in the original market make decisions without considering other parties' losses or gains due to these secondary events. Consider the example of the chemical factories and marine pollution. Chemical companies include expenses for personnel, raw materials, and equipment maintenance in their cost of production. However, they do not account for the costs of damages to fisheries caused by dripping waste liquid. Although this damage to fish eries constitutes part of the *social costs* associated with chemical manufacturing in the sense that something is lost from society, it is not included in the chemical companies' cost calculations. Moreover, chemical companies make decisions based only on their own *private costs*. Thus, in this case, the chemical companies underestimate the social costs of their manufacturing.

Figure A.4 depicts a market with external diseconomies. The downward-sloping curve D is the demand curve, and the upward-sloping curve S is the supply curve that reflects the *private marginal costs* of the producers. The *social marginal costs* are greater than the private marginal costs because of the external diseconomies, and these costs are depicted by the curve above the supply curve, namely, S°. The equilibrium price corresponding to the intersection of the demand and supply curves is p^*, and the equilibrium quantity is q^*. The consumer surplus is the triangular area of p^*ec, and the producer surplus is the triangular area of p^*ea. The total surplus is the area of ace, but this calculation does not account for the damages caused by external diseconomies. The area in which the social marginal costs exceed the private marginal costs corresponds to the marginal costs associated with the external diseconomies. Thus, when the output is q^*, the damage from external diseconomies is the area of the parallelogram $abfe$. The total social surplus, including external diseconomies, can therefore be obtained by subtracting the area of the parallelogram $abfe$ from the triangular area of ace to obtain the area of triangle bcd minus that of triangle def.

The socially optimal state, in which total surplus incorporating external diseconomies is maximized, is achieved when the marginal social cost coincides with the marginal social benefit, represented by the demand curve. Hence, the quantity of the good at the intersection of the marginal social cost curve S° and the demand curve D, namely, q°, is the socially optimal quantity of the good. In this case, the total social surplus is represented by the triangular area of bcd, and it is larger than the surplus at the market equilibrium by the triangular area of def. Note that the damages caused by external diseconomies are not zero in the socially optimal state.

The equilibrium quantity q^* exceeds the socially optimal supply q°. In general, a good that generates external diseconomies is *overproduced* relative to the socially optimal quantity. Conversely, a good that creates external economies is *underproduced* relative to the socially optimal quantity.

Several policy measures have been proposed to correct inefficiencies due to external effects. First, because the main activities associated with external economies or diseconomies are lacking or in excess, respectively, it may be possible to achieve the socially optimal state by implementing appropriate taxes or subsidies for the activities in question. In Fig. A.4, if a manufacturing or production tax corresponding to the difference between social and private marginal costs is introduced, the costs of the external diseconomies are incorporated in the cost calculations of the companies that generate them. The effective private marginal cost after taxation coincides with the marginal social cost, and the supply curve after taxation is S°. The market equilibrium after taxation is d, and the socially optimal quantity q° is produced. These tax and subsidy policies are named *Pigou policies* after their advocate.

Second, if the number of parties is small, it may be possible to improve the situation through direct negotiations between the parties involved in the externality. Additionally, because the original problem is the absence of a market for these secondary events, another good idea may be to create markets for them, thereby *internalizing* the externalities into the market mechanism. In the case of marine pollution caused by chemical production, these solutions could perhaps take the form of negotiations between the parties or the creation of a market to buy and sell pollution rights.

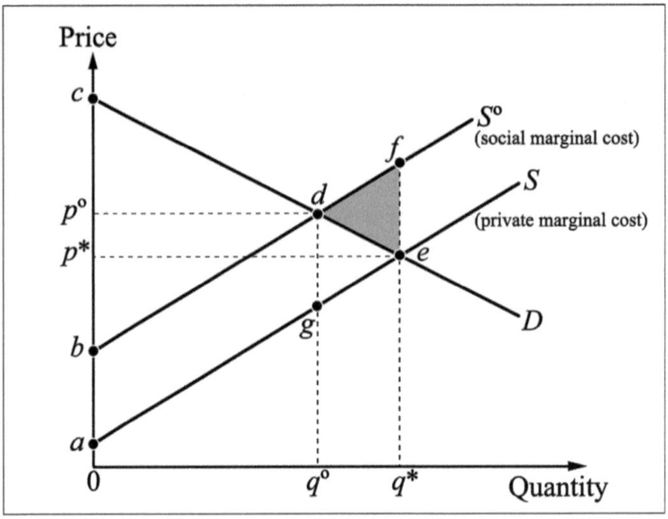

Fig. A.4 Markets creating external diseconomies

For successful negotiations between parties or internalization into the market mechanism, it is important to clearly define "pollution" as a good and assign the related rights among the relevant stakeholders. If fishermen are granted the right to use a clean sea, then the chemical companies can pay money to purchase the right to use a clean sea from fishermen. Conversely, if the right to pollute a clean sea is granted to the chemical companies, then the fishermen affected by marine pollution can buy the right to pollute a clean sea from the companies (!). The differences in the systems for allocating rights can lead to greatly different income distributions, but it is acknowledged that efficient results can be obtained under either system. This result is named the *Coarse theorem* after its advocate.

Unfortunately, whether the preferred solution is Pigou policies, negotiation between parties, or internalization into the market, the necessary information to design an appropriate policy may be difficult to obtain. It may be impossible to identify who is involved, impartiality regarding the configuration of rights and obligations may not be achieved, and the costs of negotiation may be prohibitively high. Thus, these measures are by no means foolproof for redressing inefficiencies caused by externalities.

10.7 Public Goods and the Tragedy of the Commons

If a consumer buys a hamburger and eats it, no other person can eat that hamburger. Goods and services that others cannot use if someone uses them possess the quality of *rivalriness*. If a property rights system with sufficient penalties has been established, it is easy to stop anyone from using rivalrous goods without paying compensation. This property is referred to as *excludability*. Goods that possess both rivalriness and excludability are called *private goods*. Many ordinary goods and services are private goods.

In turn, if one person is already using a public road or, more accurately, the mobility services provided by public roads, this road remains available to many other users at the same time (unless it is extremely crowded). The use of public roads is characterized by *joint-consumption*or *non-rivalriness*. In addition, it may be physically impossible to prevent non-paying users from using public roads, or the costs of collecting fees may be much higher than the revenues that would be obtained from those fees. In this case, the use of public roads is said to have *non-excludability*. Goods that possess both joint-consumption and non-excludability are called *public goods*. Some concrete examples of public goods are services related to public security, such as national defense, police, and firefighting, and services generated by social capital and infrastructure, such as public roads, parks, forest conservation and flood control projects, and so forth.

In fact, markets for public goods cannot exist. Suppose that a private company intends to provide a public good with the aim of gaining profits. Owing to the joint-consumption and non-excludable aspects of this good, all consumers can use it without paying any costs. The company cannot earn any revenue, but it still has to pay the production costs. Companies therefore do not supply public goods to the market because they cannot gain profits. Thus, markets for public goods are never realized. Like markets with externalities, public goods markets fail owing to the lack of complete markets.

When a public good is supplied, all people can enjoy its benefits simultaneously owing to its joint-consumption aspect. Thus, the social benefit from the public good can be expressed as the sum of the benefits to all individuals. As long as the social benefits outweighs the social costs of supplying the public good, it is preferable to supply it from a societal perspective (i.e., it achieves a Pareto improvement). If the sum of the marginal benefits to individuals from a public good aligns with the social marginal cost, then the provision of that good is Pareto efficient. This property is referred to as the *Samuelson condition*.

For a public good to be supplied, the production costs must be borne in some way. If the number of people in the scope of a public good's influence is relatively small, direct negotiations between individuals can be used. If a set of people can agree to share the cost of a public good in proportion with each individual's marginal benefit through negotiations, the optimal supply of the public good will be realized. This outcome is known as the *Lindahl solution*. Alternatively, if the negotiation costs are high because the number of stakeholders is large, the government can come into play. Specifically, the government asks people to declare their marginal benefits from the public good and, in turn, levies tax duties at rates proportional to the declared marginal benefits. This outcome is called a *pseudo-market solution* with government intervention.

Unfortunately, neither the Lindahl solution nor the pseudo-market solution works well in practice. Note that both methods require individuals to bear a burden based on their marginal benefits. The marginal benefit of an individual is *private information*, and only that individual can know its true value. Thus, the cost-sharing decision must be based on the declared (rather than true) values of marginal benefits. If an individual declares a high marginal benefit, that individual's share of the costs increases accordingly. Provided that others bear the expense, however, an individual can use the public good without incurring additional expenses. As a result, no one has an incentive to declare his or her true marginal benefit. For each individual, it is better to deliberately declare a low marginal benefit from the public good and free ride at the expense of others. This underdeclaration leads to an underestimation of the social benefits, which, in turn, leads to the public good being supplied below the socially optimal level. This situation is referred to as the *free rider problem*.

Such facilities as garbage incineration plants, which are indispensable to people's daily lives, are sometimes called "nuisance facilities" because they produce odor and soot, making them undesirable to be around. In the case of nuisance facilities, a similar problem to the free rider problem occurs. These facilities are needed because they enable all people to enjoy their benefits at the same time, but having one installed in one's neighborhood is seen as an inconvenience. No one is willing to take on the cost (that is, the nuisance) of these facilities. This issue is popularly referred to as the *NIMBY problem*, where "NIMBY" stands for "not in my backyard."

Incidentally, goods can be classified into four types based on their joint-consumption and non-excludability properties, as shown in Table A.3. Because joint-consumption and non-excludability are matters of degree, they do not divide clearly into a binary matrix but rather are generally treated as continuous variables. Thus, in addition to private and public goods, other concepts appear, such as *club goods* and *commons* or *common pool*.

Club goods are goods and services that can be used by a large number of members at the same time but whose use by non-paying members can be restricted or excluded (i.e., joint-consumption plus excludability). Membership sports clubs are an example. Inefficiencies may arise owing to the joint-consumption aspect, but they can be

Table A.3 Classification of goods by joint-consumption and non-excludability

		Non-excludability	
		Yes	No (excludable)
Joint-consumption	Yes	Public goods (Public security services, such as national defense, police, and firefighting, and infrastructure services, such as public roads, parks, and forestation and flood control projects)	Club goods (Membership sports clubs, performances at large theaters, the use of toll motorways, etc.)
	No (Rivalriness)	Commons (Fishery resources on the high seas, such as tuna; use of commons for grazing; etc.)	Private goods (Ordinary goods, such as food, clothing, and groceries)

kept minimal through membership restrictions, adjustments of membership fees, and allowing users the freedom to cancel their membership.

Commons and common pools are goods and services that cannot be used if others capture them but whose number of users cannot be effectively limited (i.e., rivalriness plus non-excludability). An example is fishery resources, such as tuna on the high seas. When one fisherman catches a certain amount of tuna, it increases the costs of the other fishermen searching for and catching tuna. Individual fishermen, however, do not account for other fishermen's cost increases. That is, the use of the commons creates negative externalities. Because every fisherman underestimates the social costs of catching tuna, they all try to catch more tuna than the socially optimal level. If overfishing progresses, tuna resources may be depleted. In this way, commons are utilized beyond the socially optimal level, putting them at risk of depletion. This condition is evocatively described as the *tragedy of the commons*. Policy measures to avoid the tragedy of the commons can include international agreements on the management of marine resources. However, commons face similar difficulties to those of public goods, making this problem difficult to resolve.

10.8 Monopolies and Oligopolies

A *monopoly*, in which a particular good has only one supplier, is a typical case in which the conditions for perfect competition are not met (the case of only one buyer is called *monopsony*). A monopoly may occur in several situations, including if a production technology is protected by a patent; if the establishment of a company is restricted by government licensing; if the industry has *economies of scale* in which average costs decrease as production expands, as in the case of large equipment or facilities industries, such as electricity and water supply (i.e., *decreasing cost industries*); or if *non-price competition* arises due to *product differentiation*. These factors, among others, can affect the formation of monopolies.

Because a monopolistic firm (simply, a monopoly) has no competitors, it can exert the *power of controlling price* for a good it sells. This power does not imply that a monopoly can set prices at will. Naturally, if consumers do not buy the product, the price is ineffective; price manipulation by a monopoly is therefore subject to the limitation of demand for the good. To increase the price, the monopoly firm must reduce its sales volume, and if the monopolist wants to increase its sales volume, it must lower its price.

Under perfect competition, if a firm increases its supply by one unit, its revenue increases by the same amount as the market price. A monopoly, however, must account for the discount required to increase its sales volume. On one hand, the firm may expect an increase in revenue commensurate to a one-unit increase in the sales volume. On the other hand, to increase the sales volume, the firm must also reduce the price on its prior sales, which decreases its revenue. Thus, the increase in revenue obtained from a one-unit increase in the sales volume (i.e., the *marginal revenue*) under a monopoly is less than the previous price. A monopolistic firm aiming to earn profits supplies the market with the quantity at which its marginal revenue and marginal cost are equal.

Figure A.5 depicts the equilibrium in a monopolistic market. The downward-sloping line *D*, the horizontal line MC, and the downward-sloping curve AC represent the demand curve, the constant marginal cost curve, and the average cost curve, respectively. The curve MR, which is below the demand curve, is the marginal revenue curve derived from the demand curve *D*. The monopolistic firm selects the quantity corresponding to point *e*, where the marginal revenue and marginal cost lines intersect, namely, x^m. The monopoly price is p^m, at point *a* corresponding to x^m on the demand curve *D*. The consumer surplus is represented by the triangular area of $p^m ad$, and the producer surplus is represented by the rectangular area of $p^m aep^*$; accordingly, the total surplus is the trapezoidal area of p^*ead

The quantity x^* corresponds to point *f*, where the marginal cost and the marginal social benefit, represented by the demand curve, coincide. This quantity is the socially optimal supply that maximizes the total surplus. At price p^*, which equals the marginal cost, if x^* units of the good are supplied, the total surplus is equal to the consumer surplus, given by the triangular area of $p^* fd$. In the case of Fig. A.5, the producer surplus is zero. In a monopolistic market, the equilibrium supply is x^m, which is less than the socially optimal supply of x^*, and the equilibrium total surplus is less than the social optimum by the amount corresponding to the shaded triangular area of afe. The surplus lost owing to the monopoly's existence is called the *deadweight loss*.

Several policy measures can be taken to eliminate or mitigate the undersupply and inefficiencies due to monopolies. First, given that undersupply is a problem, a government can induce a monopoly to increase its supply by granting it *production subsidies*. If a monopoly firm is granted production subsidies at a unit rate equivalent to the length of the line segment p^*c in the figure, then the monopoly's effective marginal cost becomes equal to the length of the line segment Oc. The effective marginal cost and the marginal revenue are equal at point *b*, and, thus, the firm chooses to supply x^*, the socially optimal amount. The consumer surplus increases to the triangular area of $p^* fd$, and the firm secures the rectangular area of $p^* fbc$ as a surplus a result of the subsidy. However, the government bears costs that are equivalent to the subsidy. Consequently, the total surplus is the triangular area of $p^* fd$.

A second potential policy is to employ a *marginal cost pricing regulation* to equate the marginal cost and the price. If the monopoly sets its price to equal the marginal cost, namely p^*, its revenue will be the rectangular area of $x^* fp^* O$, and the total cost will be the rectangular area of x^*ghO. Thus, the monopoly suffers losses equivalent to the rectangular area of $p^* fgh$. This loss can be compensated by, for example, a lump-sum subsidy from the government. Because the monopoly's subsidy income and the costs of the subsidy to the government are completely offset, the total surplus is once again the triangular area of $p^* fd$.

If the goods in question are electricity or something similar, in addition to the marginal cost pricing regulation, the firm could configure a *two-part pricing system* consisting of a basic fixed fee and a unit fee instead of selling the good at a single price. In other words, the monopoly sets the unit fee equal to the marginal cost p^* and collects a basic fixed fee equal to the rectangular area of $p^* fgh$ to offset the loss. In this case, subsidies for the monopolist's losses are not required. Assuming that the basic fixed fee does not exceed the consumer surplus $p^* fd$ obtained from the consumption of x^*, consumers willingly purchase this good in a two-part pricing system. Because an amount equivalent to the monopolist's losses is transferred from consumers to the monopolist in the form of the basic fixed fee, the distribution of income across the consumers and the monopoly firm changes. However, the total surplus remains at the socially optimal level of the triangular area of $p^* fd$.

For policy measures, such as production subsidies, marginal cost pricing regulations, two-part pricing systems, and so on, to work well, the government must know a monopoly's actual cost structure, and the monopoly must be properly structured to minimize costs. Because a company's cost structure is *private information*, however, it is not always provided to the government accurately. In addition, under any of these policy measures, the monopoly firms are ultimately compensated for their losses, meaning that they have no incentives to minimize their production costs. The presence of a monopoly causes a loss of surplus in the form of deadweight loss, and the various policies aiming to correct this issue create inefficiencies of their own in turn.

The above discussion focused on monopolies. Similarly, in the case of an oligopoly, in which the number of suppliers is small, the economy equally suffers from the deadweight loss caused by the price control measures pursued by these oligopolistic firms. In oligopolistic markets, strategic interdependencies between companies must also be taken into consideration.

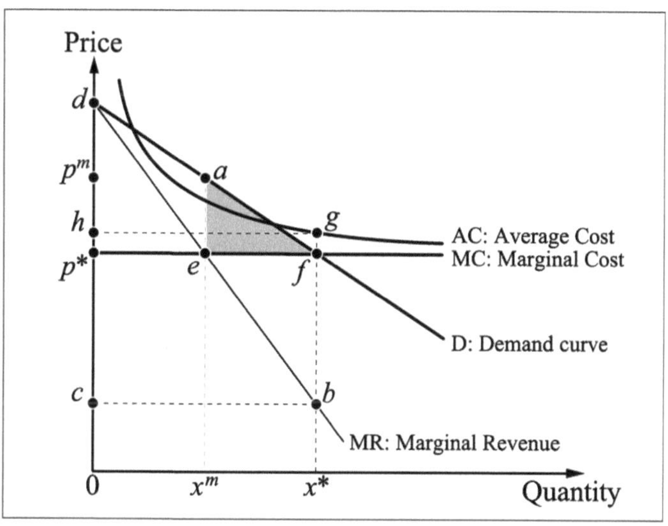

Fig. A.5 Monopolistic market

10.9 Asymmetric Information: Adverse Selection, Moral Hazard, and the Hold-Up Problem

For a given quality of a good, buyers seek cheaper alternatives, and sellers can increase their sales by correctly communicating the performance and attractiveness of their goods to buyers. In a competitive market, incentives to collect and disseminate relevant information work well, as intended. In some cases, however, it is difficult to disseminate and collect information correctly, the information may not be trustworthy, or it is advantageous to provide incorrect information. *Asymmetric information* is the condition in which one party (i.e., the seller or the buyer) has enough information and the other party lacks said information. The market mechanism fails to function well in the case of asymmetric information.

Adverse selection is a problem caused by asymmetric information that exists before a transaction is carried out. Suppose that in a usedcar market, buyers cannot distinguish between good and bad quality cars, whereas sellers are deeply acquainted with the qualities of the cars that they sell. Sellers of high quality cars will try to sell at higher prices, and sellers of low quality cars will likely sell at lower prices. Because the quality of cars is indistinguishable to the buyers, the same price must be offered for cars of either quality. If the market price is high enough that the sellers of high quality cars actually want to sell them, the sellers of low quality cars will also bring their cars to the market. Buyers, who want to avoid the risk of paying too much for a low quality car, do not buy cars at a high price (i.e., there is no demand). Then, the market price drops, the sellers of high quality cars leave the market, and only sellers of low quality cars remain. This outcome is the adverse selection phenomenon at work.

In this situation, only low quality products are spread throughout the market. This outcome is often referred to as the *principle of lemons* because defective products are commonly called lemons. It occurs because the quality of the item in question is unclear, and, thus, this situation is also referred to as the problem of "hidden attributes." In the absence of asymmetric information, high quality cars would be sold at high prices, but asymmetric information means that these sellers fail to find buyers and buyers fail to obtain high quality cars.

One way to avoid adverse selection is through *signaling*. For example, in the case of the used-car market, the seller of a car can promise to buy back a car if a defect is found within a certain period of time or attach a certificate of appraisal issued by a third party. These signals can be costly, but the sellers of high quality cars use them to reliably convey to buyers that their cars are actually of high quality. *Expending sufficient outlays on conveying information* is a type of signal, and prospective buyers trust the information in turn. In contrast to signaling, *screening* is a strategy that a party lacking information can employ to obtain information from another party that possesses information.

Unlike adverse selection, *moral hazard* is a problem caused by asymmetric information that arises after a transaction is carried out. Suppose that a company is considering hiring a salesperson for in-person sales calls at a fixed wage. The company agrees to employ and pay salespeople on the premise that they do the work as expected. The outcome of in-person sales (e.g., the number of deals closed) depends not only on the number of customers that a salesperson visits but also on whether the customers are obstinate or generous, which cannot be measured. Thus, the company cannot evaluate a salesperson's work based on the outcomes alone. In the case of a bad outcome, for example, a salesperson may argue that the result was not his or her fault but rather a product of there being too many stubborn customers. In other words, a fixed wage contract gives employees an incentive to shirk their jobs. If employees shirk, then the expected productivity is not achieved, leading to inefficiency. This problem occurs in the context of a company (i.e., a *principal*) hiring salespeople (i.e., *agents*), and, thus, it is referred to as the *principal–agent problem* or the *agency problem*. It also occurs after a transaction, and the parties' actions are not observable, meaning that it is also called the problem of "hidden actions."

The simplest way for the principal to avoid moral hazard is to monitor the agent's activities directly. This action is called *monitoring*. Although monitoring may be effective when a small number of agents are concentrated in a single office, it is too costly when salespeople are spread over a wide area, as in the case of in-person sales, making it an unrealistic choice. If a principal-agent contract is well designed, it may be possible to encourage an agent to voluntarily conform to the principal's wishes without direct monitoring. This solution is referred to as an *incentive contract*. In the case of a traveling salesperson, for example, a wage contract that stipulates a low fixed payment plus a commission based on the number of closed deals may increase the salesperson's incentives to make more efforts toward sales calls. Because salespeople may choose not to sign an employment contract that offers only a commission, a low fixed salary is introduced as an additional incentive to participate.

If no asymmetric information is present and a contract containing clauses that cover all conceivable contingencies (i.e., a *complete contract*) can be concluded, then the principal can achieve the *first best result* in terms of efficiency. If, however, information is asymmetric, it is not possible to include contractual clauses based on items that cannot be verified by a third party (e.g., a court). Hence, principal-agent contracts inevitably become *incomplete contracts*. Furthermore, if a contract is incomplete, only inefficient *second best results* can be obtained. For example, in the case of a traveling salesperson, because the salesperson cannot prove whether a client is stubborn, the employment contract cannot include a clause that stipulates a wage payment conditional on whether a client is stubborn. The fixed payment portion of the incentive contract described above, for example, places an additional burden on the employer that would not be necessary if perfect information were available. This issue prevents the realization of efficient outcomes.

Various other problems arise in the case of incomplete contracts. For example, consider a manufacturing company (i.e., principal) that ordered custom-made parts from a sub-contractor (i.e., agent) under a verbal promise to pay a certain price for the parts but is now requesting a price cut just after the parts are completed and are ready to be delivered. If the agent cannot demonstrably prove the existence of the verbal promise and the custom-made parts cannot easily be resold to other parties, then it must accept the principal's request. One party attempting to manipulate a situation to its benefit when the other party has no recourse is called the *hold-up problem*.

If the hold-up problem can be anticipated in advance, an agent will not undertake an order from the principal in the first place, and the transaction will not take place. Thus, to realize a profitable transaction (from an individual or societal perspective), the principal must persuasively indicate to the agent that he or she will not engage in *opportunistic behavior* at the agent's expense. Someone creating a situation in which he or she is forced to take a certain action is referred to as a *commitment* to that action. In the previous example, if the principal can make a commitment to pay, he or she can gain the agent's trust and, accordingly, the transaction will be formally carried out. For example, depositing the full amount of money in escrow with a court is a possible means of commitment. Another means of commitment is making an advance payment. Notably, a commitment by the principal may in turn induce moral hazard or opportunistic actions on the part of the agent, creating a reverse hold-up problem.

10.10 Discounted Present Value

Households determine their current activities by considering various events in their *life cycles*, such as the extent of their education, where and how long they work, when they retire, how they will support themselves after retirement, and so on. Companies also develop management strategies for production, inventory, and capital investment by establishing prospects for future sales and market trends. To analyze these long-term economic activities, the element of time must be clearly defined and appropriately incorporated into any discussion of economic agents' evaluations of the present and future.

Consider the following problem. A very generous person offers two proposals: A, an immediate payment of 5 million JPY in cash, and B, a payment of 5 million JPY in cash in one year. Which of these proposals is more advantageous? Here, we assume that the selected proposal is carried out with certainty. It is inappropriate to think of A and B as identical choices even though they both provide 5 million JPY. For many people, this distinction is self-evident. If the financial markets operate well, proposal A is clearly more beneficial because it immediately provides 5 million JPY in cash. That cash can be used to purchase a *financial asset* that will pay interest, meaning that this choice offers the principal of 5 million JPY plus interest after one year. At the time that proposal B is realized (i.e., one year later), proposal A offers more money than proposal B does according to the amount of interest.

The rate of return on financial assets is called the *nominal interest rate*, or simply the *interest rate*. For example, if the nominal interest rate is 3% per annum (nominal interest rate $= 0.03$), the combined principal and interest on 5 million JPY is 5.15 million JPY after one year. This amount is calculated using the formula principal $\times(1+$ nominal interest rate). The sum of the nominal interest rate and one is called the *gross interest rate*. Thus, 5 million JPY today with an interest rate of 3% per annum is equivalent to 5.15 million JPY after one year. Conversely, we can calculate the amount of money today that is equivalent to the 5 million JPY after one year offered in proposal B. To obtain this value, it suffices to divide 5 million JPY by the gross interest rate. The amount obtained is 4.854 million JPY ($\approx$ 5 million/1.03), and this amount is called the *discounted present value* of 5 million JPY in one year. Naturally, proposal A is more advantageous than proposal B when the discounted present values are compared.

Generally, *discounting* refers to dividing amounts of money at different points in time by the gross interest rate to convert them into comparable present values. The nominal interest rate is also a *discount rate*. The discounted present value of 5 million JPY after one year is calculated by dividing it by the gross interest rate once, whereas the discounted present value of 5 million JPY after two years is calculated by dividing it by the gross interest twice. That is, 4.713 million JPY ($\approx$ 5 million $\div$ 1.03 $\div$ 1.03) is the discounted present value of 5 million JPY after two years, given an interest rate of 3% per annum. This process corresponds to an inverse calculation of *compound interest*.

Because the interest rate is not always constant over a long period of time, the interest rate in each period must be accounted for when calculating the discounted present value of an amount in the distant future. For example, if the annual interest rate up to one year from now is 3%, but the annual interest rate one to two years from now is expected to be 5%, then the discounted present value of 5 million JPY after two years is calculated as 5 million $\div$1.03 $\div$ 1.05 $\approx$ 4.623 million. The process of discounting to obtain proper present values is important to various types of economic activities, such as companies' investment plans, households' mortgage decisions, and people's choices of pension and insurance premiums.

Incidentally, people's well-being is determined not by a nominal level of income but rather by the quantity of goods and services that can be purchased with that income, that is, *real income* (= nominal income $\div$ price level). Calculations to determine the real discounted present value of income must account for price fluctuations.

Suppose that an individual currently has 100,000 JPY in cash and that the nominal interest rate is 3% per year. If the price of 1 kg of rice is 1,000 JPY, then this individual can buy 100 kg of rice ($= 100,000 \div 1,000$). Thus, the nominal value of 100,000 JPY in cash corresponds to the real value of 100 kg of rice. Conversely, if this individual purchases financial assets with 100,000 JPY in cash, he or she will obtain 103,000 JPY in one year. Because an additional 3 kg of rice can be purchased with that interest in one year, the nominal interest rate of 3% also increases the real value by 3%. If, however, the price of rice rises by 1% over the course of a year to 1,010 JPY per kg, the amount of rice that can be purchased only increases by approximately 2 kg ($1.98 = 103,000 \div 1,000 - 100$). The rate of change in the real value (in terms of the volume of rice) is therefore approximately 2%. In other words, the rate of change in the real value resulting from a nominal interest rate of 3% and a price increase rate of 1% is only 2%, which is obtained by subtracting the price increase rate from the nominal interest rate.

To consider fluctuations in real values within an economy, which includes a wide variety of goods and services, we must use the *inflation rate* instead of using rates of change in the prices of individual goods and services. As the above example shows, the rate of change in the real value can be expressed as the difference between the nominal interest rate and the inflation rate. This rate is called the *real interest rate.* The relationship "real interest rate = nominal interest rate – inflation rate" is called the *Fisher equation.* The discounted present value of future real income must be calculated using the real interest rate.

The nominal and real interest rates reflect market assessments of the value of current income relative to future income. It is also important to consider households' subjective assessments of real income today and in the future. For example, imagine that you are going to eat one of your favorite cookies. Whether you eat it today or tomorrow, you will feel equally happy (in terms of utility) when you eat it. However, if you compare eating a cookie today and eating it tomorrow from today's perspective, it likely seems more beneficial to eat it today. Eating it tomorrow happens after a day has passed, and you have to patiently wait one day to consume it, which means that waiting seems less desirable. *Spending time to put up with something incurs a subjective cost.* The percentage decrease in utility after one period relative to the current utility is called the *subjective discount rate.* The subjective discount rate indicates the degree to which a household weighs the current point in time, that is, it indicates a household's "impatience." The *lifetime utility* is the overall level of utility that a household can obtain from long-run consumption activities over a lifetime. It can be expressed as the *sum of the present values of the utilities (i.e., instantaneous utility) from consumption at each point in time discounted using the subjective discount rate.*

Column 15. The Constitution of Japan and human rights

Much of this book focuses on legal relationships under private law, and it rarely touches on issues covered under public law (for more on the relationship between private law and public law, see Column 9). Thus, this column briefly outlines the most basic regulations regarding human rights (all articles are from the Constitution of Japan).

The Constitution of Japan stipulates that respect for human rights is an important value and, furthermore, that the highest purpose of basic human rights is the dignity of the individual. Basic human rights, along with popular sovereignty and pacifism, form the three major principles of the Japanese Constitution. General human rights include the right to pursue happiness as a comprehensive basic right (Art. 13) and equality under the law (Art. 14). Specific human rights include the right to exclude state intervention, social rights that guarantee the right to substantive equality, the right of human rights protection, the right to claim state affairs, and the right to suffrage.

The right to freedom can further be divided into rights to mental, economic, and personal freedom. Accordingly, regarding the right to mental freedom,

Article 19 guarantees freedom of thought and conscience, Article 20 guarantees freedom of religion, Article 21 guarantees freedom of expression, and Article 23 guarantees academic freedom. The prevailing view is that restrictions on mental freedom should be recognized under stricter standards relative to restrictions on economic freedom (i.e., double standards).

Economic freedom is defined as the freedoms of residence, relocation, and choice of occupation (Art. 22) and guaranteed property rights (Art. 29), which are said to be regulated by public welfare. The regulatory objectives are divided into passive objectives to prevent, eliminate, and mitigate dangers to health and life and positive objectives to protect socially and economically vulnerable people based on the philosophy of the welfare state. Additionally, a theory requires strict rationality for regulations related to passive objectives, proposing that judicial examinations should be conducted from the viewpoint of necessity, rationality, and LRA criterion.

Finally, social rights are human rights that guarantee protections for the socially and economically vulnerable and aim to achieve substantial equality based on the ideals of the welfare state. The right to life (Art. 25), the right to receive education (Art. 26), the right to work (Art. 27), and fundamental labor rights (Art. 28) are all stipulated in the Constitution. Judicial precedent claims that the right to life cannot be guaranteed by constitutional provisions alone. However, some theories state that an objective minimum standard of living can be determined to some extent and, thus, that standards stipulated in individual and specific statutes may be judged unconstitutional. The standardization of working conditions and the idea of basic labor rights are based on the idea that employees are generally at a disadvantage relative to their employers when trying to establish conditions for their work. Basic labor rights (i.e., the right to organize, the right to bargain collectively, and the right to act collectively) aim to place employees on an equal footing with employers. Theoretically, it is useful to understand that a judicial review of these constraints must be conducted under fairly strict standards.

Index

A

Act on Specified Commercial Transactions (ASCT), 8
Act on the Promotion of Global Warming Countermeasures, 210
Actuarially fair, 133
Advance disposal fee, 214
Adversary system, 17
Adverse selection, 108, 135, 239, 260
Agency theory, 49, 60
Agent. *See* agency theory
Agreement on Trade-related Aspects of Intellectual Property Rights, 30
Alternative transaction obligations, 157
Analysis
  normative a., 15, 16, 192
  positive a., 15, 16, 192
  quantitative a., 15
Anglo-American law, 161, 190
Antimonopoly Act, 72
Antitrust law. *See* Antimonopoly Act
Appropriability, 35–37
Asymmetric information, 107, 134, 260, 261
Automobile Recycling Law, 216, 219, 220, 222

B

Backward induction, 251
Benefits and counter-benefits, 133
Berne Convention, 30, 38
Building ordinance, 229
Business judgment rule, 57

C

Causal relationship, 15, 189, 191
Cease and desist order, 73, 76
Certainty equivalent, 243
Change of circumstances, 154
Civil Code, 12–14, 18, 19, 21, 24, 25, 47, 52, 68, 77, 98, 102, 103, 112, 151, 153–155, 157, 158, 160, 186–188, 227, 228
Coase theorem, 224, 234
Commitment, 65, 262
Commons, 223, 232, 257
  tragedy of the c., 223, 226, 233
Companies Act, 46, 47, 51–55, 57–59, 62–64
Company
  joint-stock c., 46
  with a board of directors, 58
  with committees, 58
Competition law, 72
Compound interest, 263
Conflicting interest transactions, 52
Conflict of interest, 58
Consumer surplus, 75
Containers and Packaging Recycling Law, 214, 215, 218
Continental law, 162
Contract
  binding force of the c., 159
  breach of c., 152
  complete c., 171, 172, 177, 261
  employment c., 102, 103
  for work, 103

T. Yanagawa et al. (eds.), *Econo-Legal Studies*,
https://doi.org/10.1007/978-981-16-5145-8

freedom of contracts, 47, 48
incentive c., 261
incomplete c., 169, 172, 174, 178, 179, 261
Copyright Act, 27, 28, 30, 38, 39
Cost
fixed c., 246
marginal c., 77, 245
marginal c. pricing regulation, 258
private c., 252
private marginal c., 252
social marginal c., 217, 252
transaction c., 160, 172, 224, 225, 234
variable c., 245
Creation laws, 27, 28

D
Damages
obligation to mitigate d., 150, 160, 163, 169, 177
ordinary d., 156
punitive d., 190
right to claim d., 52, 153–155
special d., 156
Deadweight loss, 75, 258
Demand curve, 213, 245, 246, 253, 258
Derivative lawsuit, 51, 55, 56
Design for the environment, 215, 220
Director
board of directors, 46, 53–55, 57, 59
directors' remuneration, 58
representative d., 51
Discounted present value, 263
Discussion-oriented city planning, 234
Dismissal, 112
abuse of the right to dismiss, 112, 115
adjustment d., 113
for disciplinary reasons, 113
ordinary d., 113
regulations, 114
District plan, 231
Double marginalization, 78, 81, 82
Dual partition of common space, 227
Due care, 199, 202
Duty
of care, 47
of loyalty, 52, 54
to monitor, 54, 55

E
Econo-legal studies, vi, 2
Economic welfare, 11, 77, 243
Economies of scale, 257
Efficiency, 11–13, 46, 66, 67, 75
Efficient breach, 160, 169
Employee
non-regular e., 102
regular e., 102
Employment
indirect e., 102
contract, 102, 103
English law, 150
Equivalence, 133
Excludability, 226, 255
Expectation interest, 165
Extended Producer Responsibility (EPR), 214, 217
External benefits, 195
Externality, 211, 252

F
Fairness, 11–13, 66, 75, 111, 145, 161
First fundamental theorem of welfare economics, 246
First-to-file, 33
Fisher equation, 264
Free riding, 78, 256
Funded method, 137

G
Game
chain store g., 250
extensive-form g., 250
strategic-form g., 248
tree, 250
General designation, 86
Generational accounting, 138
Good
club g., 256
experience g., 40
normal g., 245
private g., 255
public g., 255
Government failure, 14

H
Hand rule, 200
Hold-up problem, 262
Home Appliance Recycling Law, 214–217, 219, 220
Human capital, 116

I

Immaterial, 23
Impediment of fair competition, 81, 82
Impossibility of performance, 154, 155, 179
Incentive, 198, 203, 209, 211, 212, 214, 215, 221, 235, 240, 249, 251, 261
  contract, 261
Income effect, 245
Income redistribution, 11, 112, 118, 122, 129, 134, 146, 193
Innovation, 31, 35, 75, 218
  process i., 36
  product i., 35, 36
Insurance
  and welfare principles, 128
  health i., 125, 127, 132, 134, 139, 141
  long-term care i., 125, 129, 139–141
  social i., 125–128
Intellectual property, 23
Intellectual Property Act, 27
Internalization of external benefits, 195
Interpretation (method), 15
Inventing around, 32, 34

J

Japan Fair Trade Commission (JFTC), 72
Joint-consumption, 255
Judicial precedent, 161

L

Land ownership, 24, 29, 226, 227, 229
Landscape, 223, 225, 232
Law and economics, v, 2
Law of demand, 245
Legal stability, 235
Legislation (method), 15
Leniency, 97
Liability
  product l., 217
  strict l., 186, 201–203
Liberalism, 11
Libertarianism, 11
Life cycle, 217, 262
Lindahl solution, 255
Lock-in, 87, 96

M

Mandatory laws, 41
Marginal benefit, 246
Marginal net benefit, 246
Marginal willingness to pay, 213
Market
  comprehensiveness of markets, 244
  definition of the m., 97
  dual structure in the labor m., 115
  equilibrium, 245
  external labor m., 106
  failure, 14, 31, 75, 108, 247
  internal labor m., 106
  mechanism, 244
Means test, 128, 144
Merger, 25, 46, 63, 72, 97
Minimum intervention, 229
Minimum Wage Act, 108, 109
Monitoring, 261
Monopoly, 88–90, 257
Monopsony, 110, 111, 257
Moral hazard, 108, 136, 143, 145, 260
Mundell's theorem, 130

N

Nash equilibrium, 203, 249
National Health Insurance (NHI), 139
National minimum, 124
Negligence
  comparative n., 157
  liability, 186, 188, 198, 200–203, 205
Neighboring relations, 228
NIMBY problem, 256
Non-excludability, 255
Non-price competition, 78, 257
Non-rivalriness, 255

O

One share, one vote, 46, 48
Opportunism, 116, 170
Optimization, 240
Ownership, 3, 23, 24

P

Pacta sunt servanda, 159, 163, 170
Pareto
  criterion, 247
  efficiency, 75, 247
  improvement, 247
Paris Convention for the Protection of Industrial Property, 30
Patent Act, 27, 28, 30, 36
Pay-as-you-go, 137
Pay-as-you-throw, 214
Payoff
  function, 248

matrix, 249
Perfect competition, 108, 244, 247, 257
Power of controlling price, 257
Price taker, 244
Principal, 49, 60, 261
Principle
of lemons, 260
statutory p., 162
Prisoners' dilemma, 250
Private information, 256, 259
Private monopolization, 72, 74
Producer surplus, 75, 88, 246
Product differentiation, 81, 257
Pseudo-market solution, 255
Public assistance, 122, 124–126, 142, 143
Public health, 126
Public pensions, 126

R
Rate, 262–264
Rationality, 10, 116, 233, 265
Real income, 263
Recycling, 215
optimal amount of r., 217
responsibility for r., 217, 218, 220, 221
Resale Price Maintenance (RPM), 76
procompetitive effect of RPM, 78
Right
appraisal r., 63, 64
personal r., 228
property r., 29, 226, 227
to avoid contracts, 153, 157
to claim the contracted object, 153
to demand performance, 153, 159
to demand substitute goods, 154
to life, 117, 265
to payment, 153
Risk, 241
allocation, 194
-averse, 242
diversification, 123
-loving, 242
mitigation, 123
-neutral, 242
premium, 243
selection, 135
Rivalriness, 254
Rule of law, 15

S
Safety net, 123
Samuelson condition, 255
Schumpeterian hypothesis, 74
Screening, 260
Separation of ownership and management, 47, 48
Servitude, 227, 234
Shareholder
controlling s., 50, 62–65
general meeting of shareholders, 47, 49, 58, 59, 62, 64, 65
minority s., 50, 62, 64
Signaling, 260
Skills
firm-specific s., 116
general s., 116
Social
benefits, 126
capital, 127, 255
cost, 252
dilemma, 233
expenditure, 127
surplus, 192, 253
welfare, 125, 126, 128, 192
Social security
benefits, 127
law, 133, 135
Specific performance, 173, 175
Substitution effect, 245
Supply curve, 245
Synergy, 62

T
Tangible objects, 26, 28
Tax
deductions with benefits, 144
for climate change mitigation, 210
negative income t., 143
Pigouvian t., 211, 212, 224
Theory of distinction between civil and criminal liability, 190
Tie-in. *See* tying
Tinbergen's theorem, 130
Tolerable limit, 228
Torts, 186
Total surplus, 192
Total willingness to pay, 213
Trade indication laws, 27
Trademark Act, 27, 30

Two-part pricing, 258
Tying, 86, 87, 89, 90, 92

U
Uncertainty, 241
Unfair trade practices, 72, 73, 76, 86
United Nations Framework Convention on Climate Change, 210
Unlawful download, 39
Unreasonable restraint of trade, 72
Usufruct, 227
Utilitarianism, 11
Utility, 11, 106, 131, 192, 193, 239
  expected u., 131, 242
  expected u. theorem, 242
  function, 241
  instantaneous u., 264
  lifetime u., 264

V
Voluntary laws, 41
von Neumann-Morgenstern (vNM) utility function, 242

W
Working poor, 108
Wrongful act deterrence function, 194

MIX
Papier aus verantwortungsvollen Quellen
Paper from responsible sources
FSC® C105338
www.fsc.org

If you have any concerns about our products,
you can contact us on
ProductSafety@springernature.com

In case Publisher is established outside the EU,
the EU authorized representative is:
Springer Nature Customer Service Center GmbH
Europaplatz 3, 69115 Heidelberg, Germany

Printed by Libri Plureos GmbH
in Hamburg, Germany